LARS TOFT-ERIKSEN, ED.

Melgaard + Munch

LARS TOFT-ERIKSEN, ED.

Melgaard + Munch

The End of It All Has Already Happened

Artworks:

Bjarne Melgaard and Edvard Munch

Texts:

Lars Toft-Eriksen
David Lomas
Bjarne Melgaard interviewed by Lars Toft-Eriksen
Patricia G. Berman
Øystein Sjåstad

Graphic design:

Snøhetta

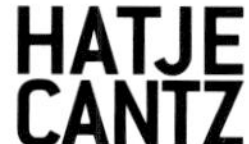 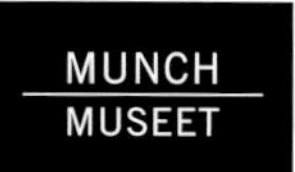

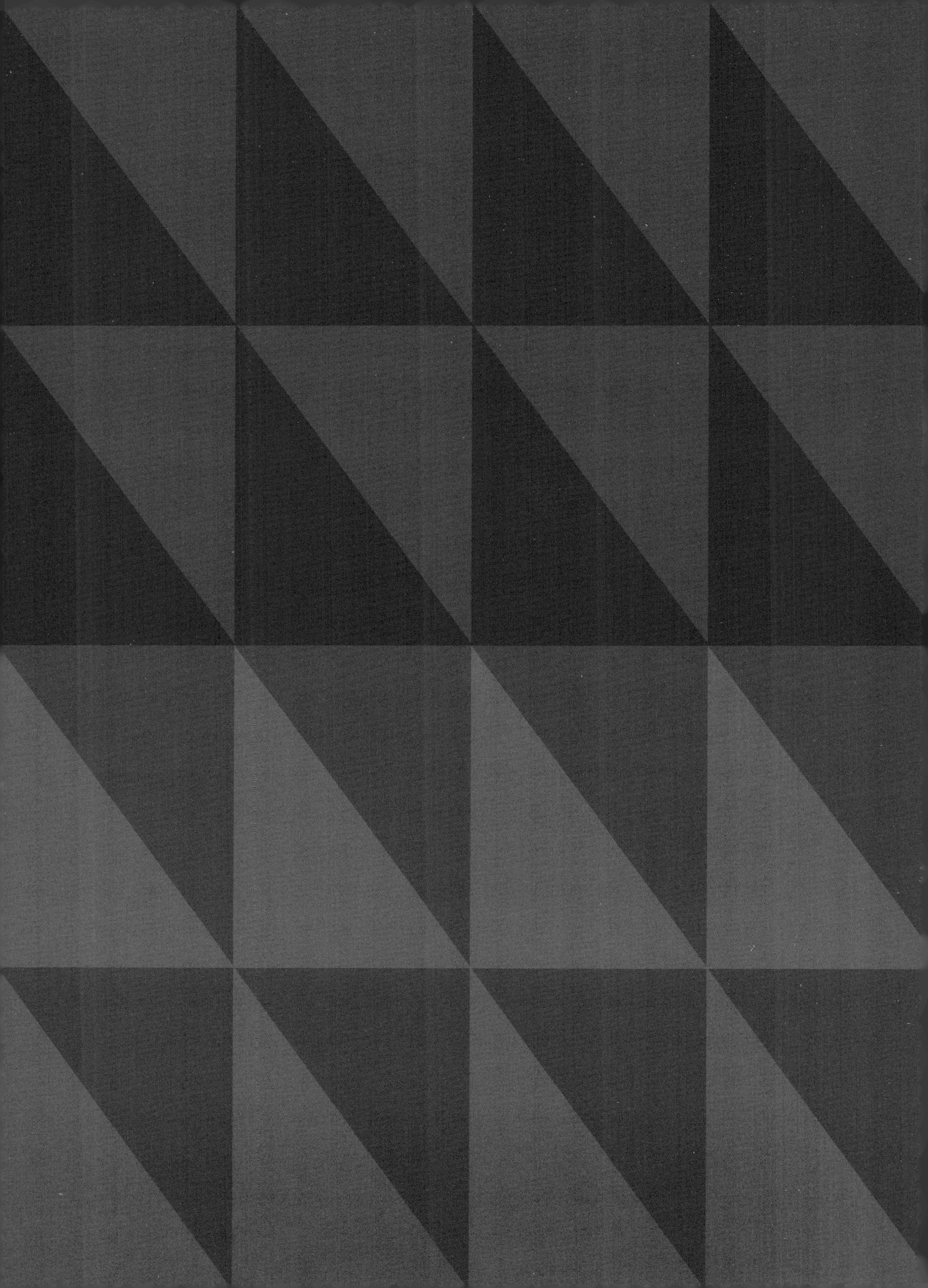

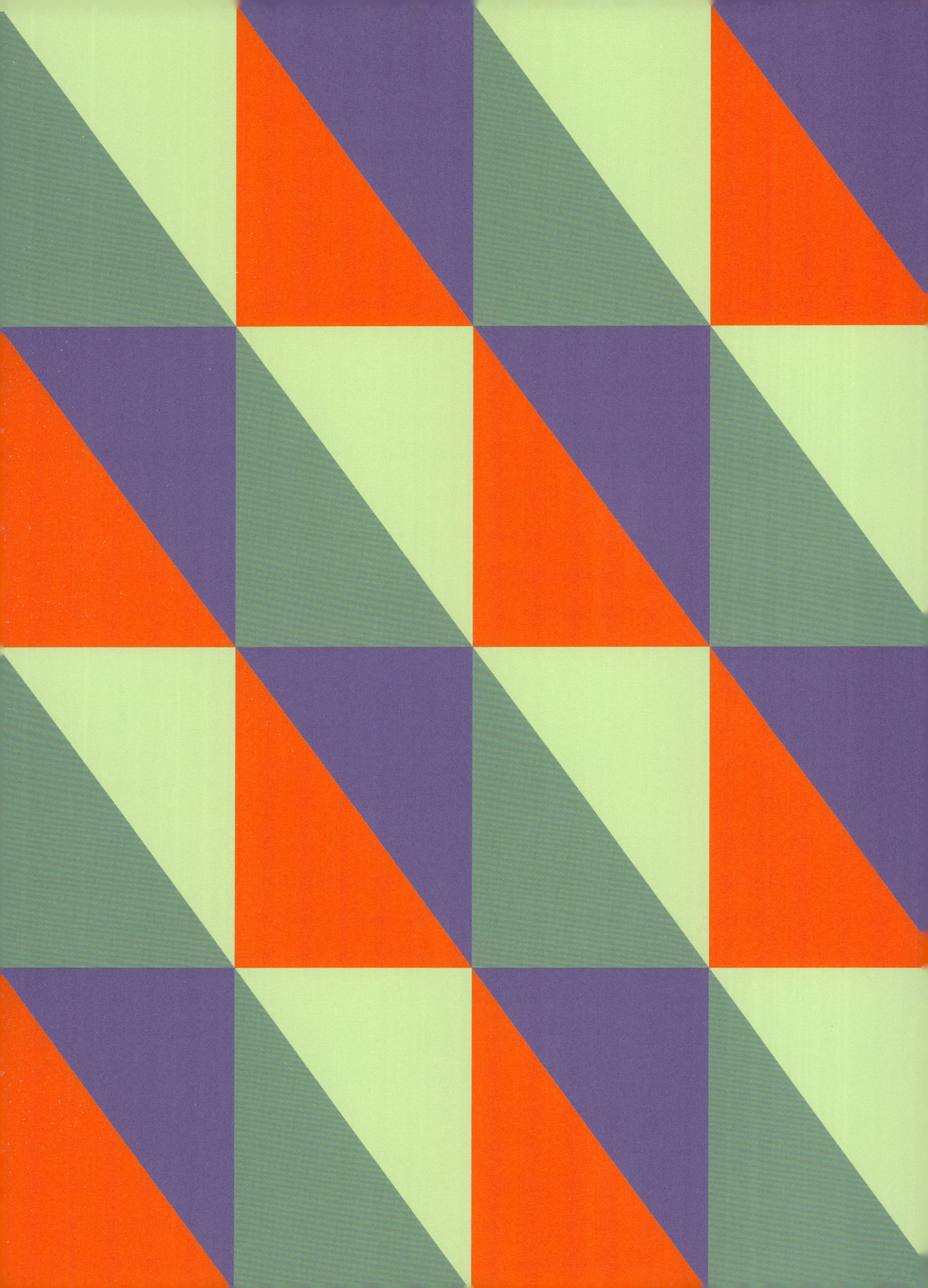

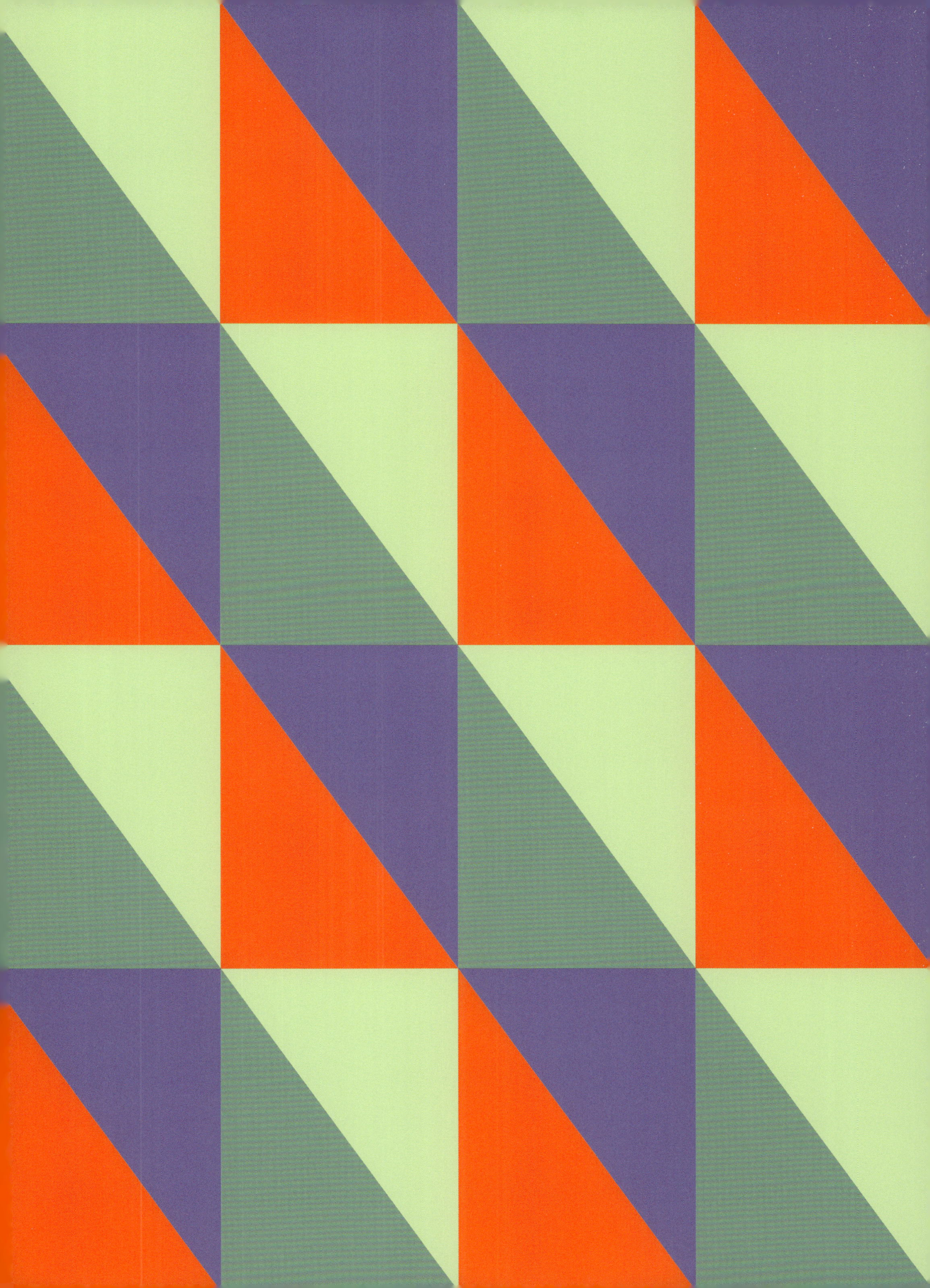

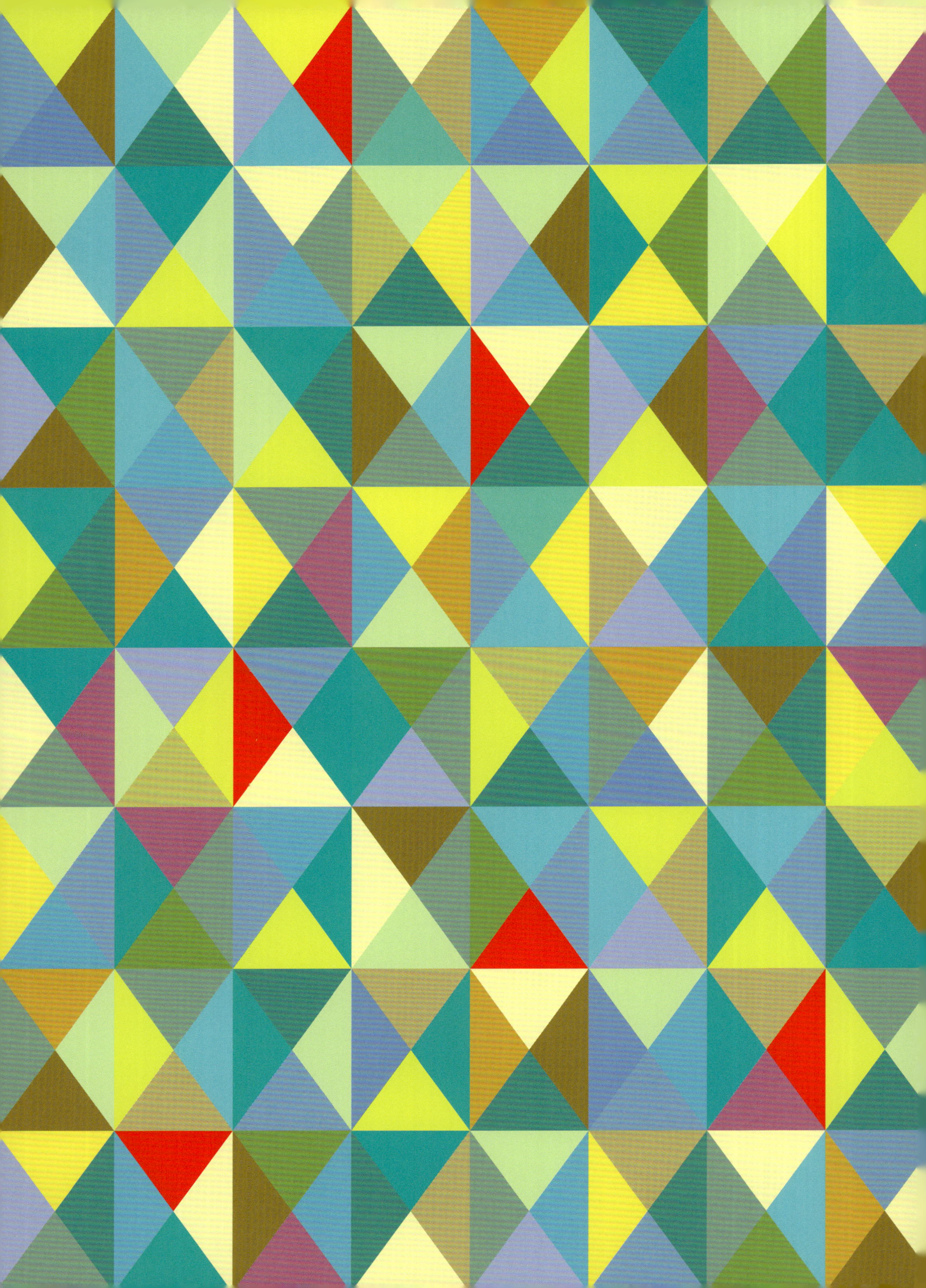

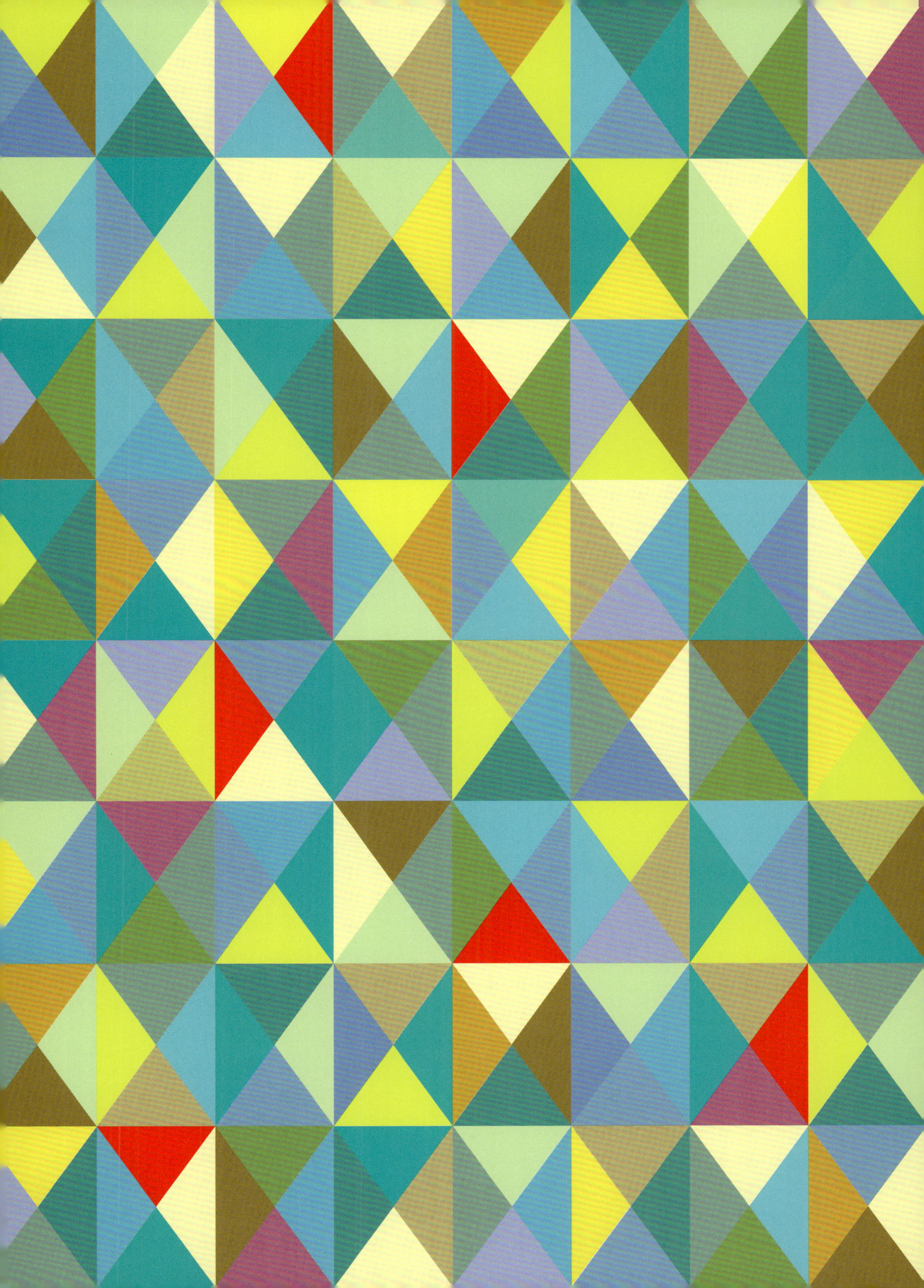

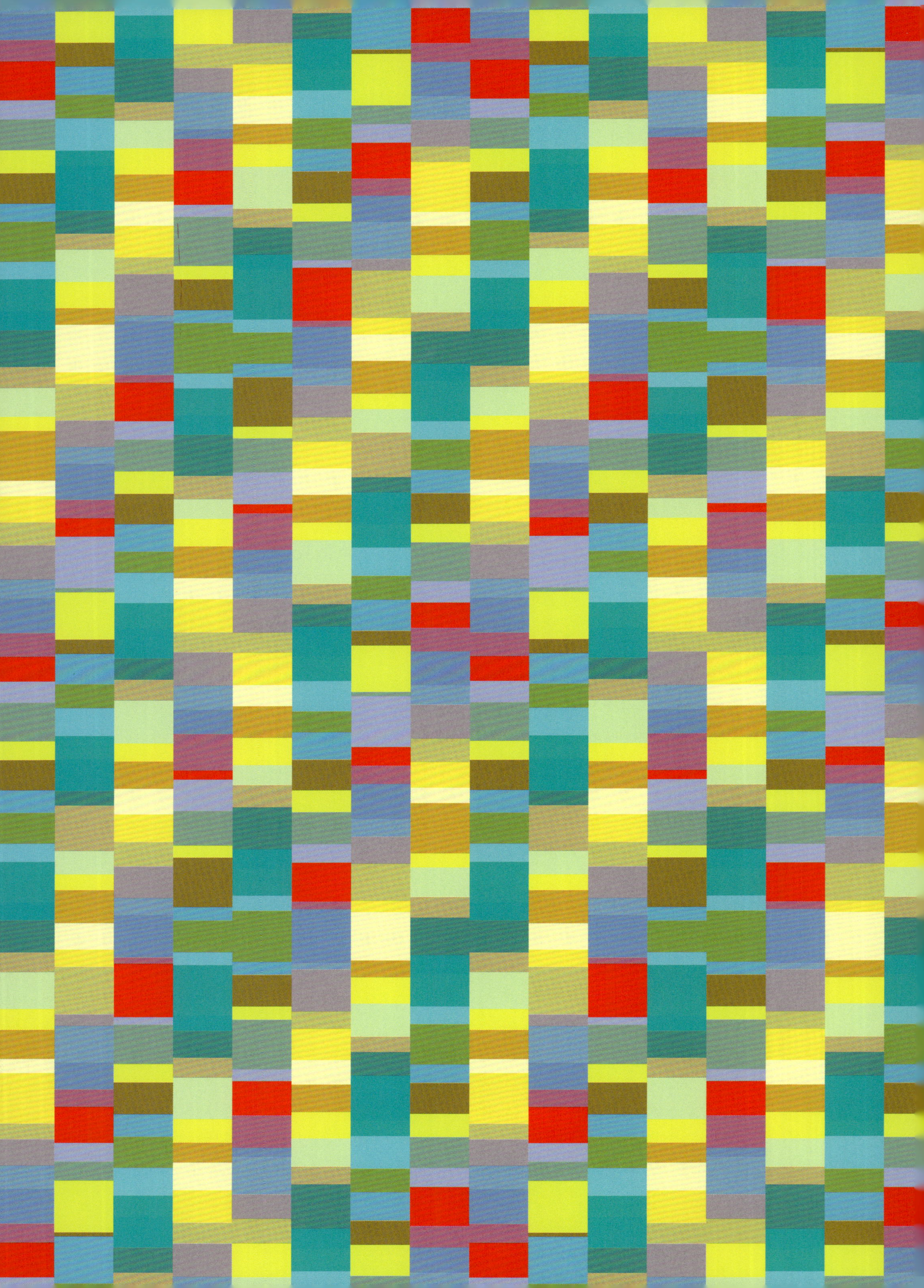

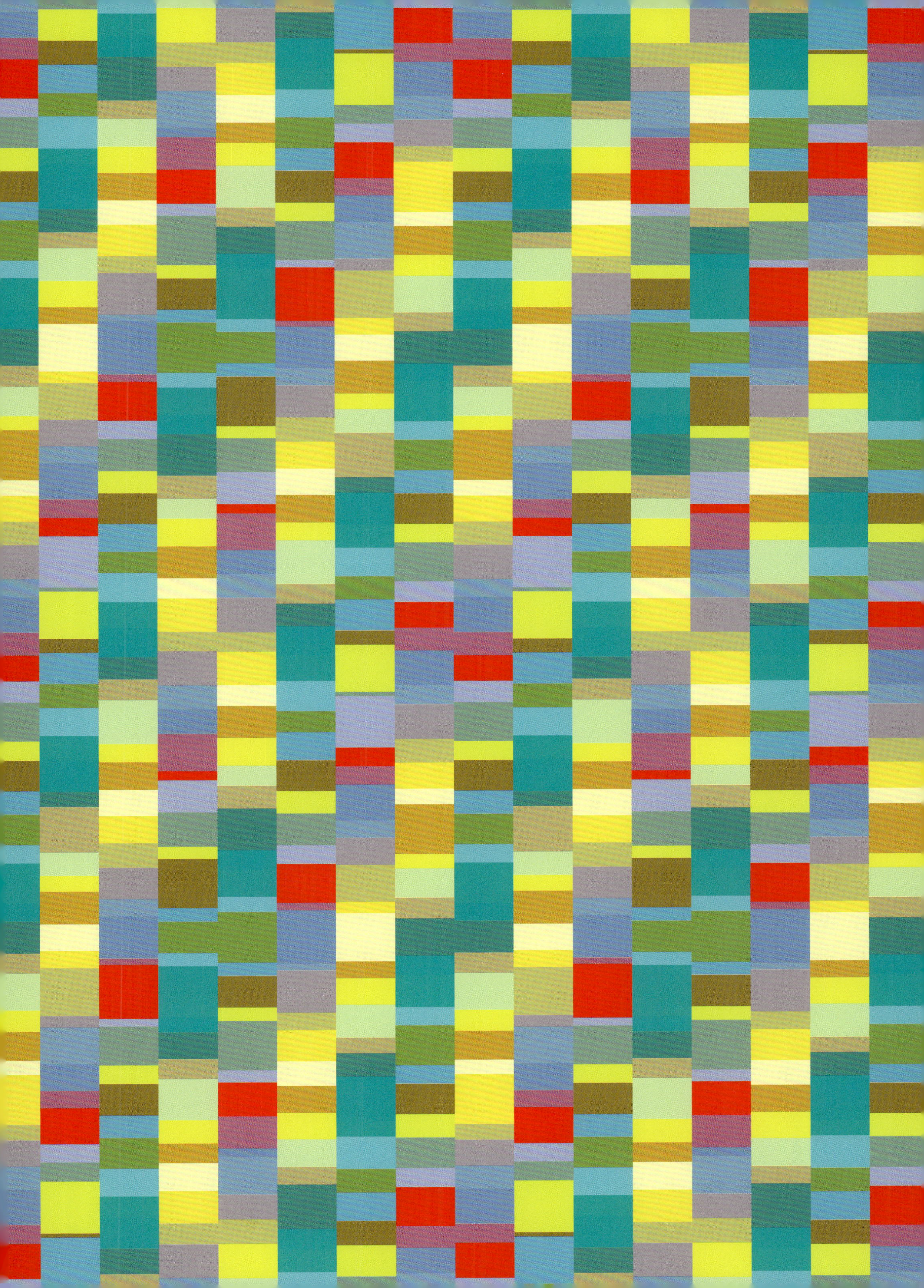

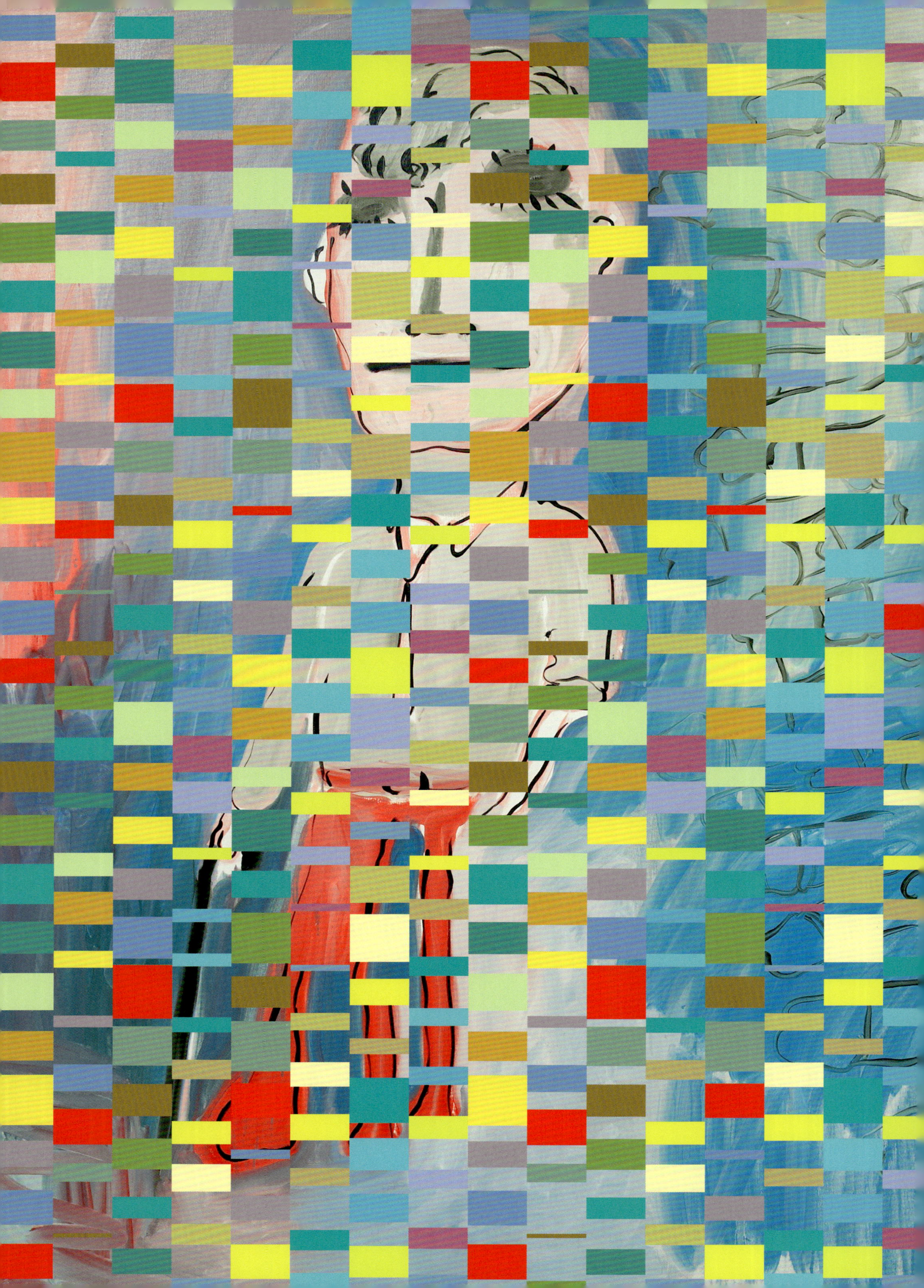

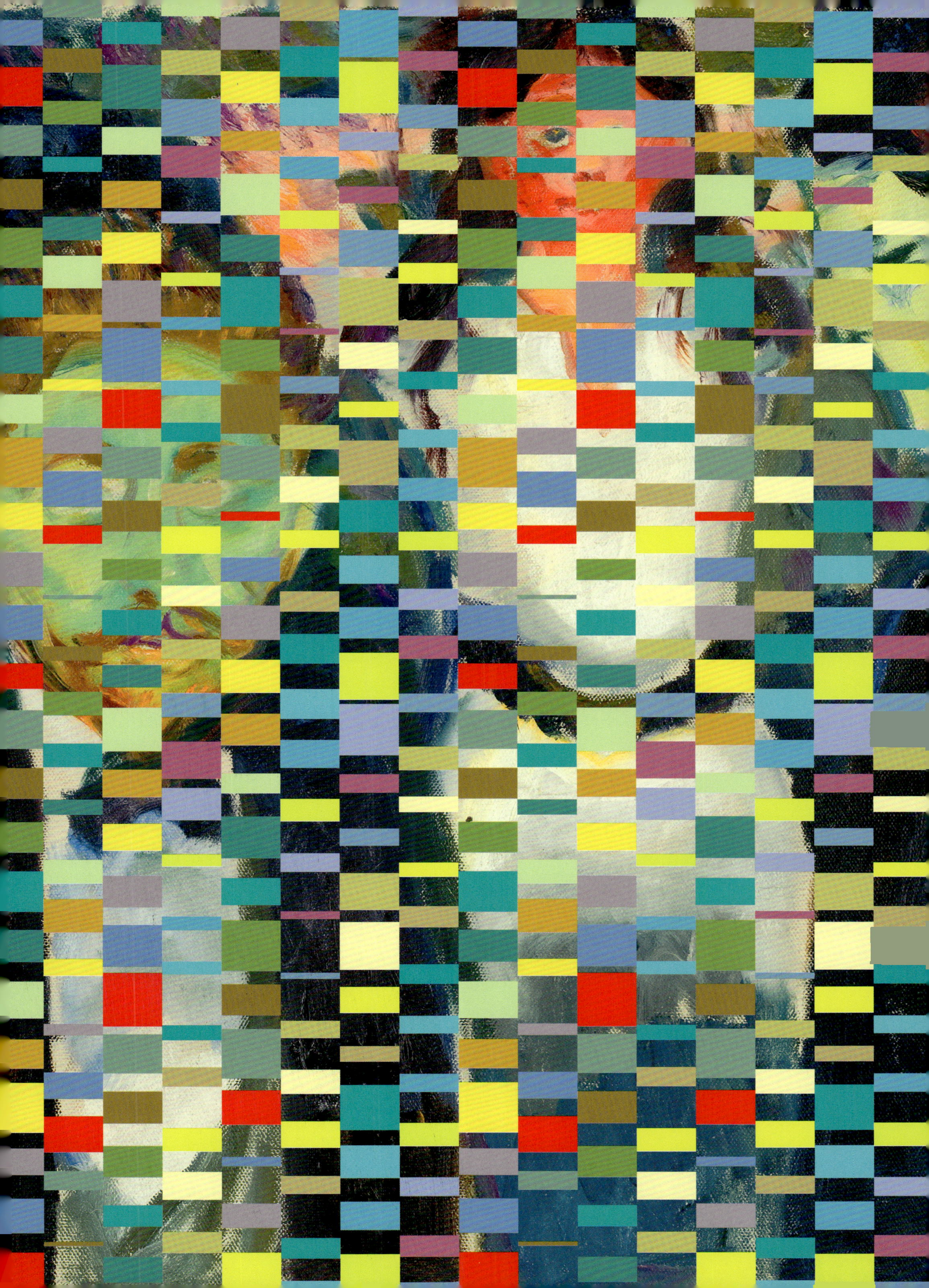

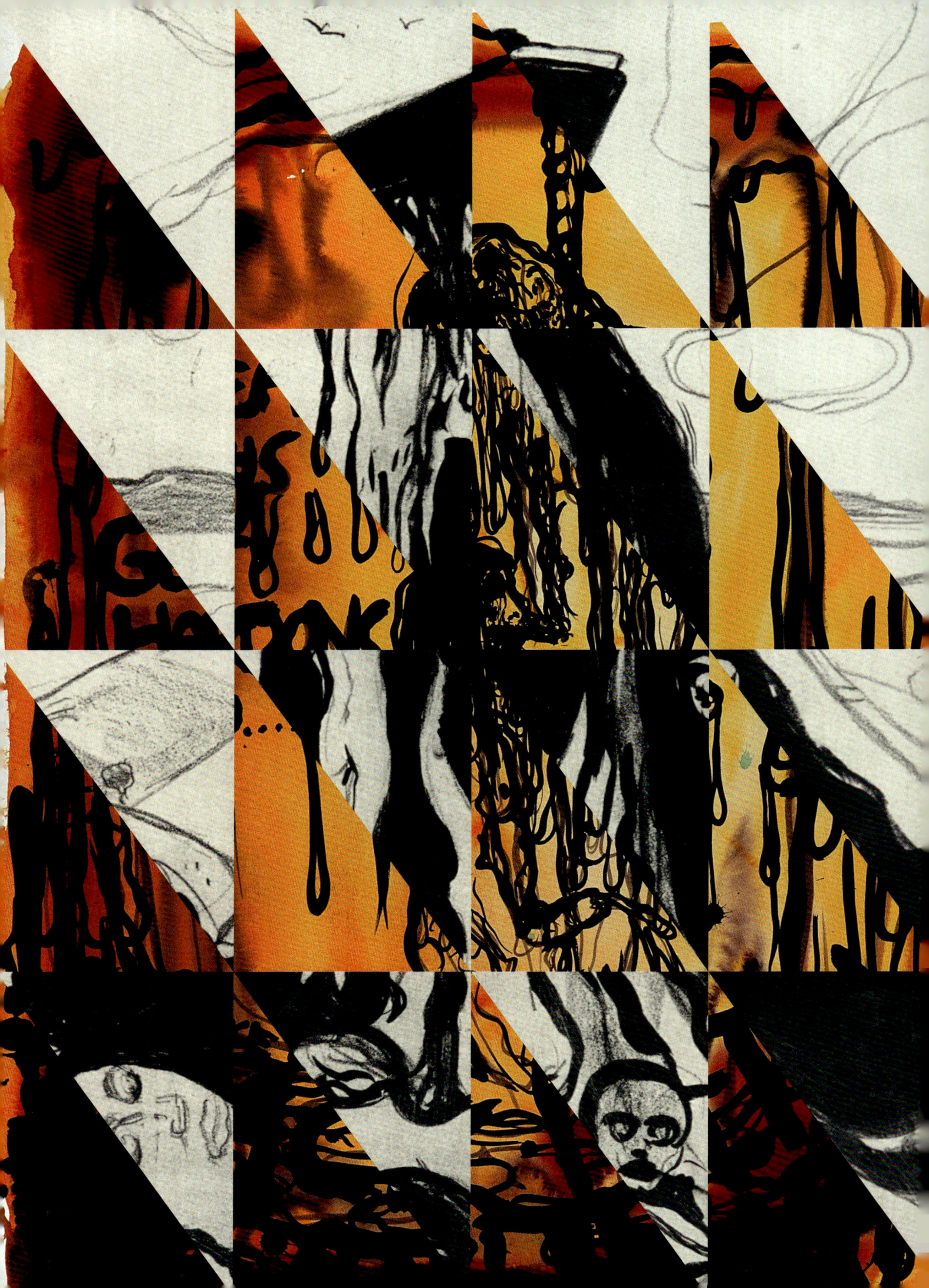

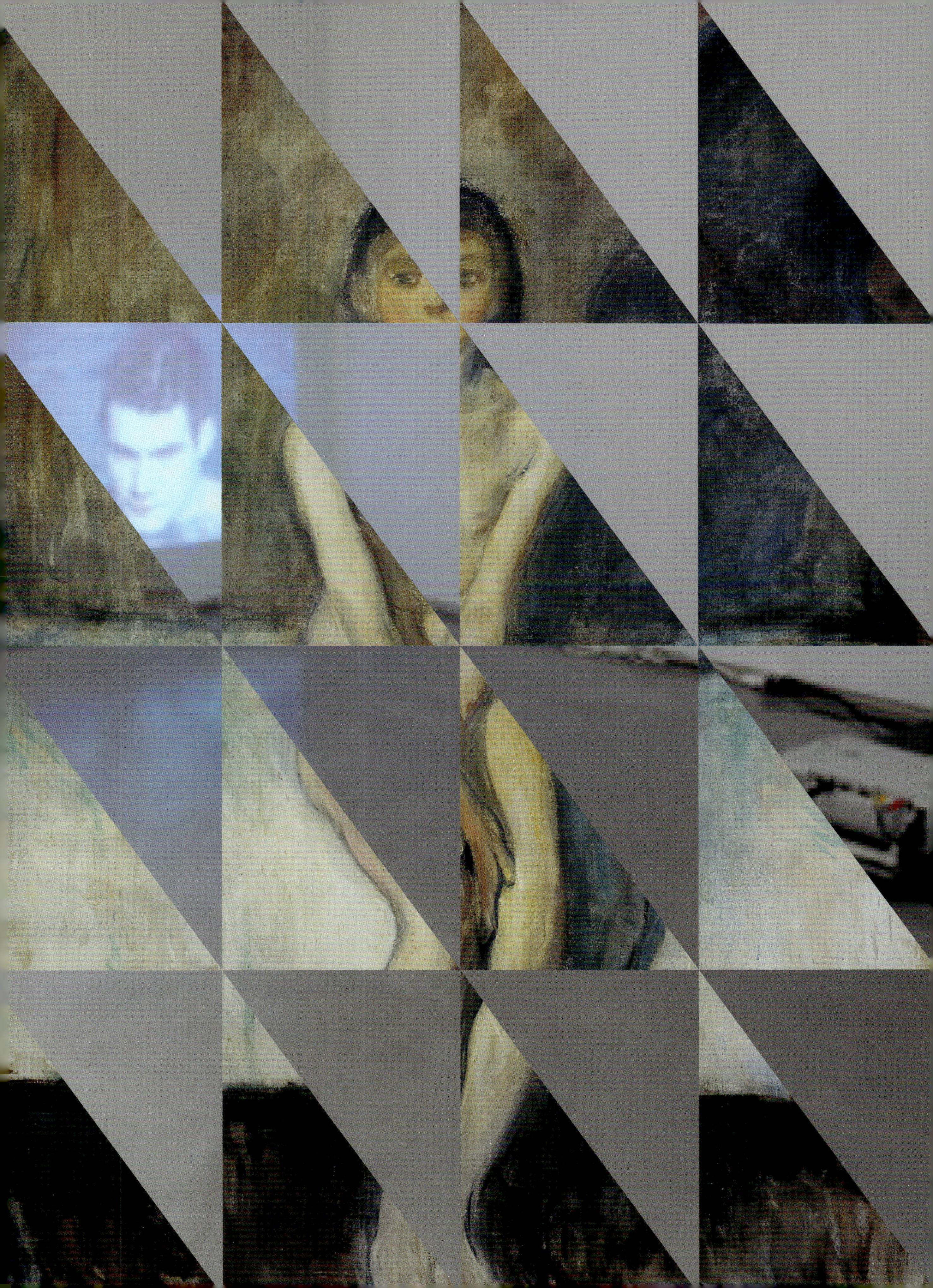

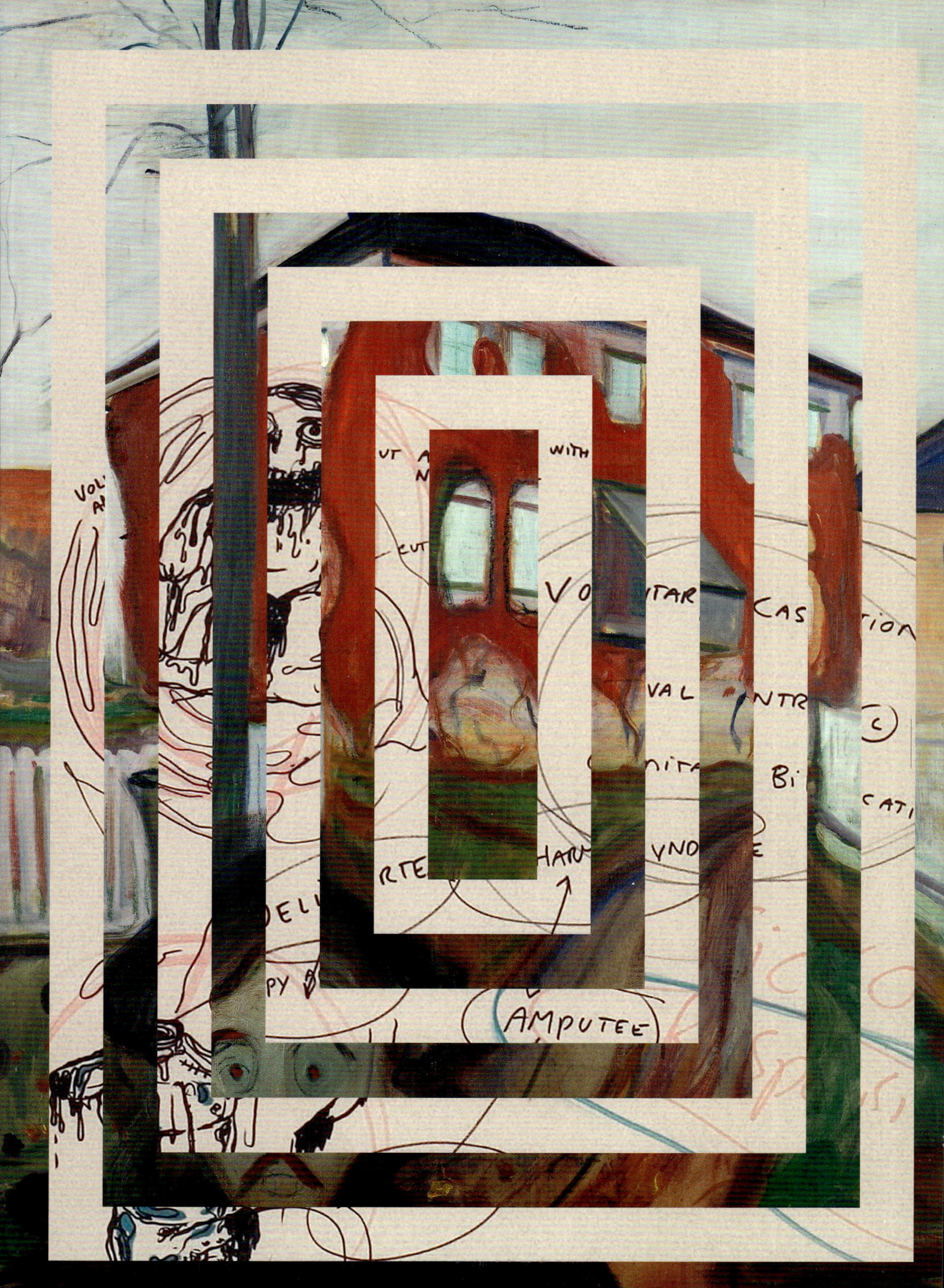

VOLUNTAR
CAS
TION
WITH
VOL
A
CUT
VAL
NTR
(c)
ita
Bi
CAT
RTE
HAN
VNO
E
DELI
PY
AMPUTEE

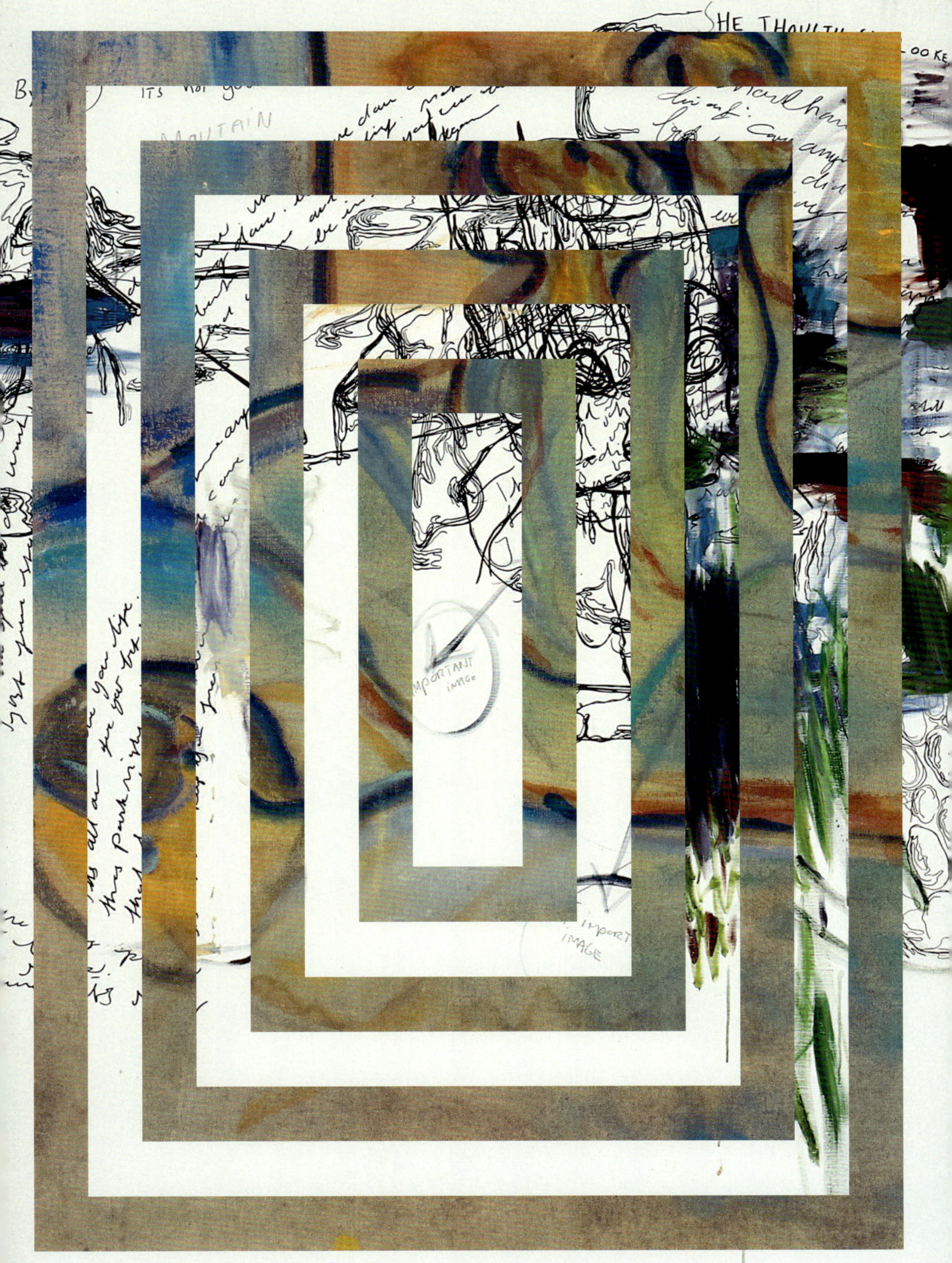
SHE THOUGHT
ITS not good
MOUTAIN
IMPORTANT
IMAGE
IMPORT
IMAGE

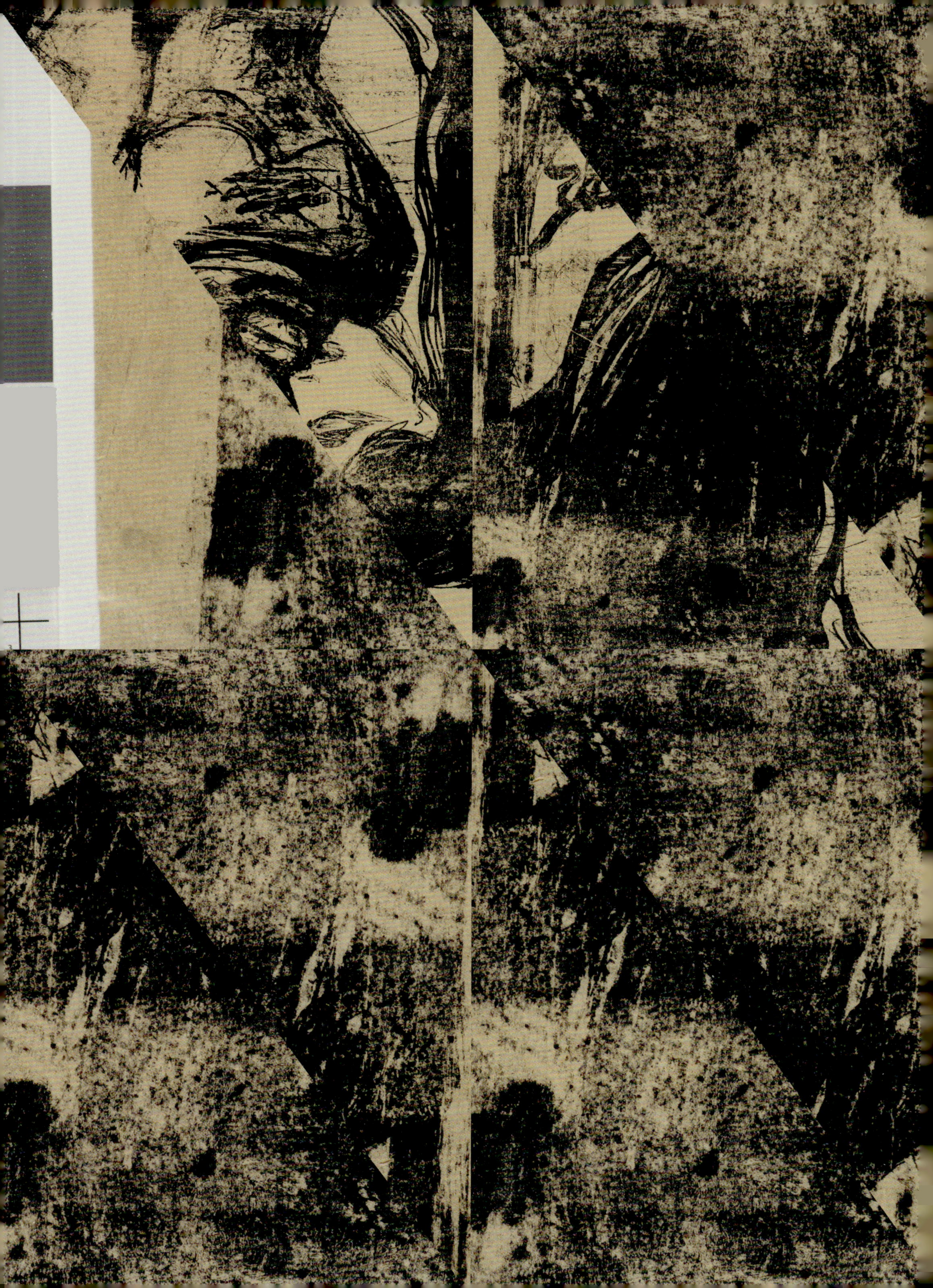

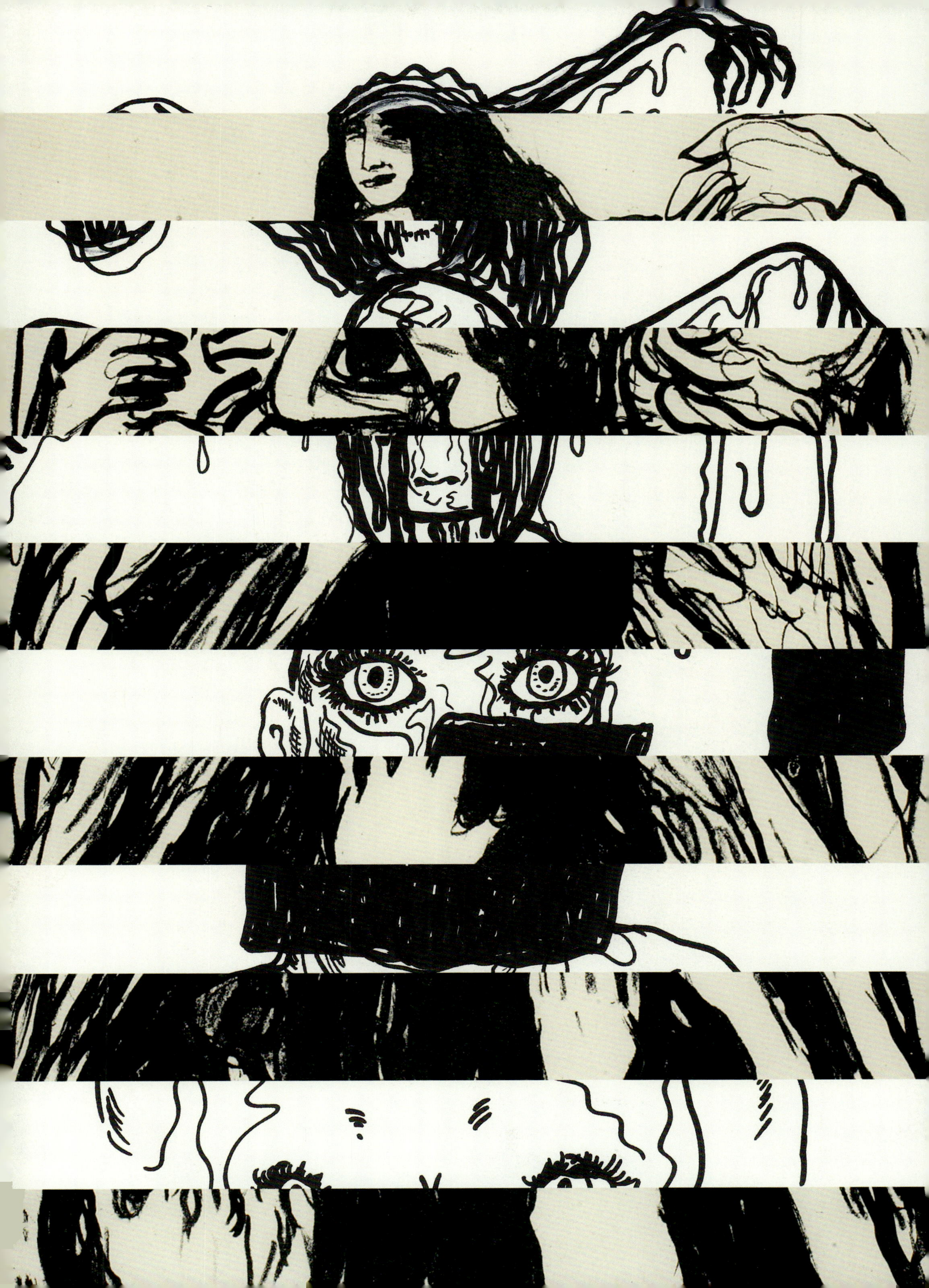

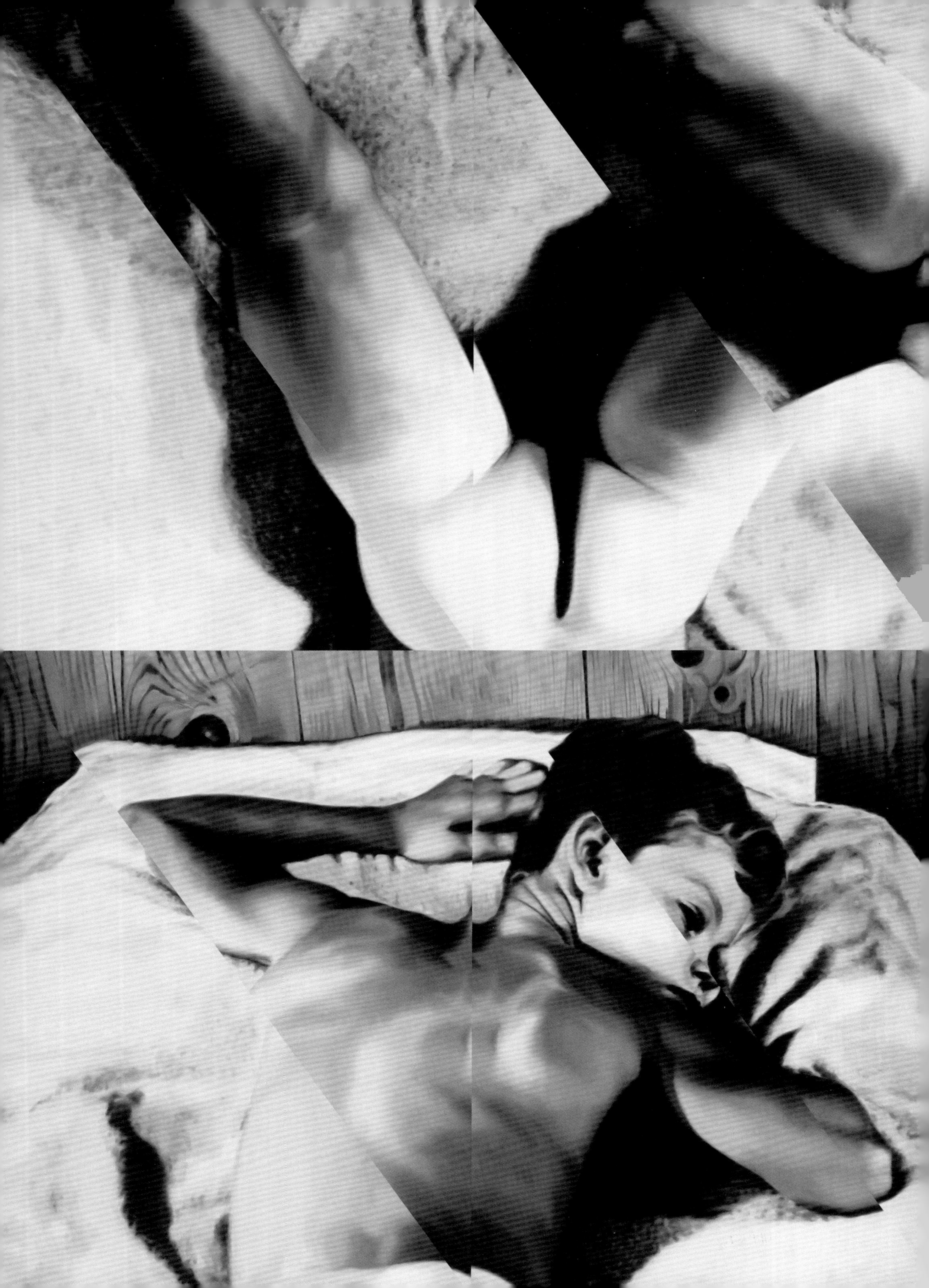

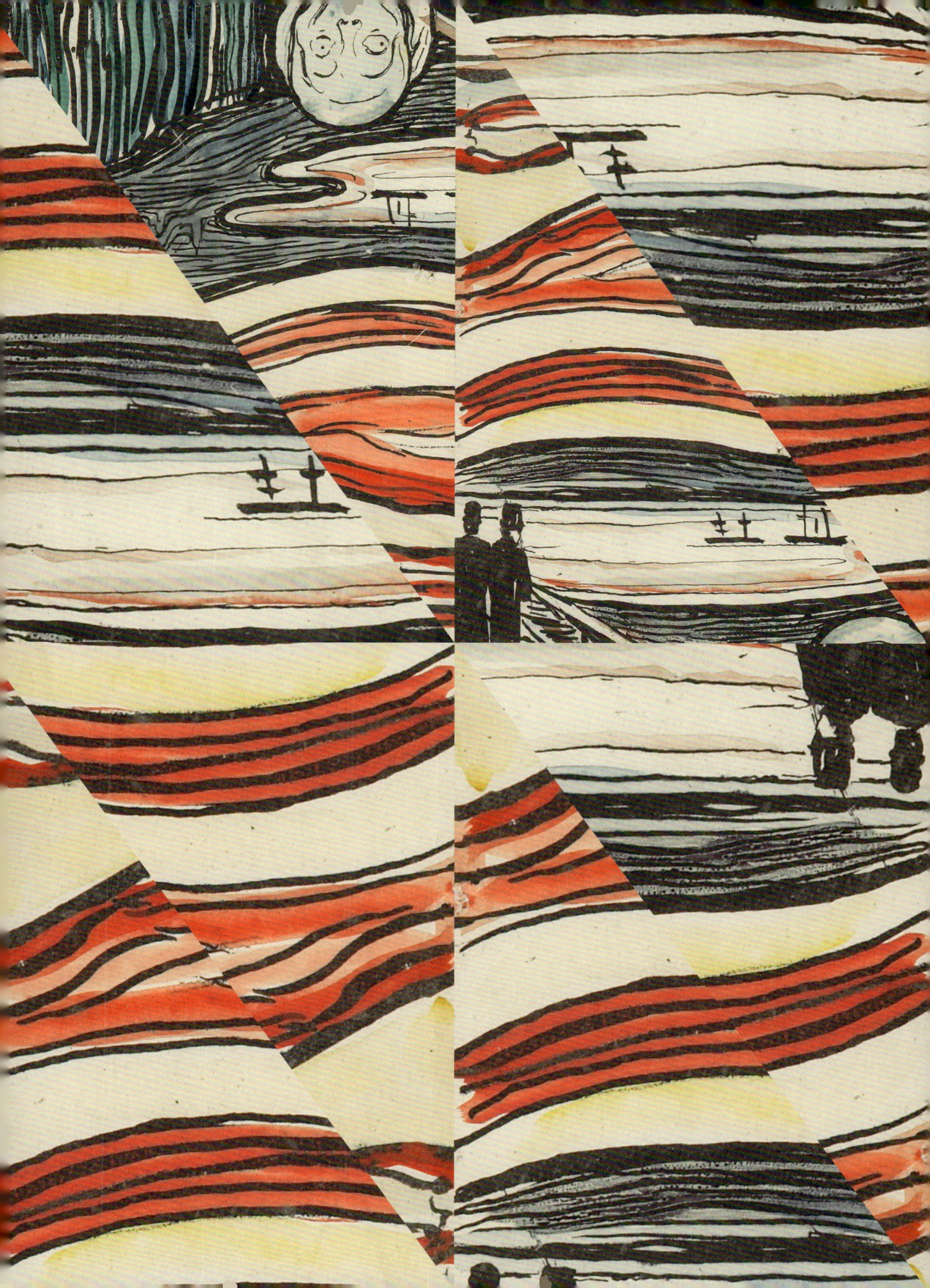

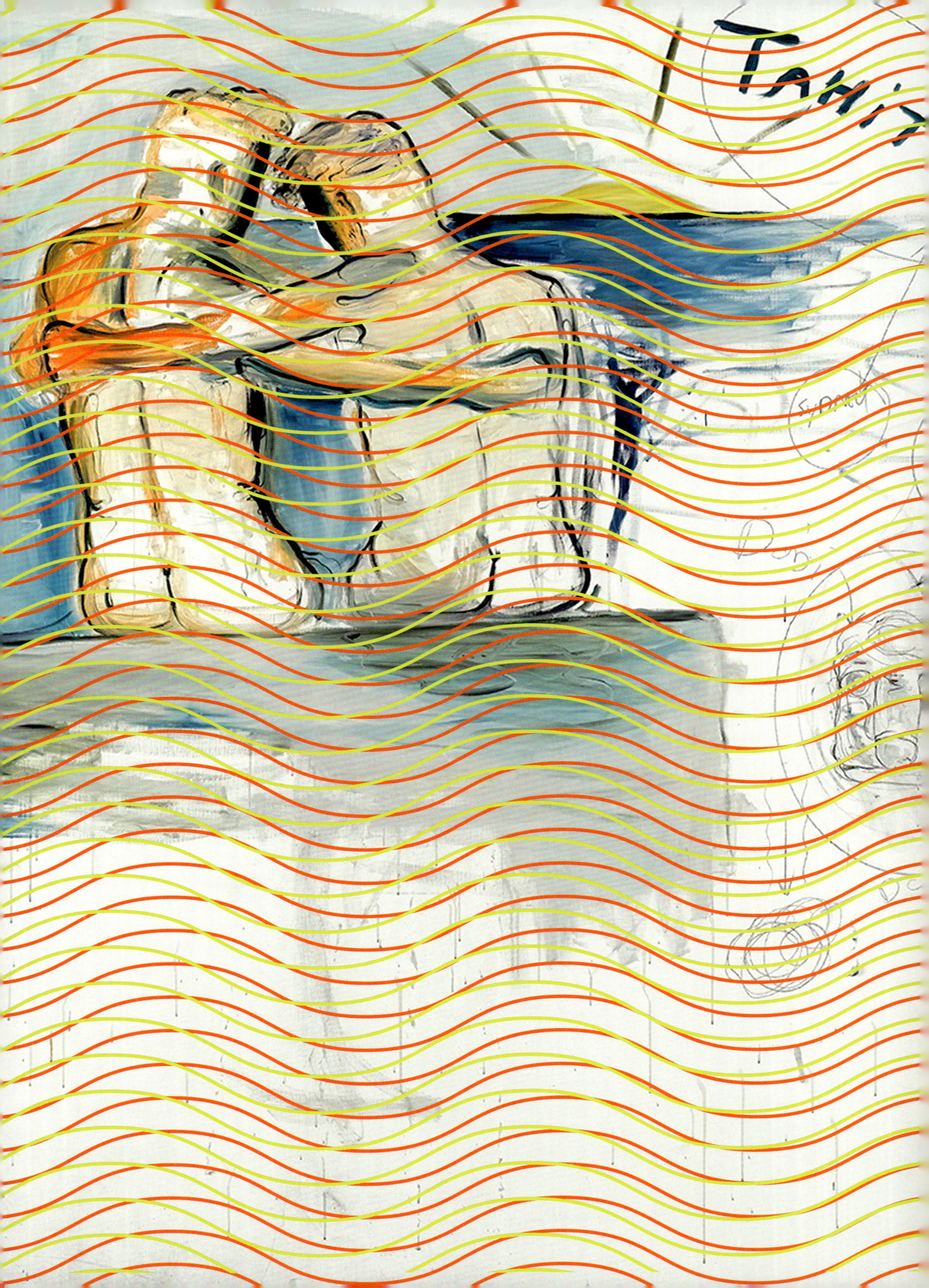

Tahiti
Sydney

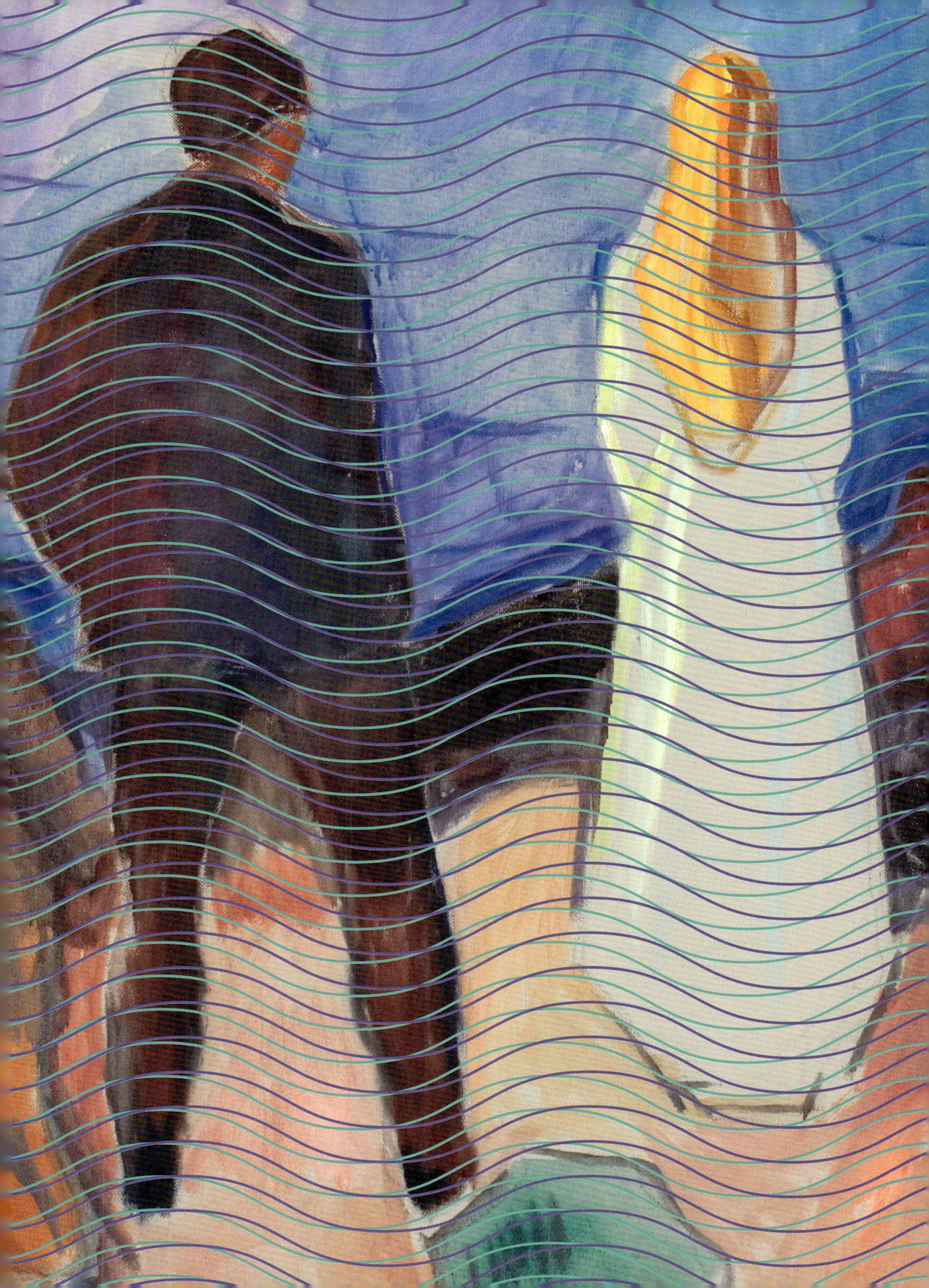

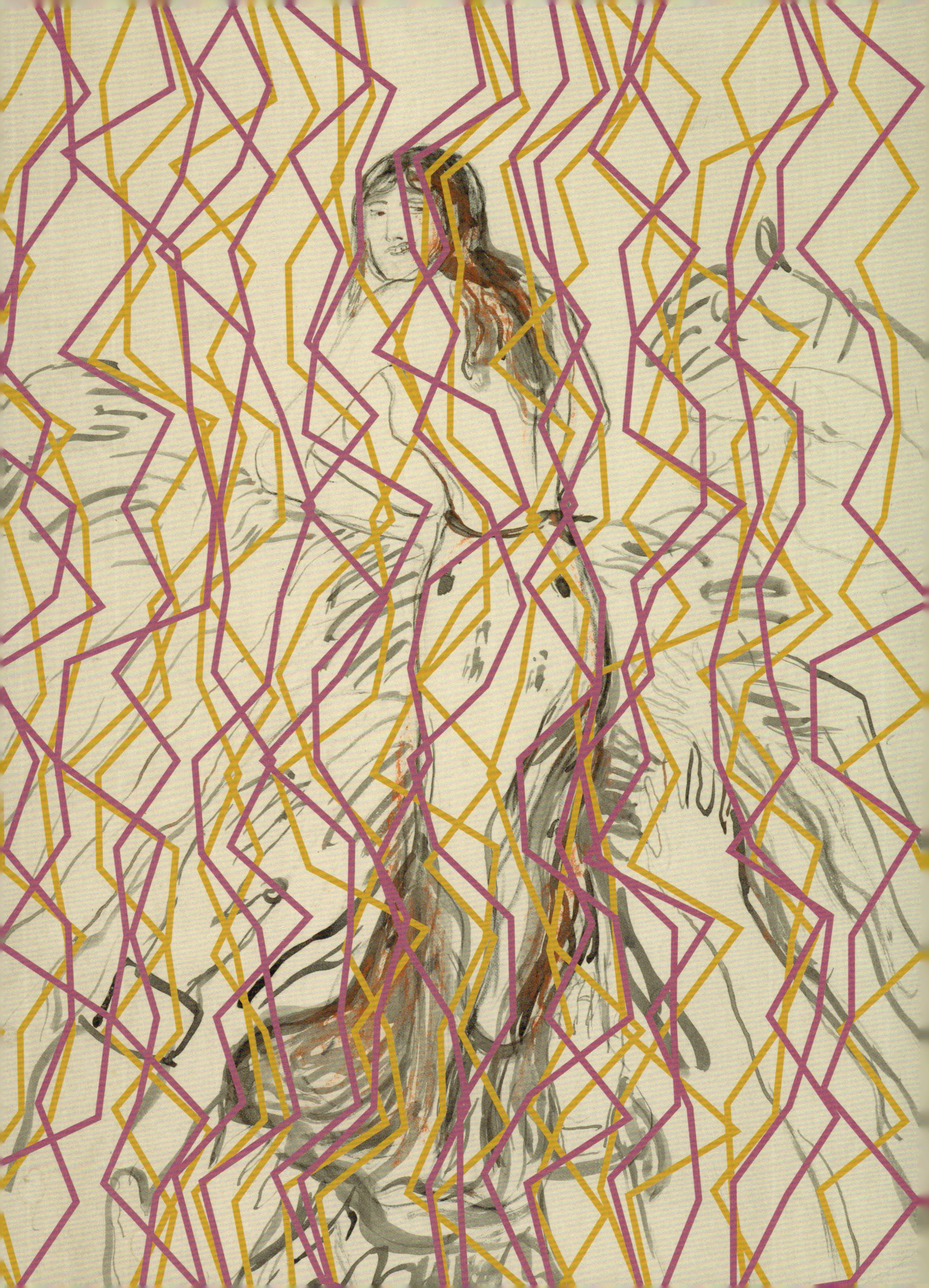

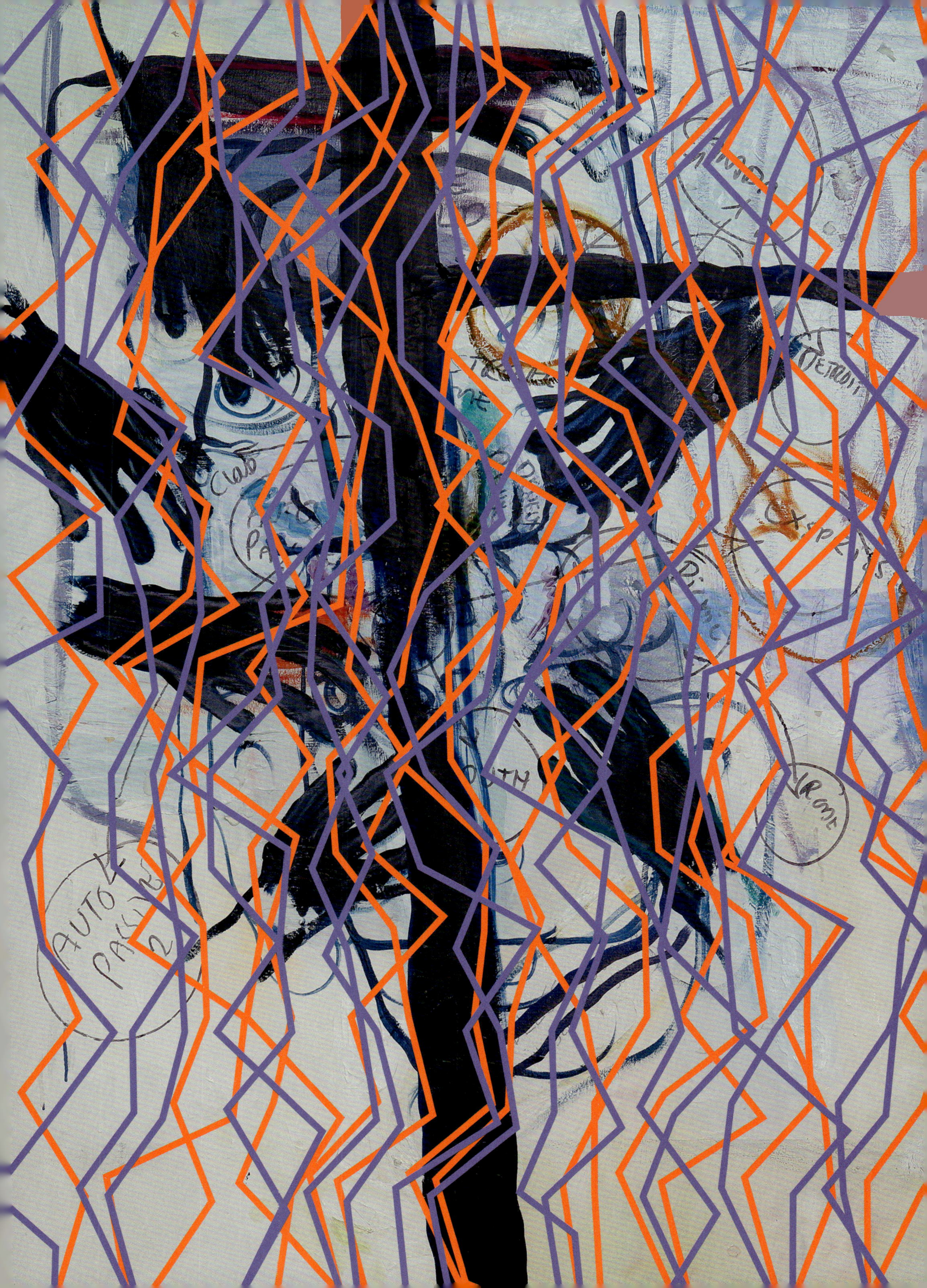

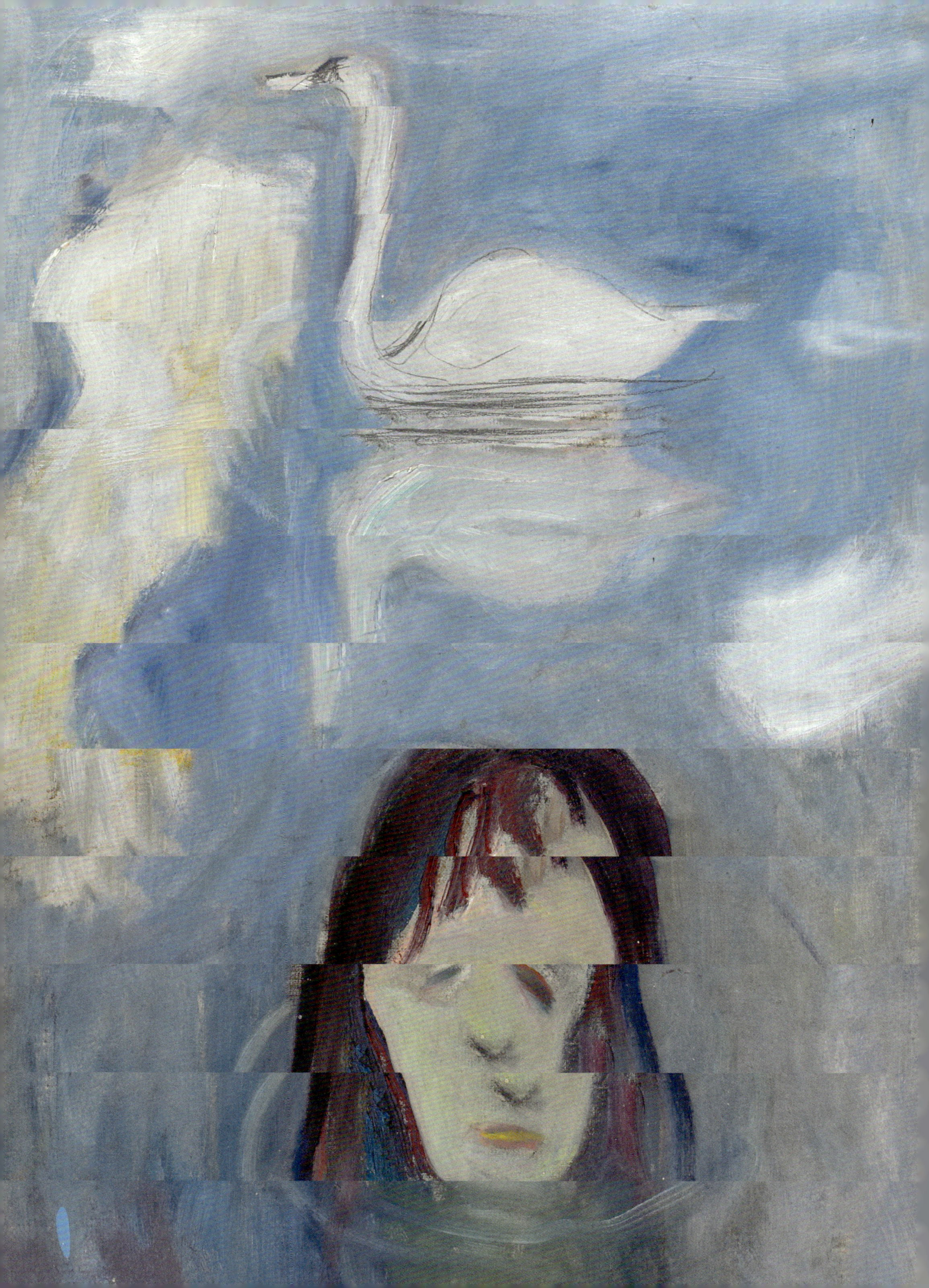

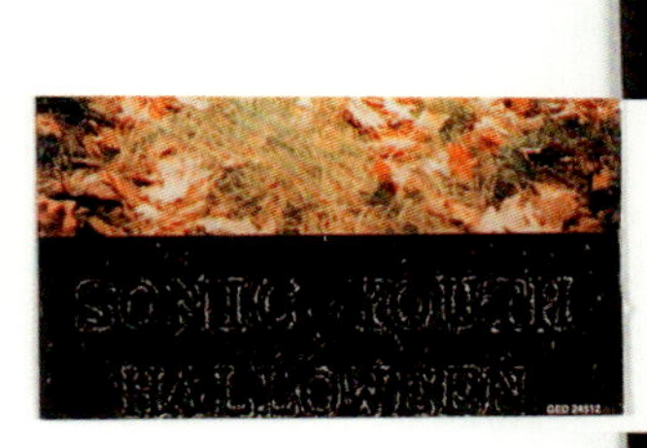

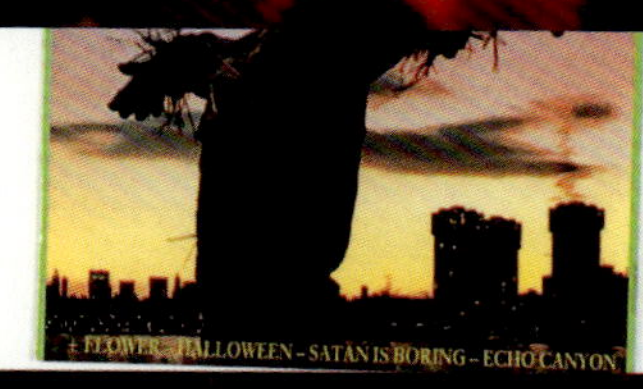

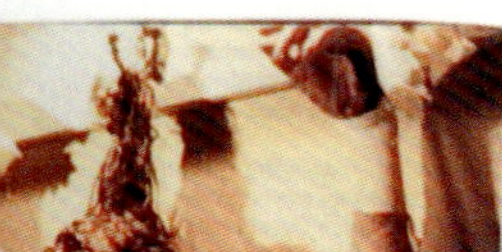

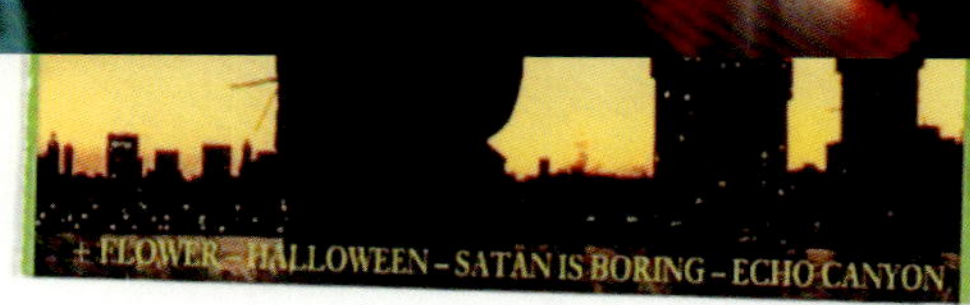

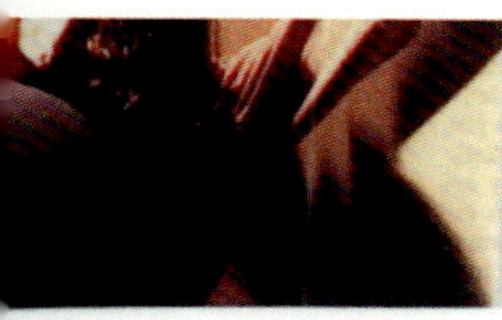

YES....

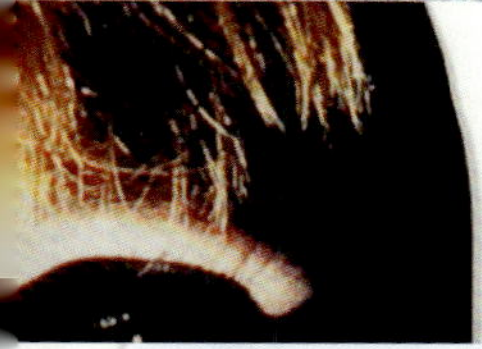

...er of '84...Billy Psycho is shot in the kneecaps. Ed Koch and Keith Hernandez split up ...ks bad for their careers. Bruiser Brody got stabbed. Rev. Sharpton has plenty of extra ...r' tickets, real cheap. The second Tommy Dog single is in the shops, though not Some ...hich hasn't opened yet. No Gap on St. Marks, Times Sq.-as indoor-mall is still 10 years ...hy bother setting the "scene," when Sonic Youth's connecton to it just sells them short? ...fucking times did the words "lower-east-side" figure prominent in someone's confused ...ght and more precise than Chinatown-TriBeCa-Hoboken for sure, but slow-thinkers were ...k to box Sonic Youth into a ghetto so small it's zip code was stolen.

...or not, Bad Moon Rising, and its preceding single "Death Valley '69" (w/ Lydia Lunch) were ...res, you had to admit it, even if you were busy watching the gate at the rock/art internment

YES...

The autumn of '84 featured some incredible Sonic Youth shows in NY that hardly anyone saw (this wasn't so unusual prior to the release of Bad Moon)...I remember a scorching 15-minute set at the Pyramid that ended with the plug being pulled (and the Lady Bunny punching Bob Bert in the eye) I got into a big argument with Timmy 'Noise The Show' Sommer on the walk home 'cause he thought I said "kill the fucking homos" when in fact I told him to blow his nose. (Years later, Tim would have an almost identical exchange with Michael Bolton prior to a VH-1 on-air interview, too bad he never got those ears checked out.) Thanksgiving at Maxwell's in front of 15 people, everything was going swell until Thurston decided to reenact the entire first side of Black Flag's "Family Man."

Bad Moon made its initial splash in the UK, where Richard Thompson lookalike Paul Smith had released it on his new Blast First imprint. The album was originally scheduled to come out on Cabaret Voltaire's Colecovision label, but the company went bust during the whole video game crash of '84. US release came shortly thereafter on the poorly financed, barely distributed Homestead label, an operation whose previous achievements included releasing early titles by Thor and Virgin Steele (years later I remember reading that the bass player for this band was a member of the Buttafuoco clan, but maybe

it's LIKE THAT

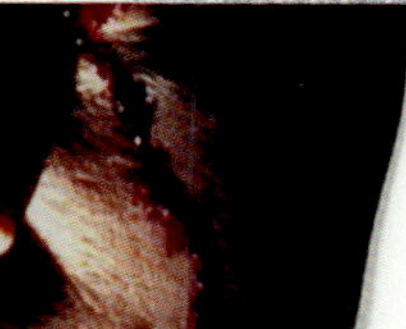

...copies of the "Death Valley" 7" and to this day it is estimated that this single has outsold the rest of the

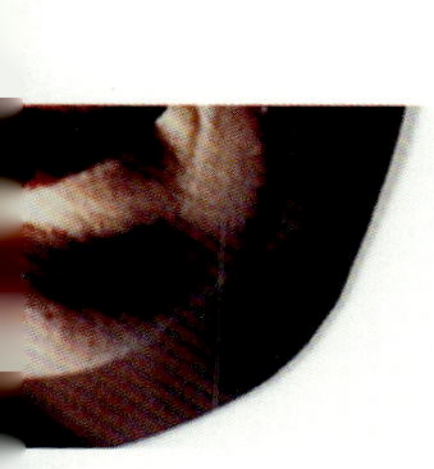

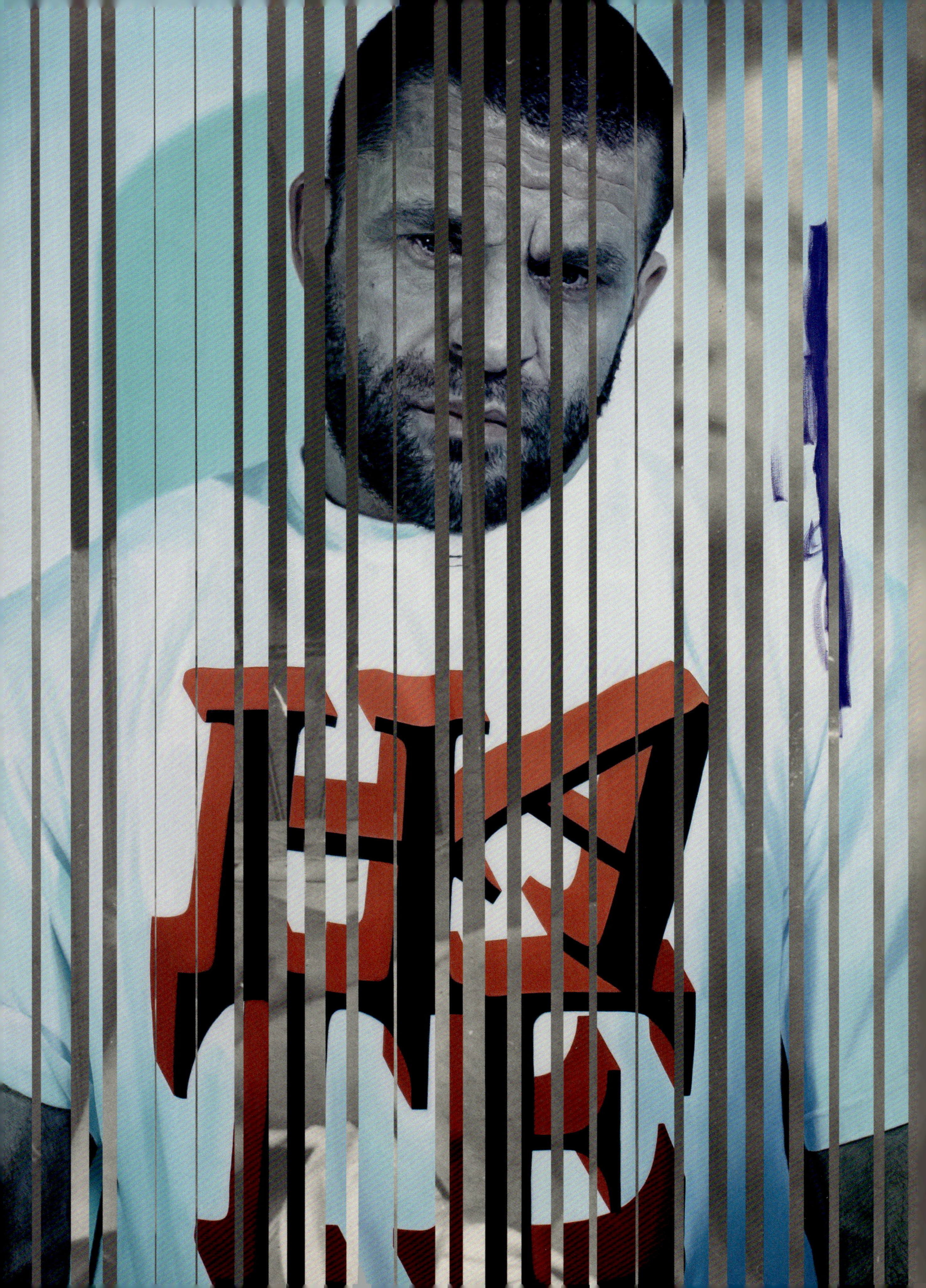

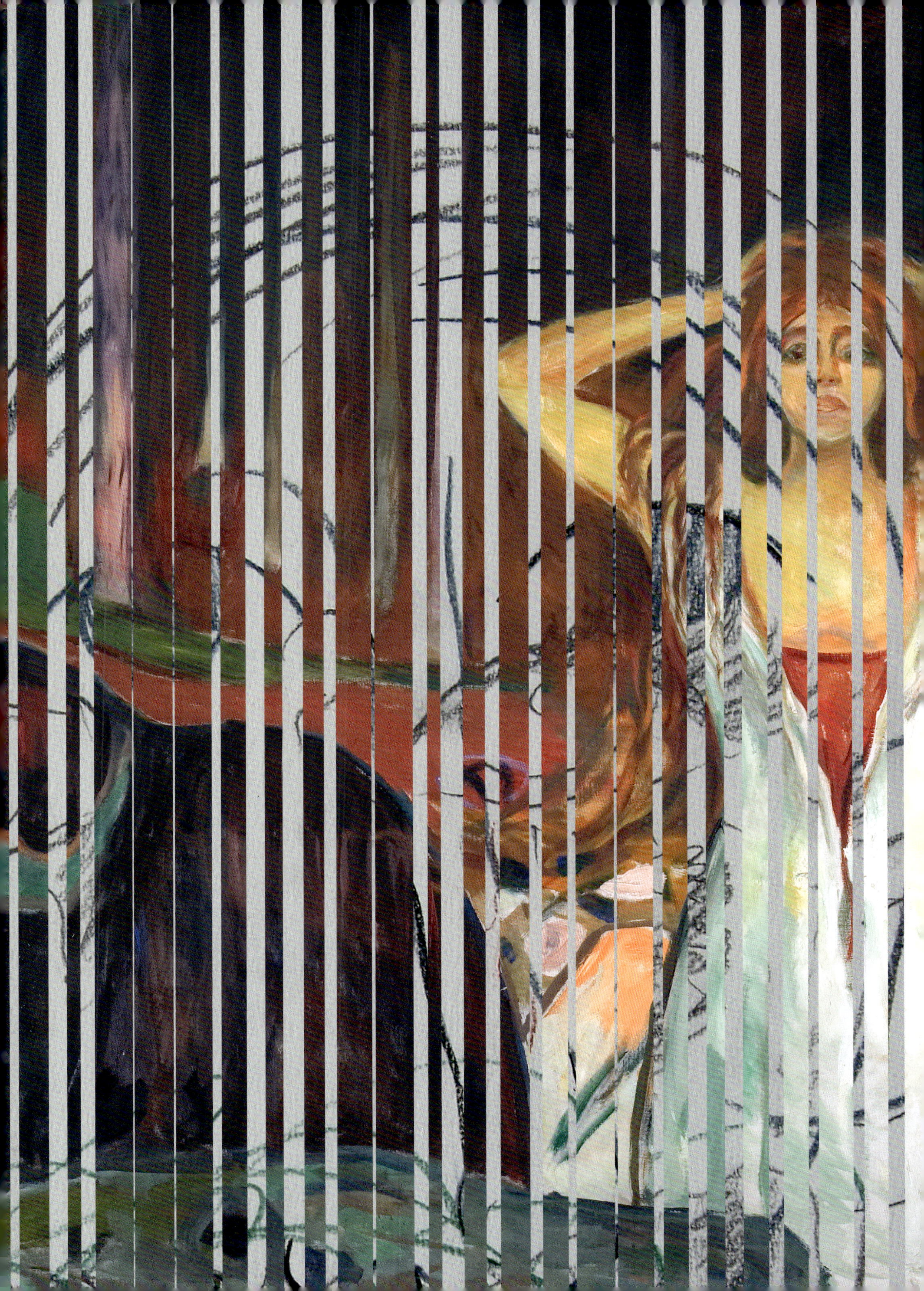

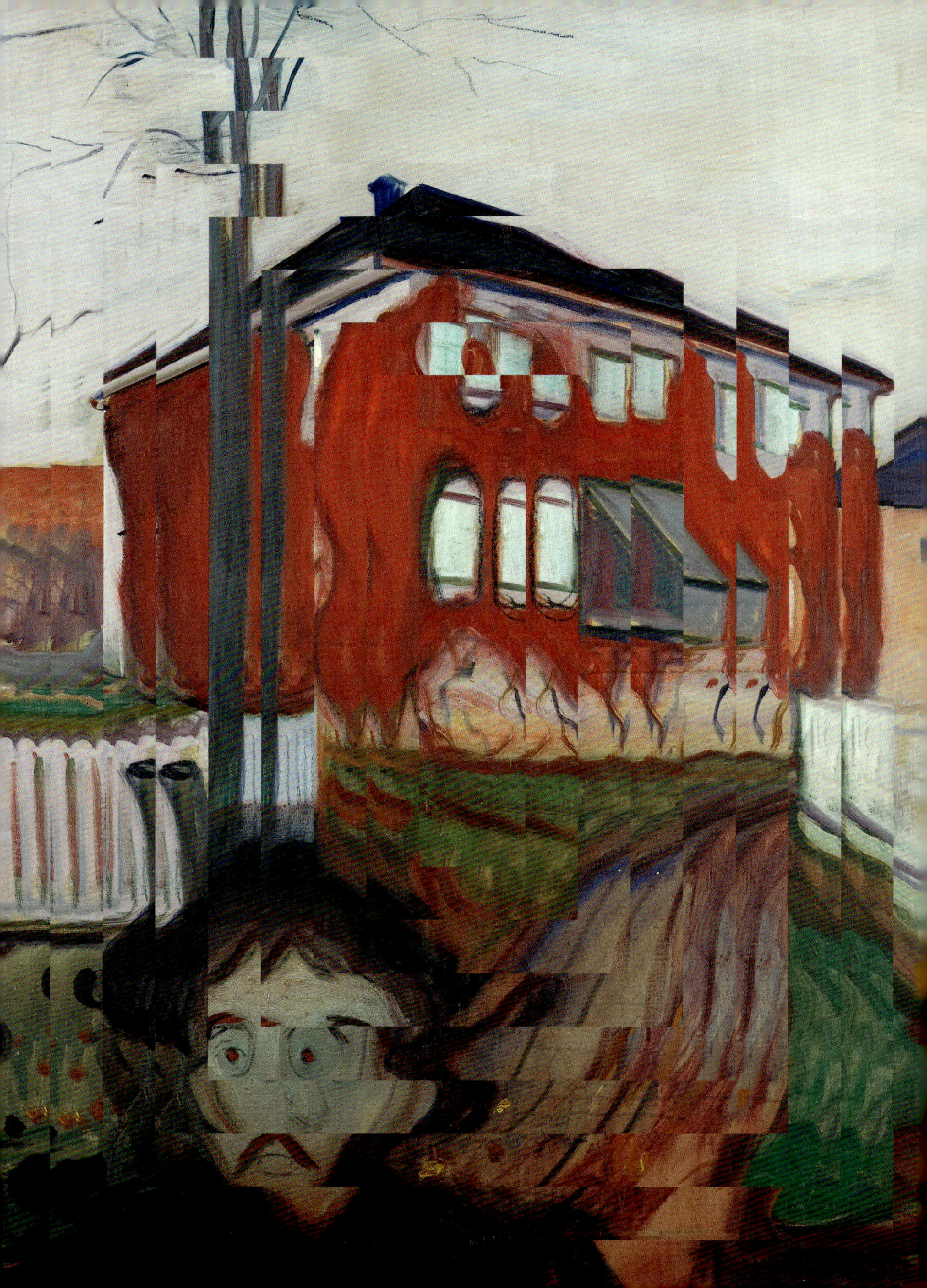

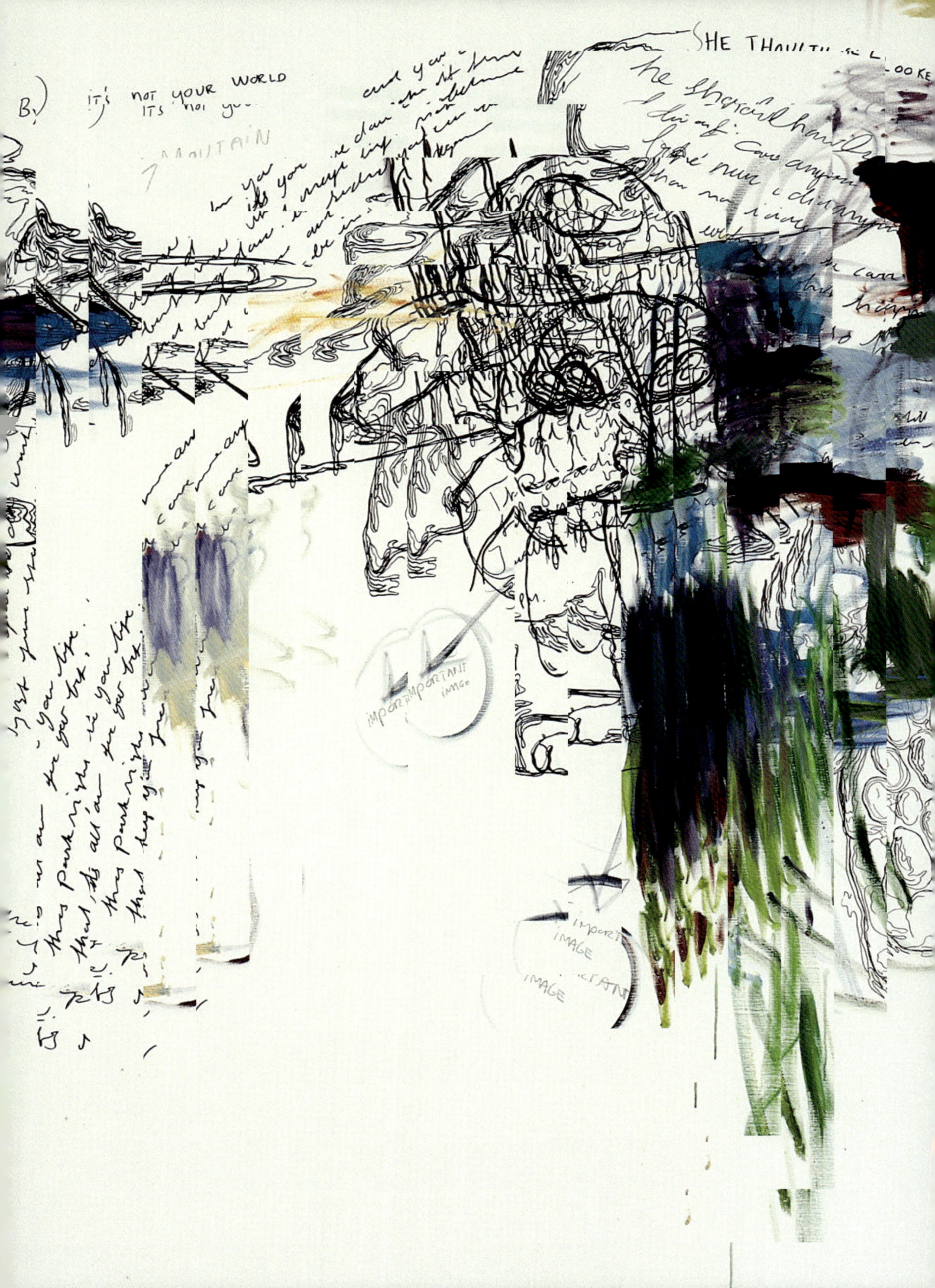

B.)
it's not your world
its not you
MOUTAIN
SHE THAULT HE LOOKE
IMPORTANT IMAGE
IMPORT IMAGE
IMAGE

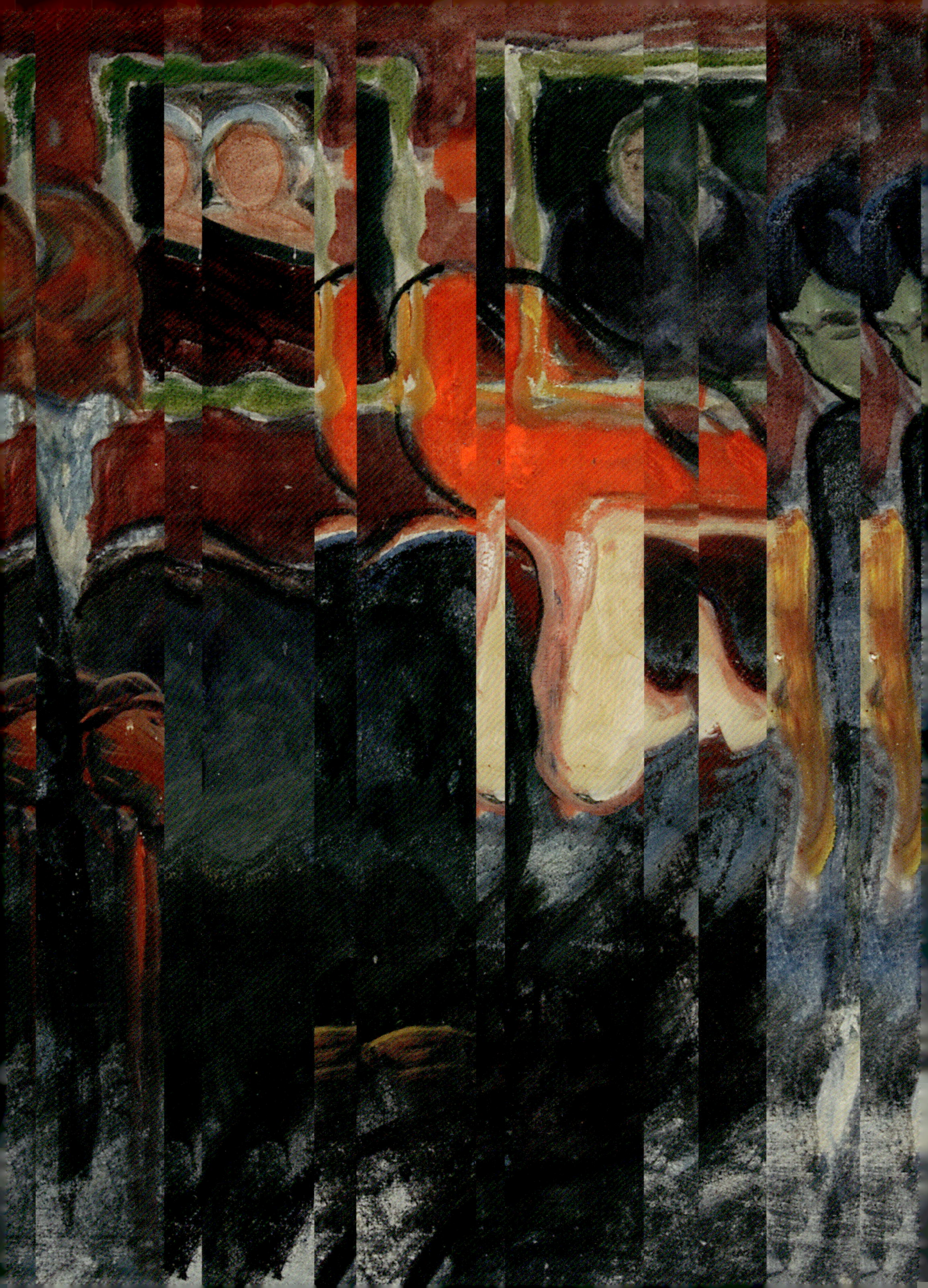

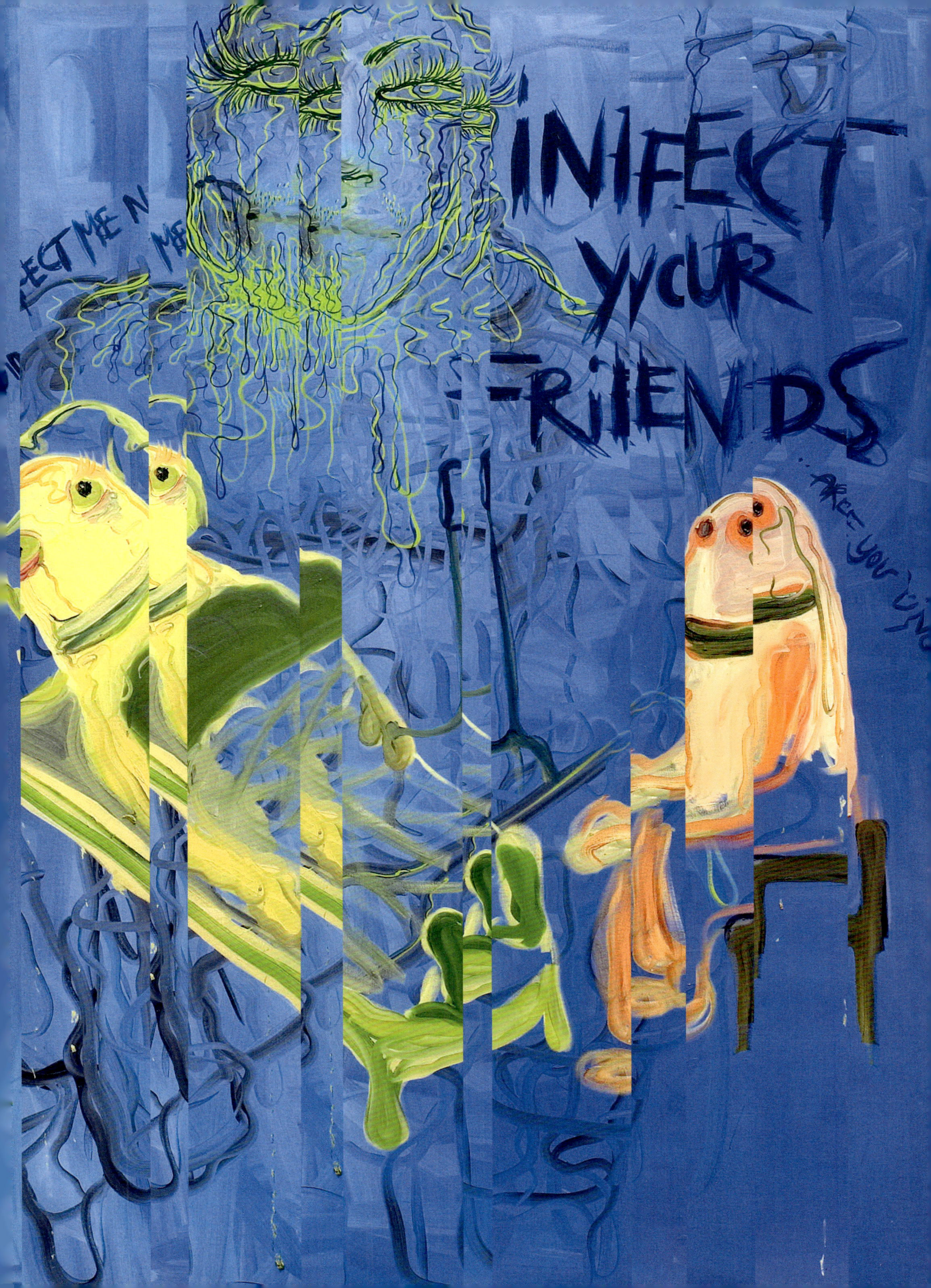
INIFECT
YVCUR
FRIIENDS
ECT ME N ME

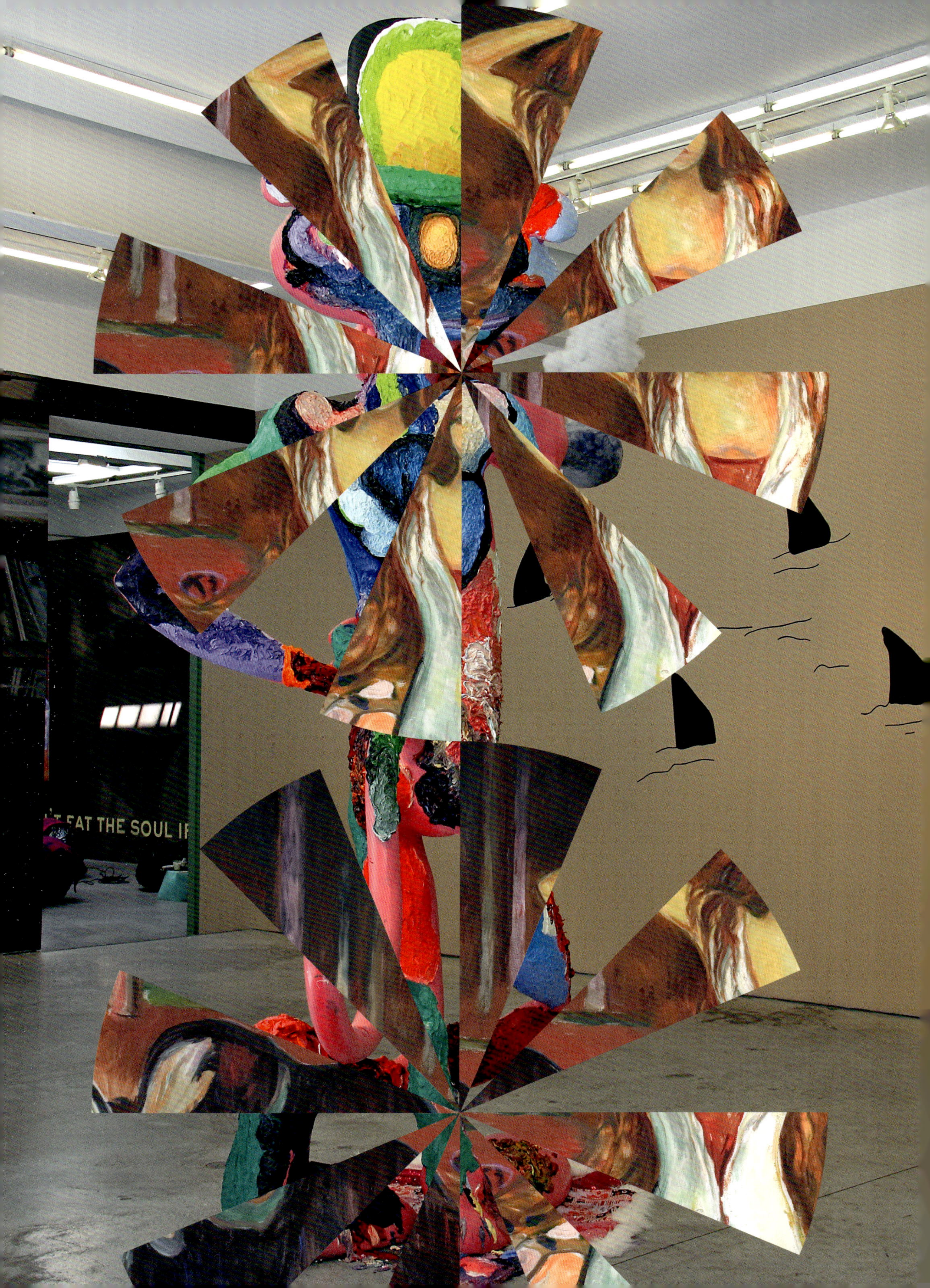
T EAT THE SOUL IF

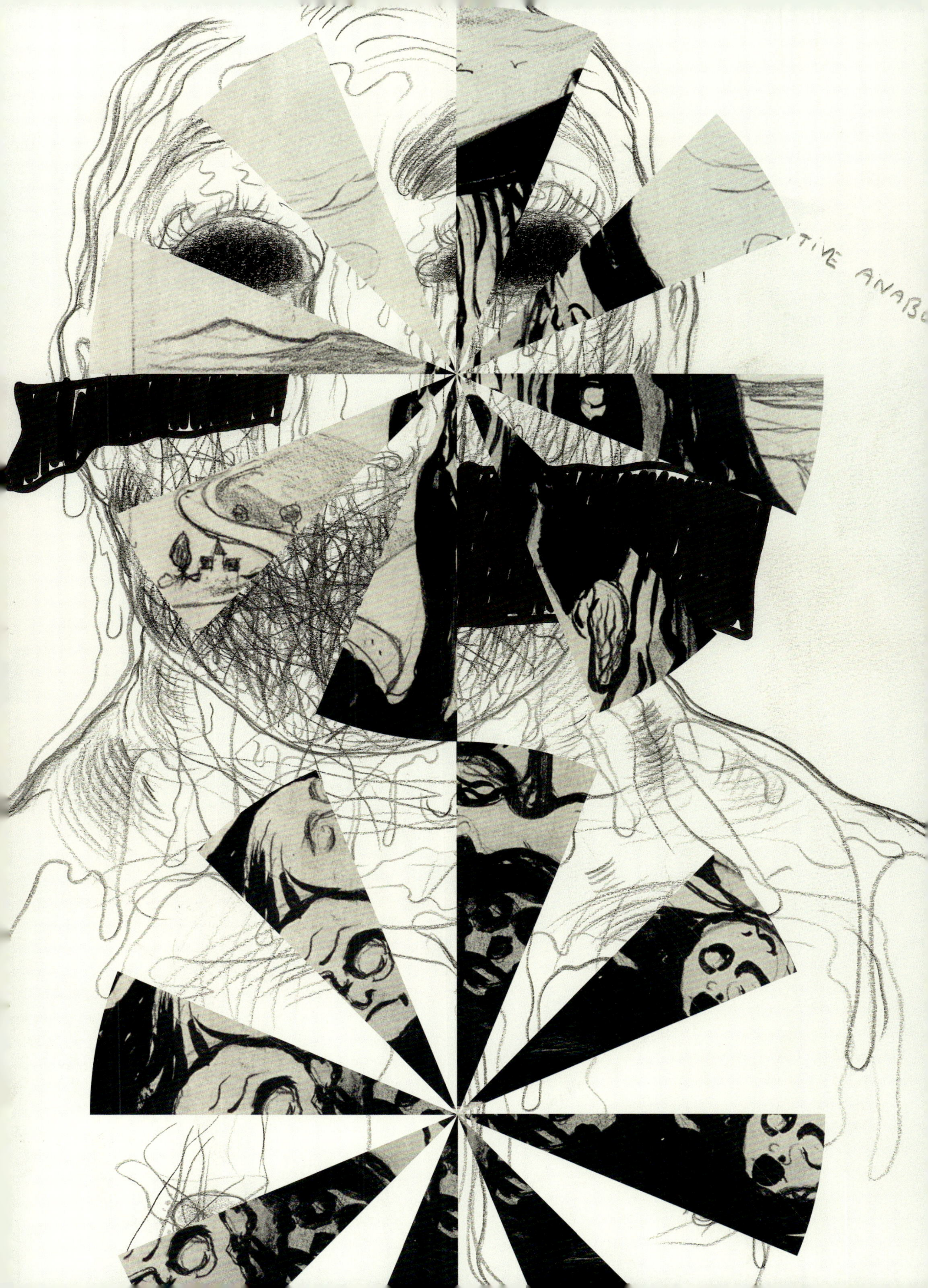
TIVE ANABO

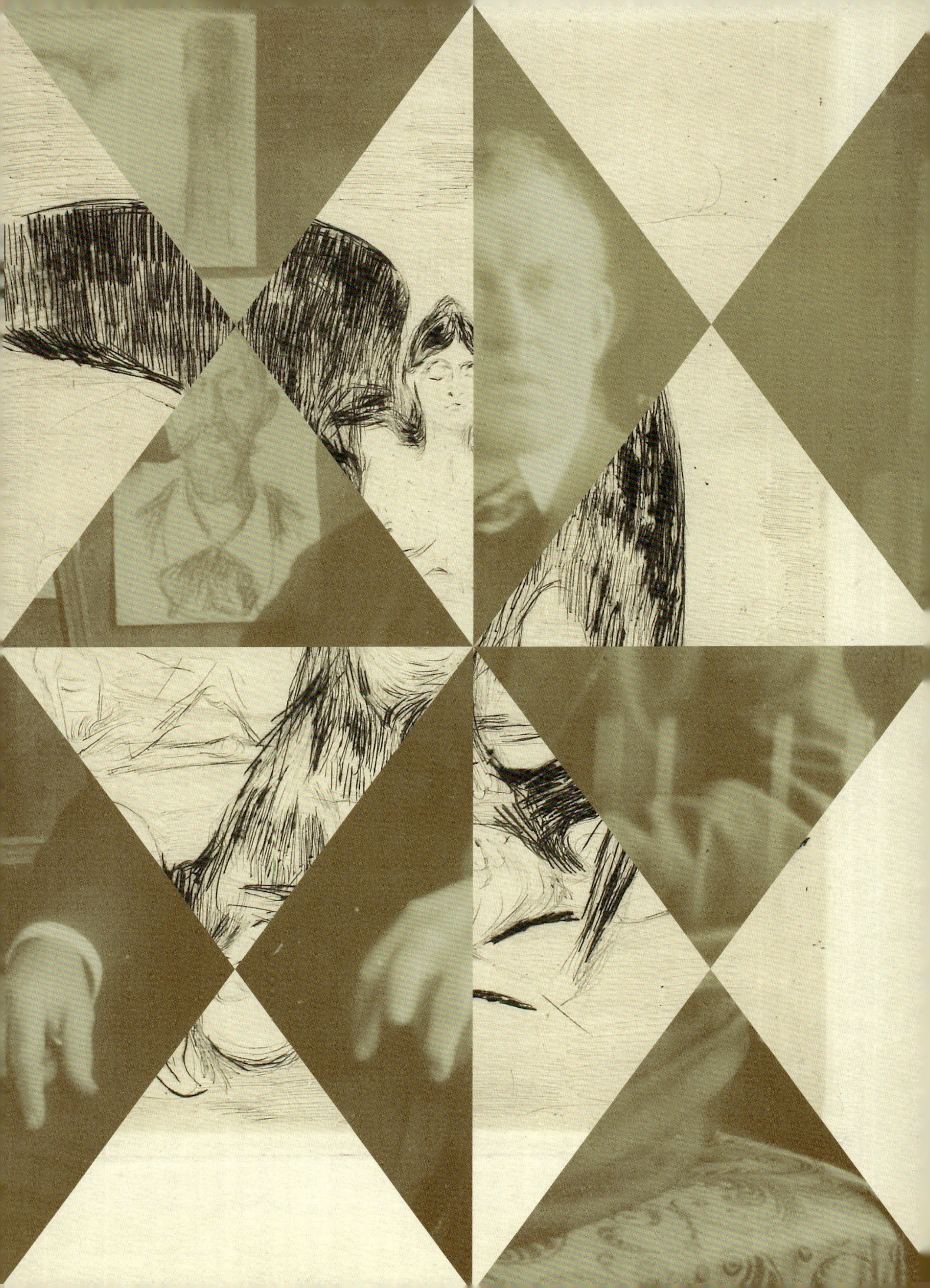

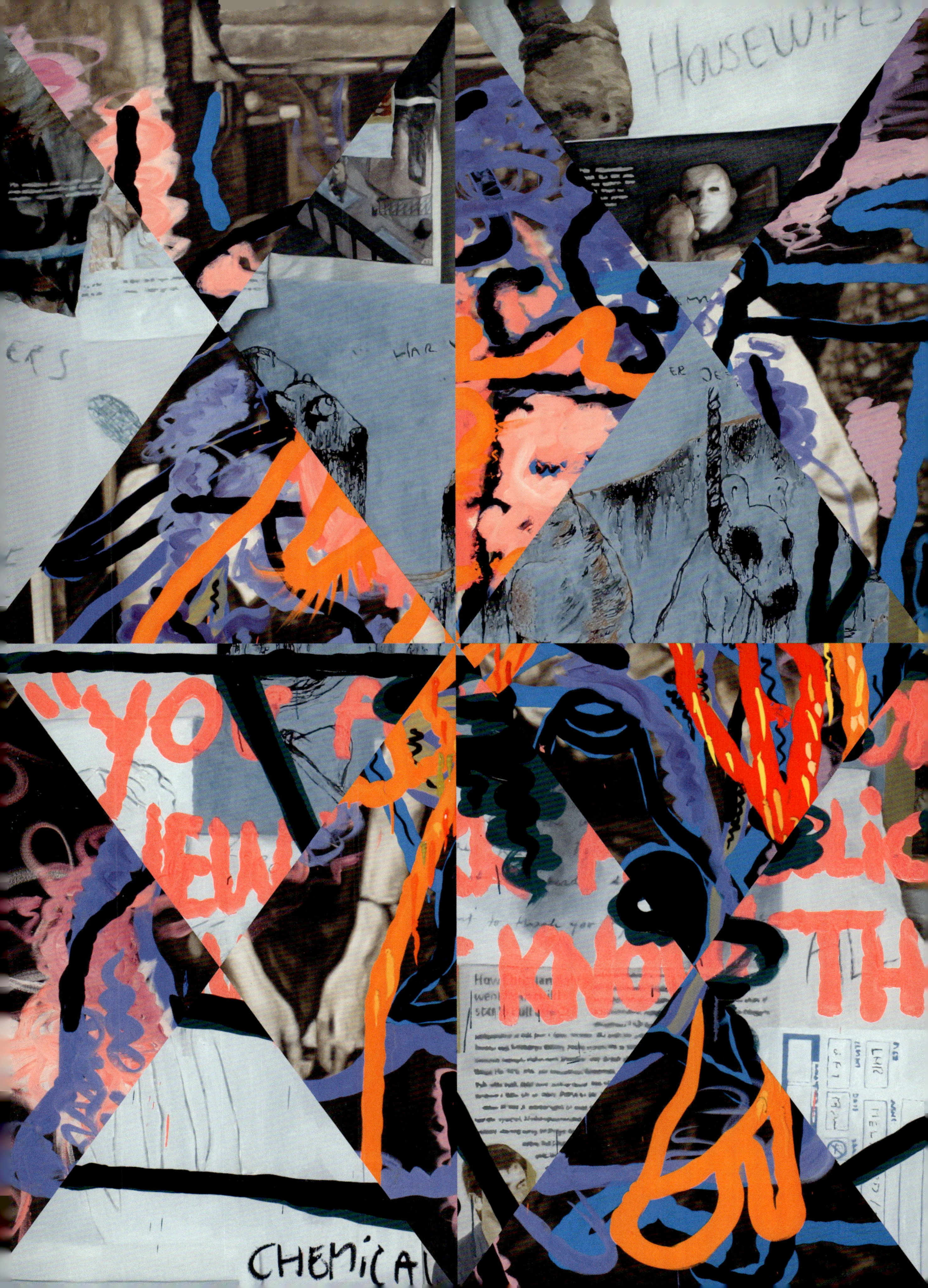
HOUSEWIFES
CHEMICAL

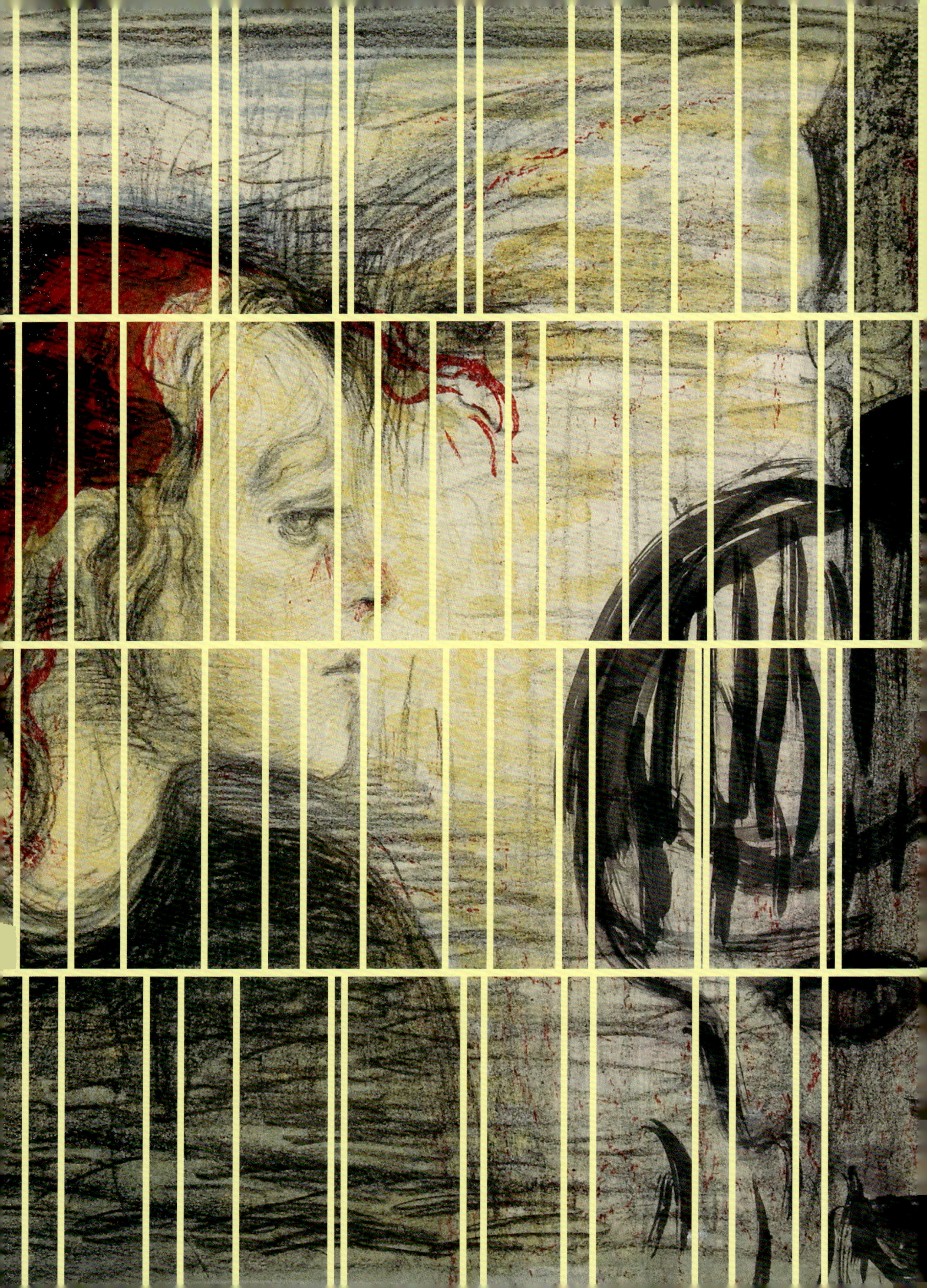

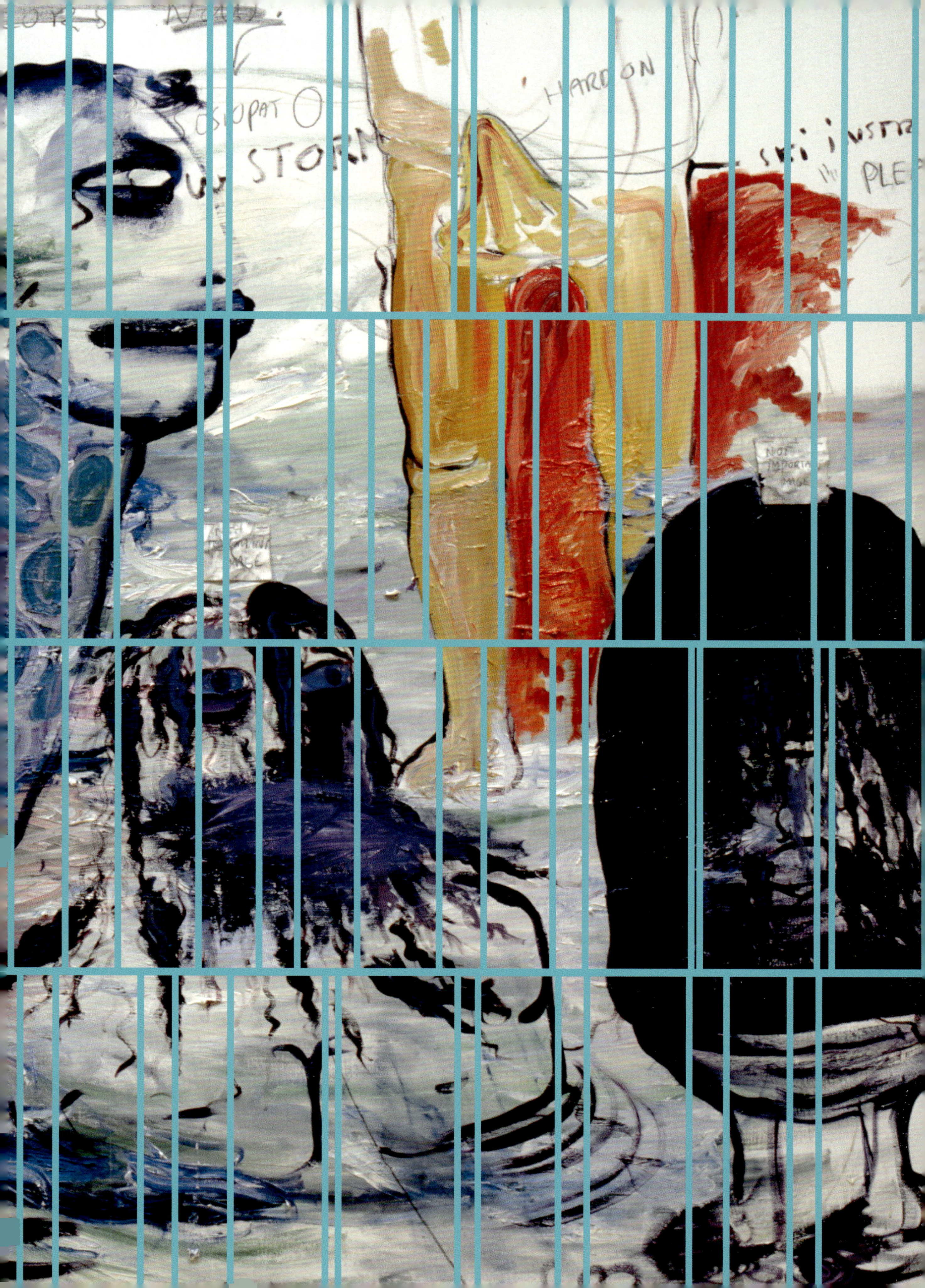

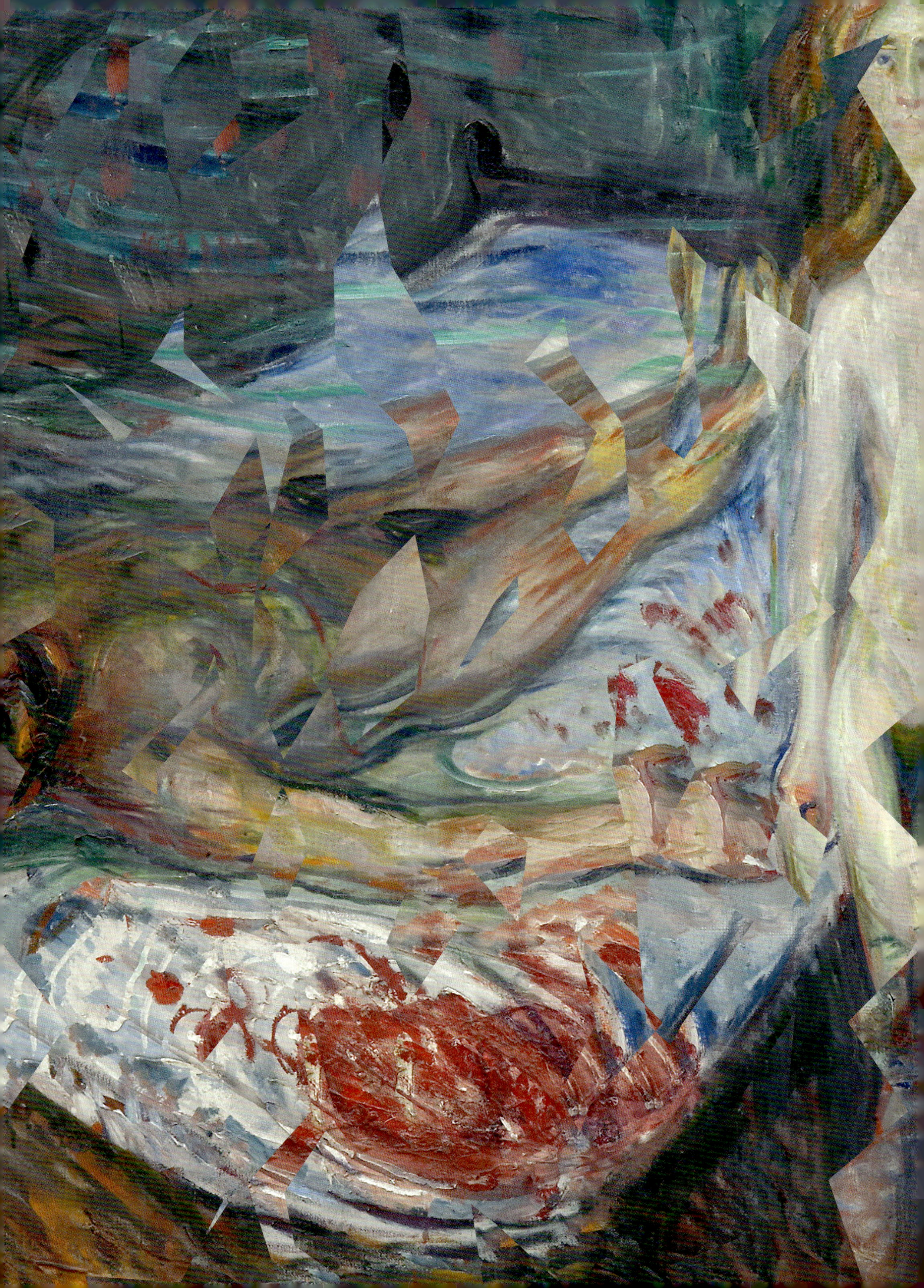

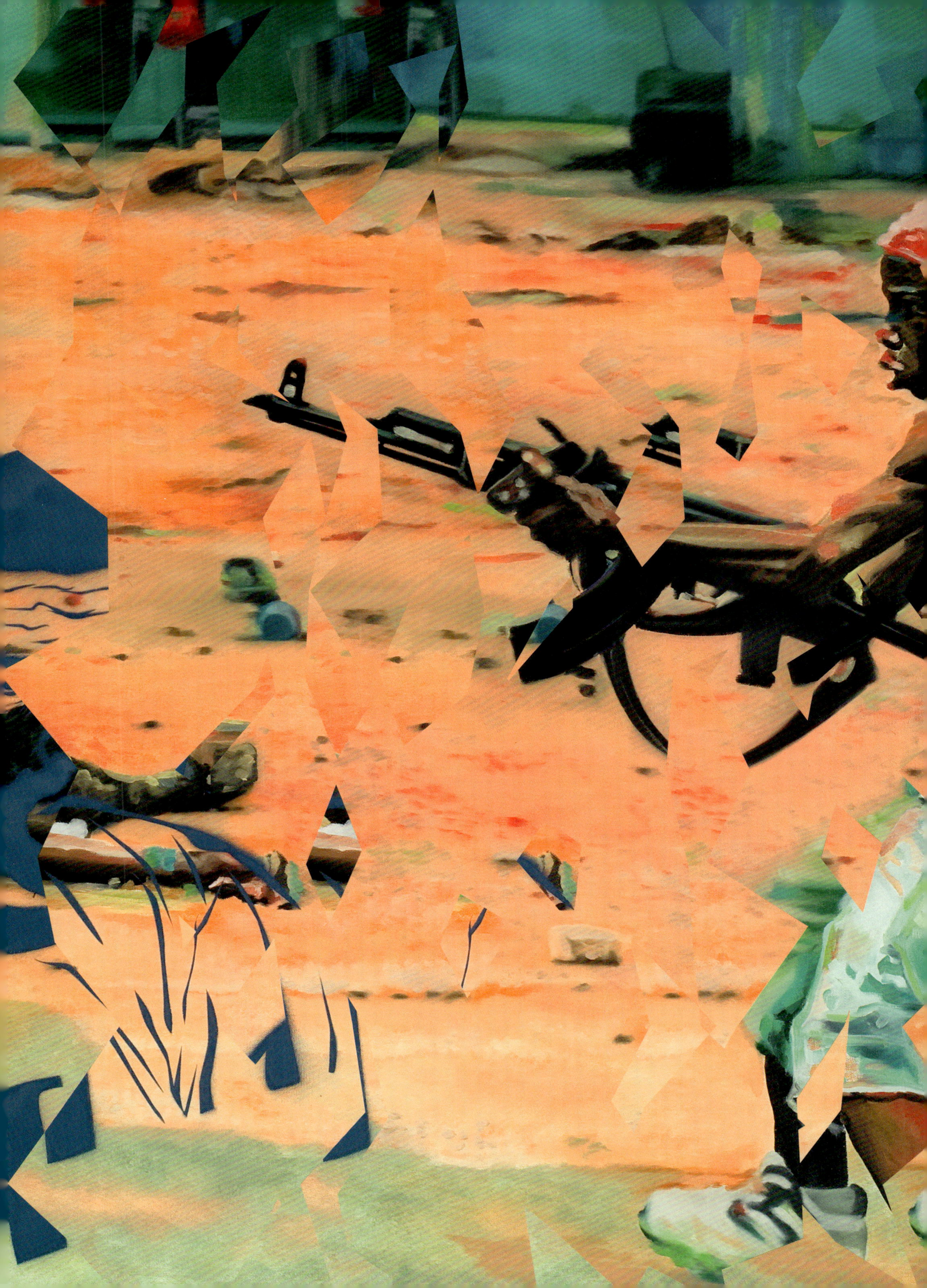

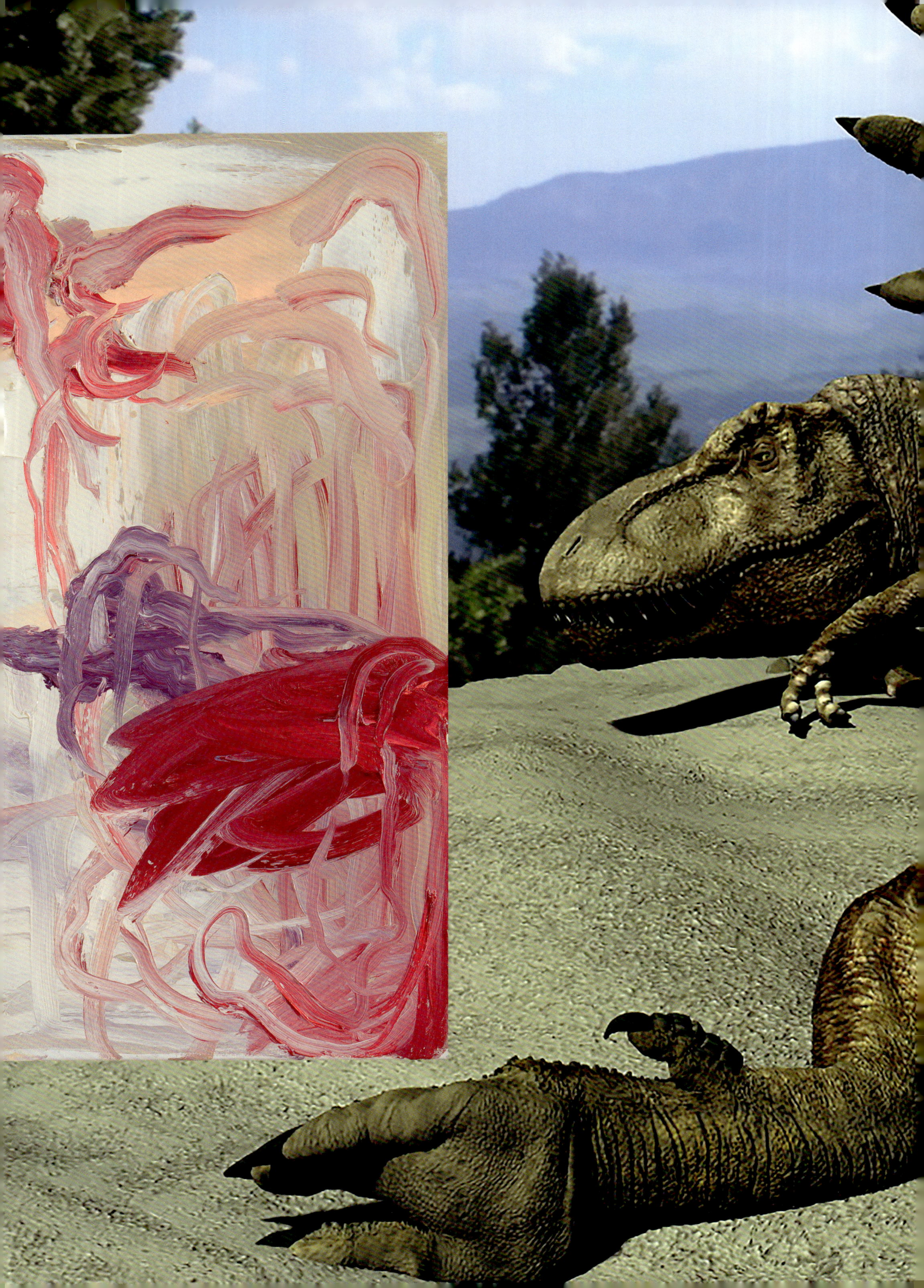

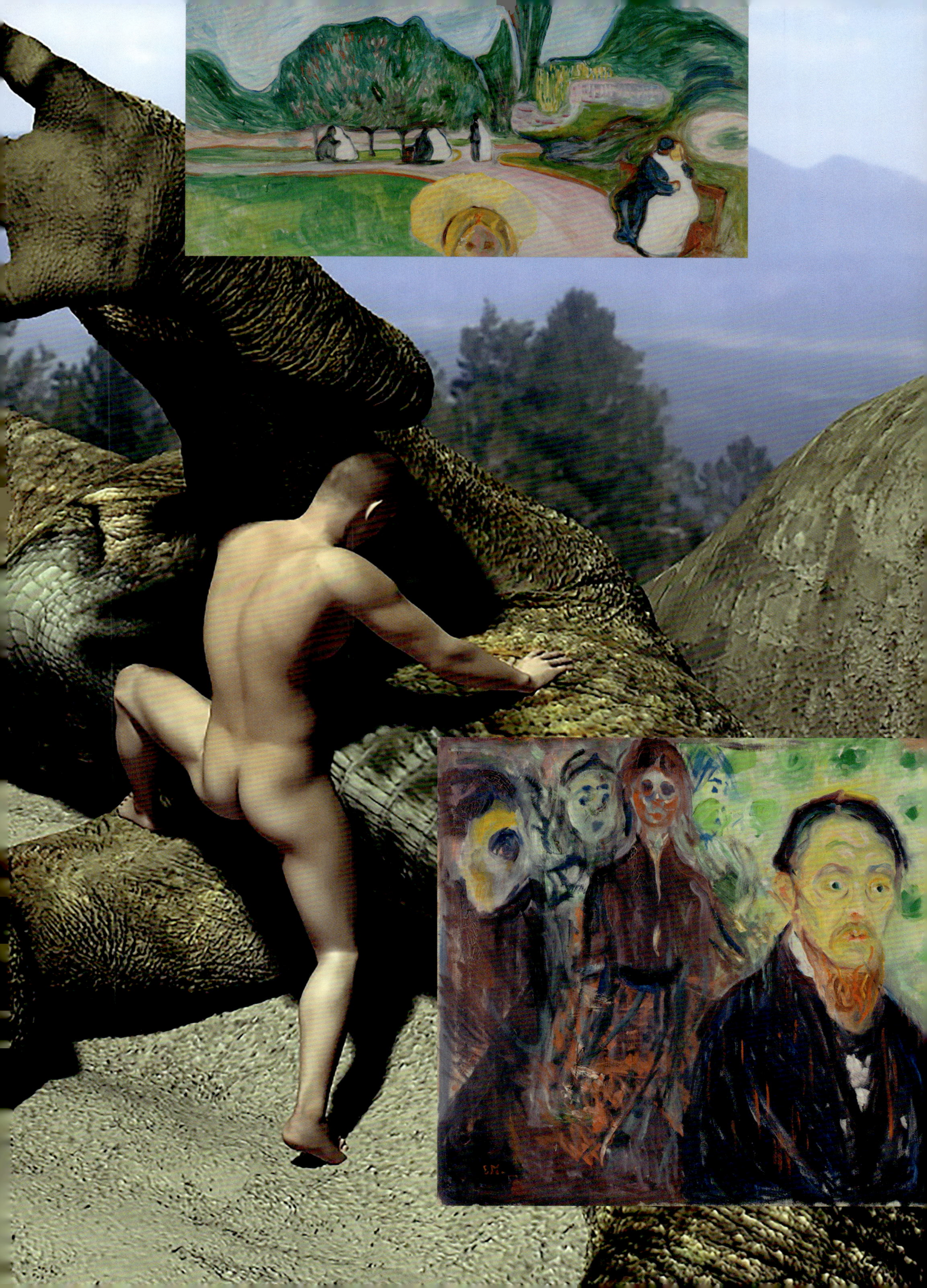

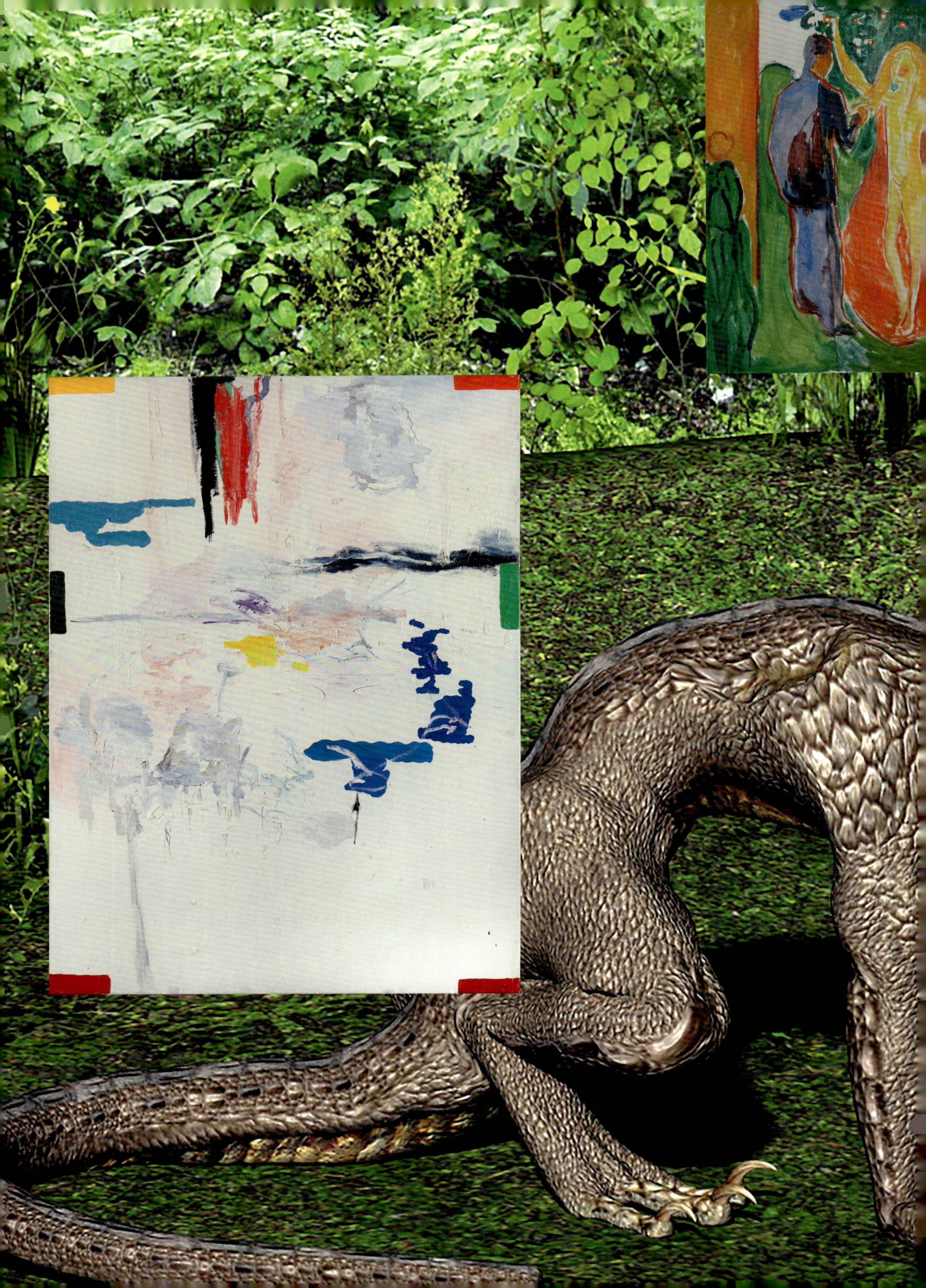

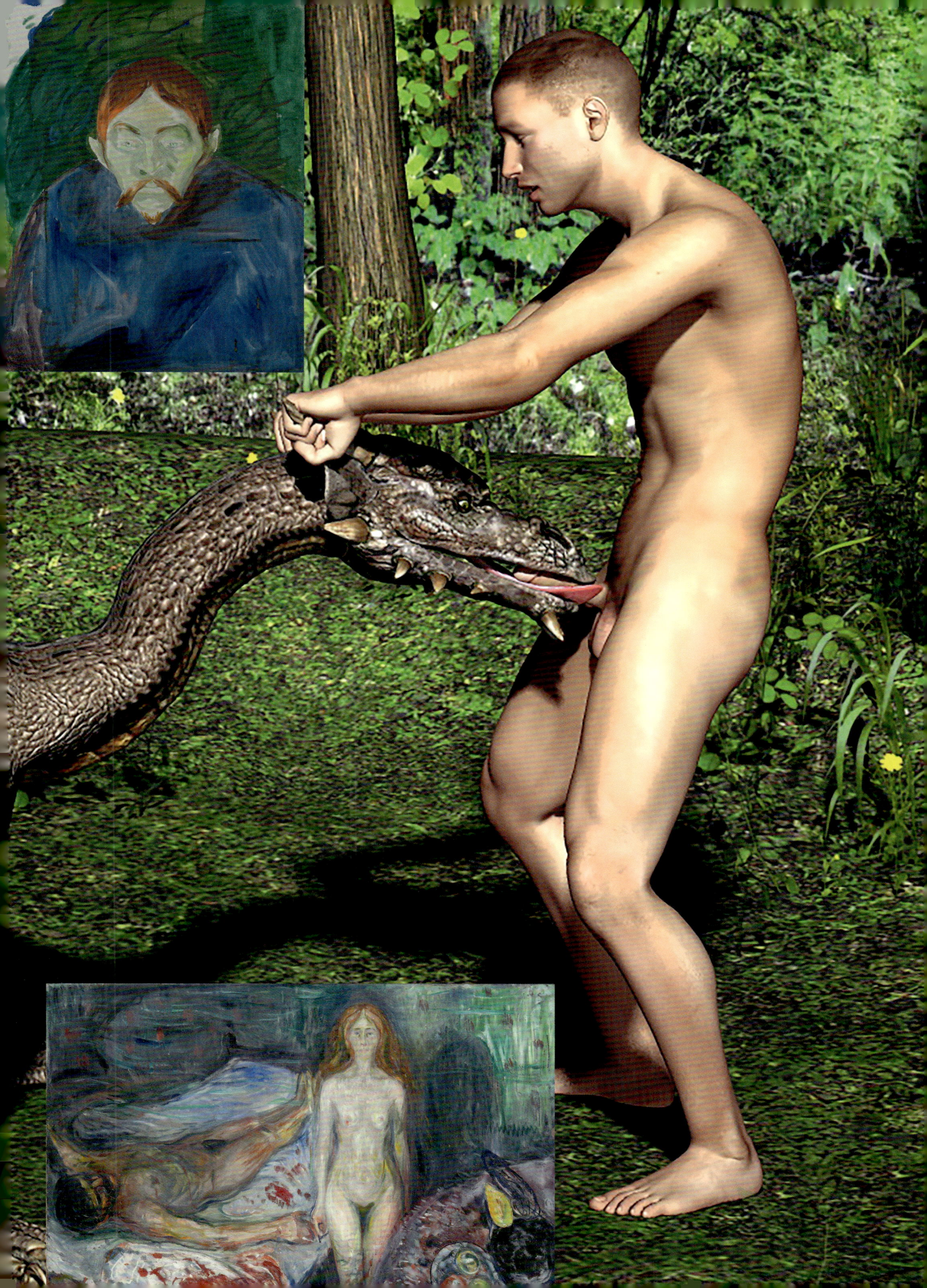

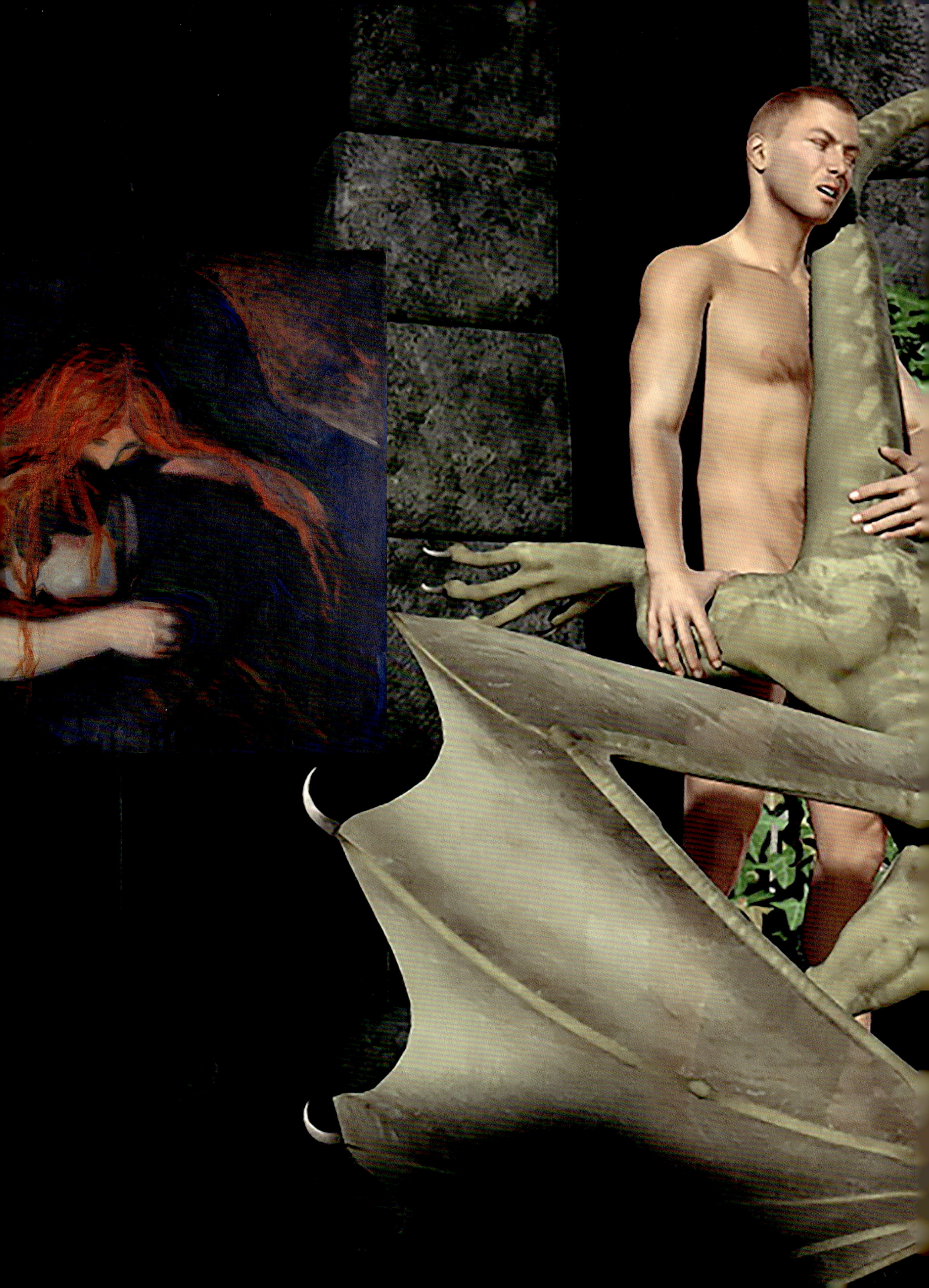

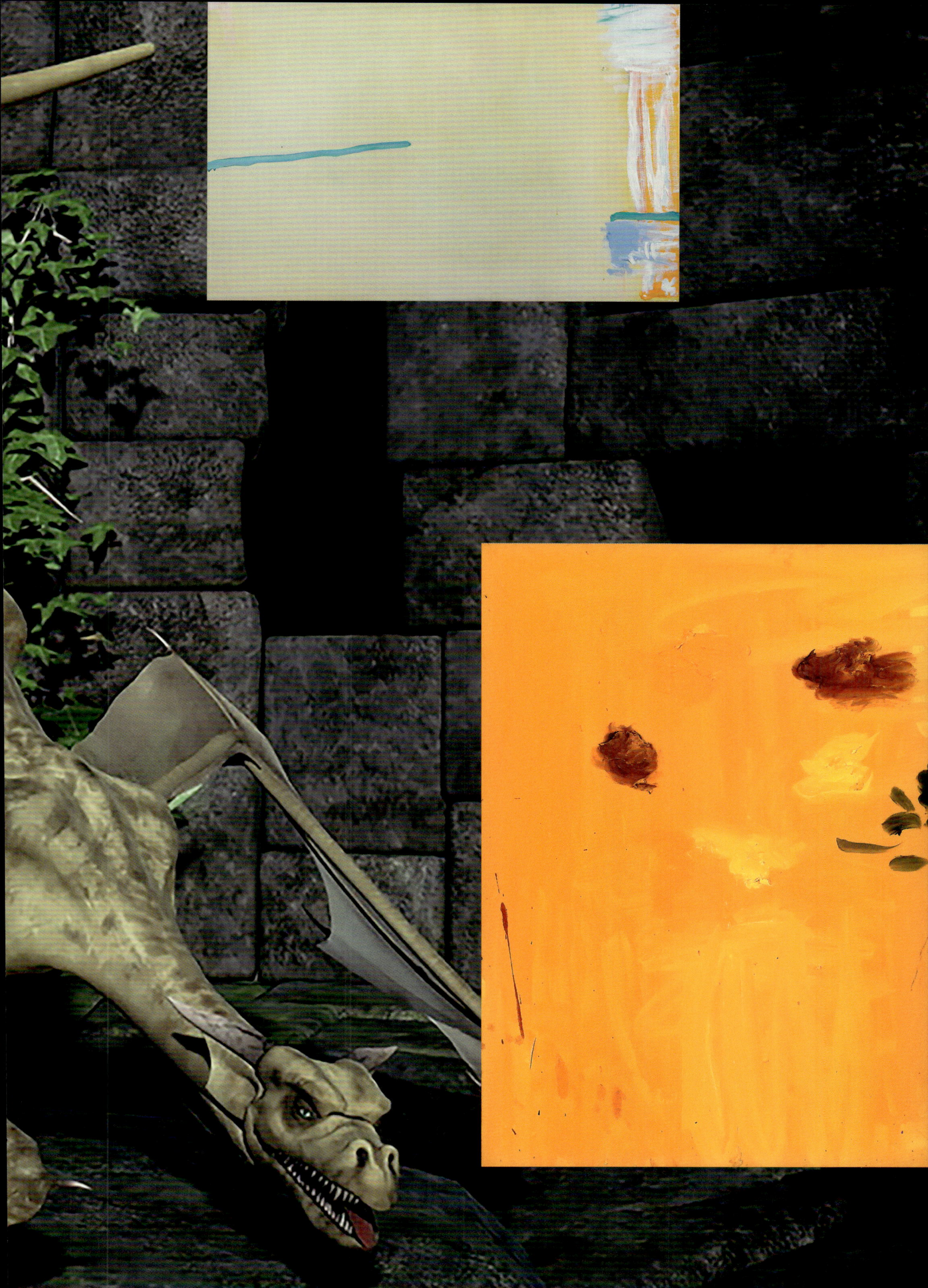

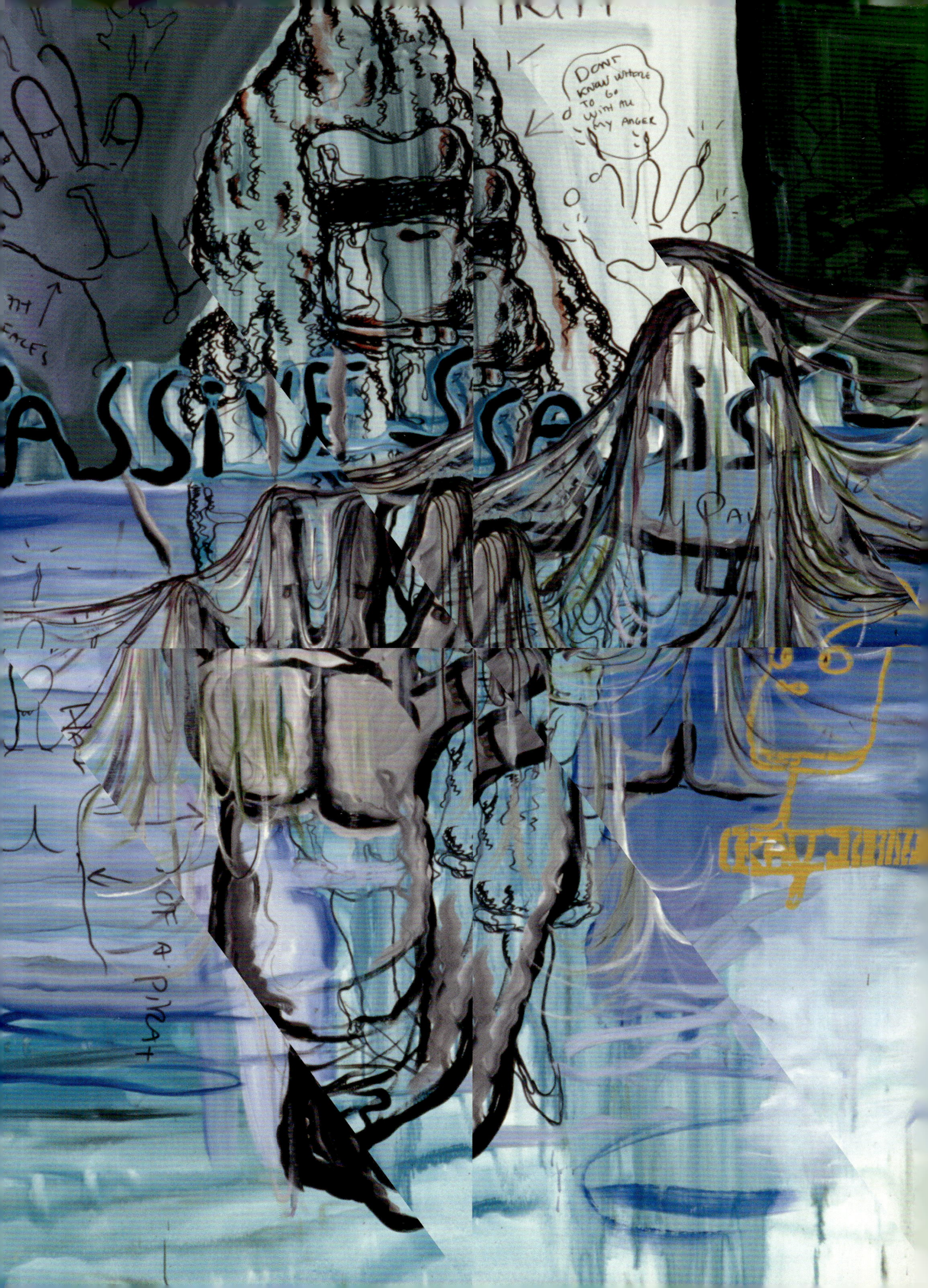
DONT
KNOW WHERE
TO GO
WITH ALL
MY ANGER
MASSIVE SCANDAL
OF A PIRAT

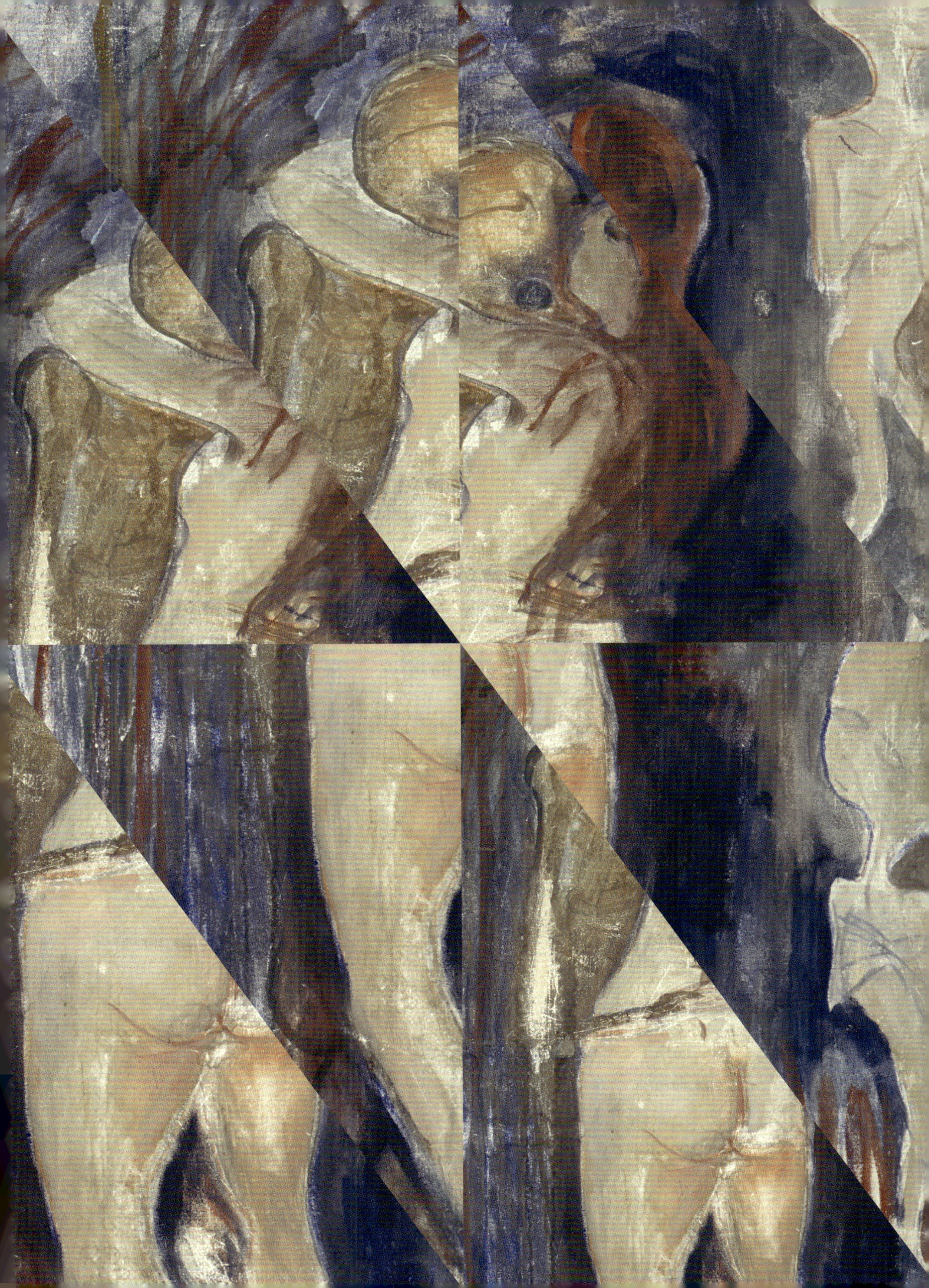

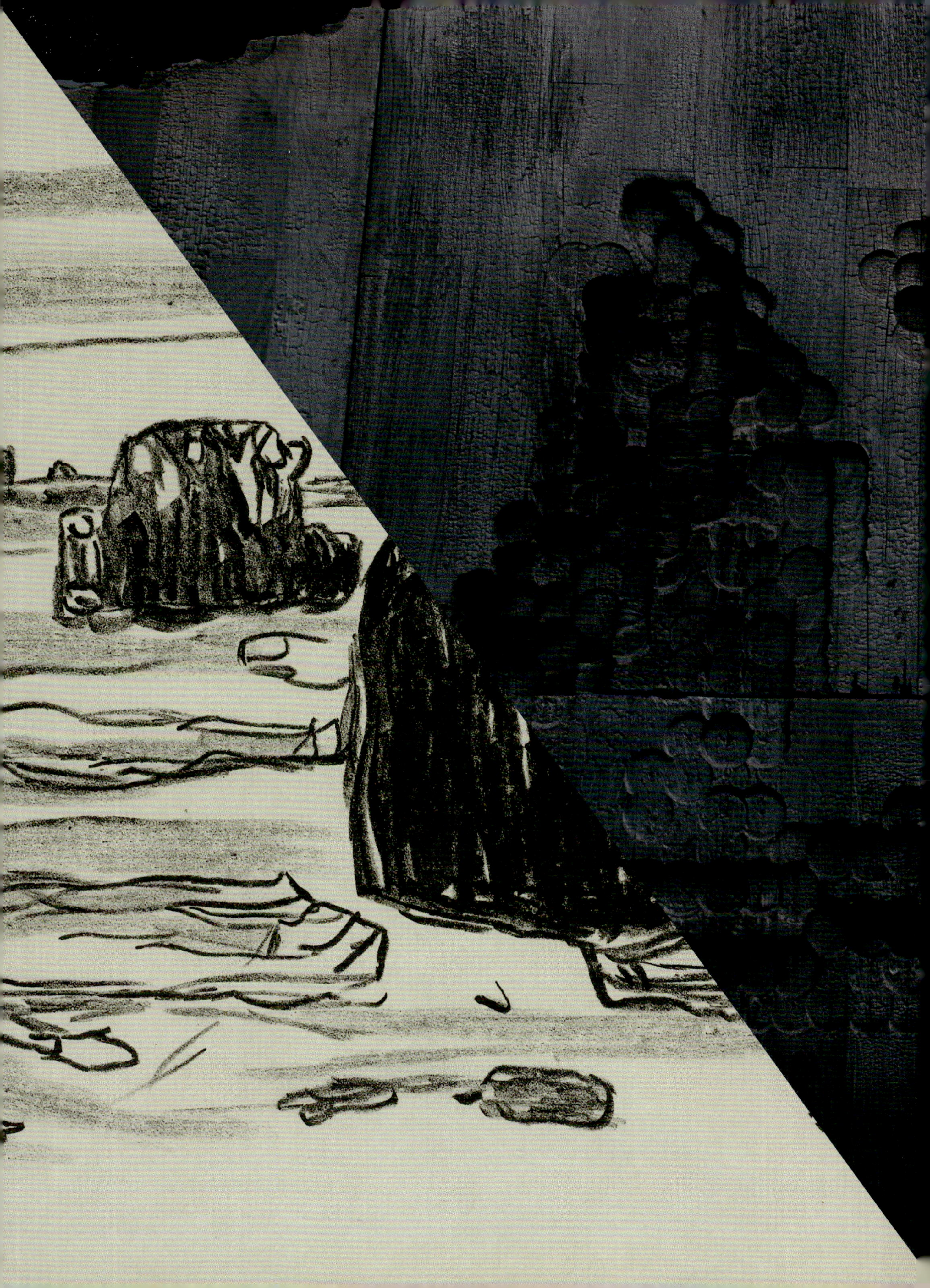

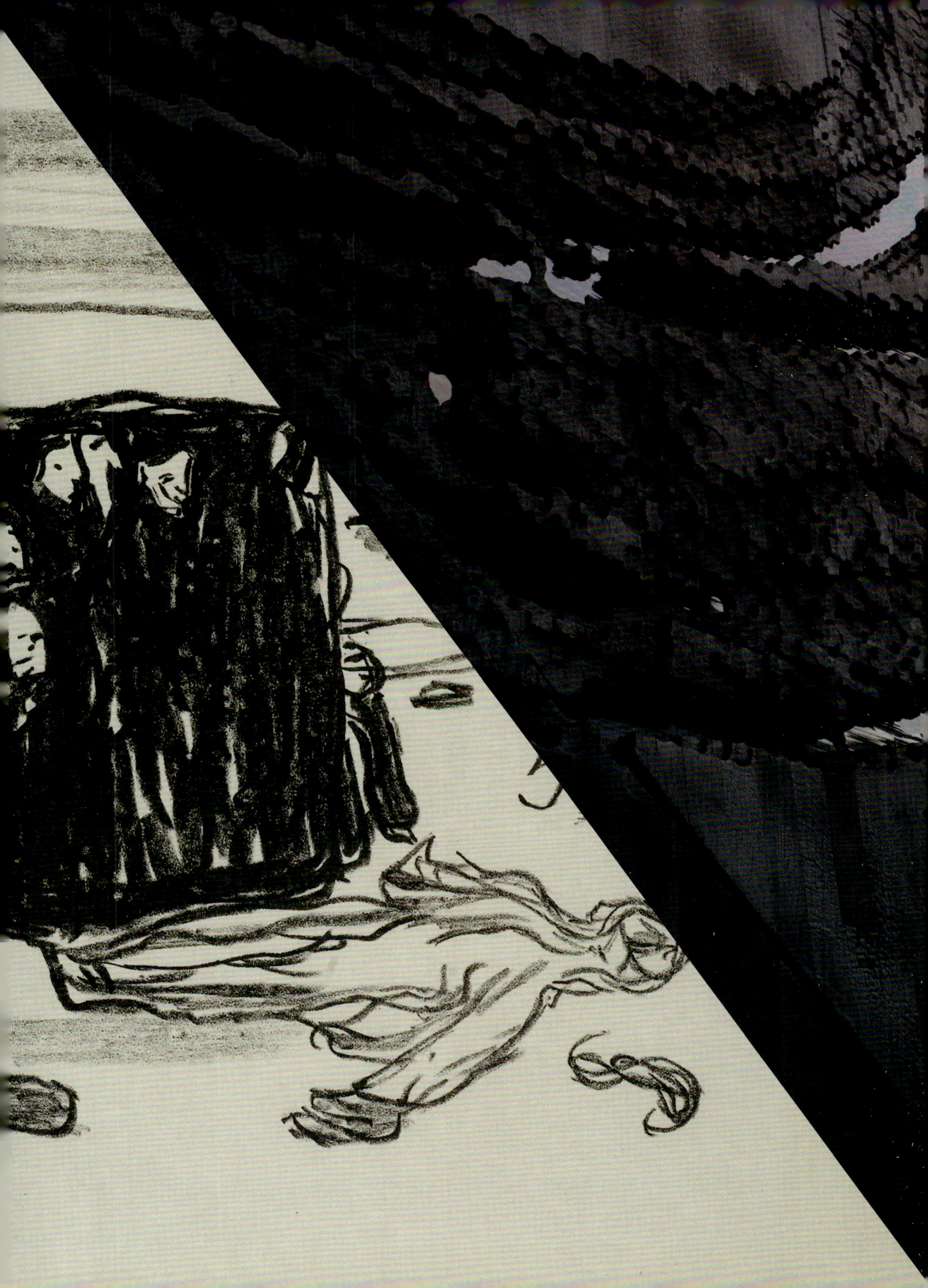

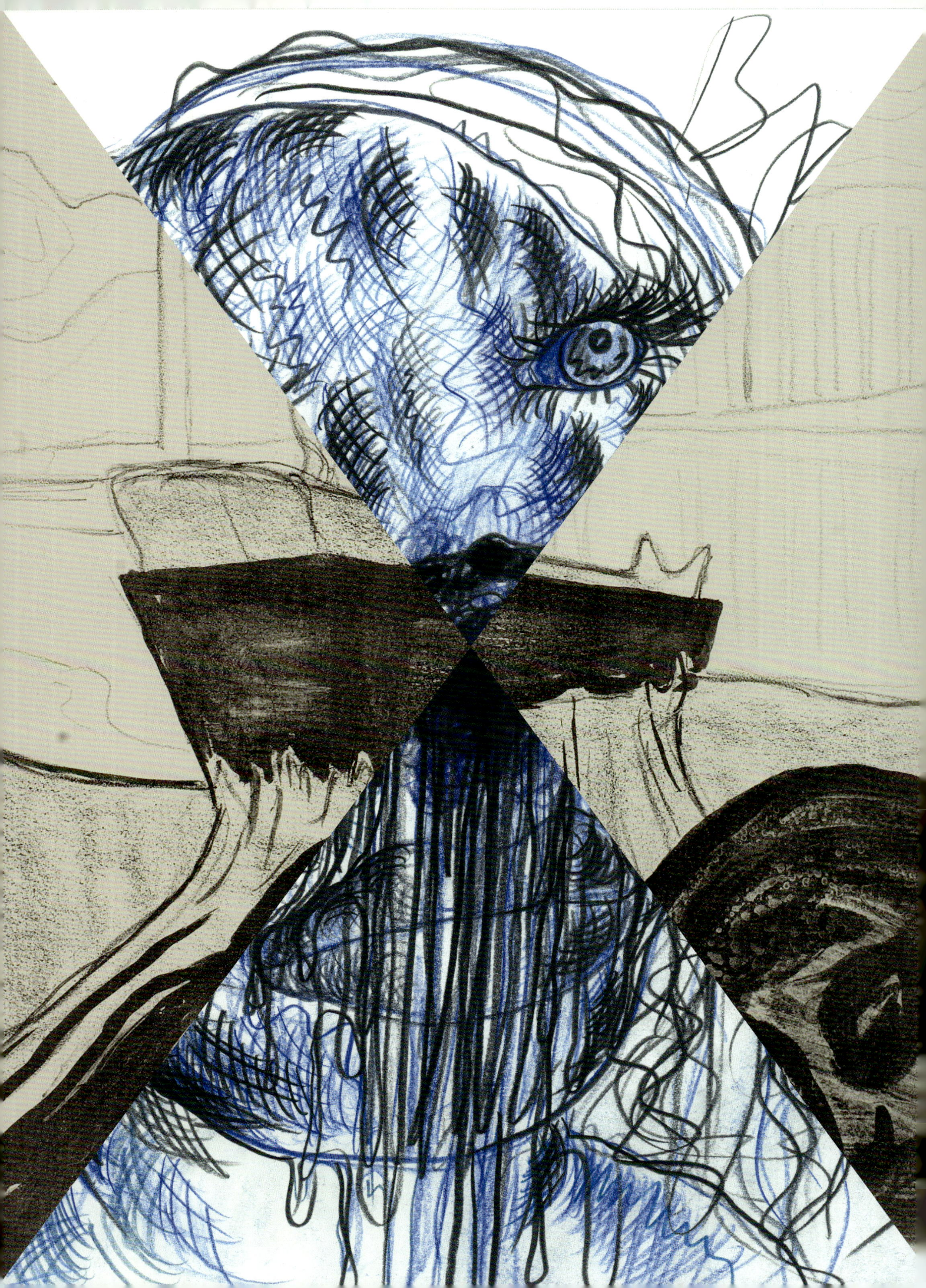

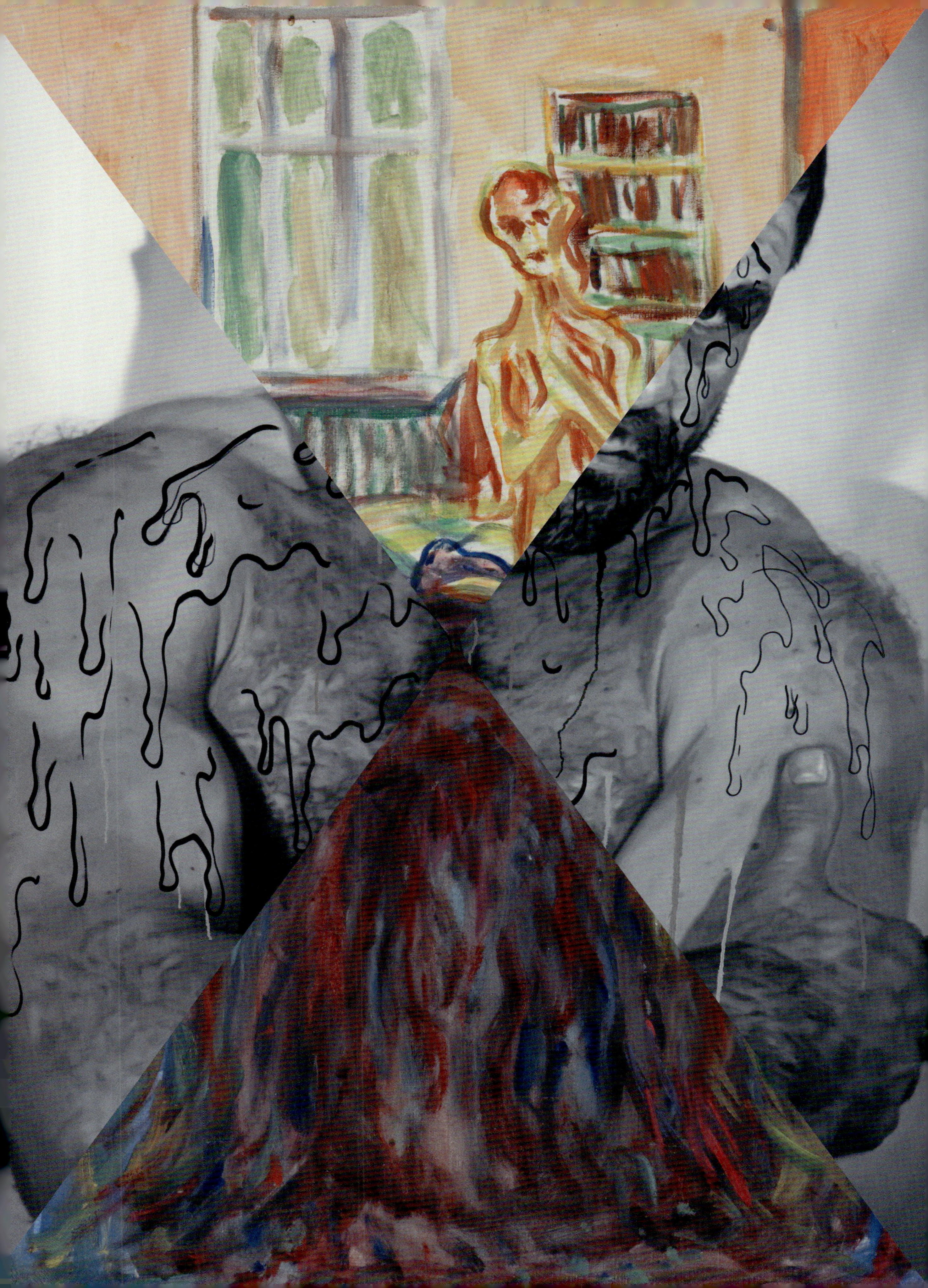

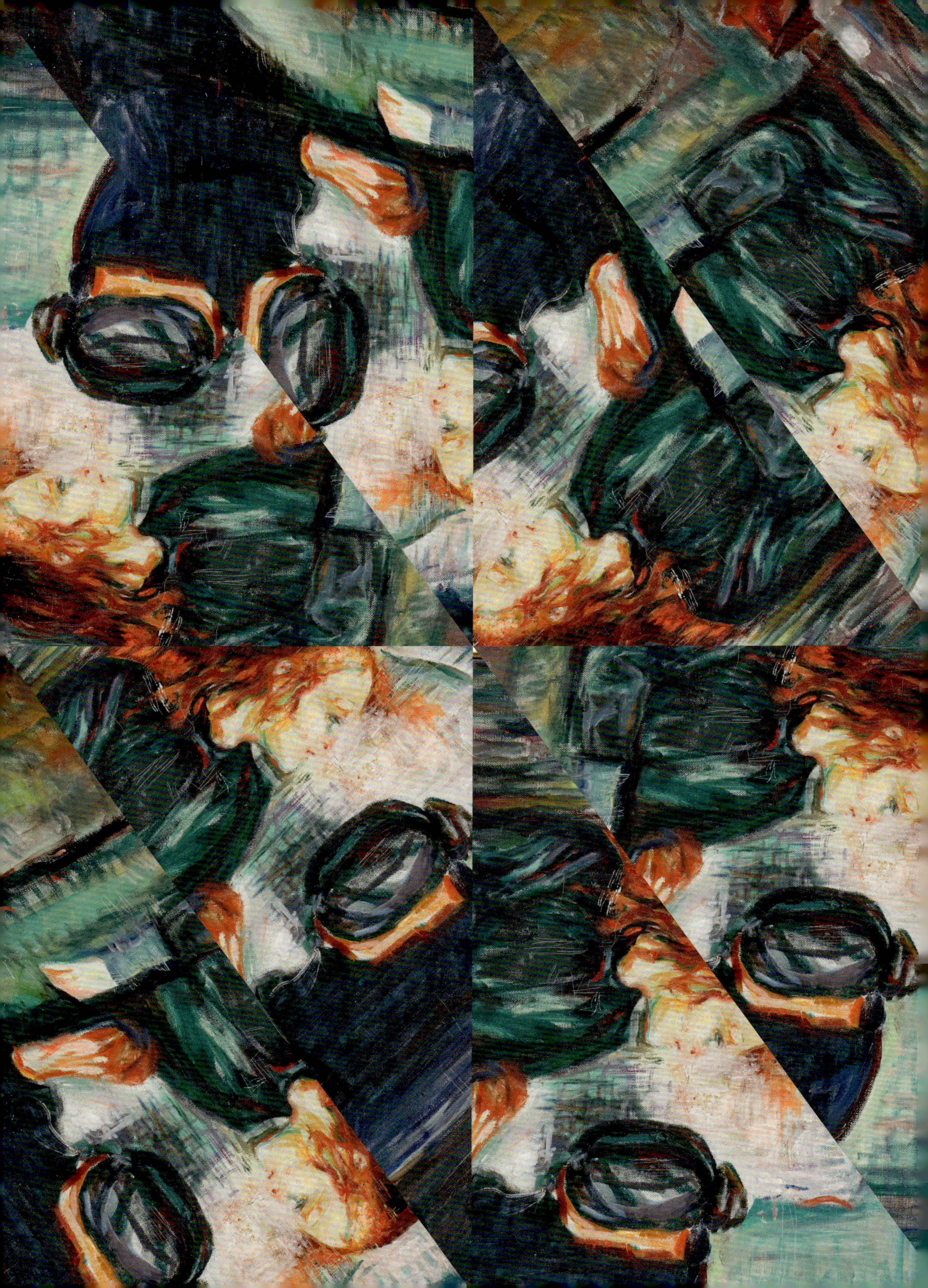

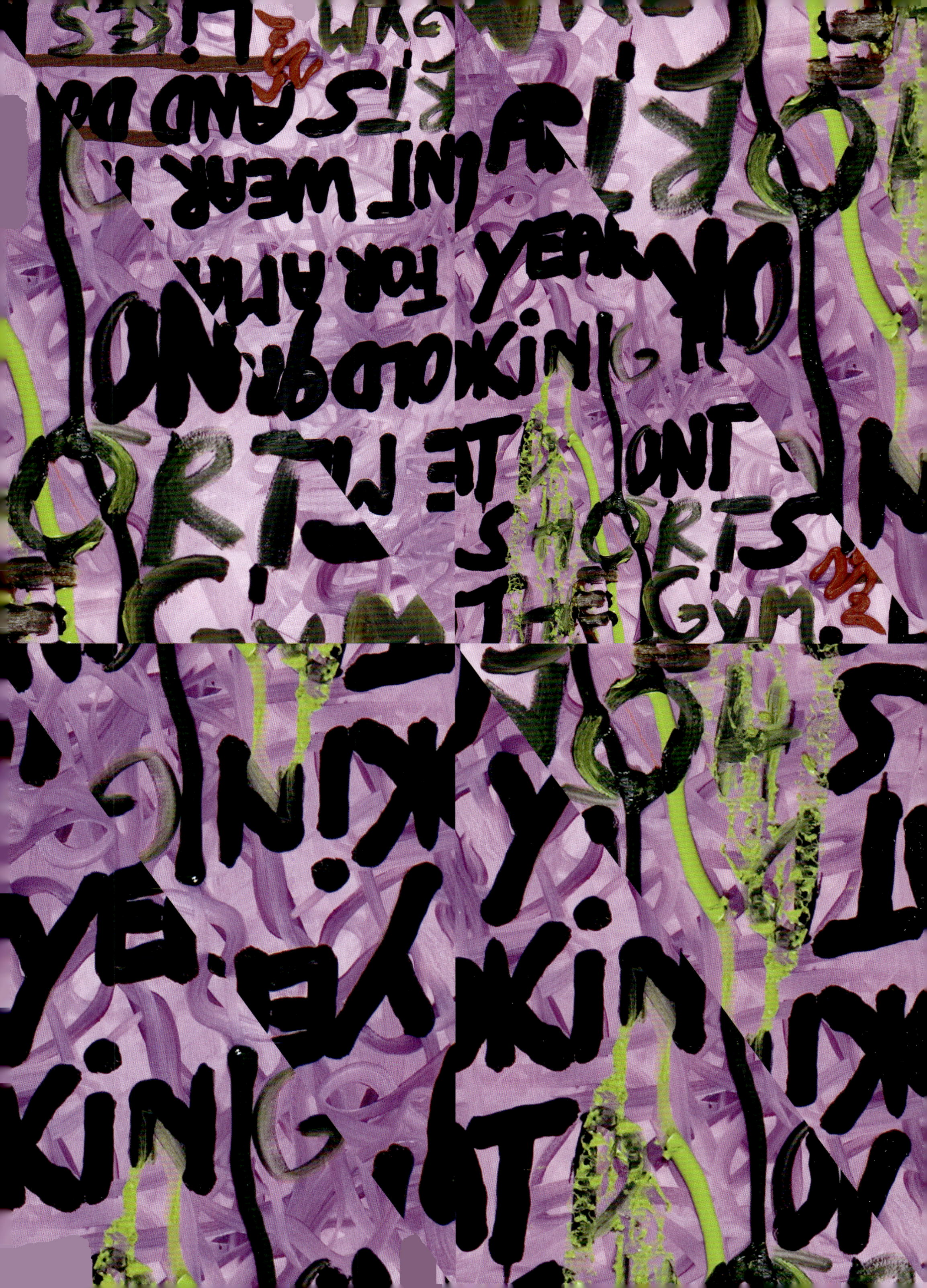

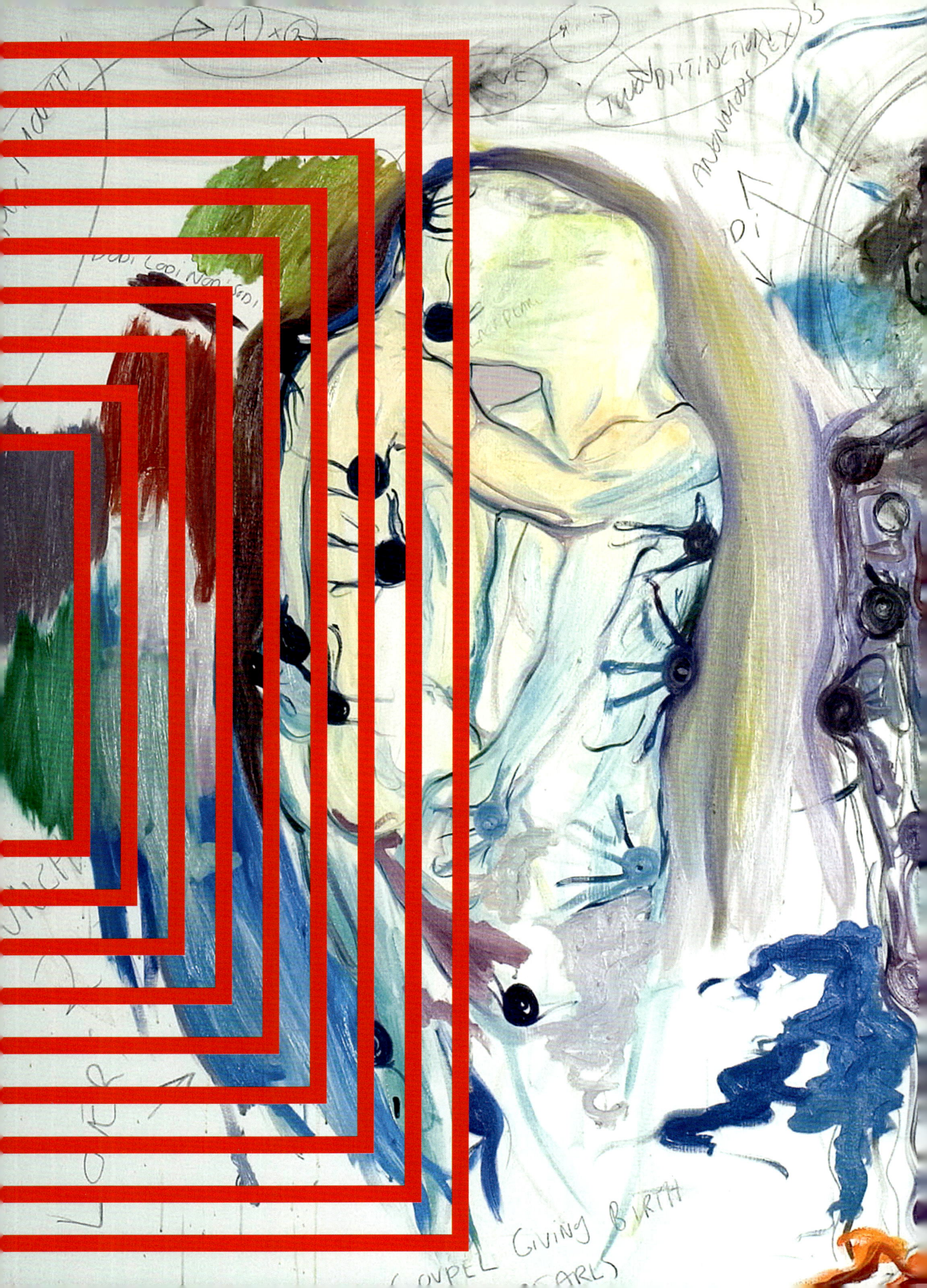
LOVE
TWO DISTINCTION SEX
ANONYMOUS
D.I.Y.
COUPLE GIVING BIRTH
PEARLS
LOVER

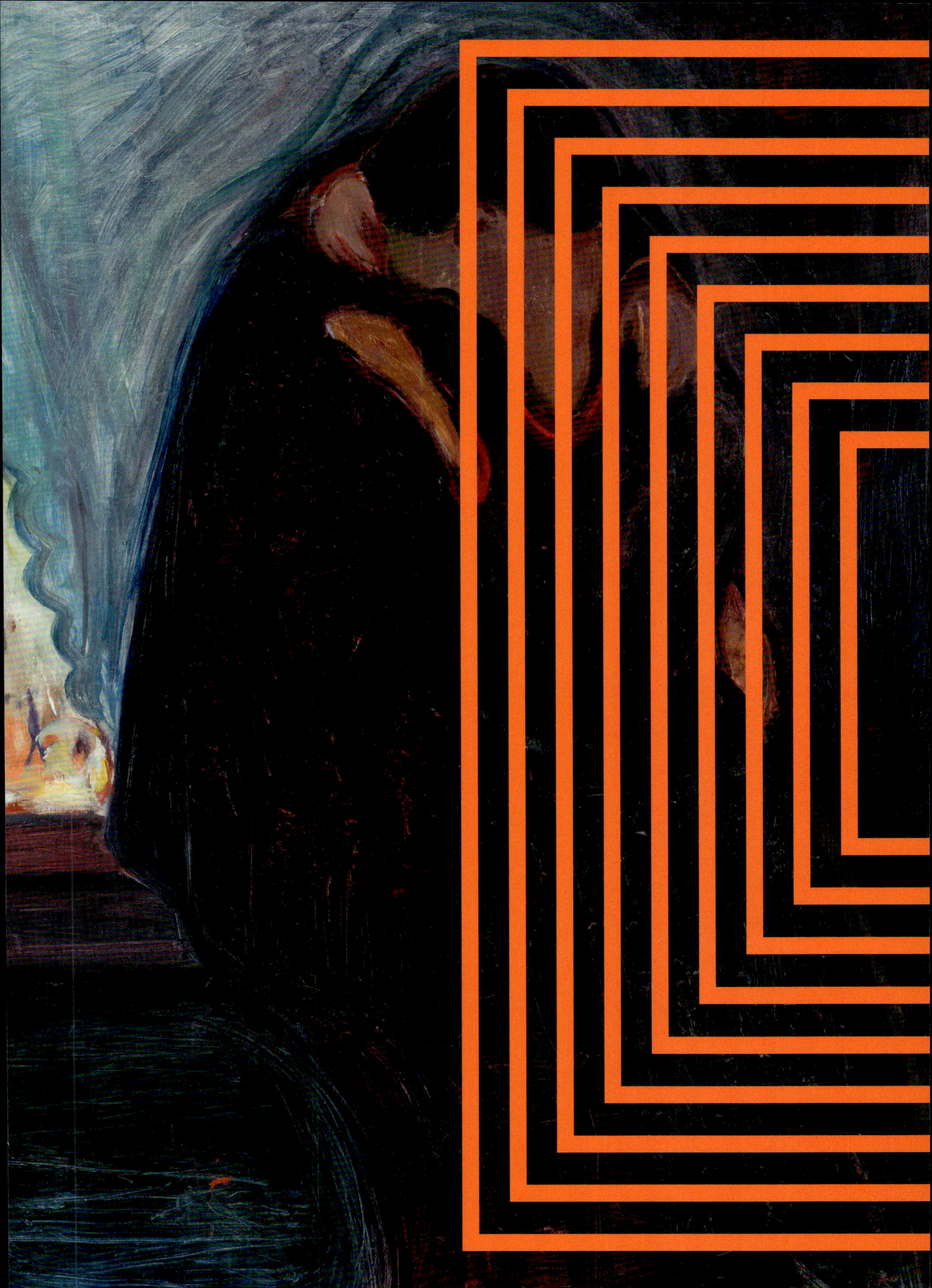

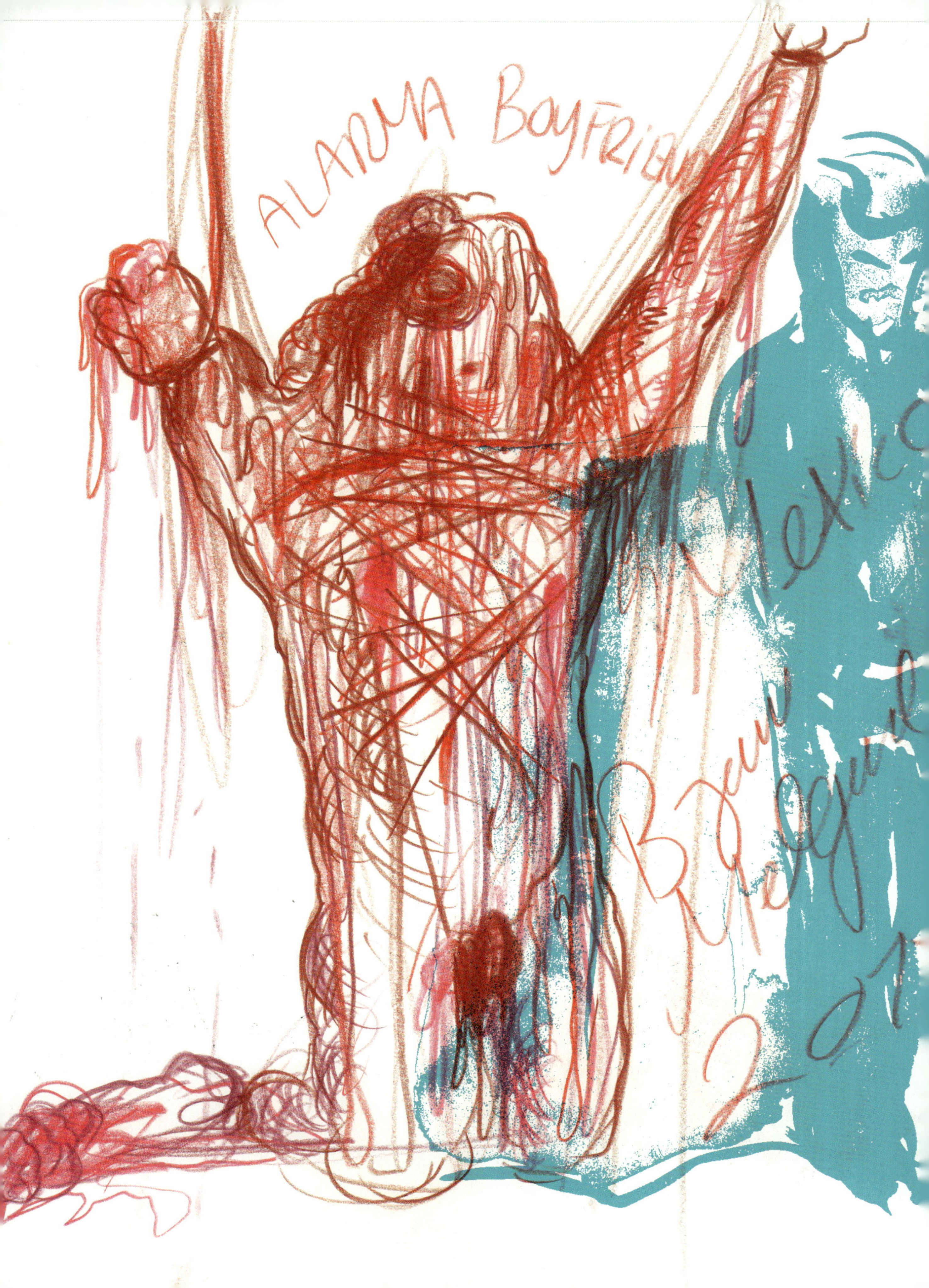

ALARMA BoyFRIE

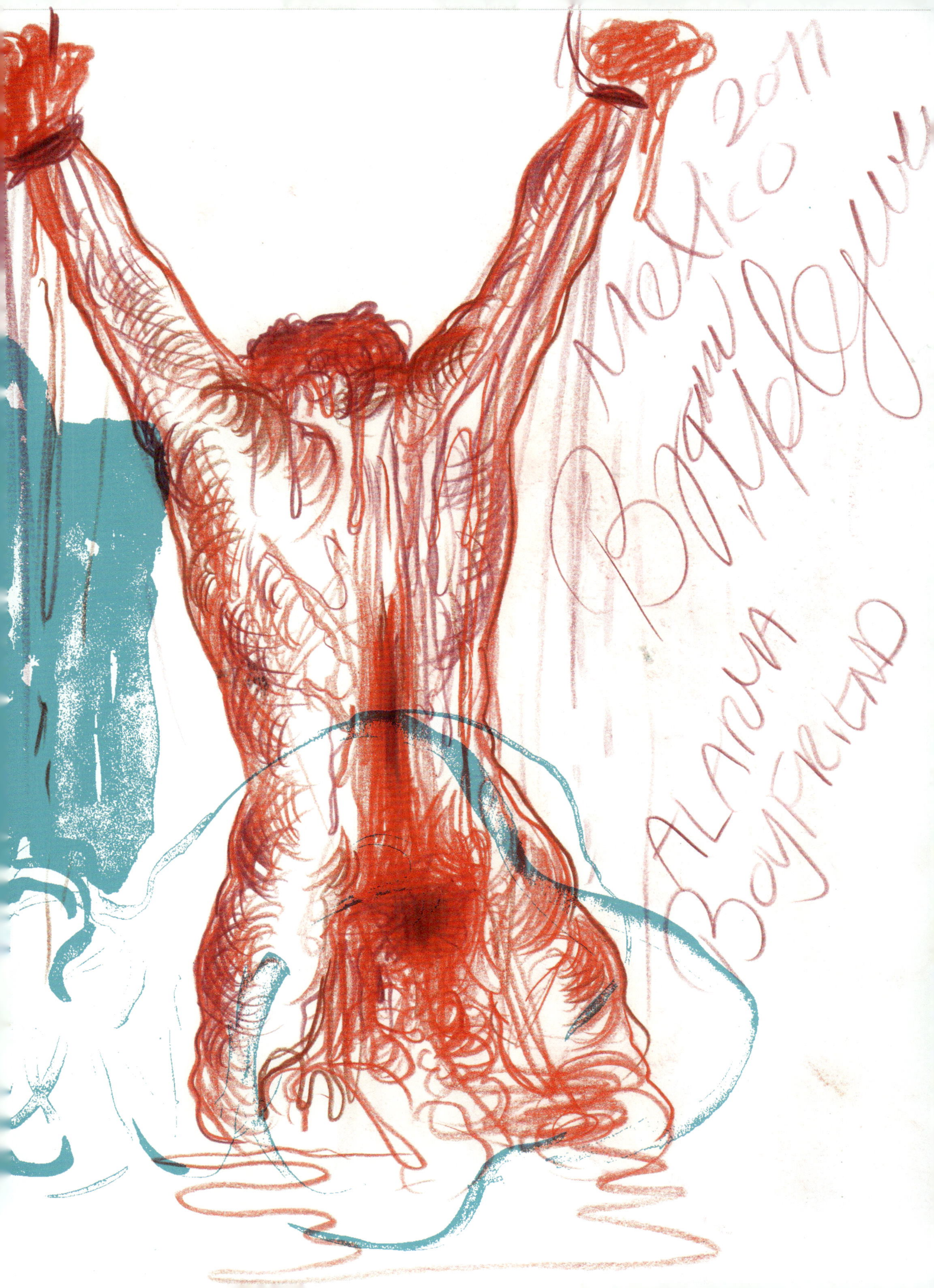

Mexico 2011
Alanya
Boyfriend

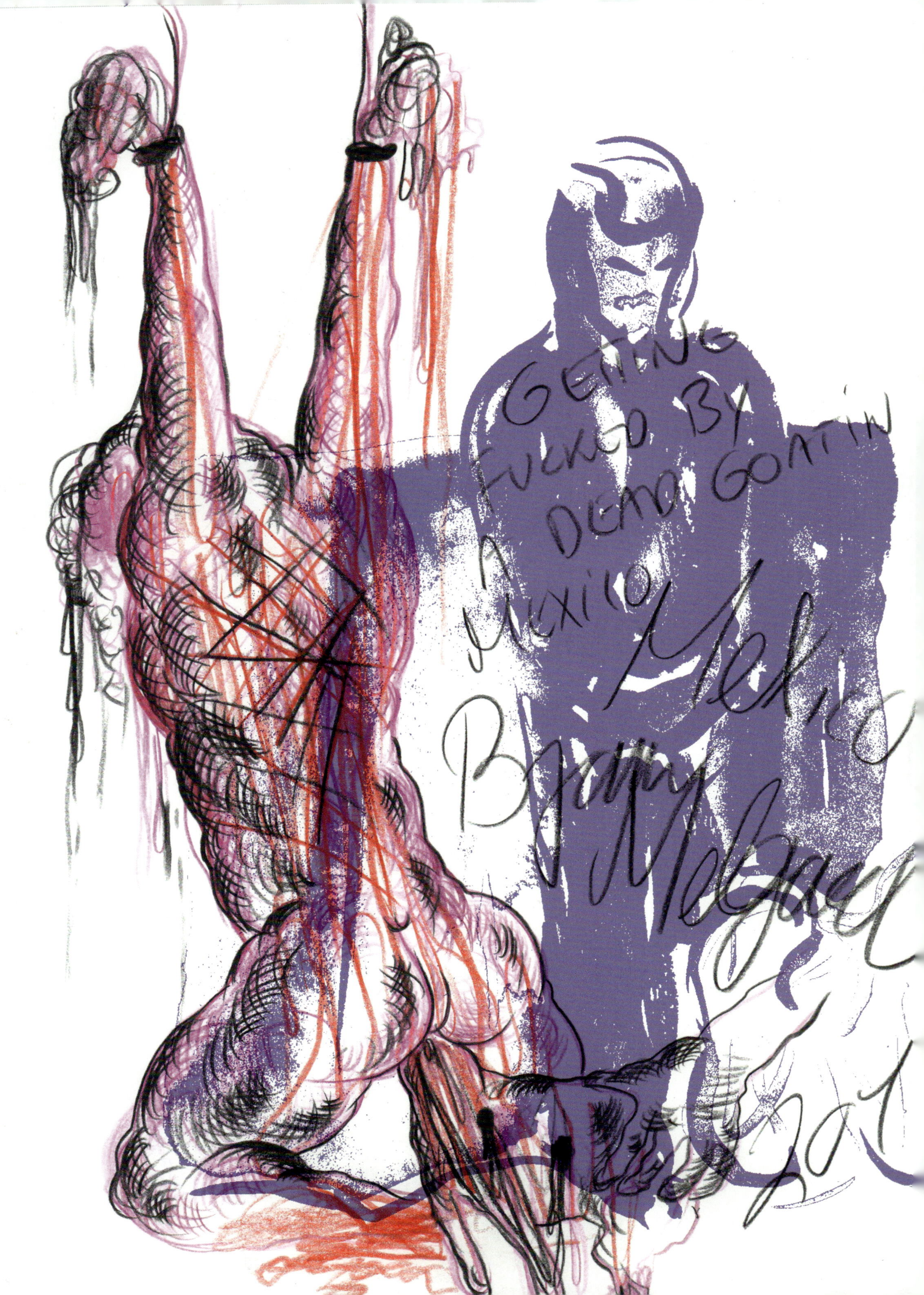

GETTING FUCKED BY DEAD GOAT IN MEXICO

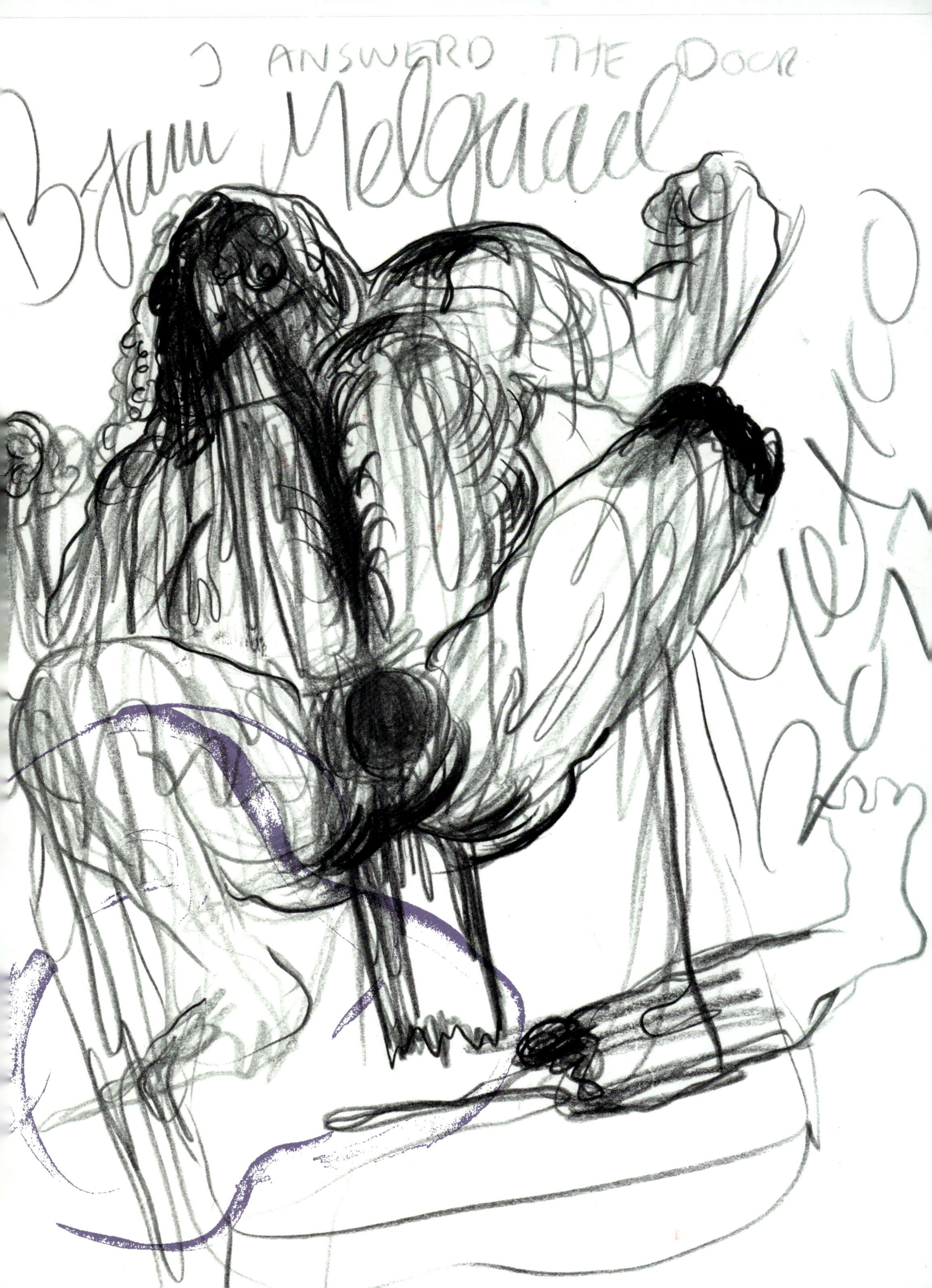

I ANSWERD THE DOOR
Bjarne Melgaard

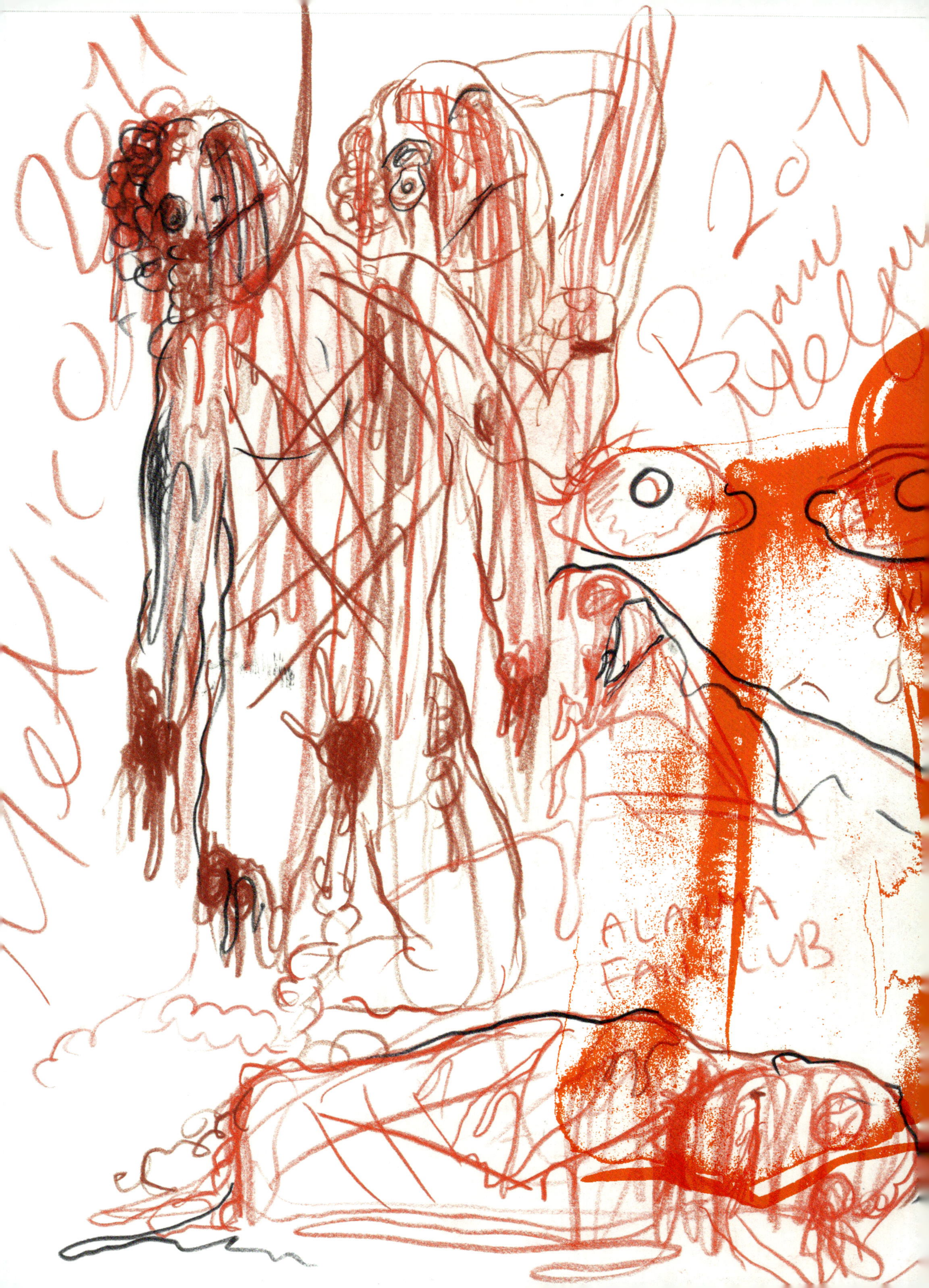
ALABAMA
FAN CLUB

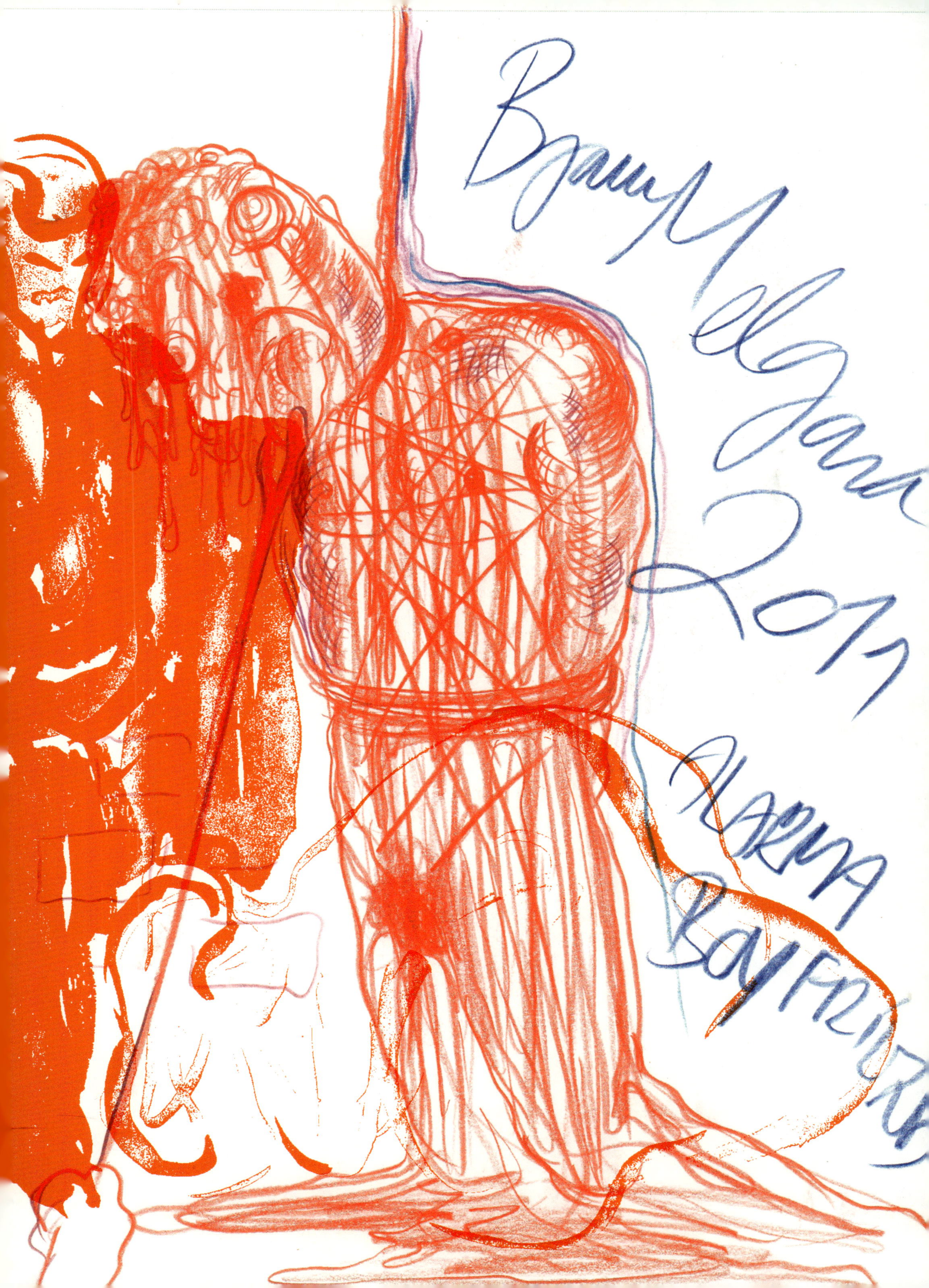

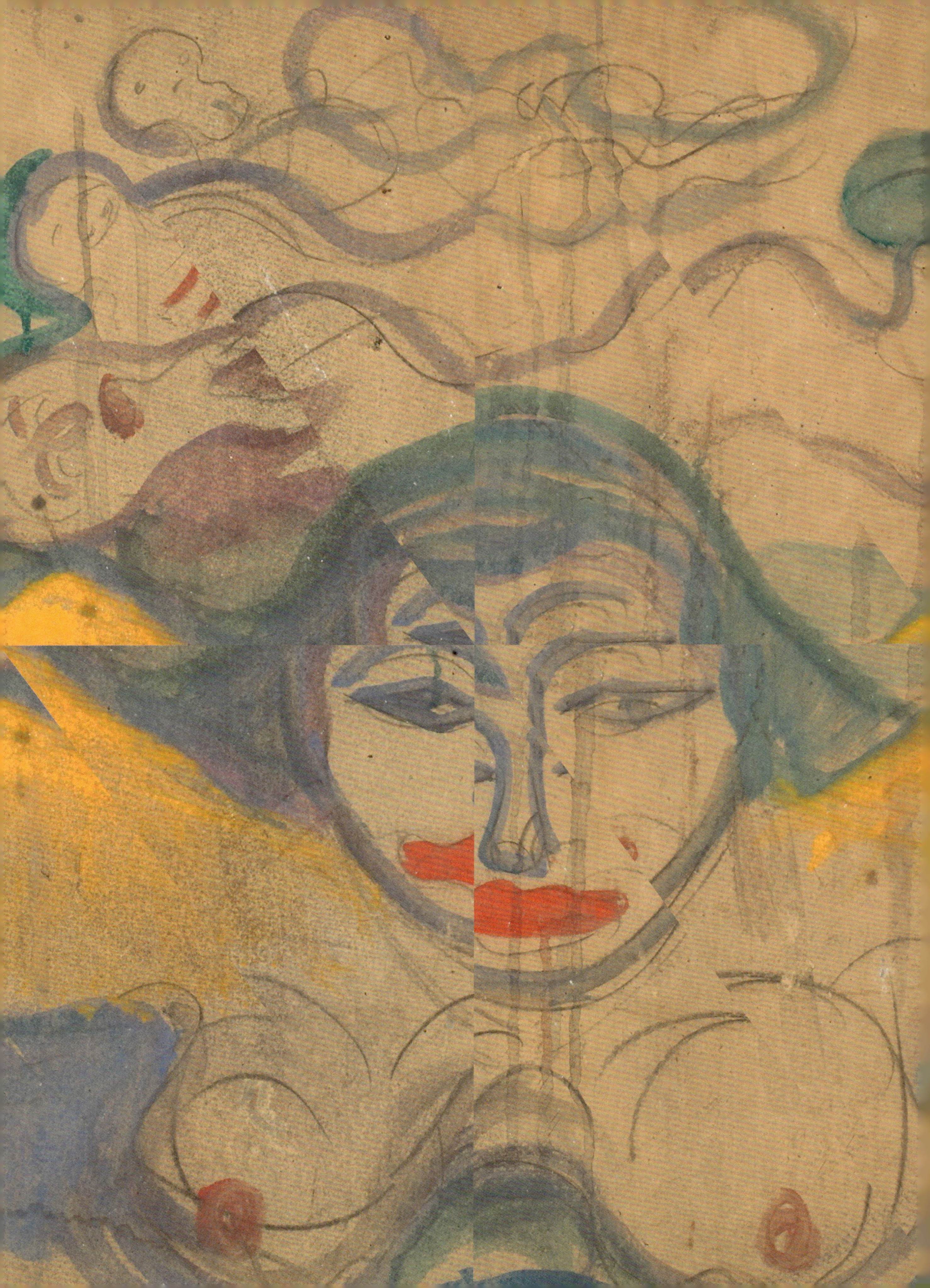

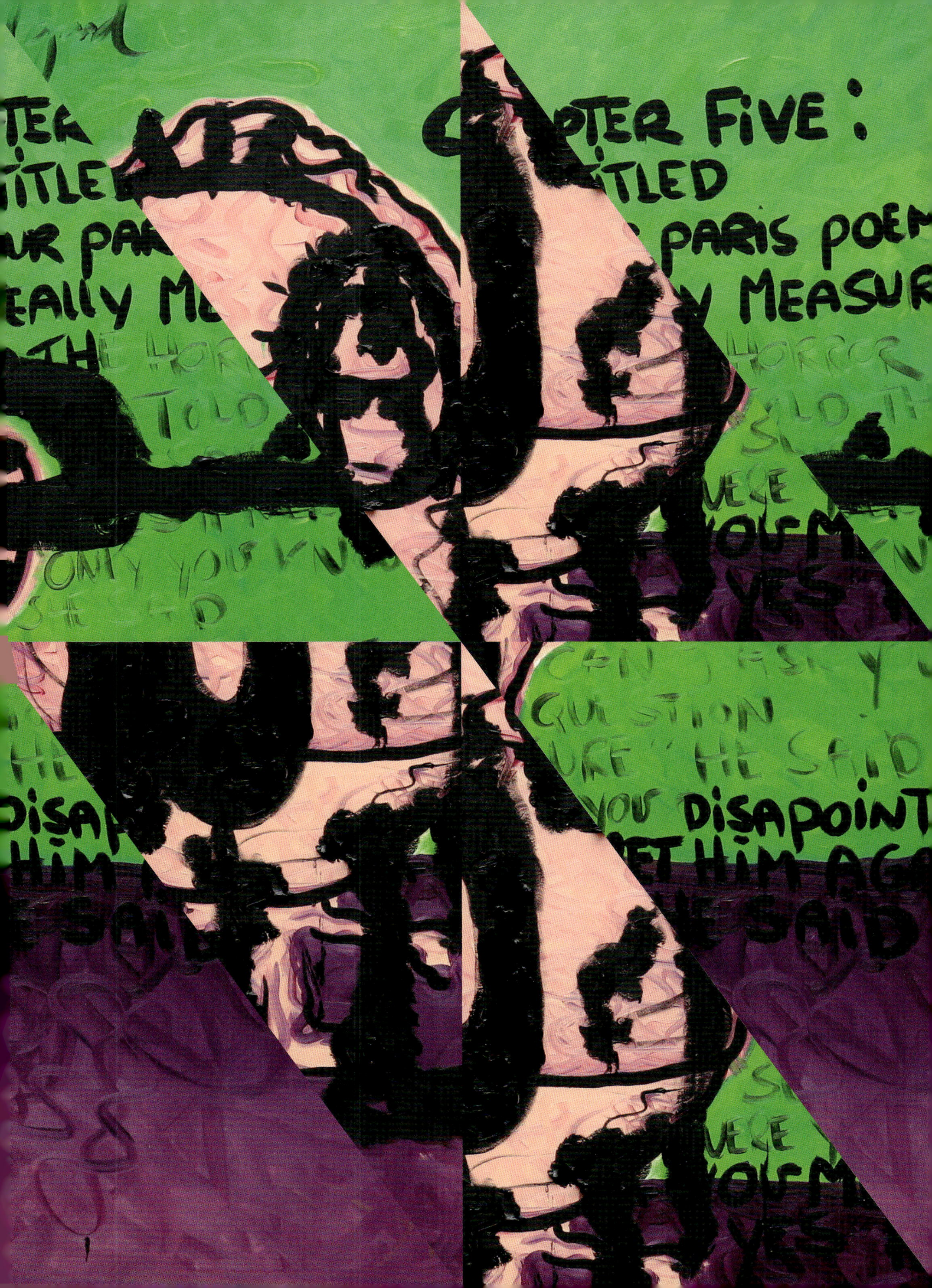
PTER FIVE:
TITLED
PARIS POEM
MEASUR
CAN I ASK Y
QUESTION
URE HE SAID
YOU DISAPOINT
HIM AG
HE SAID

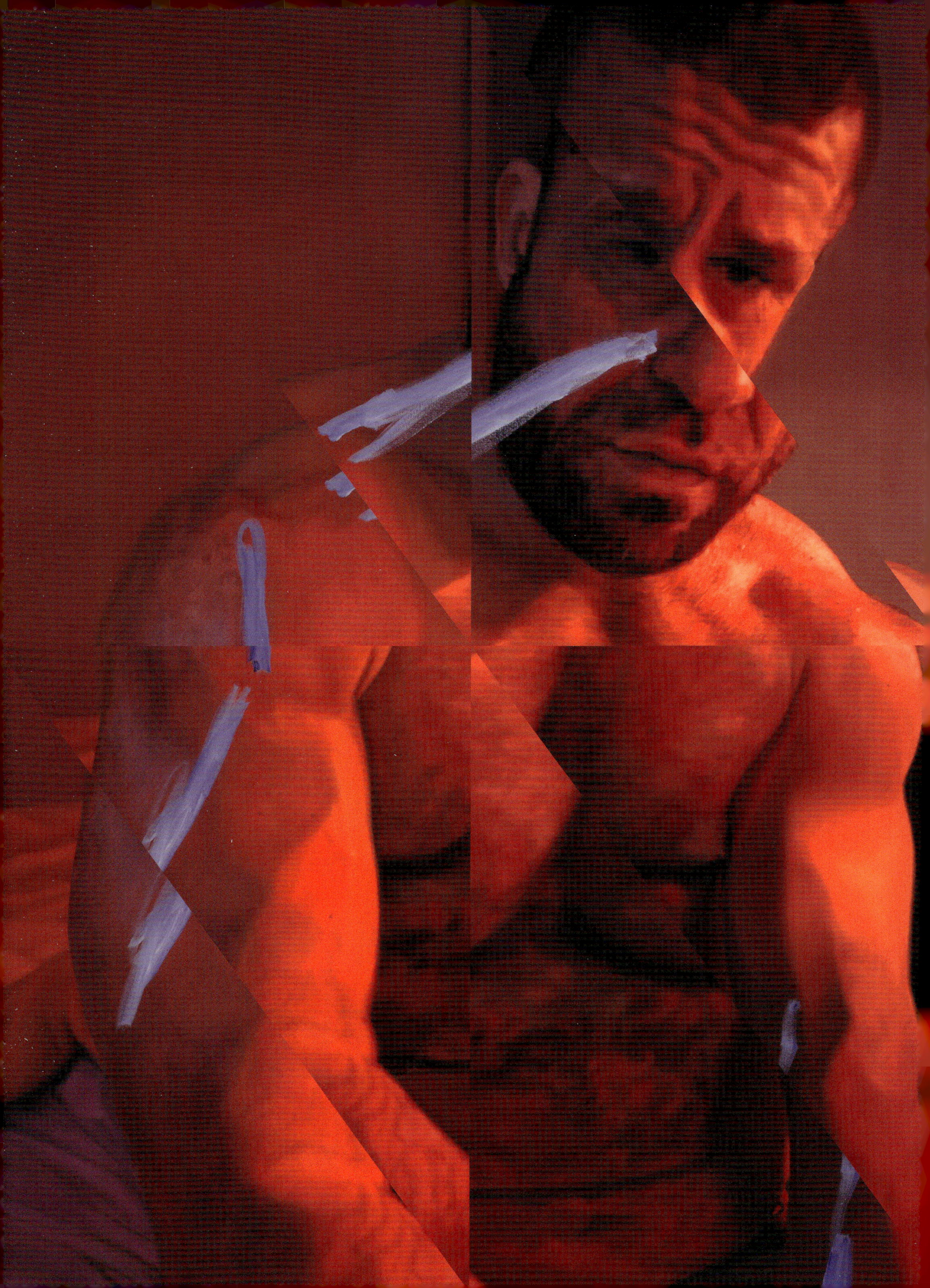

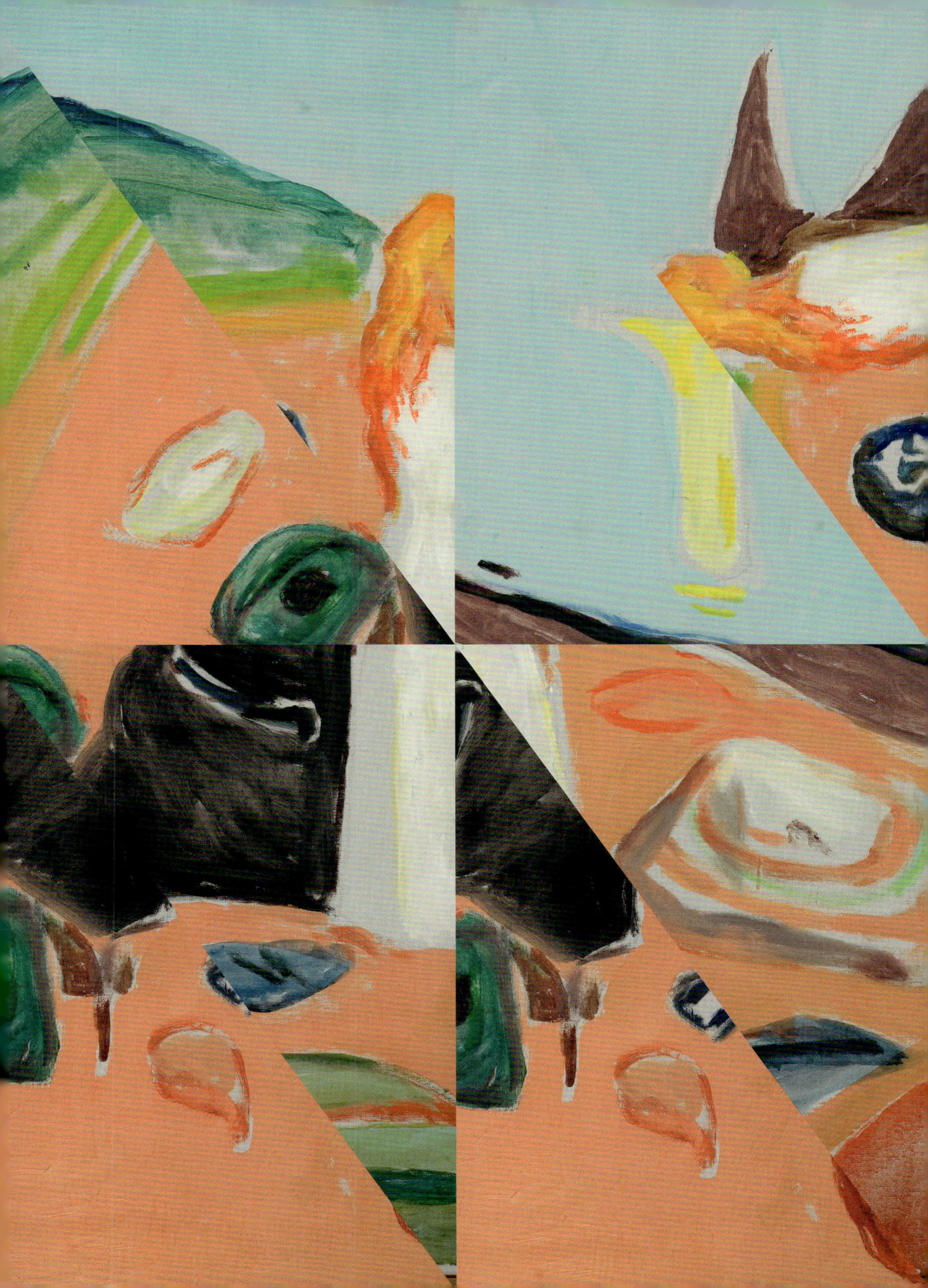

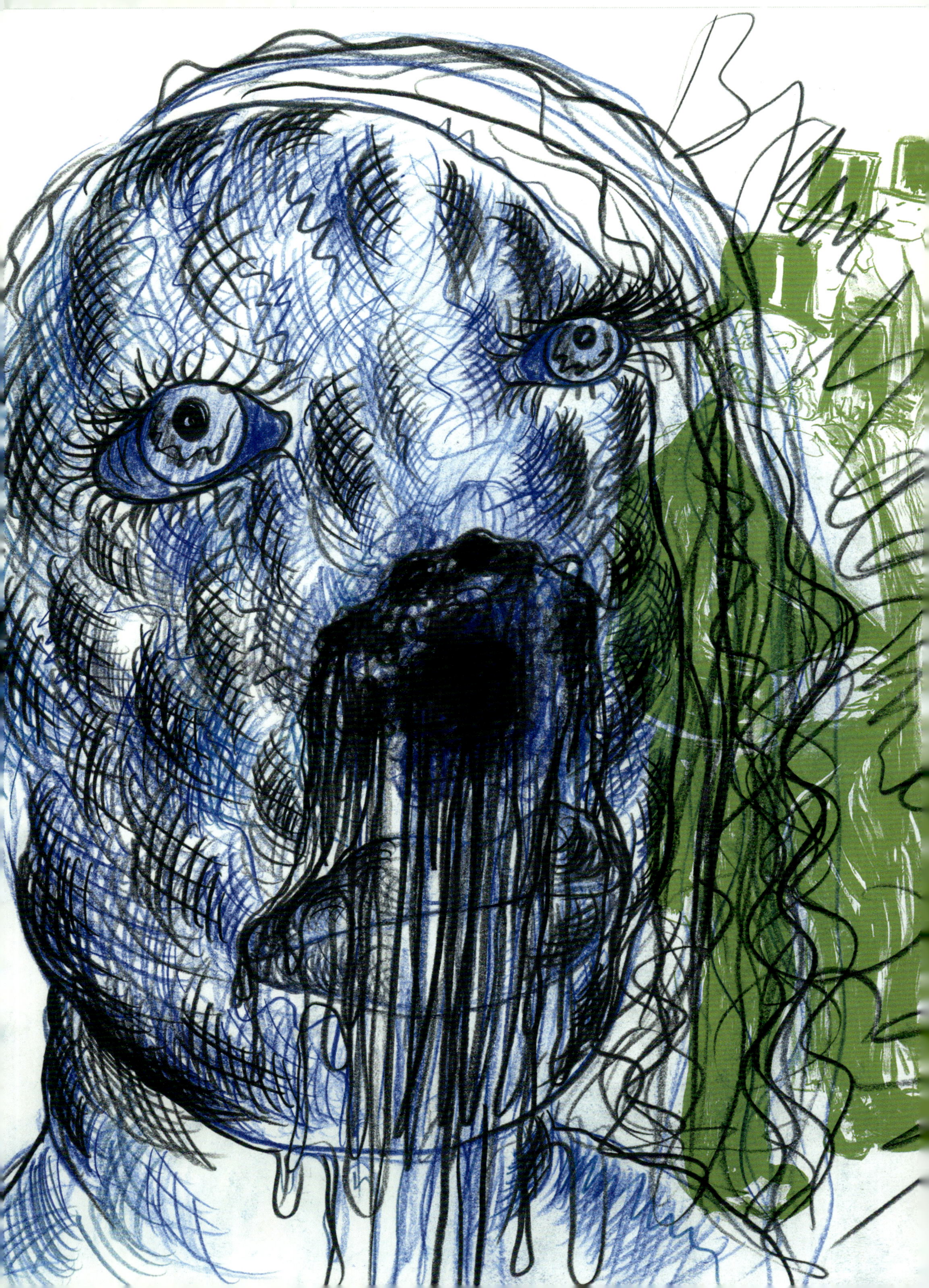

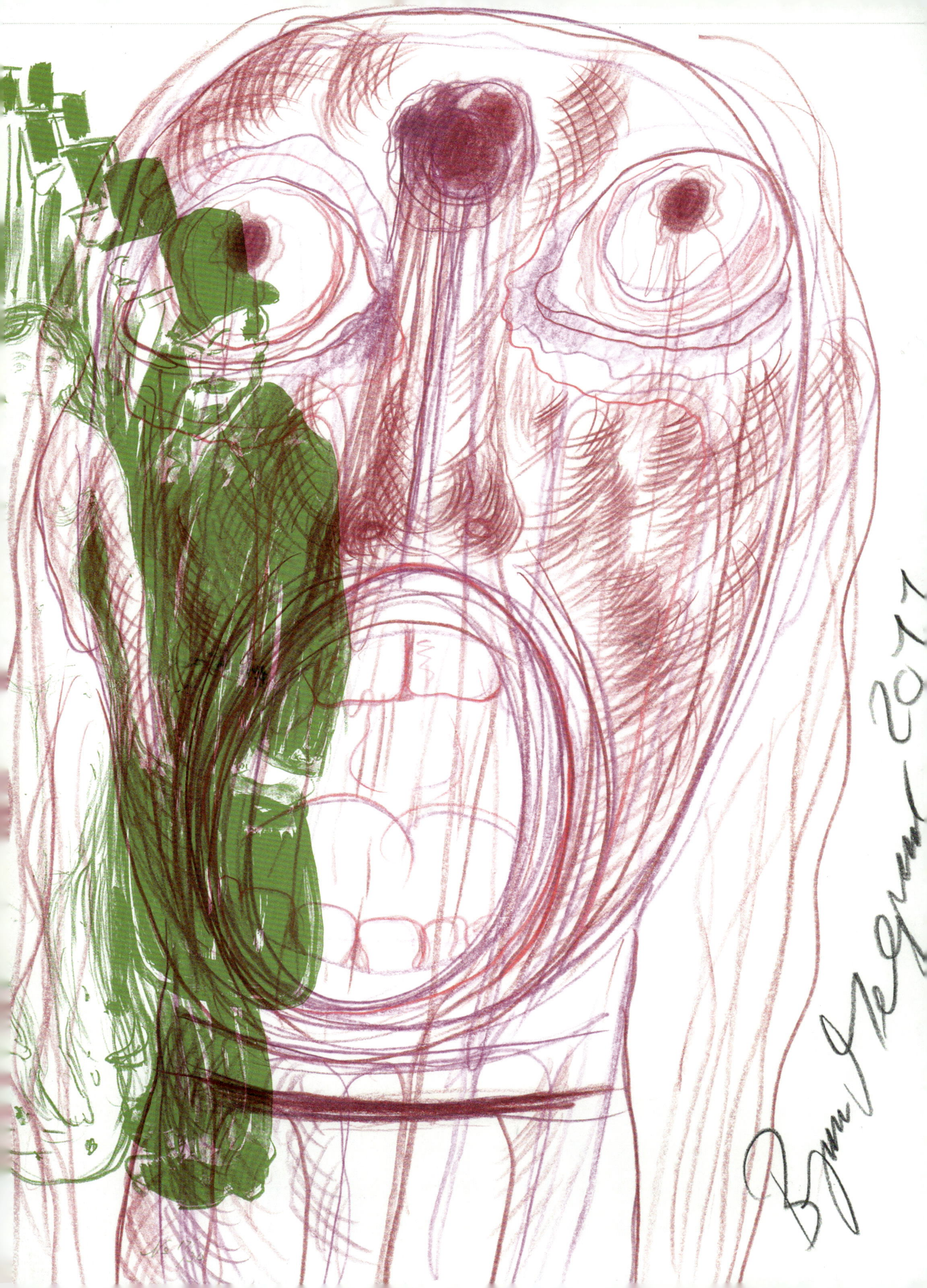
Bjarne Melgaard 2011

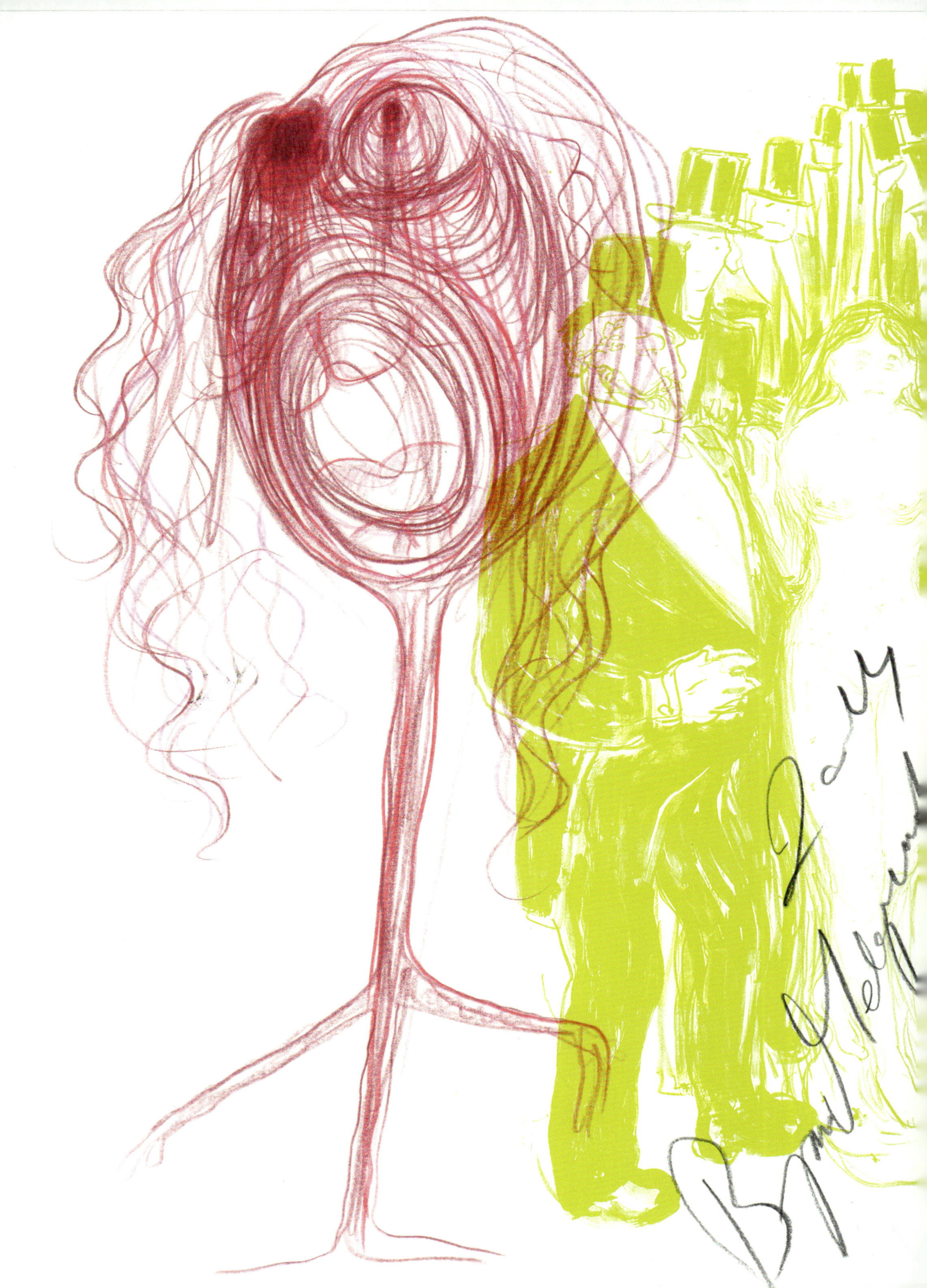

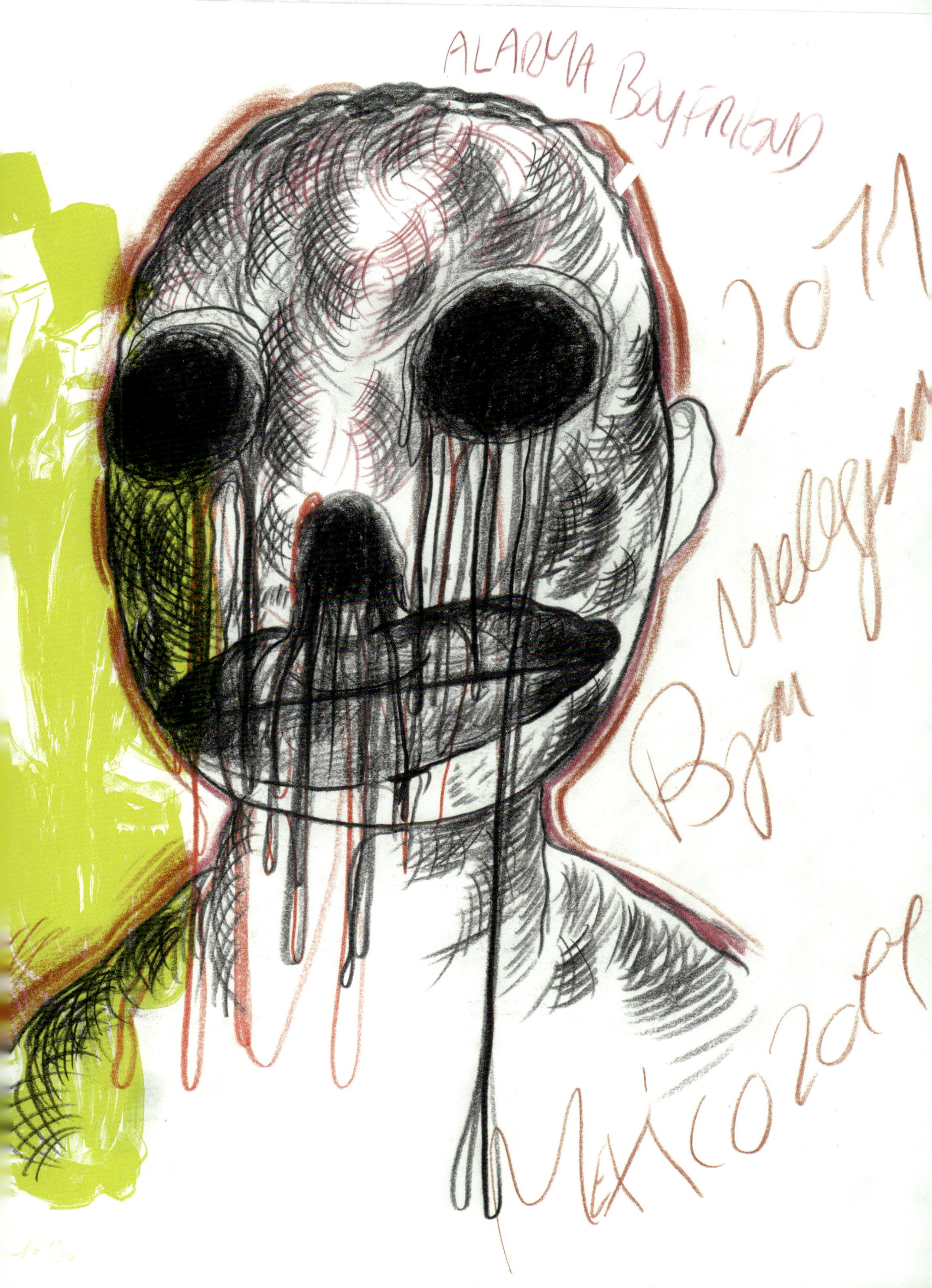

ALARMA BOYFRIEND
2011
Mellgren
Bylm
México 2011

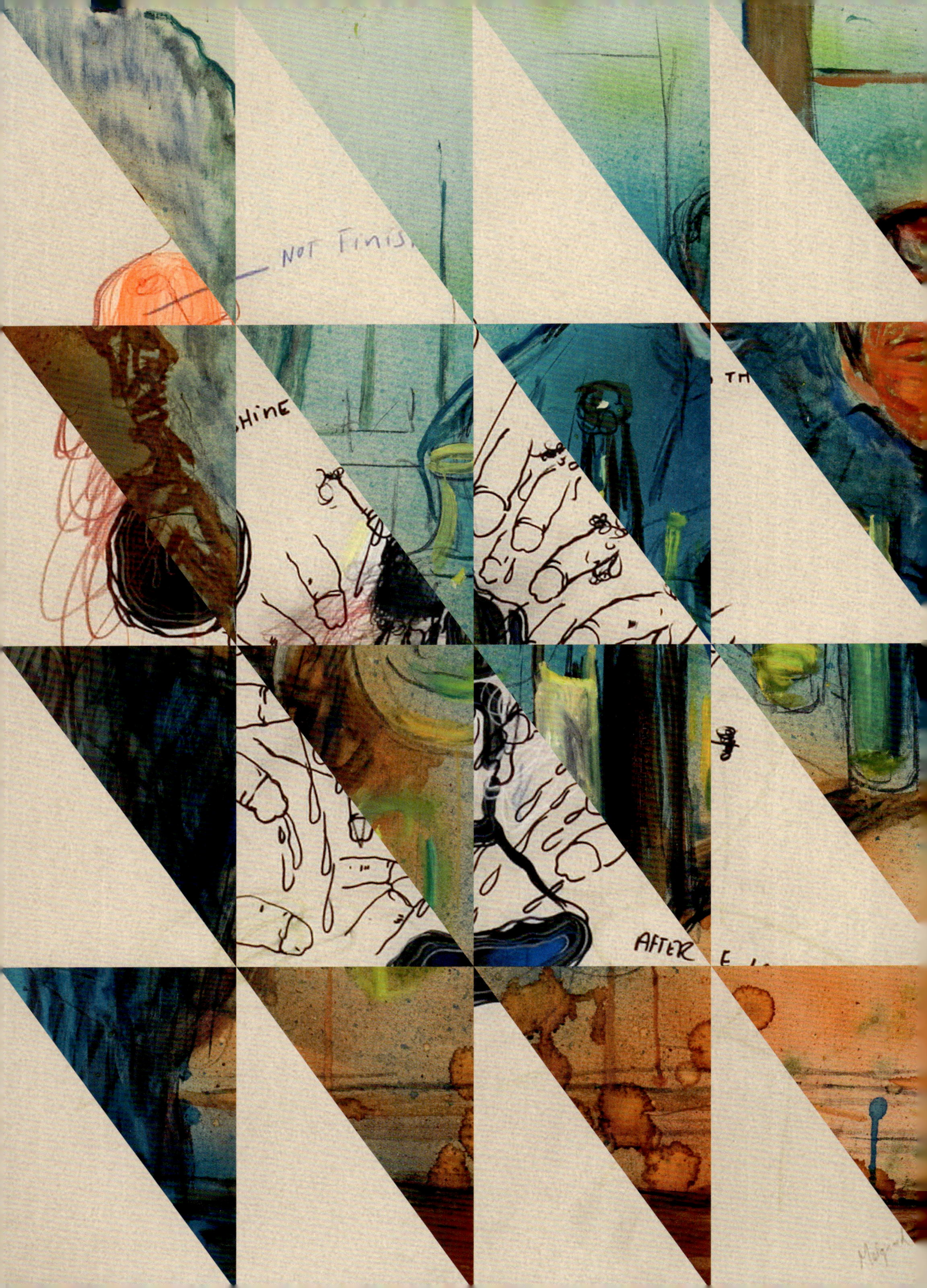
NOT FINIS.
SHINE
TH
AFTER

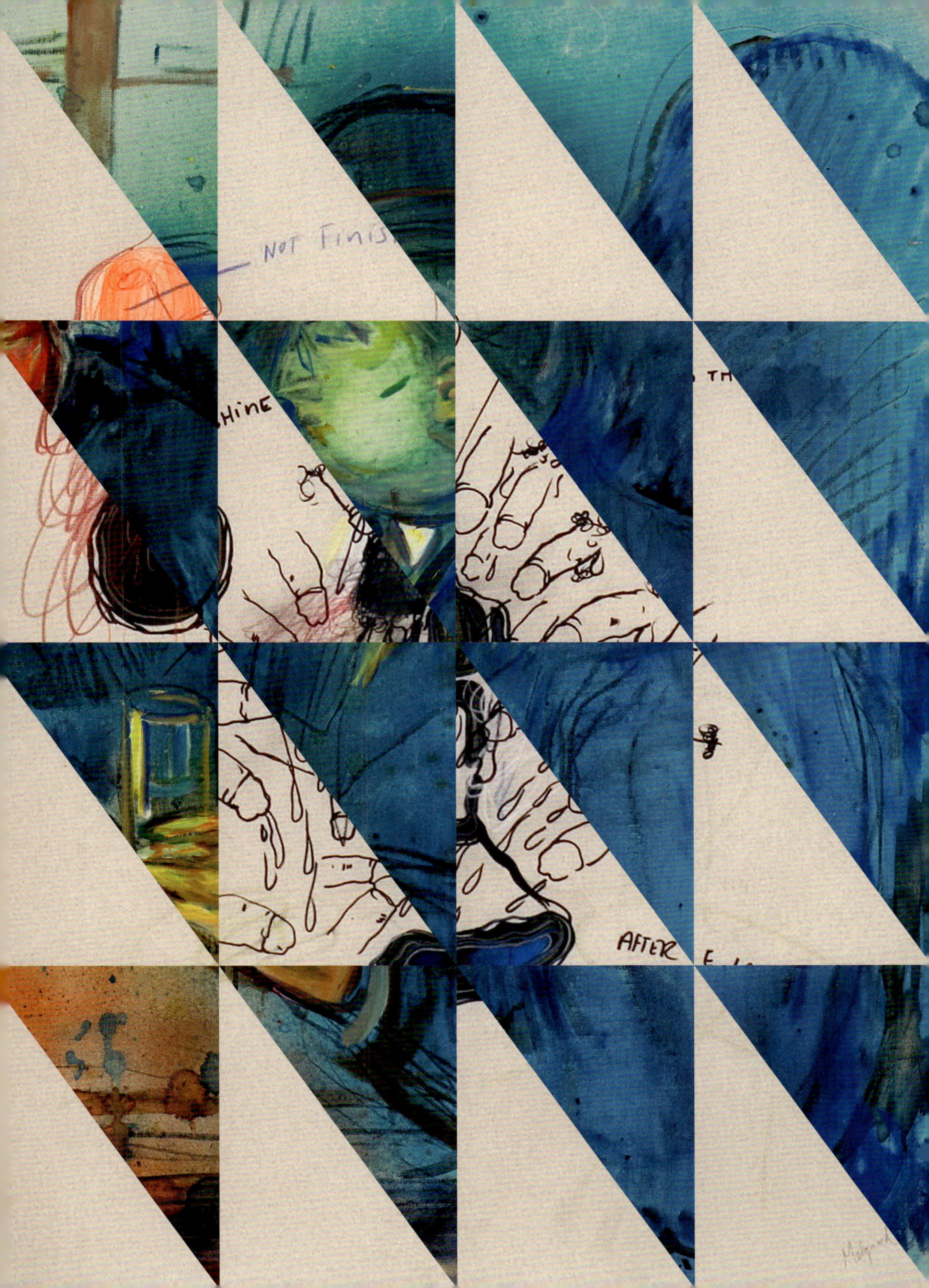

NOT FINIS
HINE
TH
AFTER

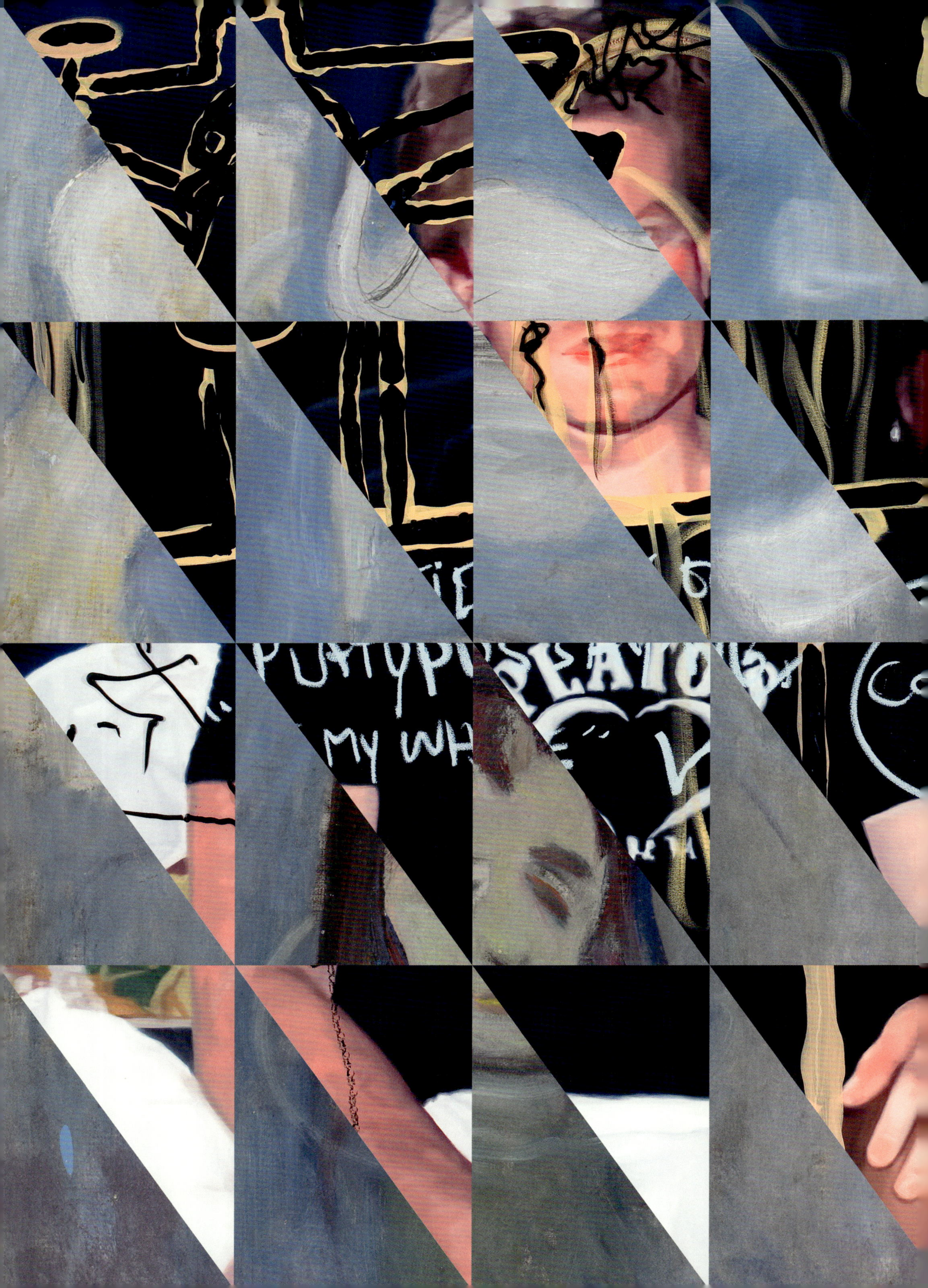
PUSSY PUSSY PLATO
MY WH

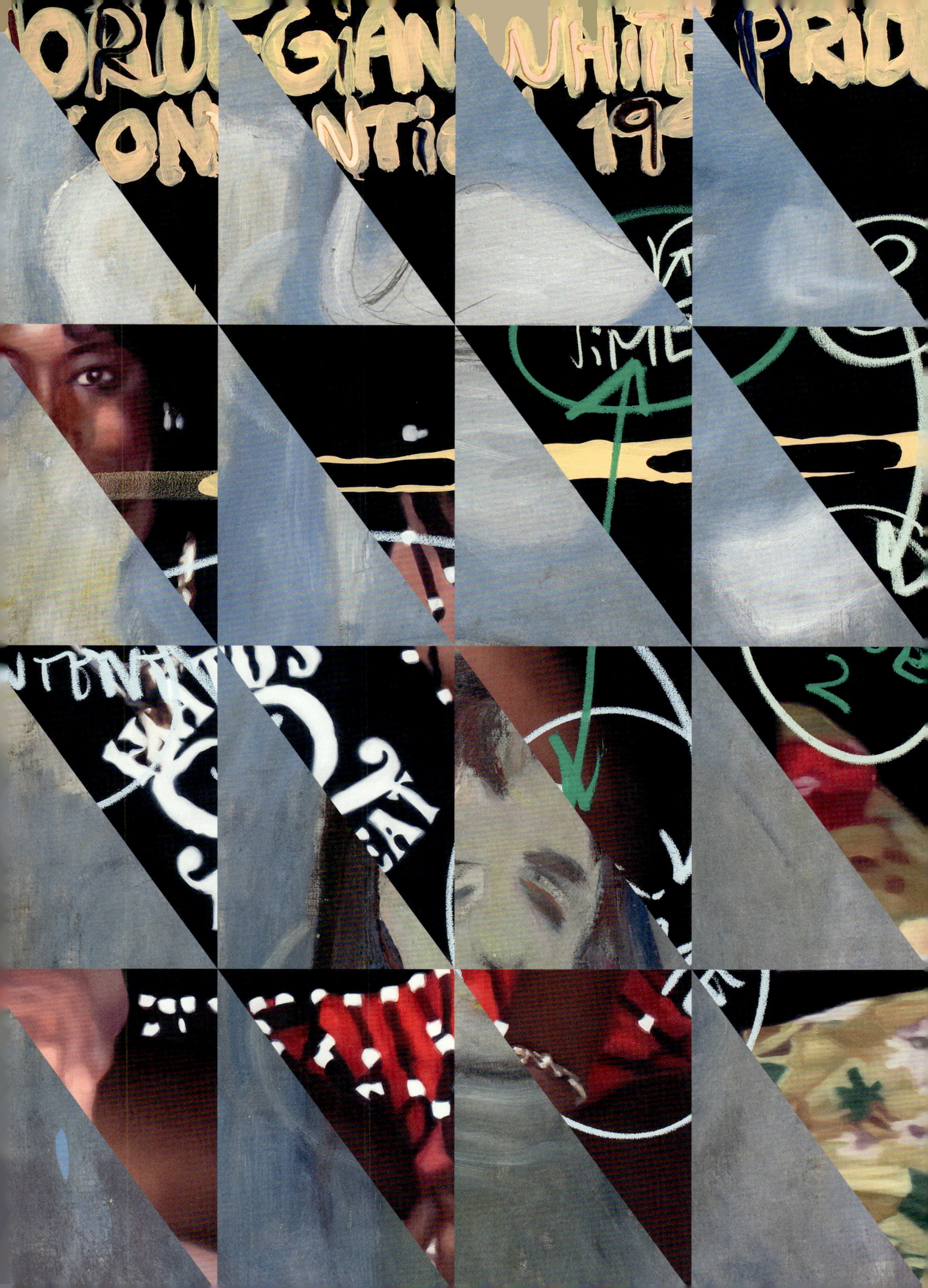

NORWEGIAN WHITE PRIDE
CONVENTION 19
TiME

ARE

JUST … ont ya … ll HiM

"TE… HiM WA… ."
- THAT you Saw … AGAIN

…nt Fi… …lison … n, Fi…
IND… EN A P… AND A …ENT iT AND L…
THAT owhere … TRANLUC… T AND L
"WHO CAN you TURN TO NOW " you A

"SN… HiM "
TiGER …liED TO …iminATE …OES Th
LiKE A … BLACK FOG… &CLOUD AROUND
…PHONE CALL; WHAT you

DiA…
3 0 … 2002

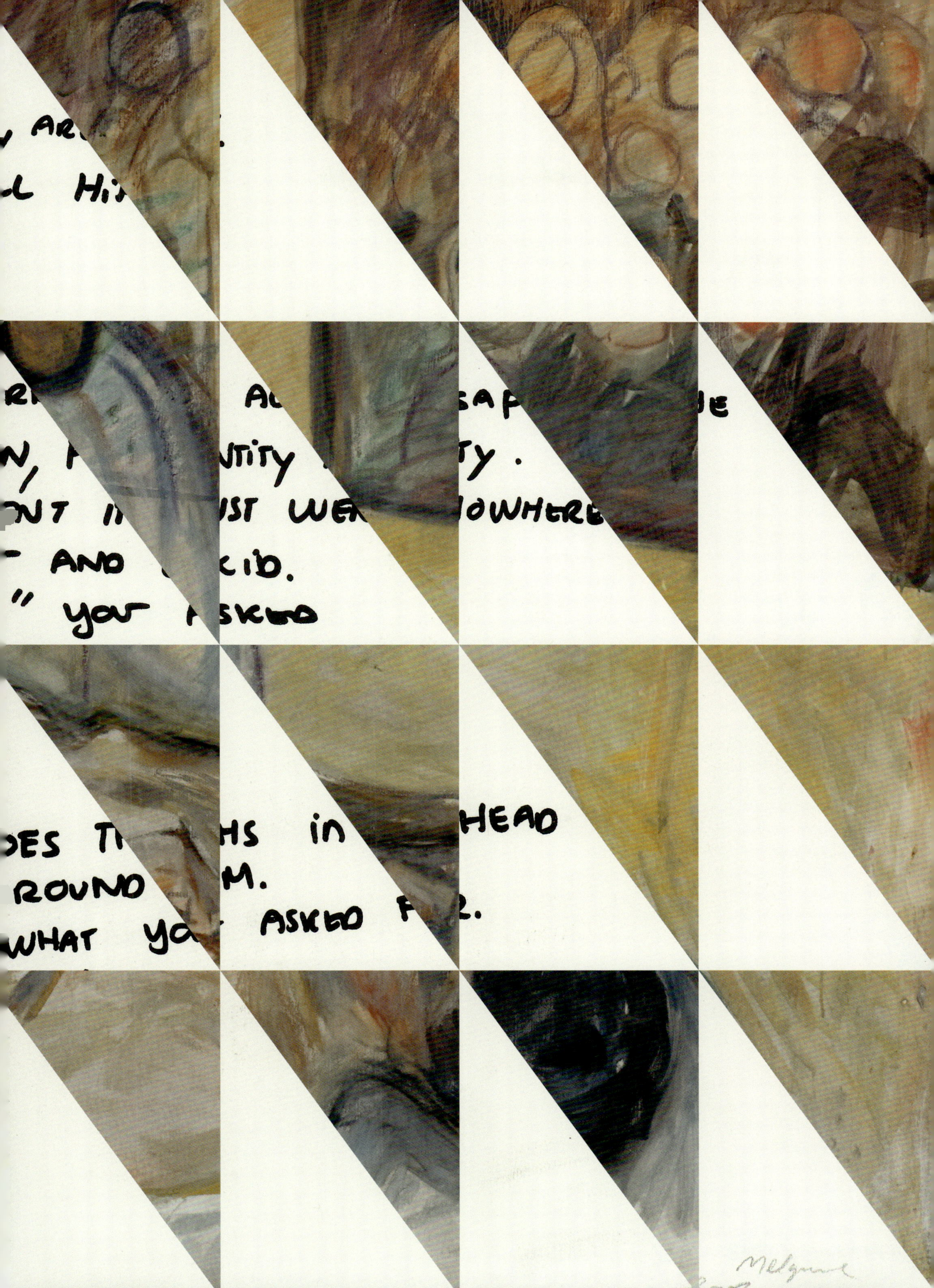
ARE
HIS
A
NTITY   TY.
NT I   ST WE   OWHERE
AND   CID.
" your ASKED
DES T   HS in   HEAD
ROUND   M.
WHAT yo   ASKED F R.

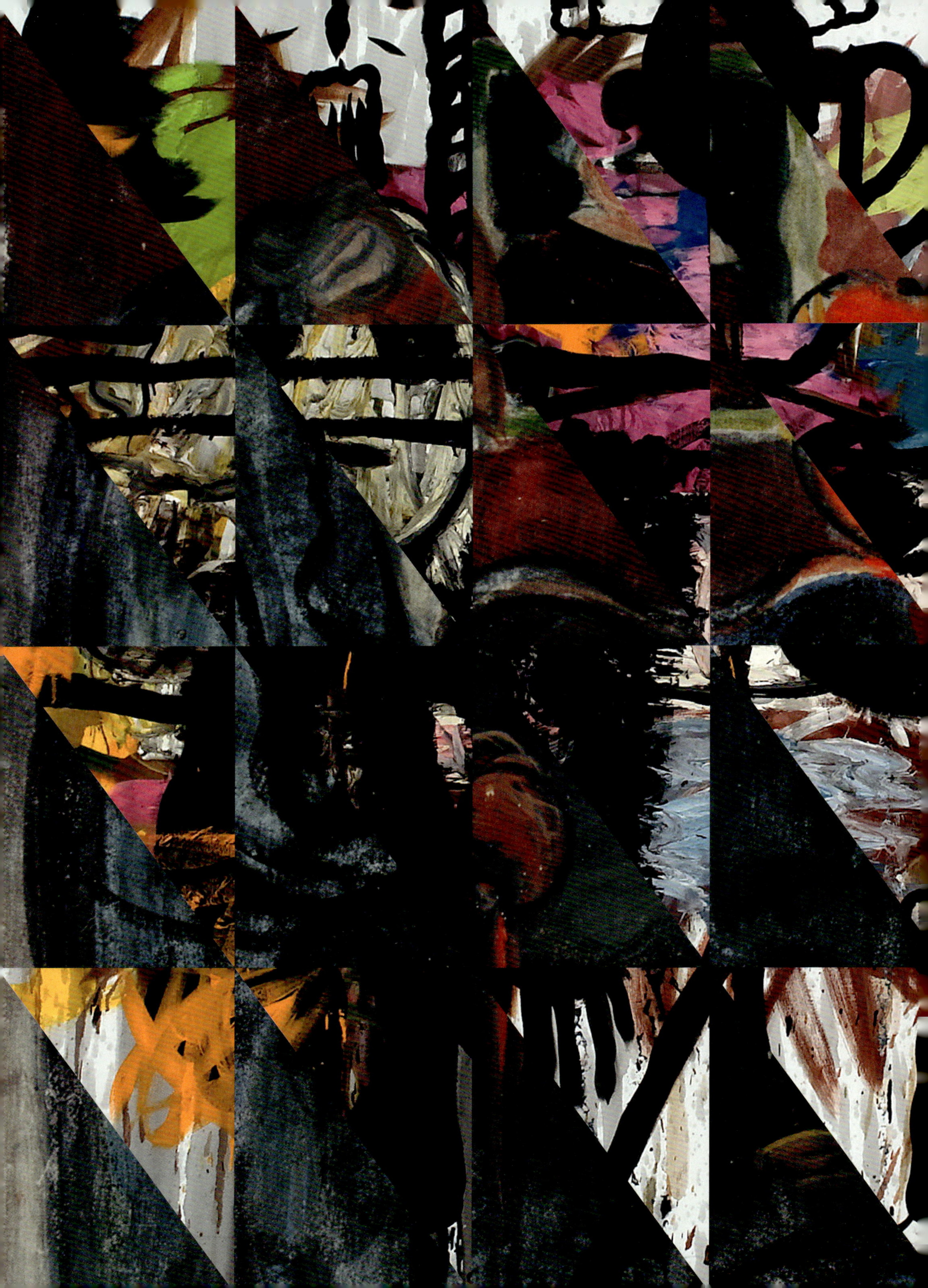

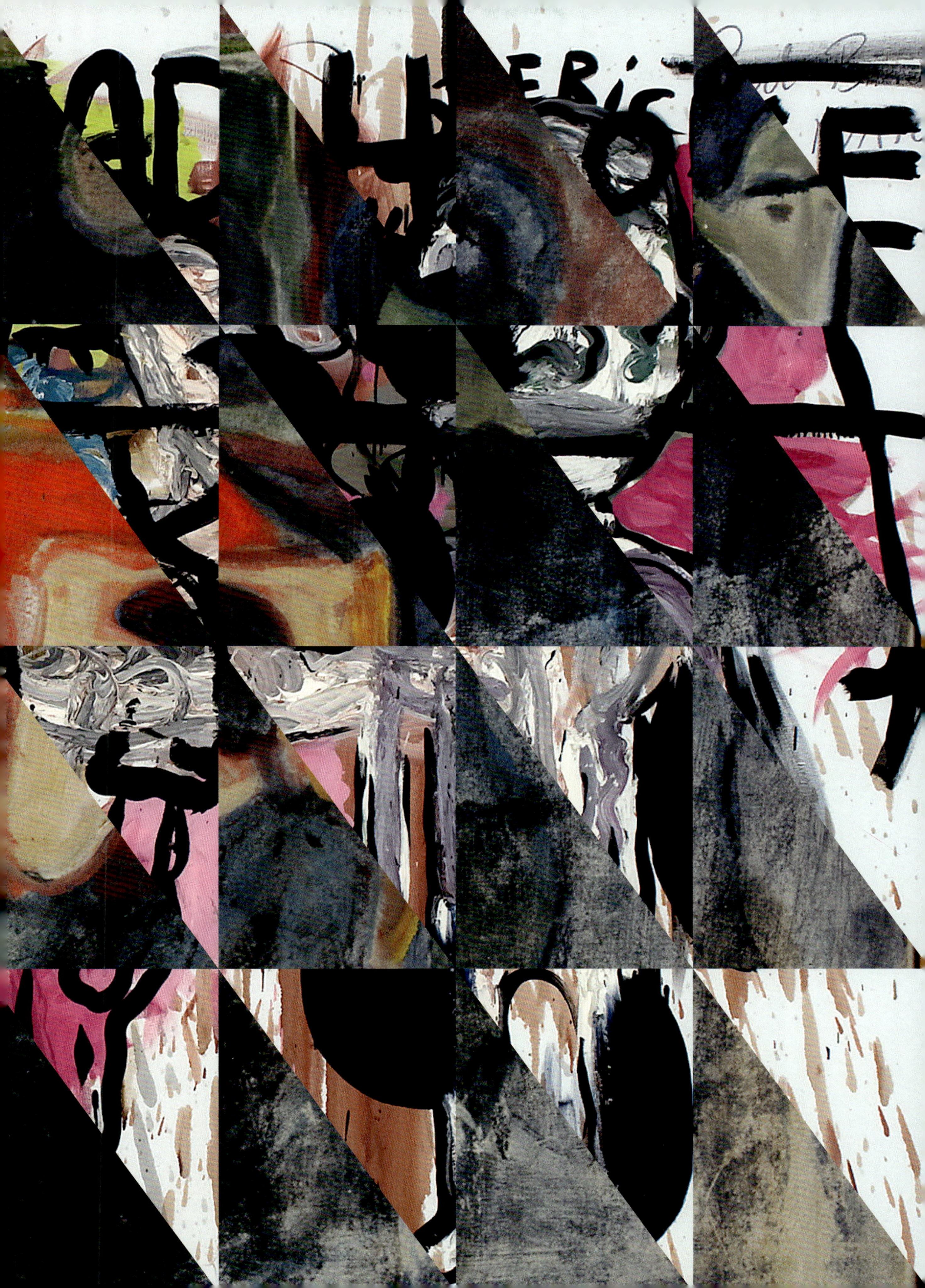

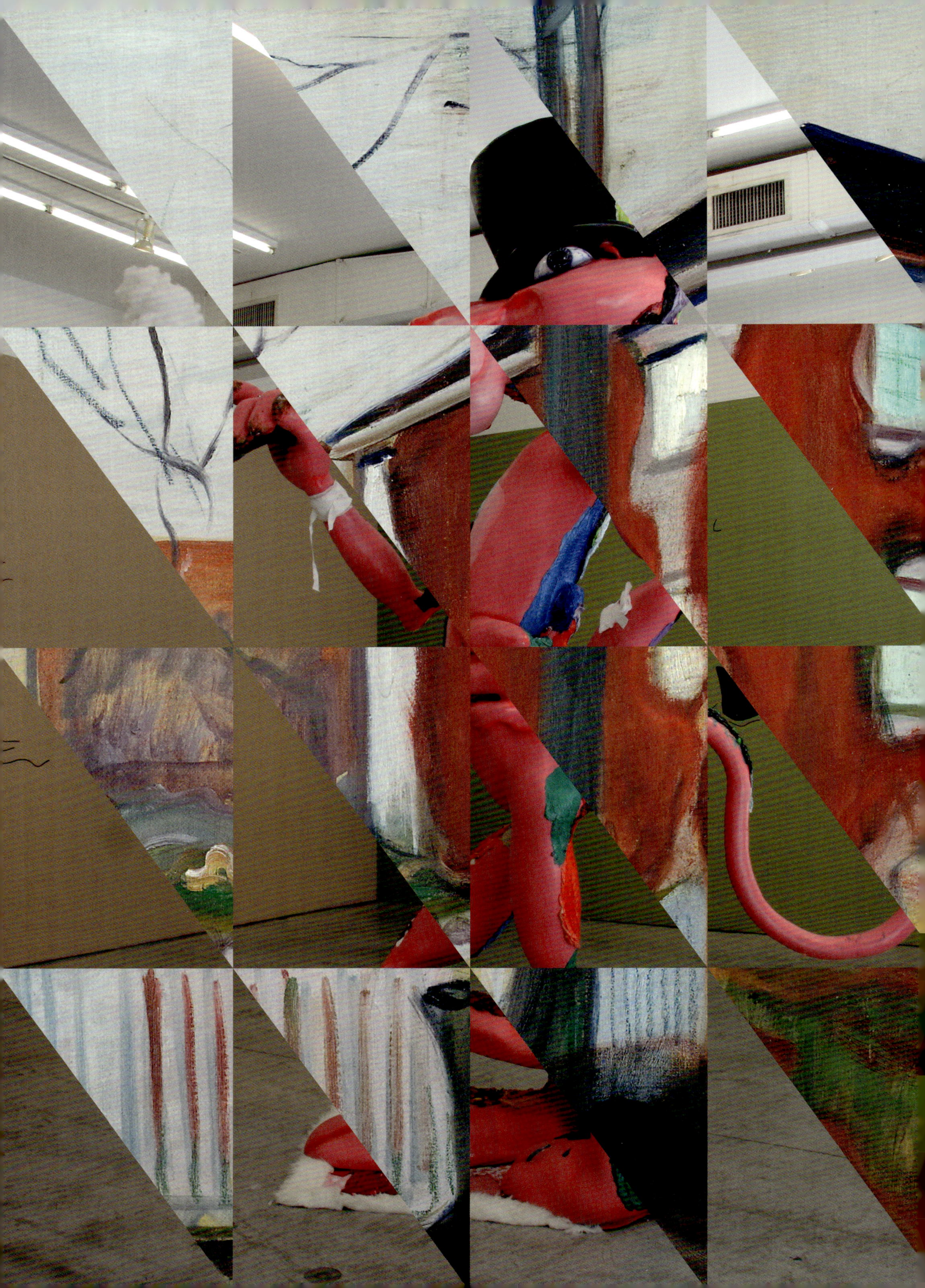

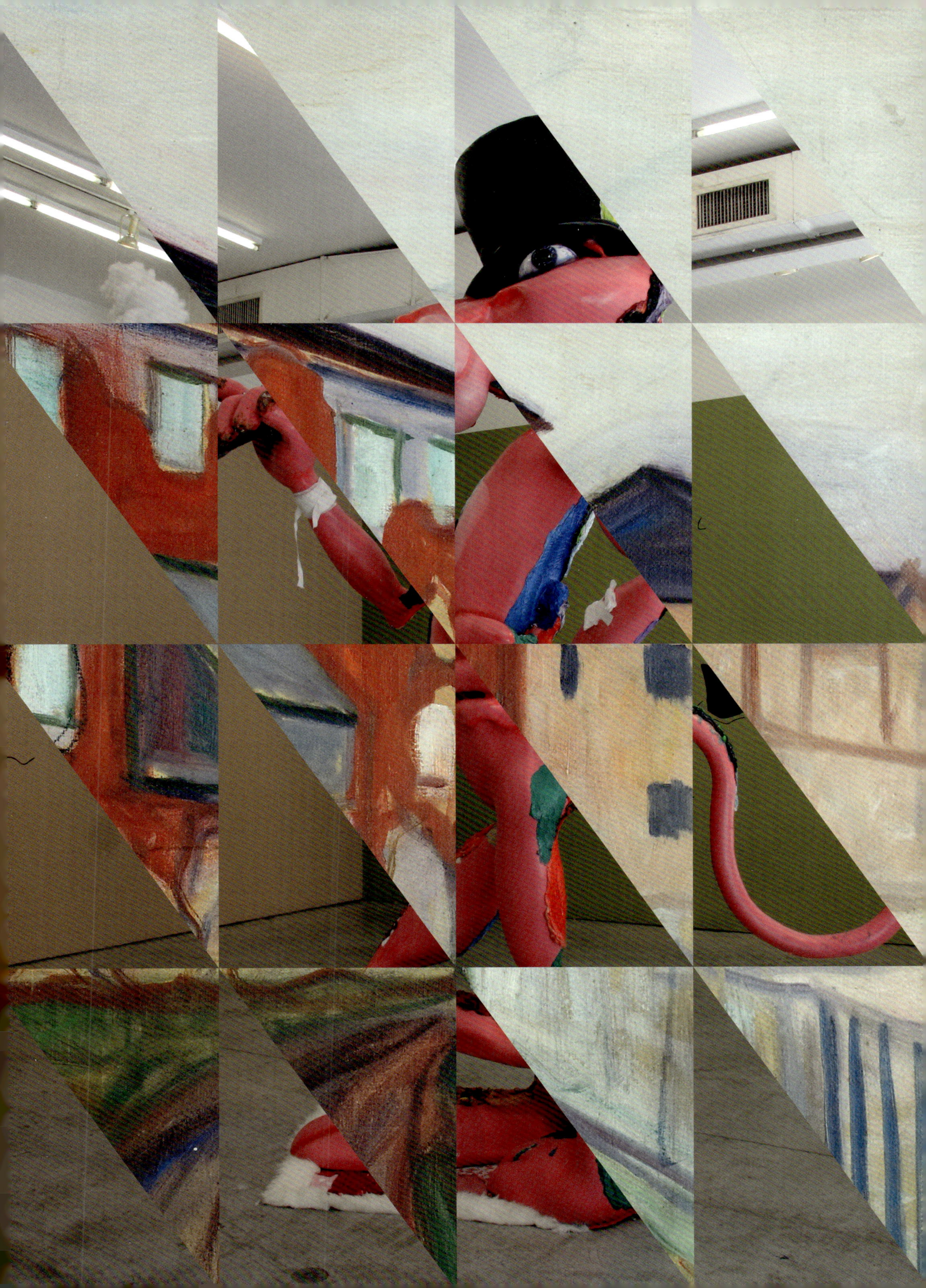

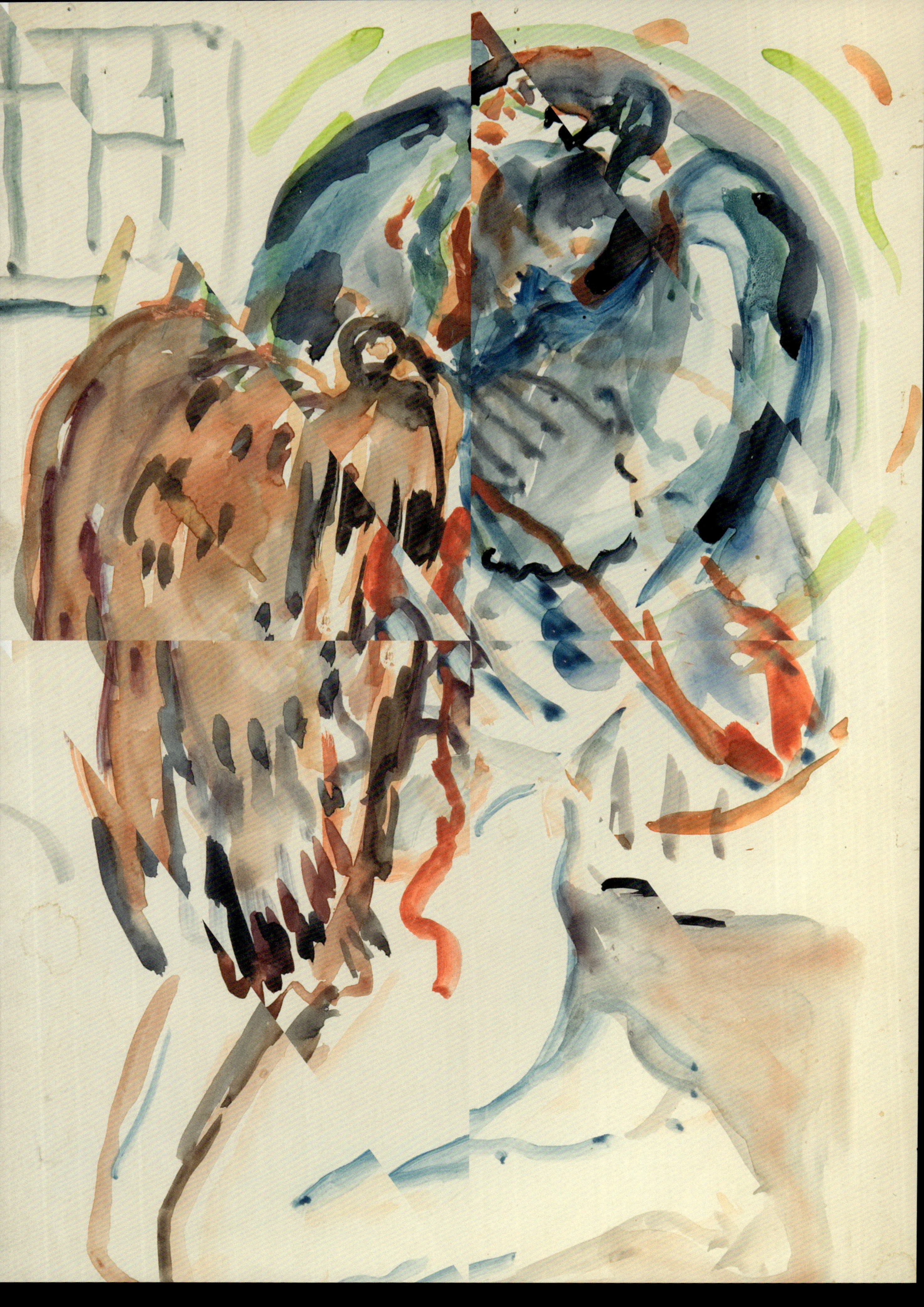

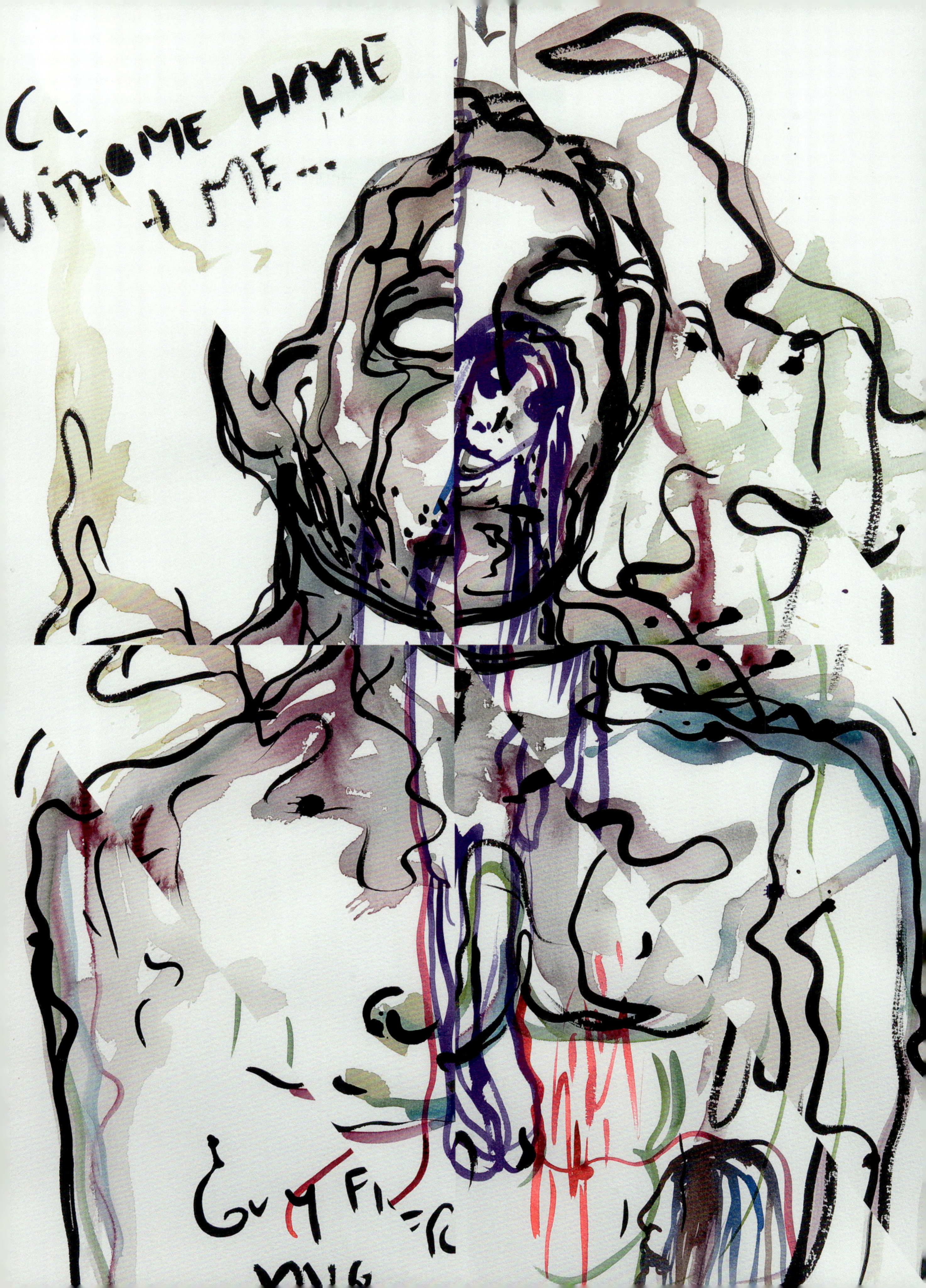
C. OME HOME
ME...
GuY FiER
MiG

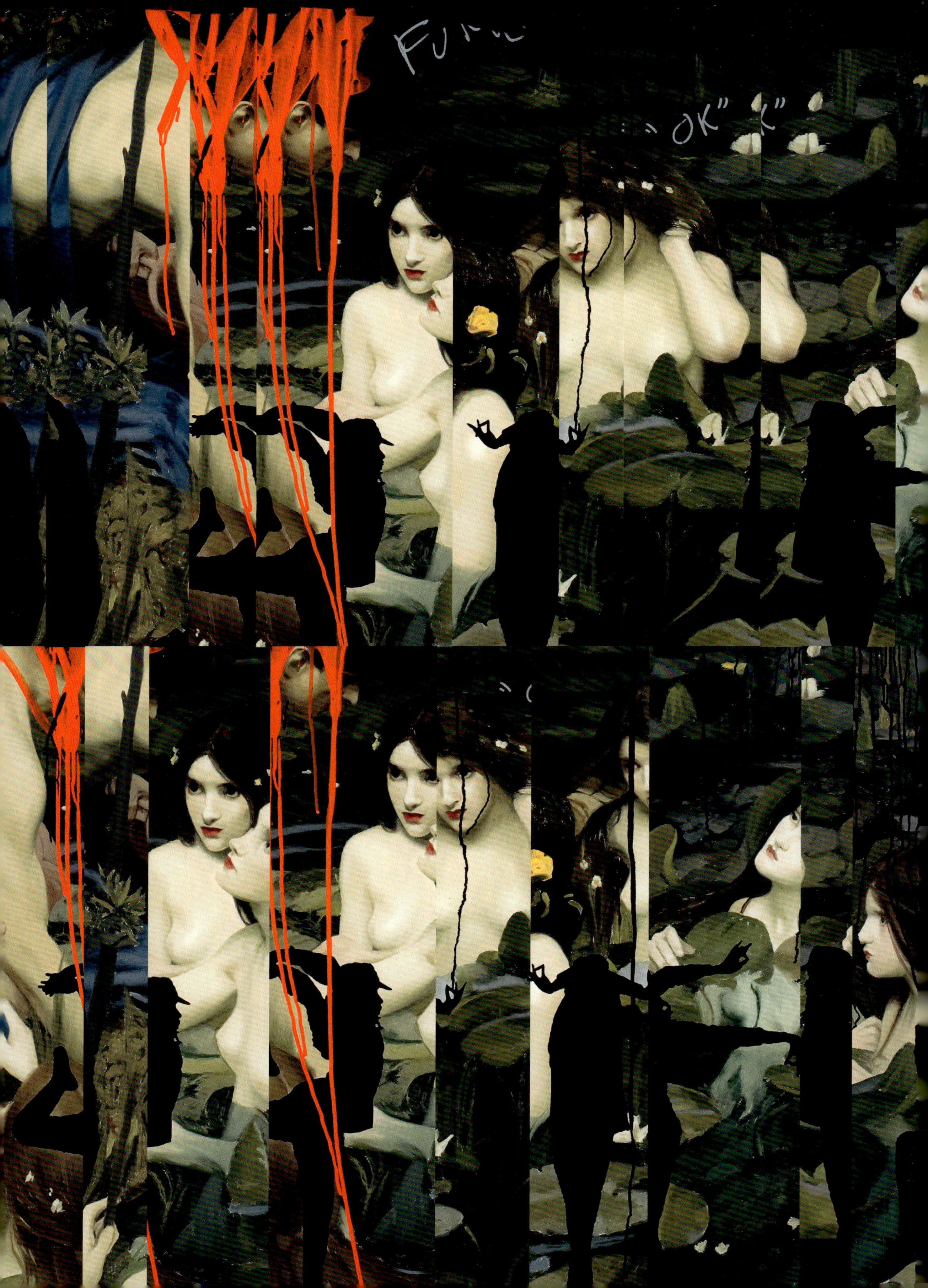
Full
"OK" "?"

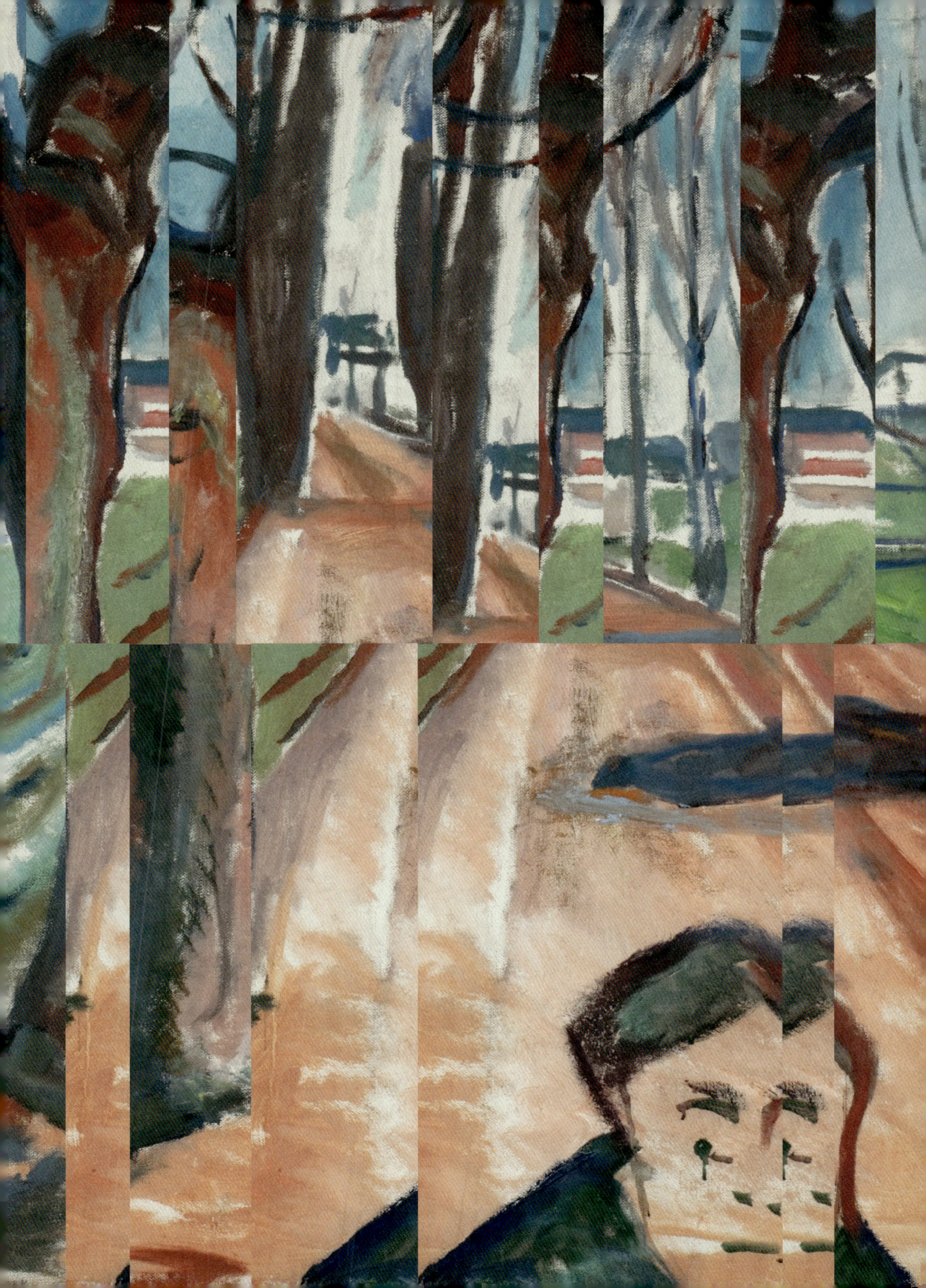

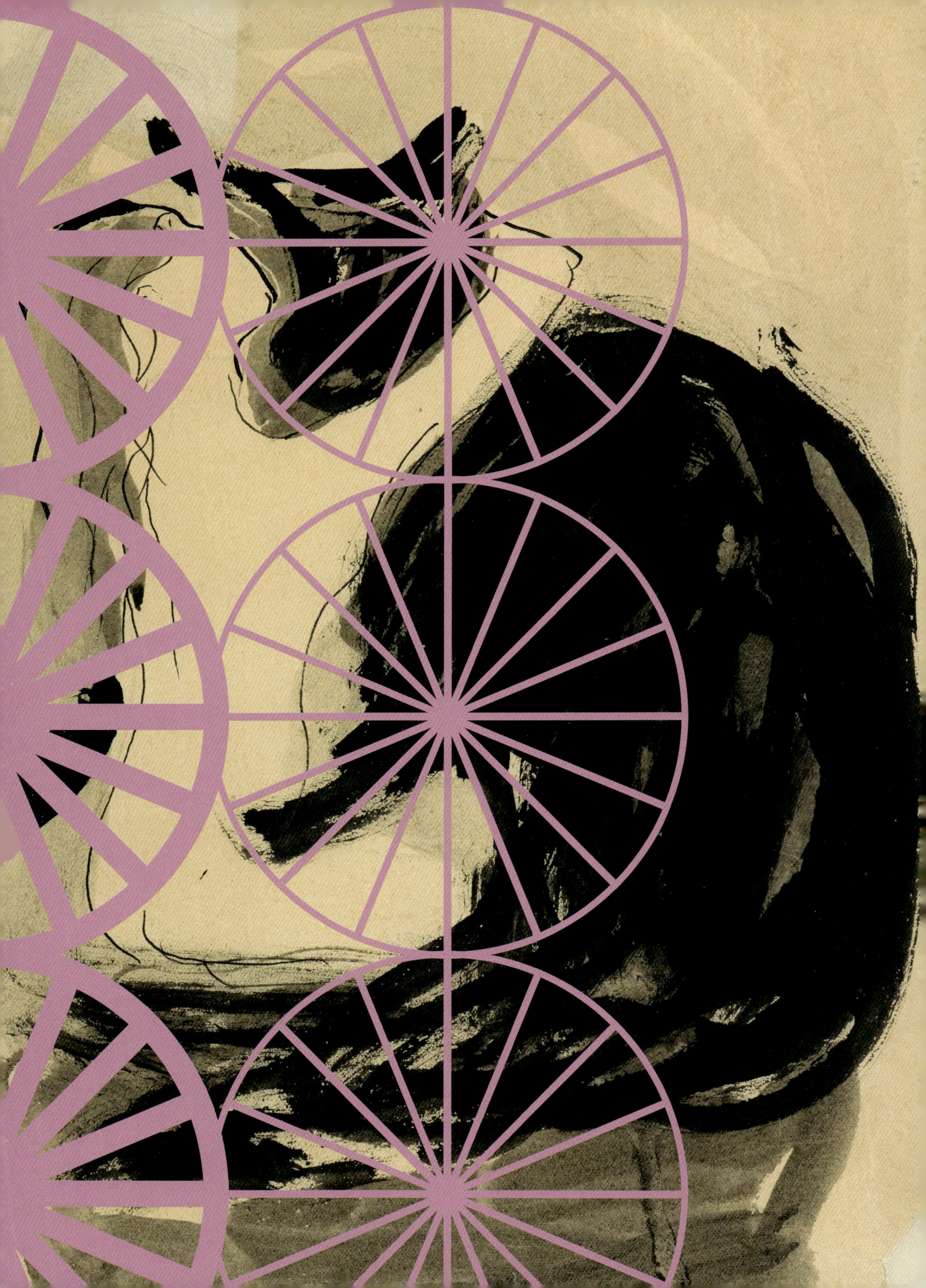

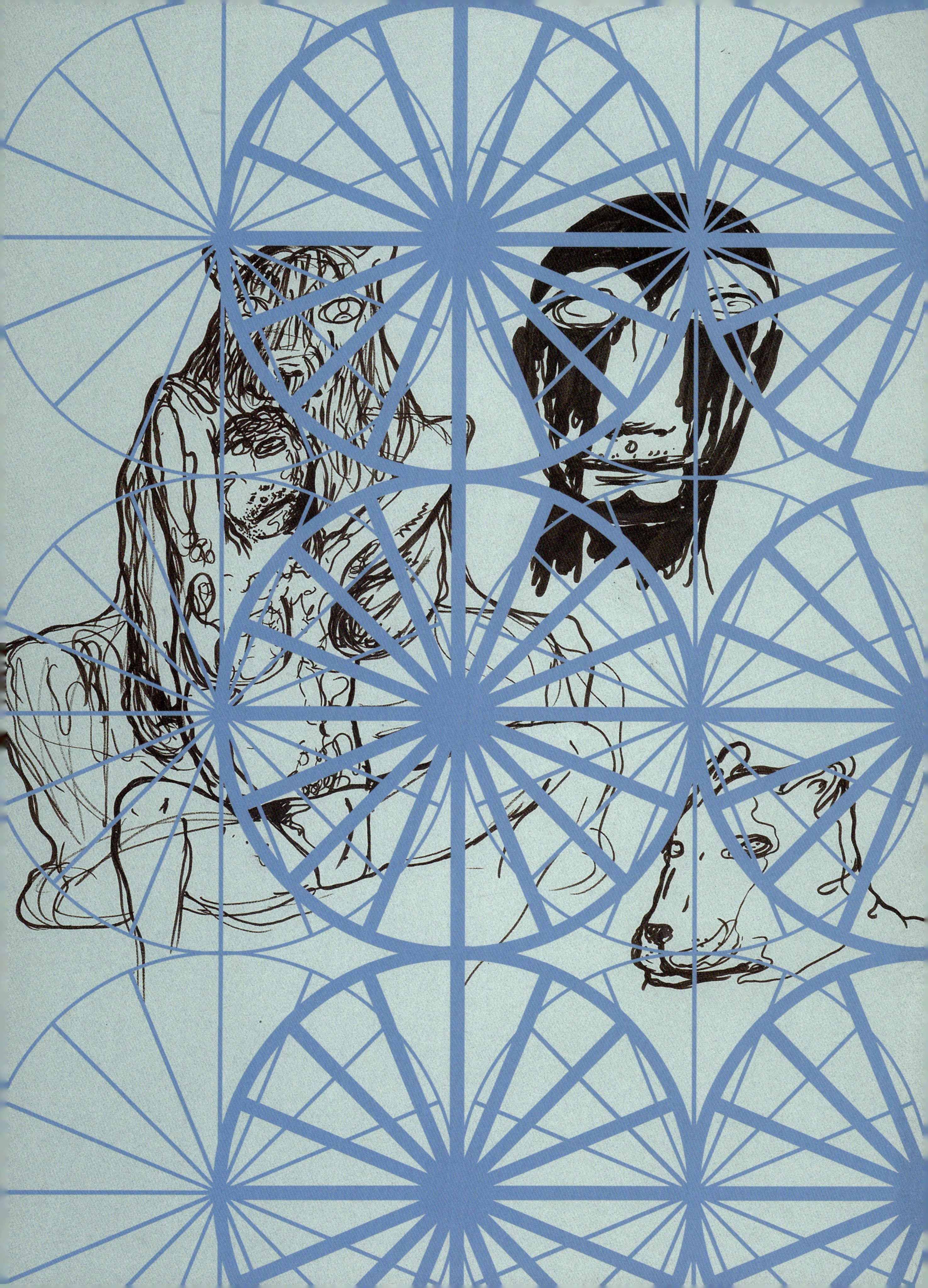

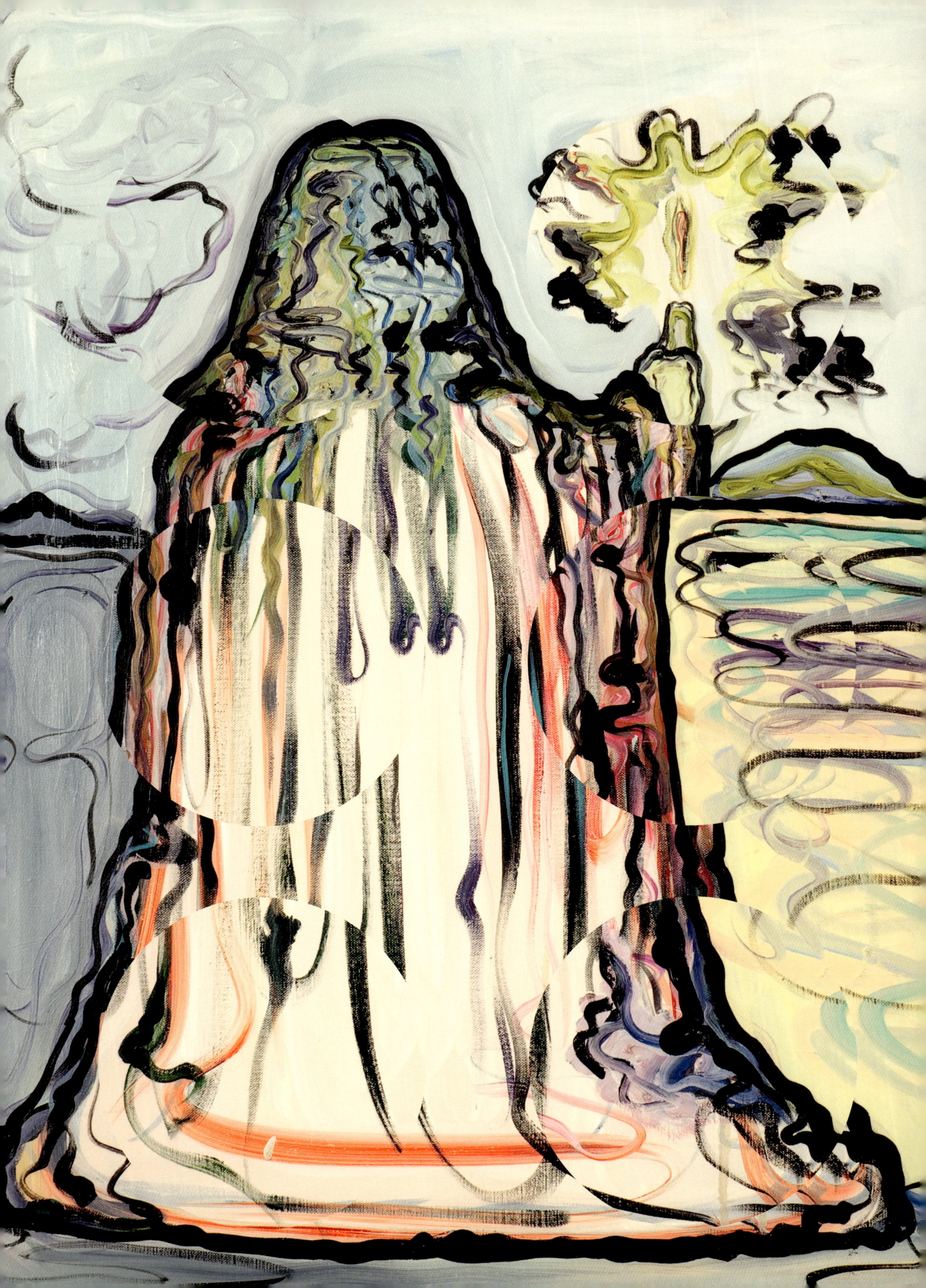

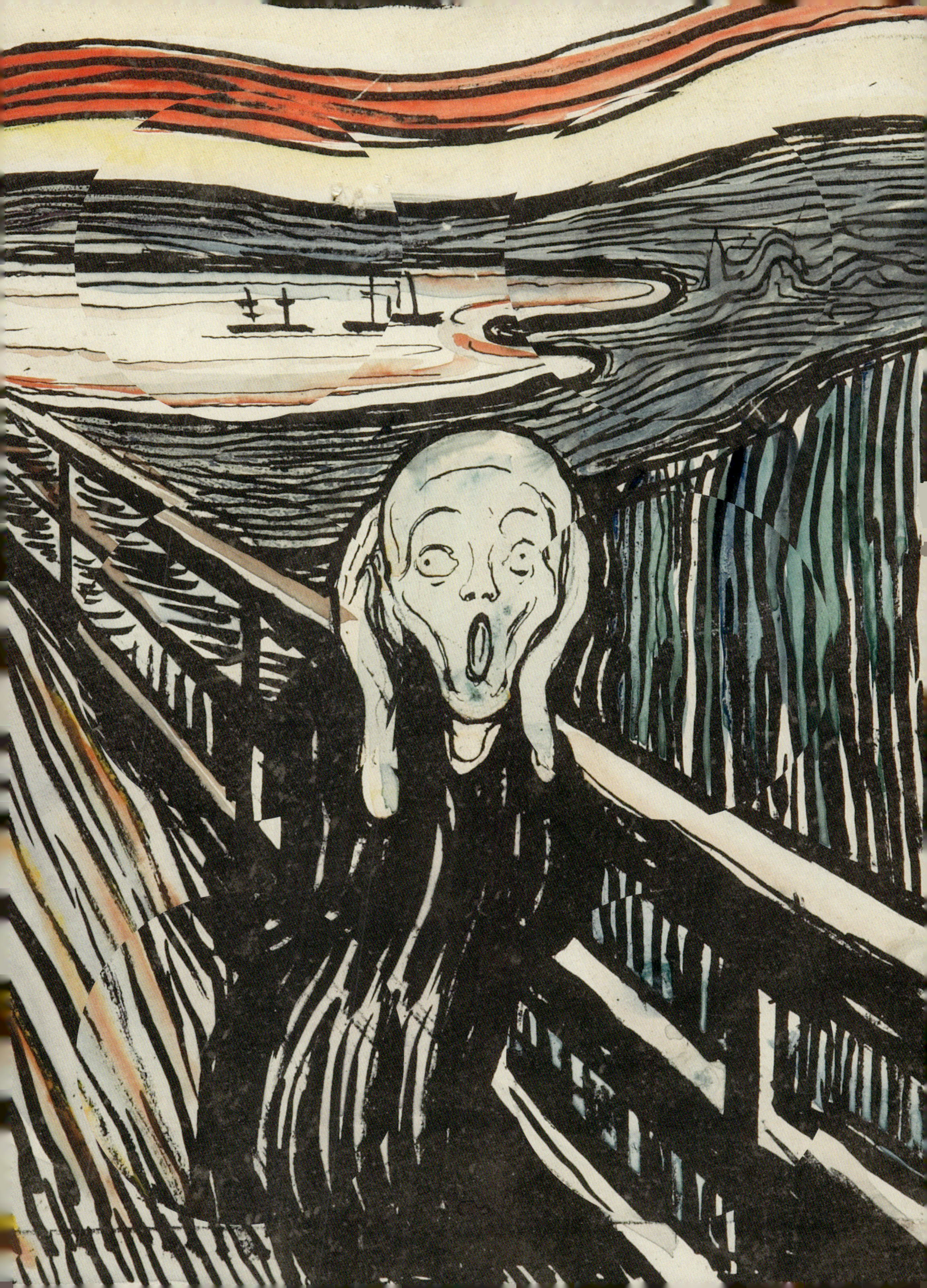

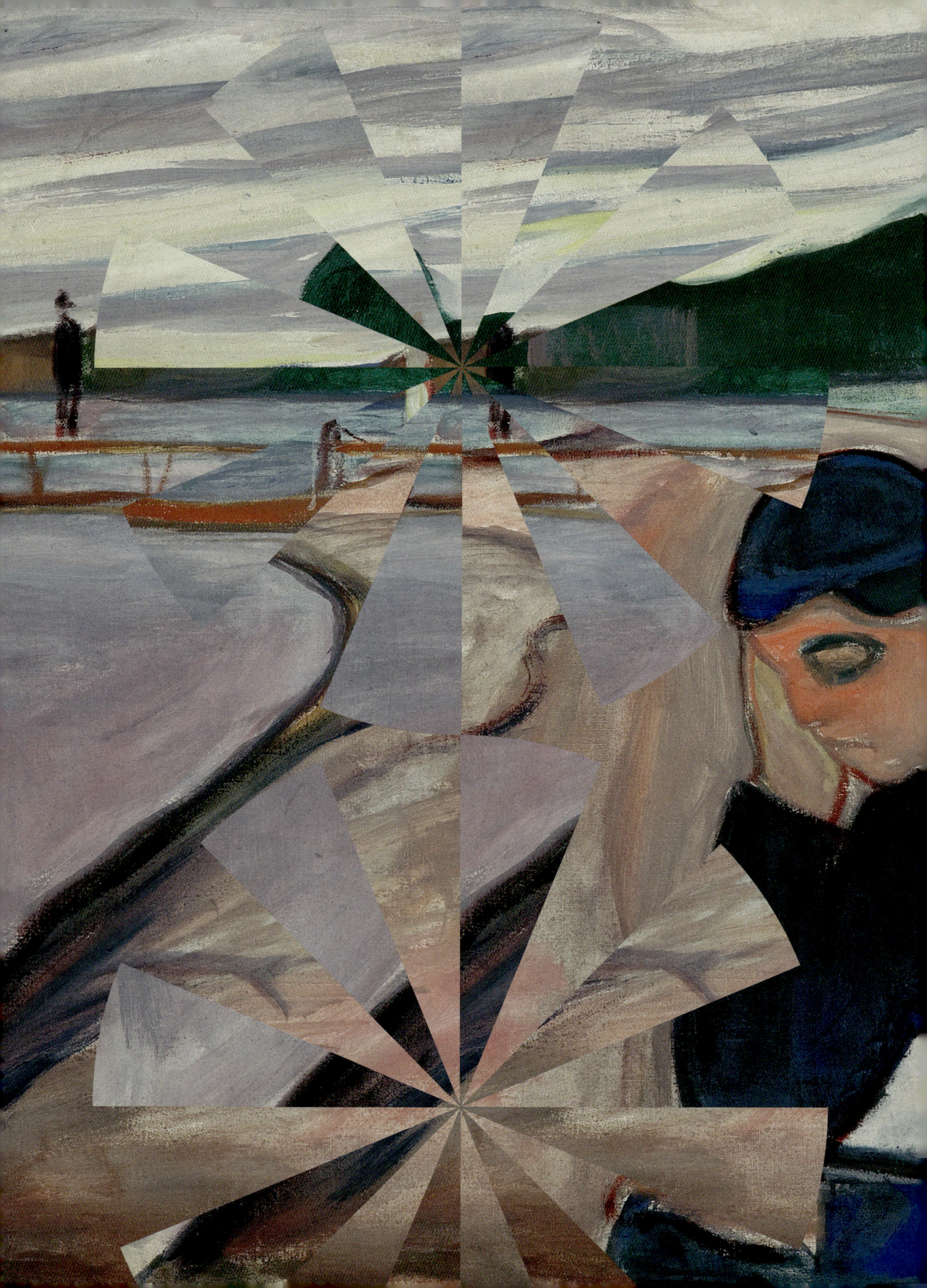

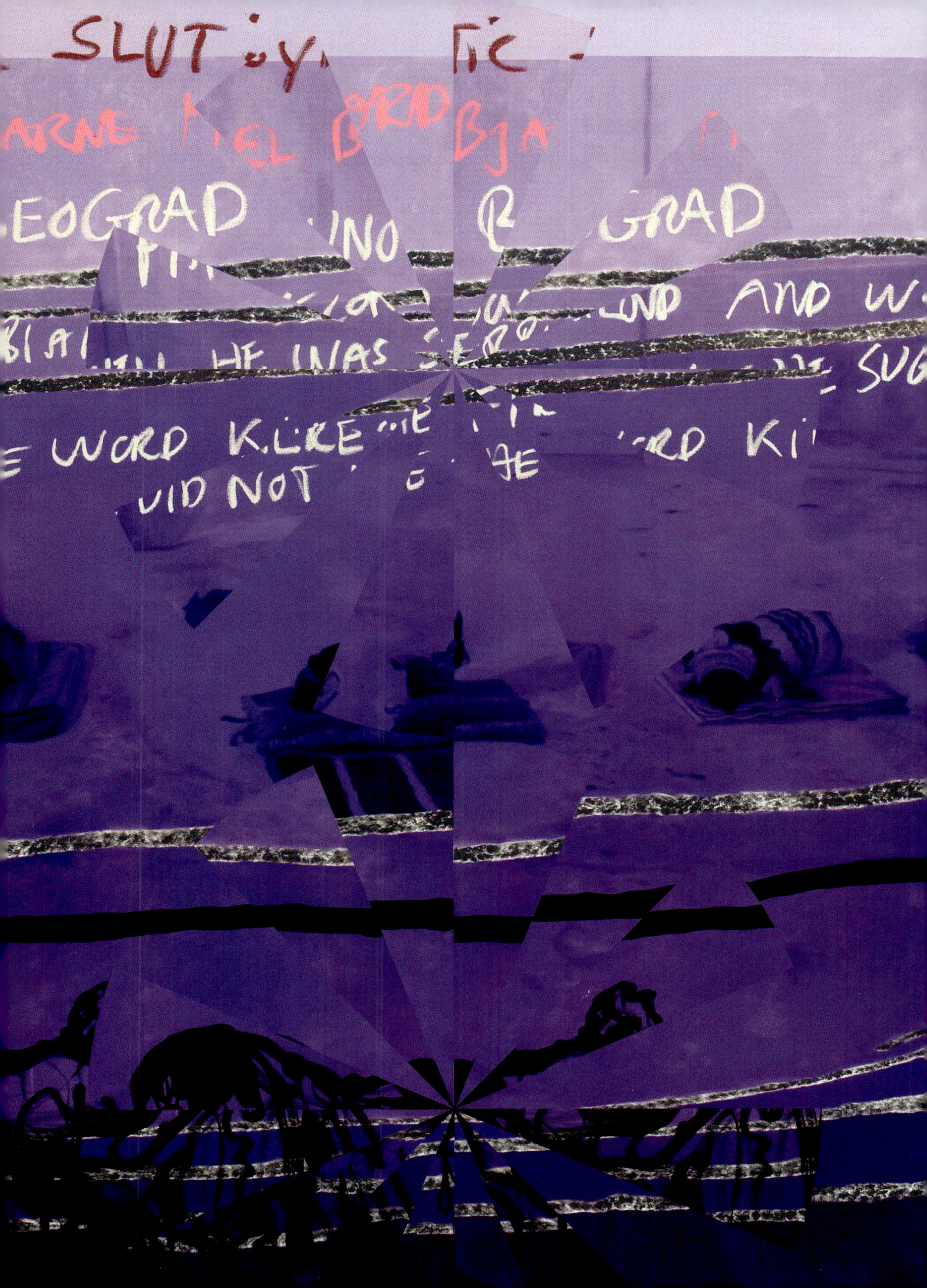

SLUT ... TIC

...ARNE ...EL B...RD ...BJA...

...EOGRAD ...INO R...GRAD

...ND AND W...

BLA... HE INAS SE... ...E SUG...

...E WORD K.IRE... ...RD KI...

...VID NOT ...

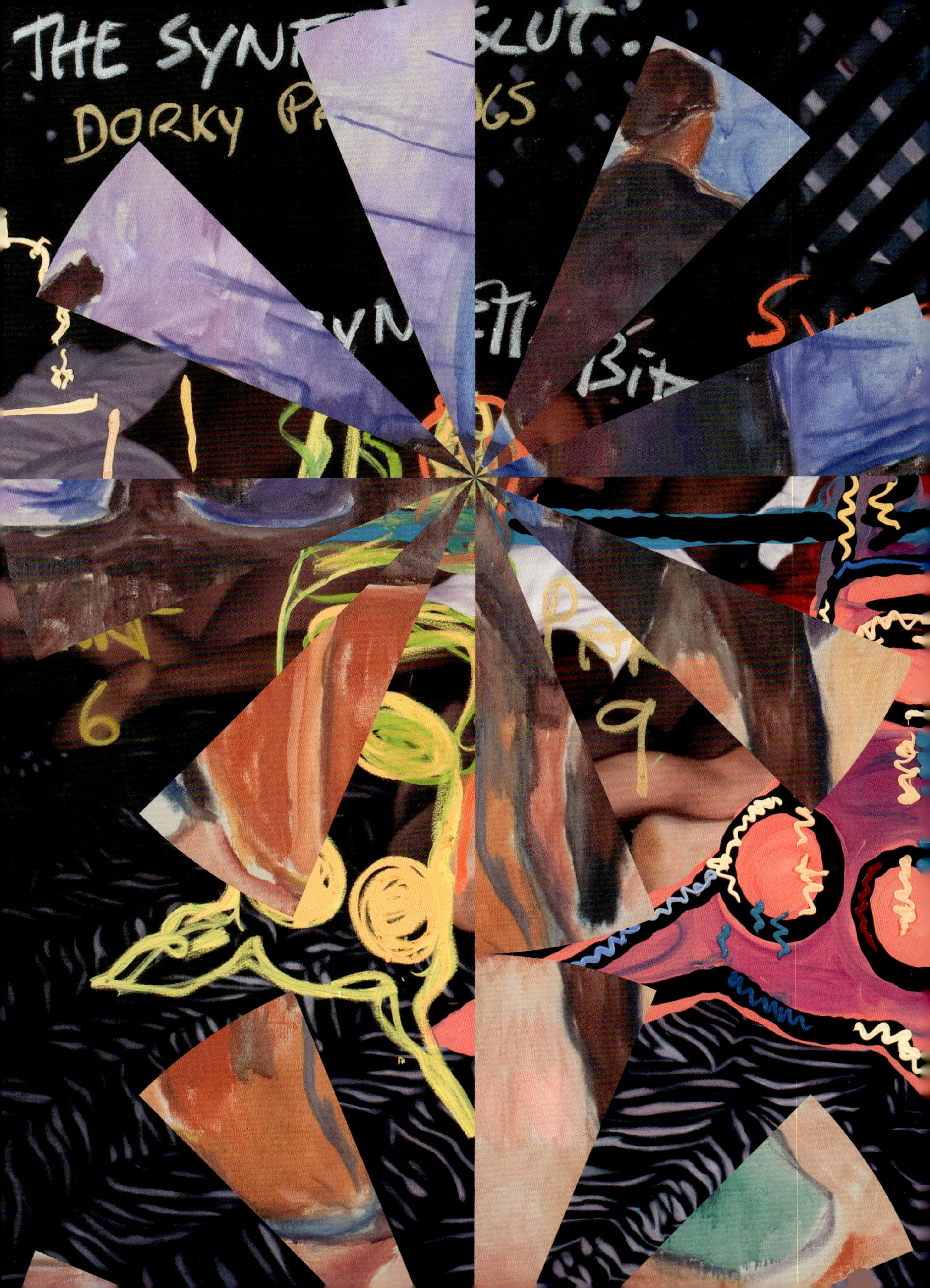

THE SYNTHETIC SLUT:
DORKY PAINTINGS

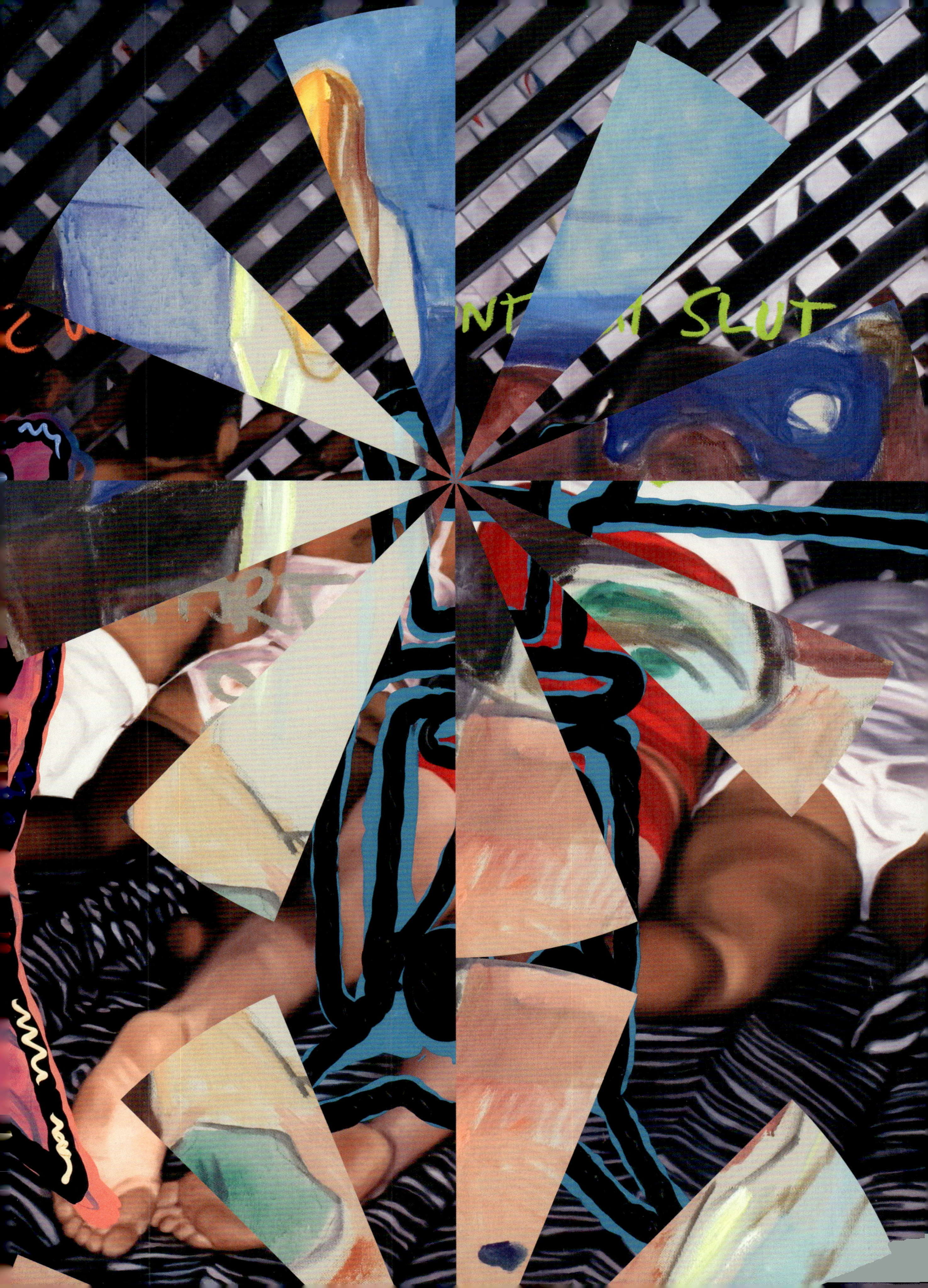
SLUT

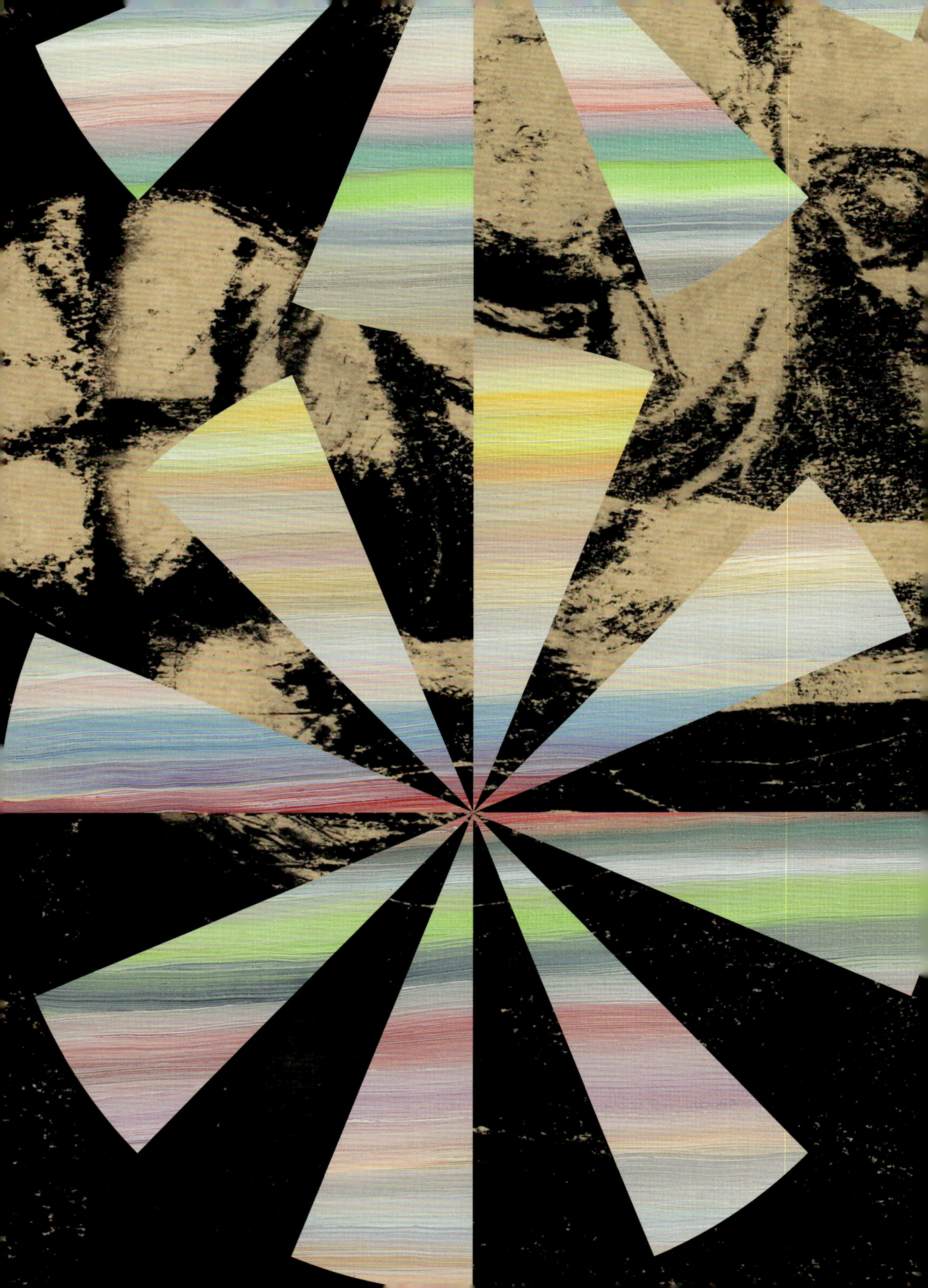

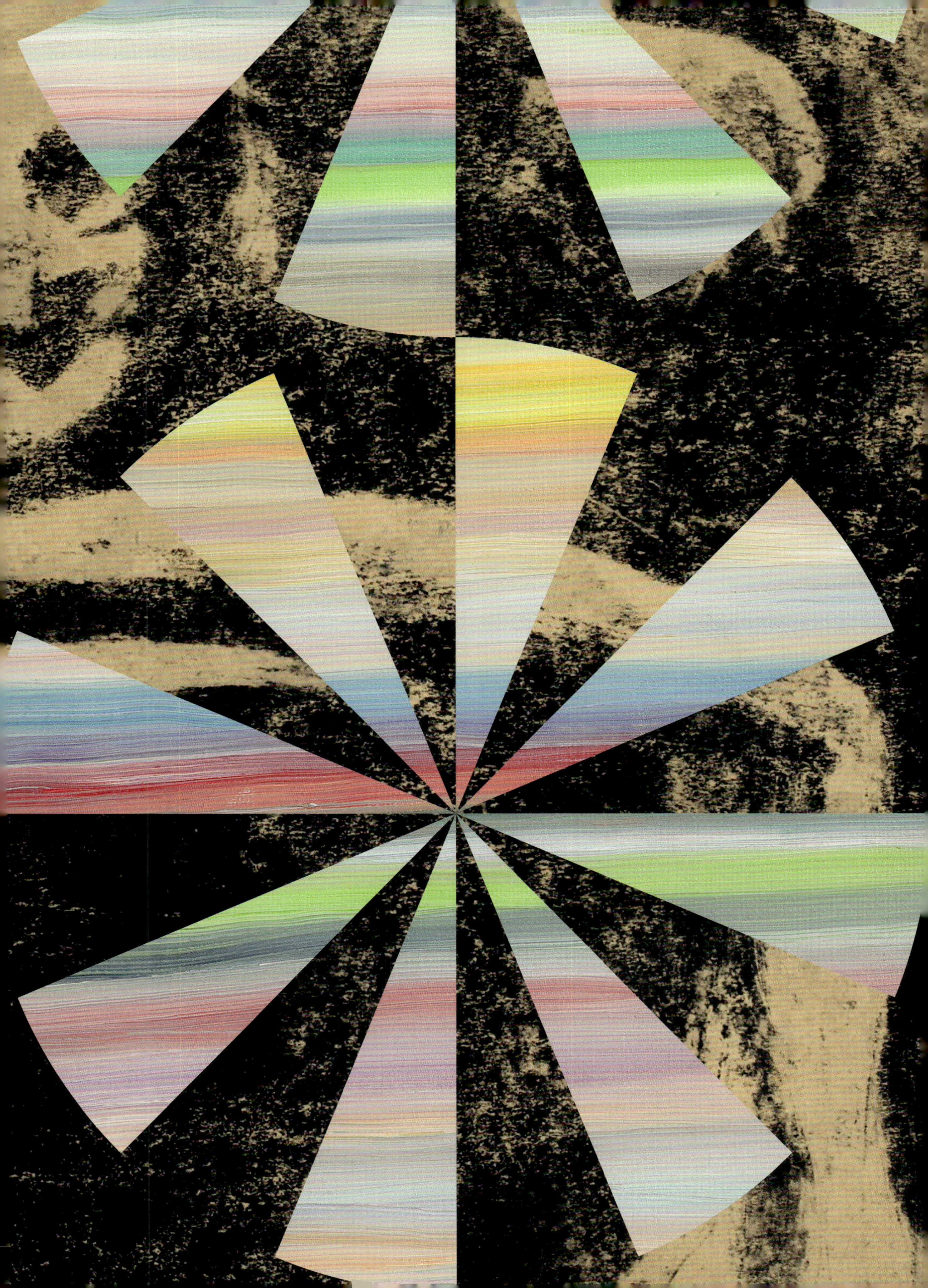

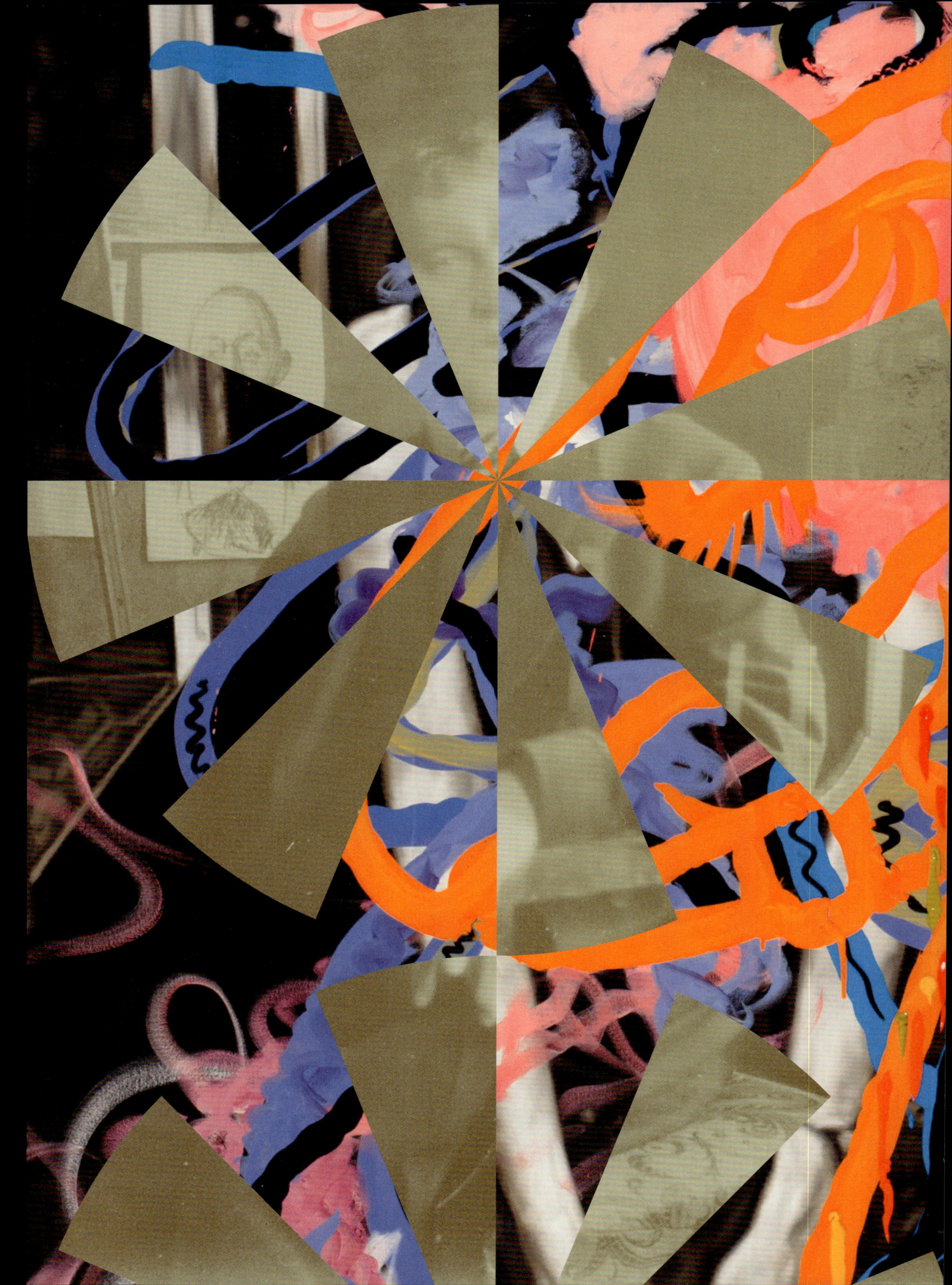

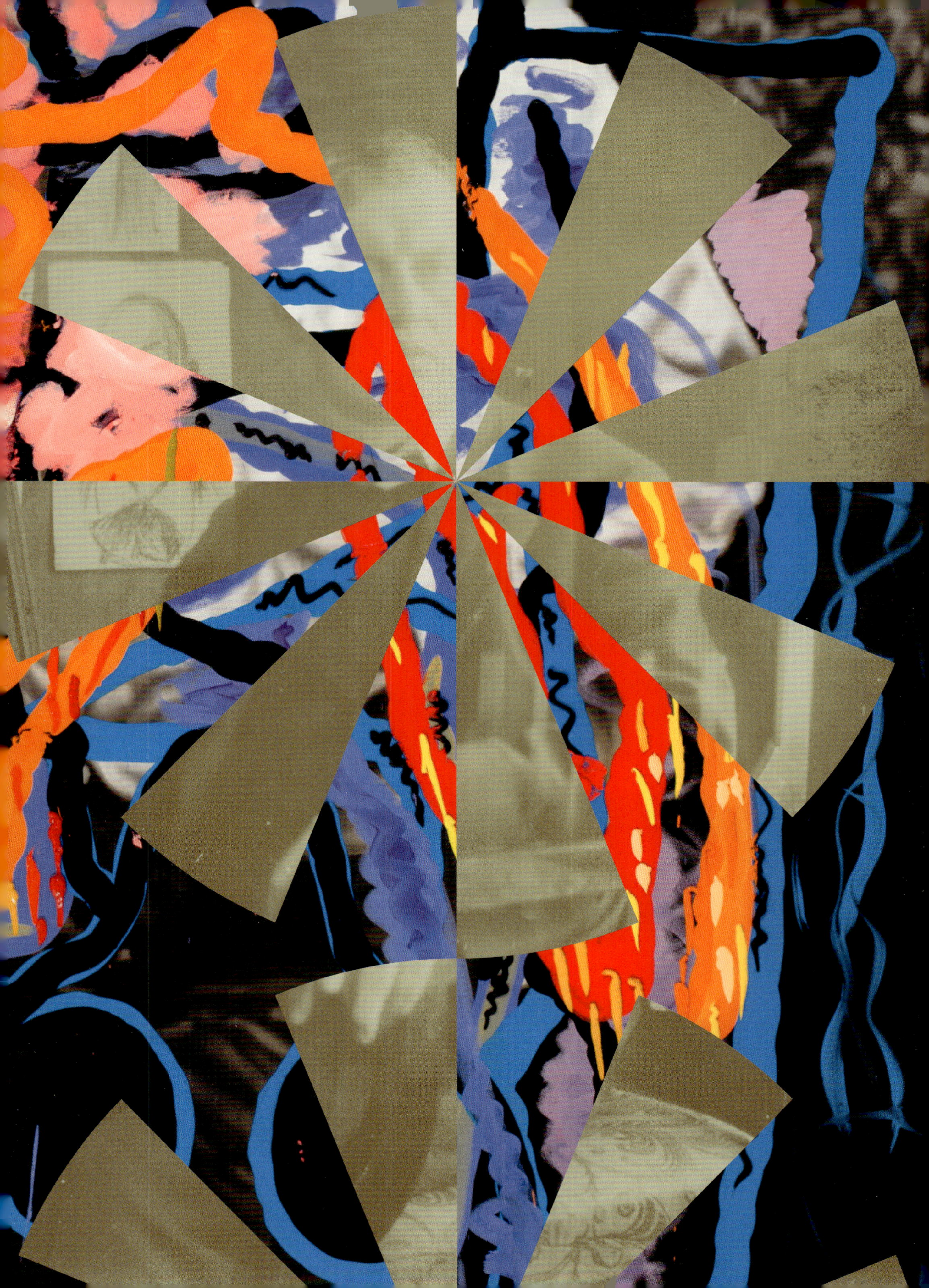

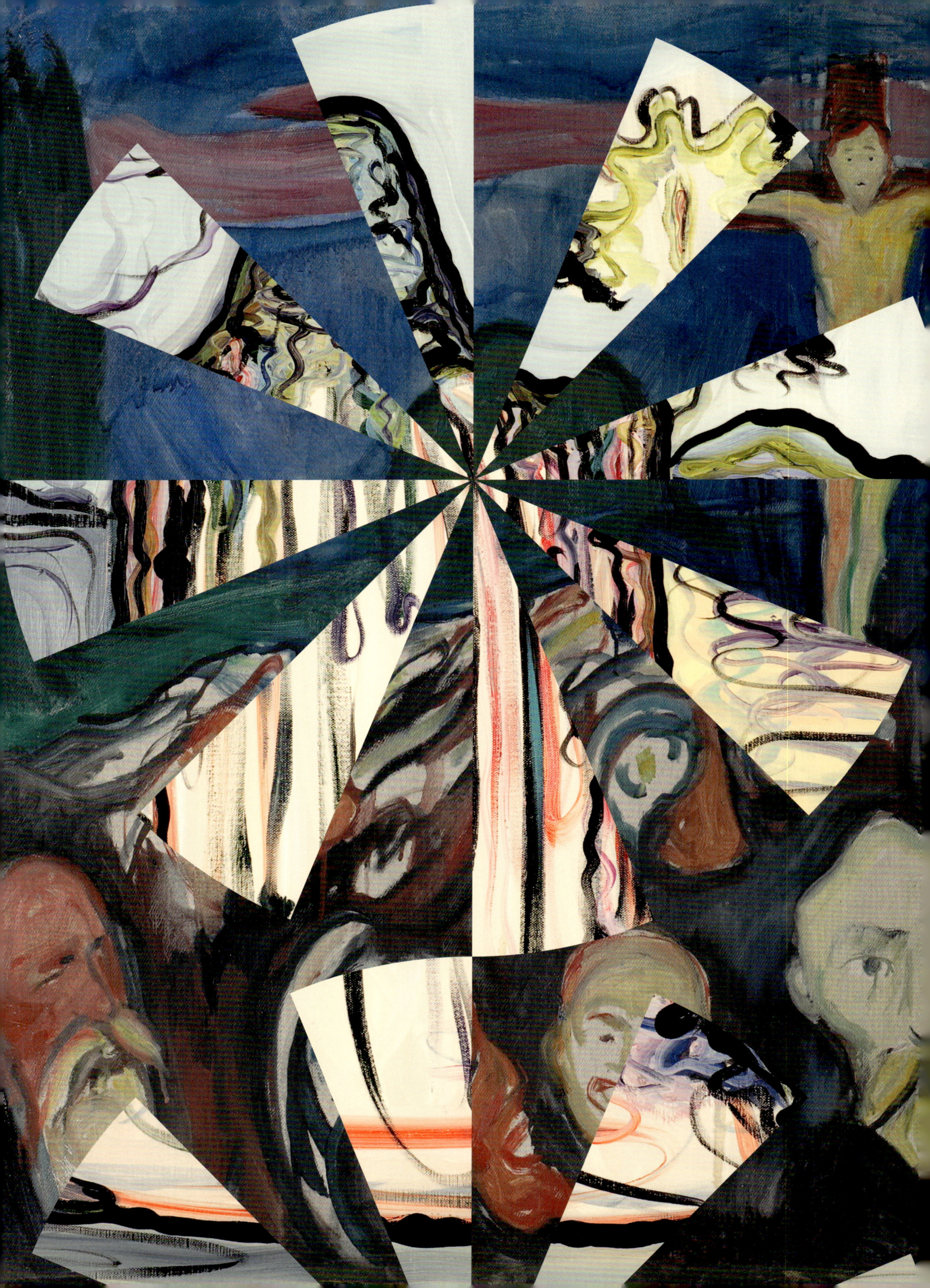

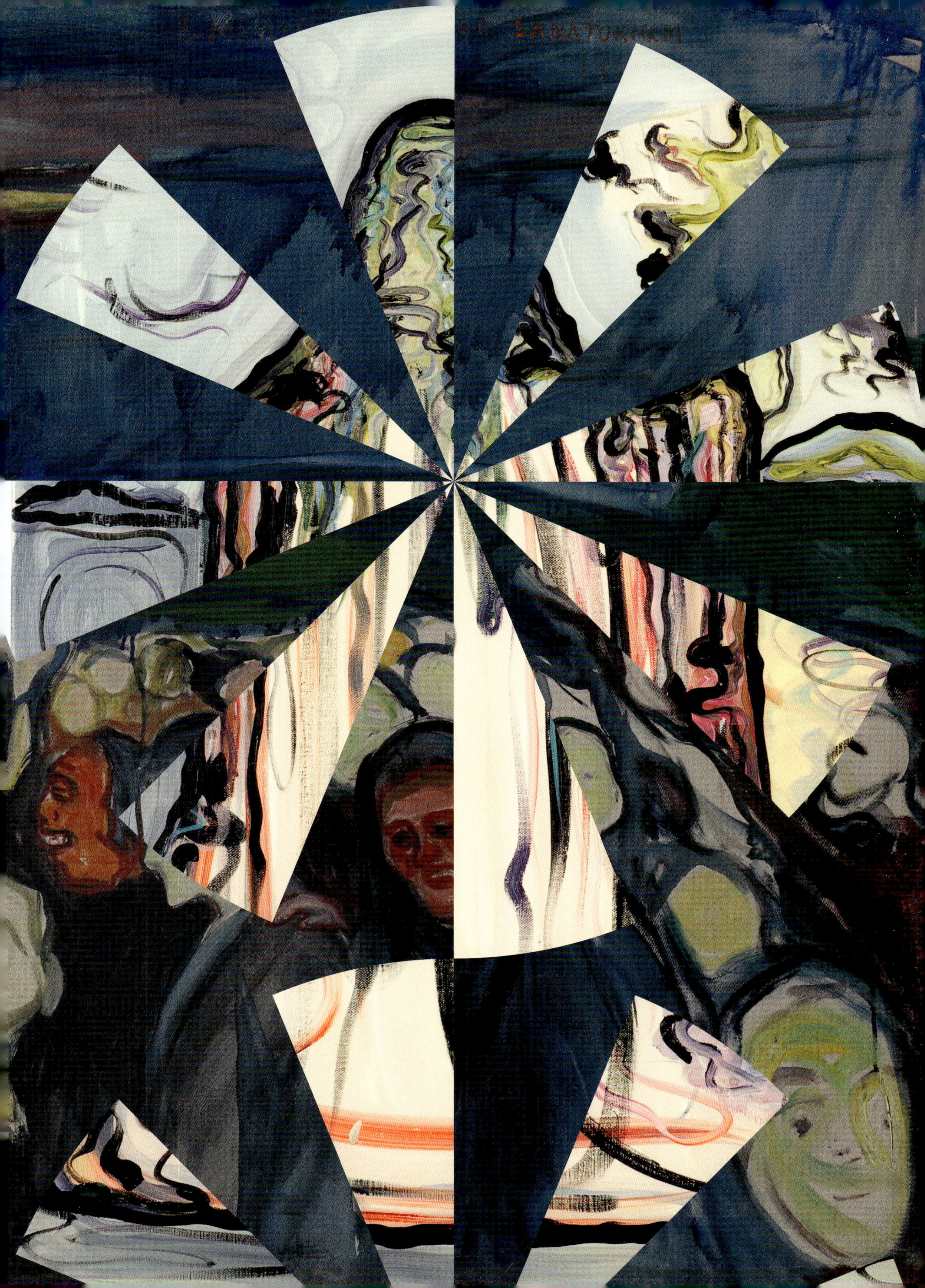

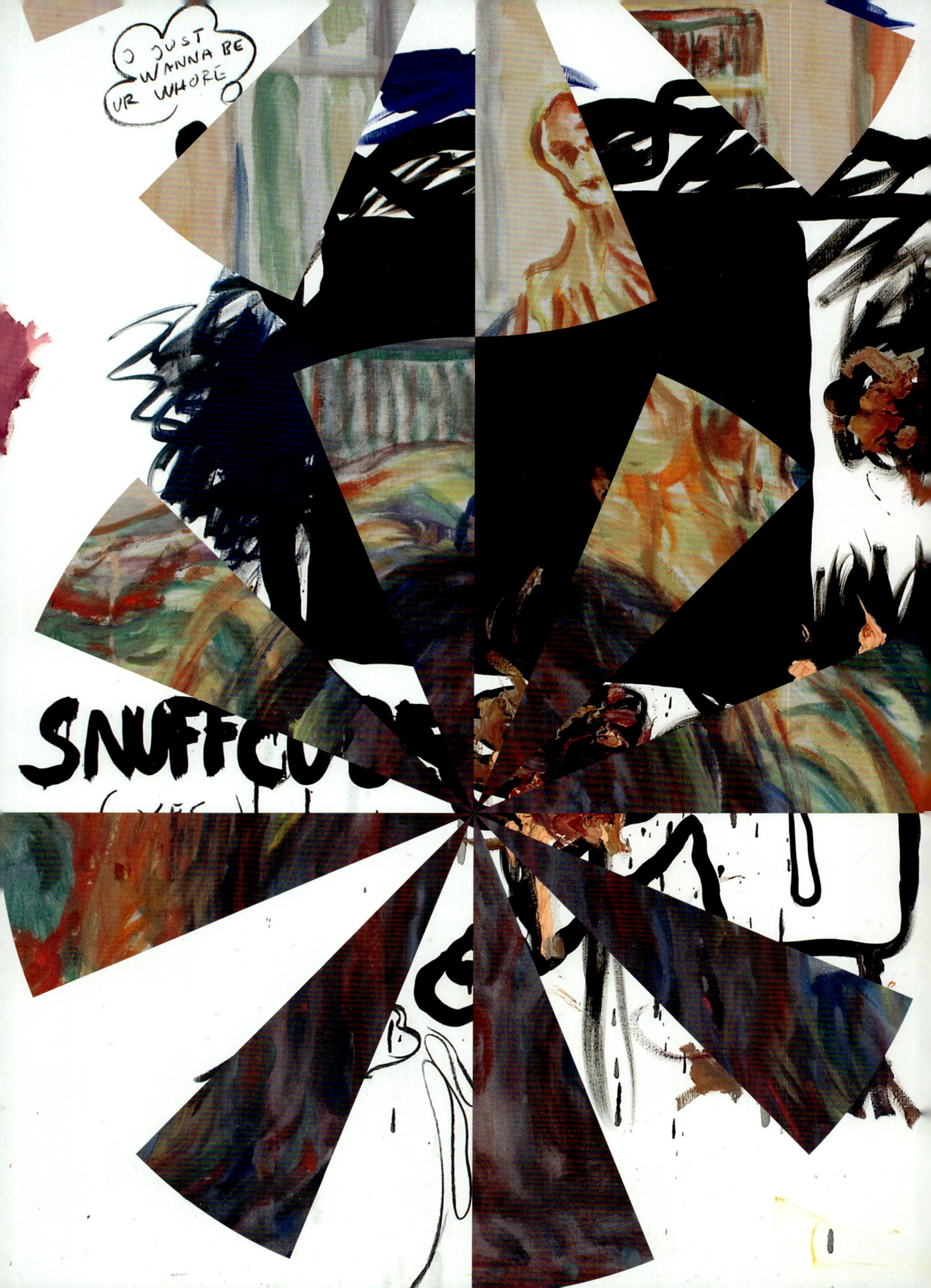
I JUST WANNA BE UR WHORE
SNUFFCU

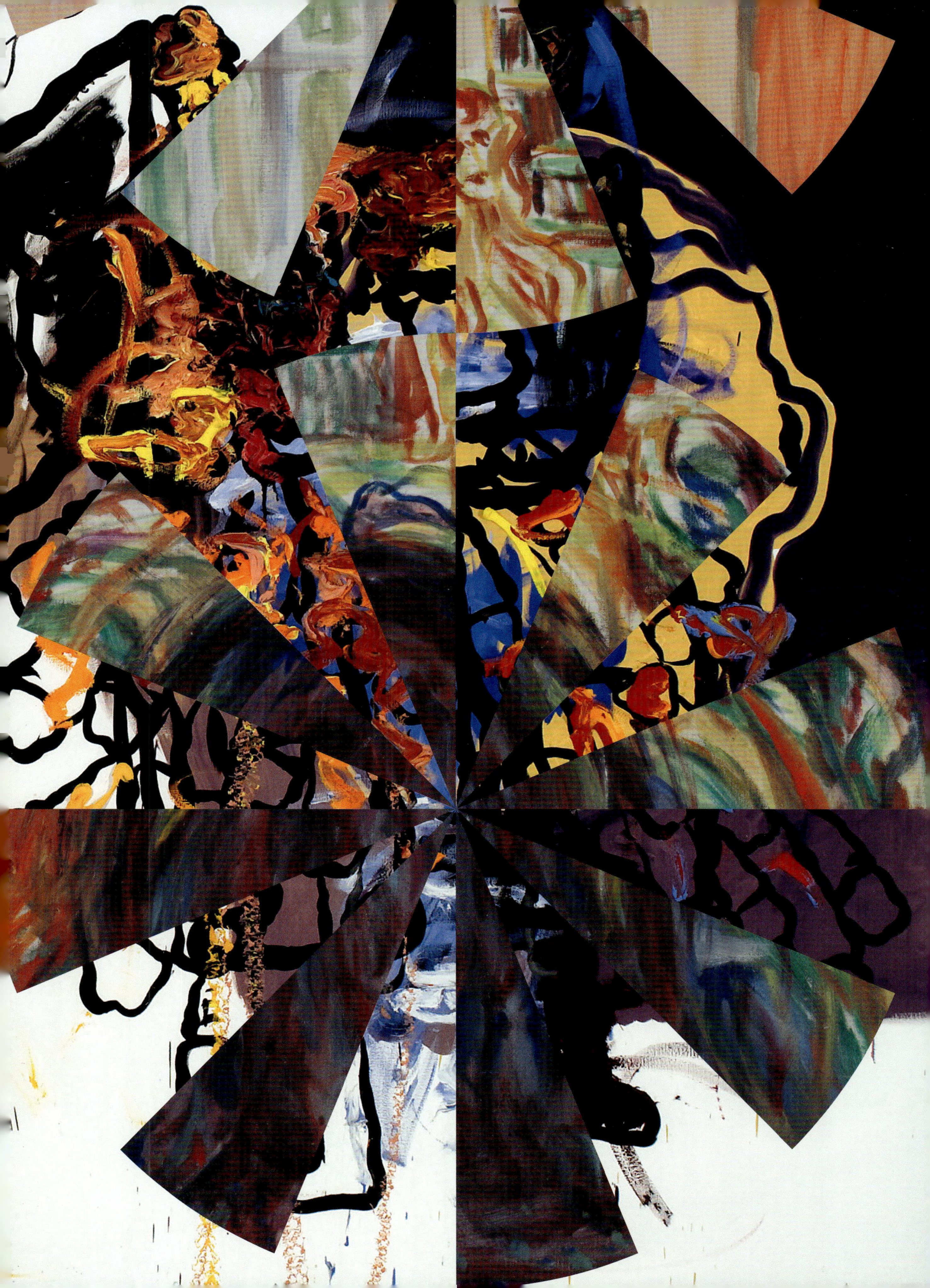

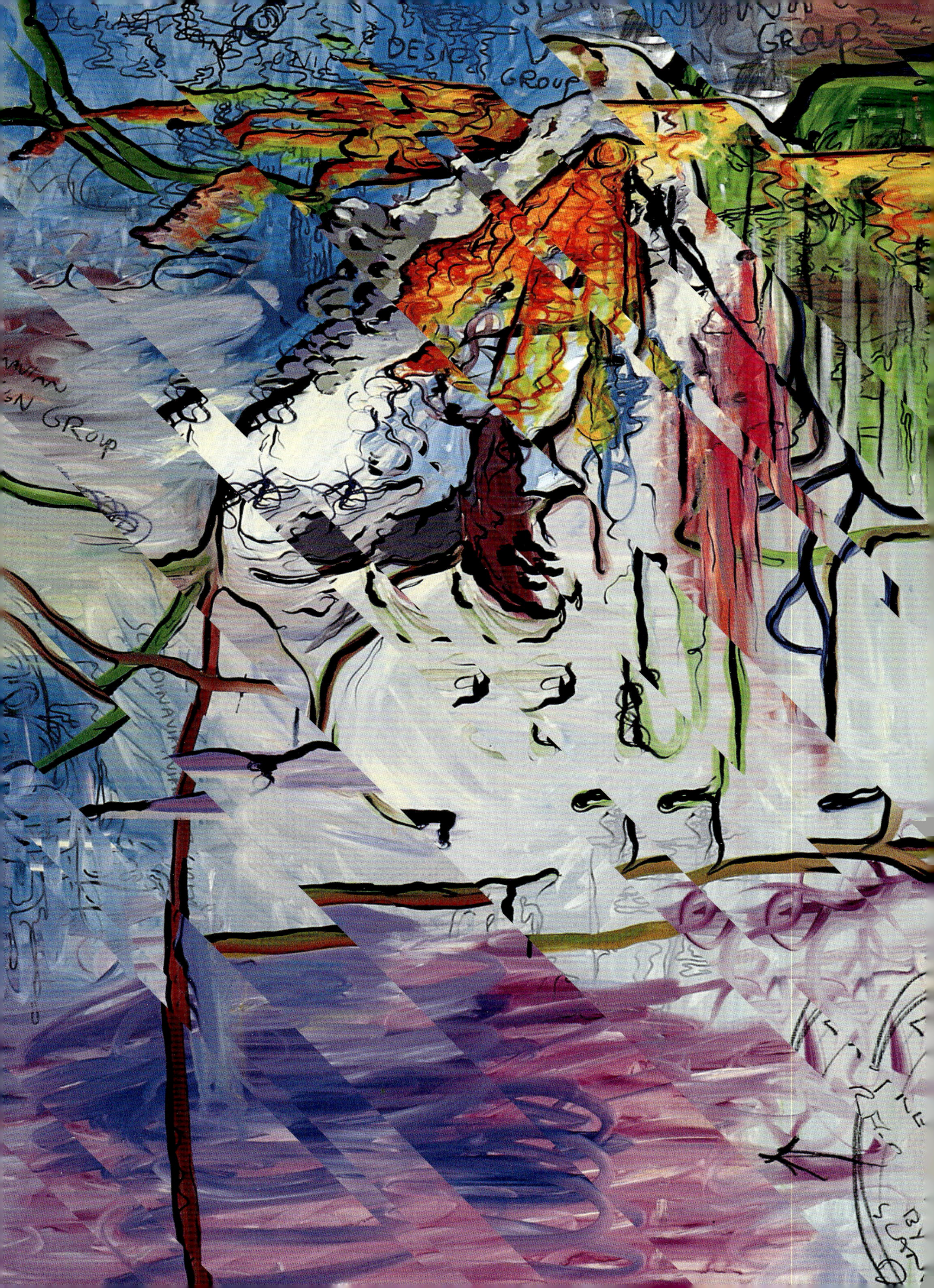

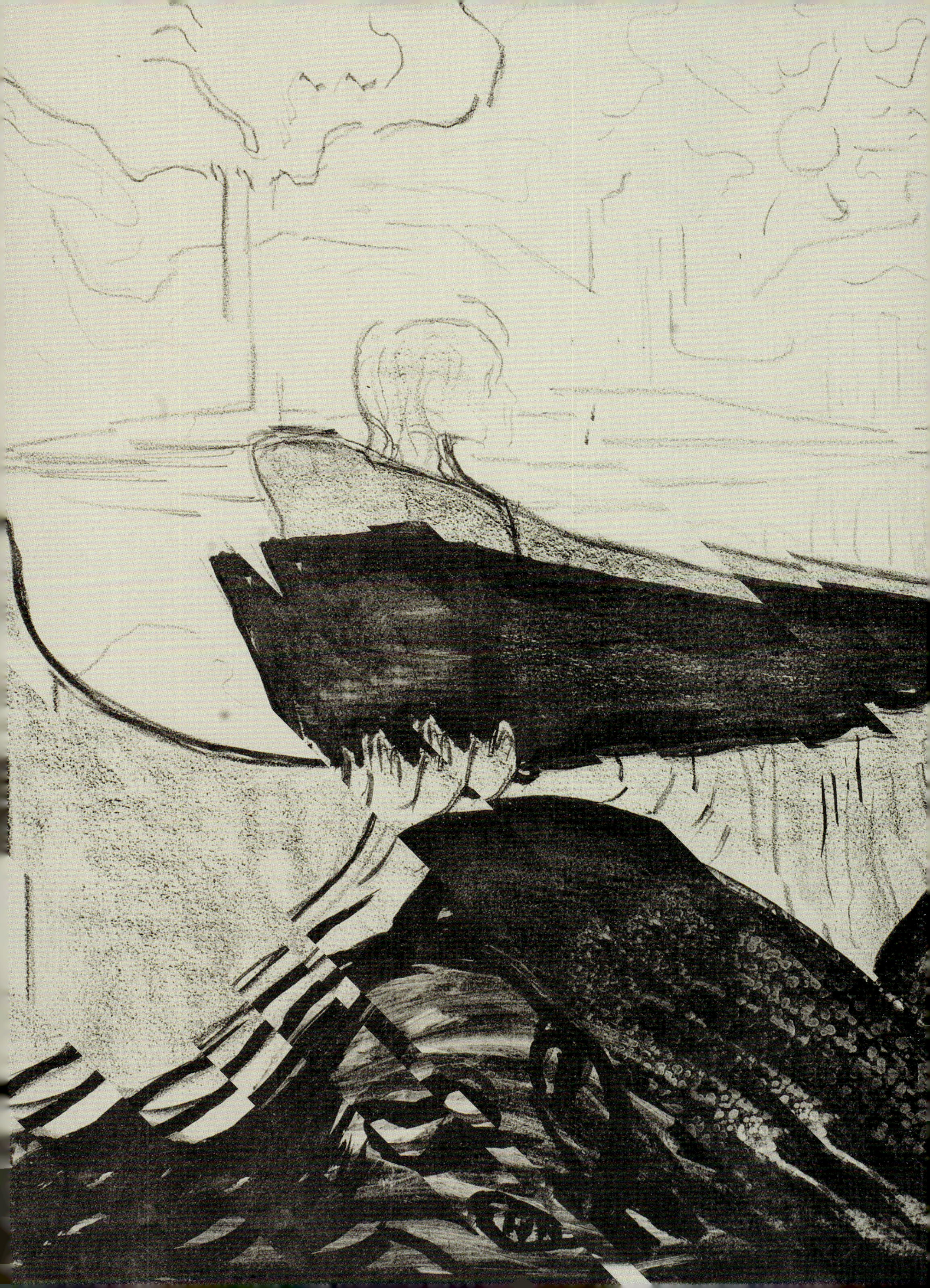

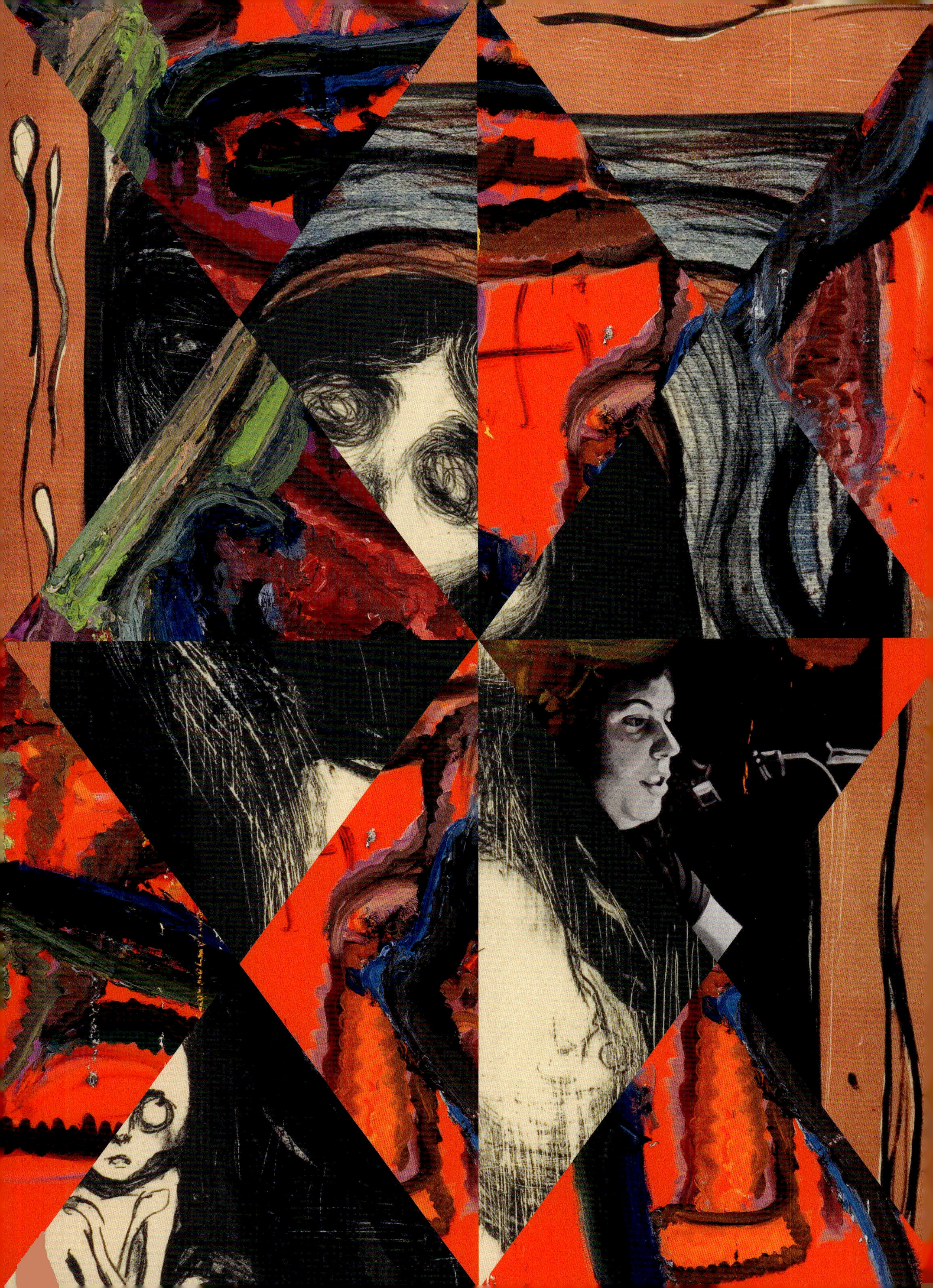

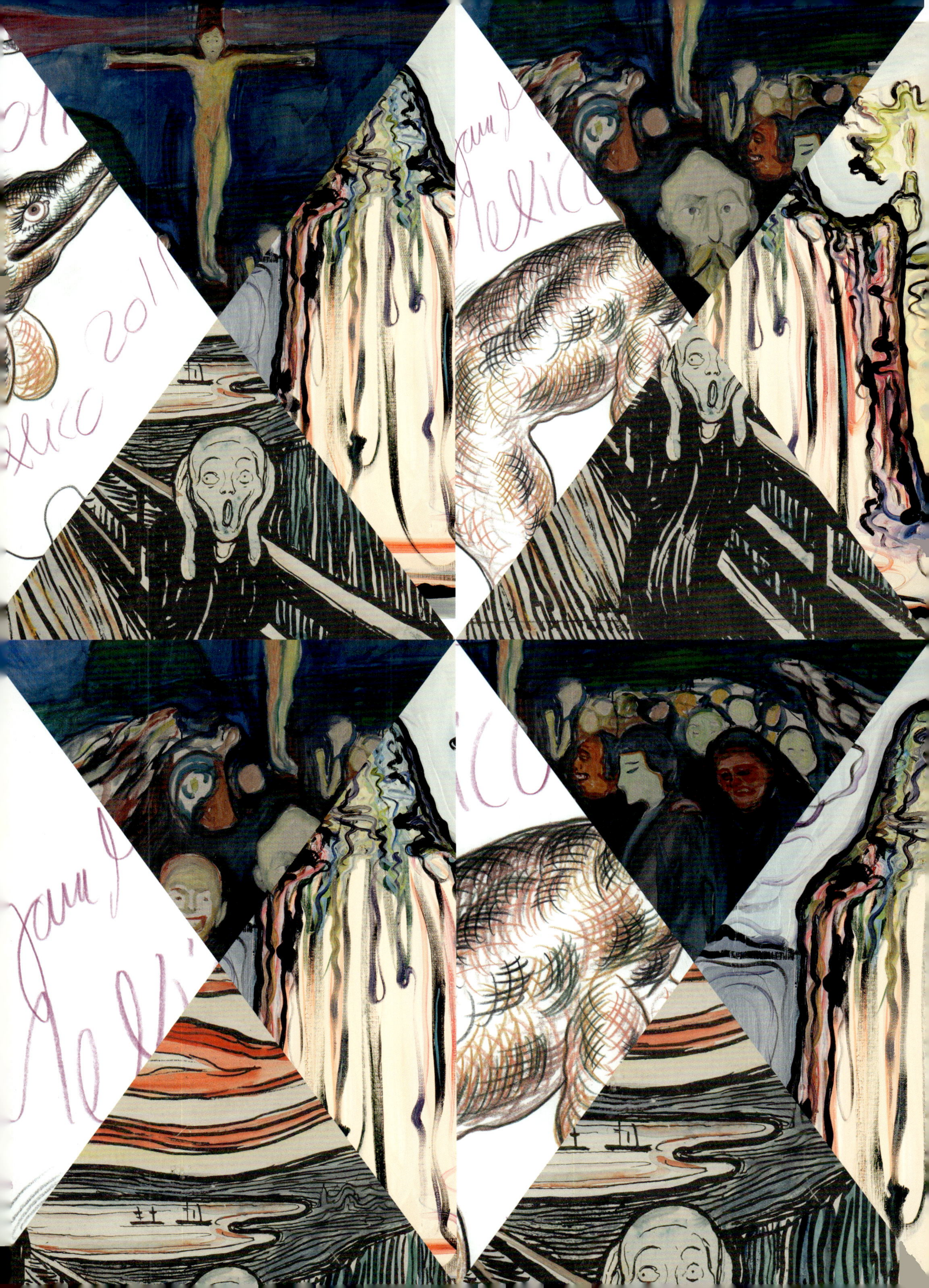

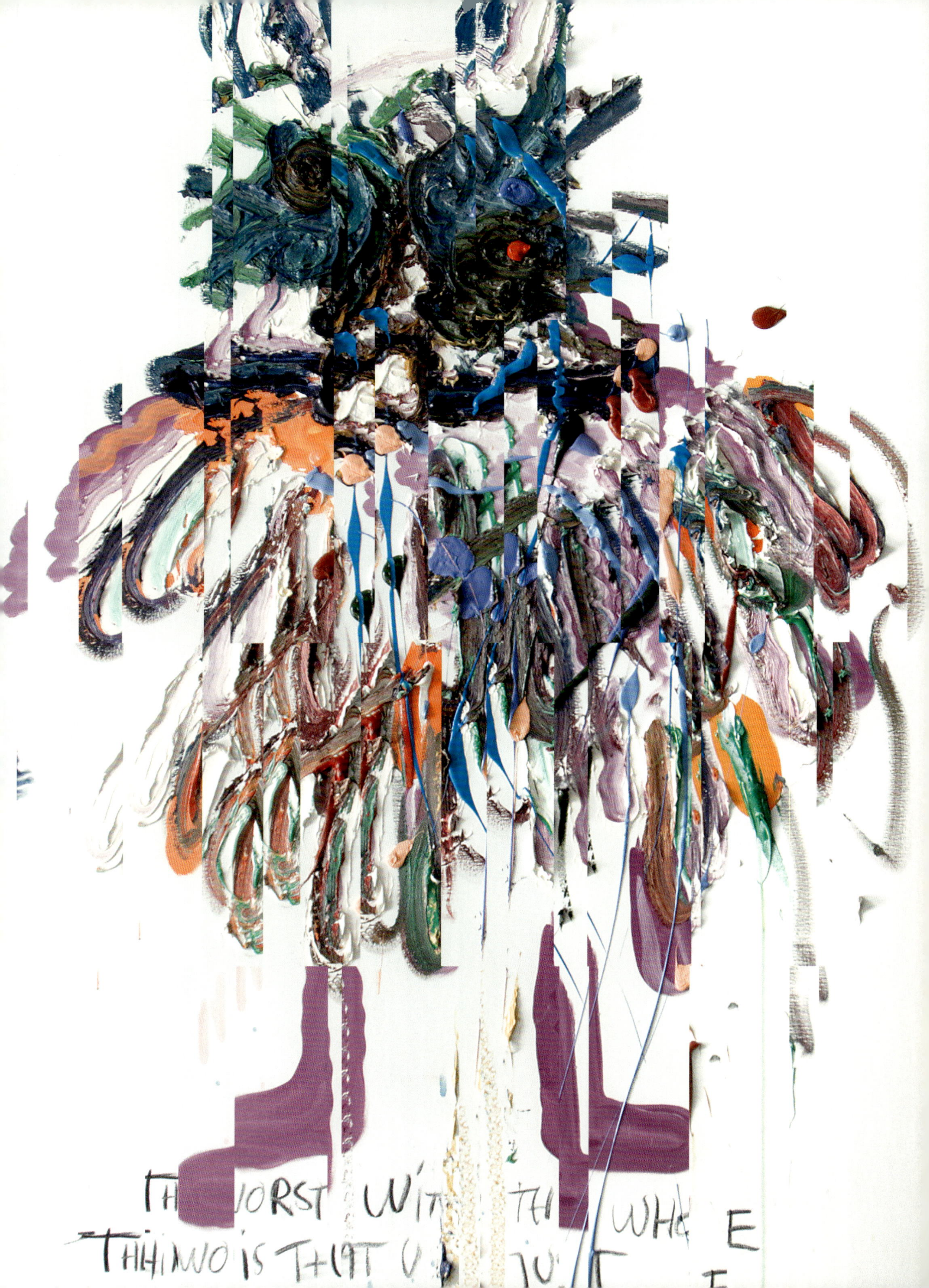
TH ORST WIT   TH   WH E
THINO IS THAT U   JU T   E

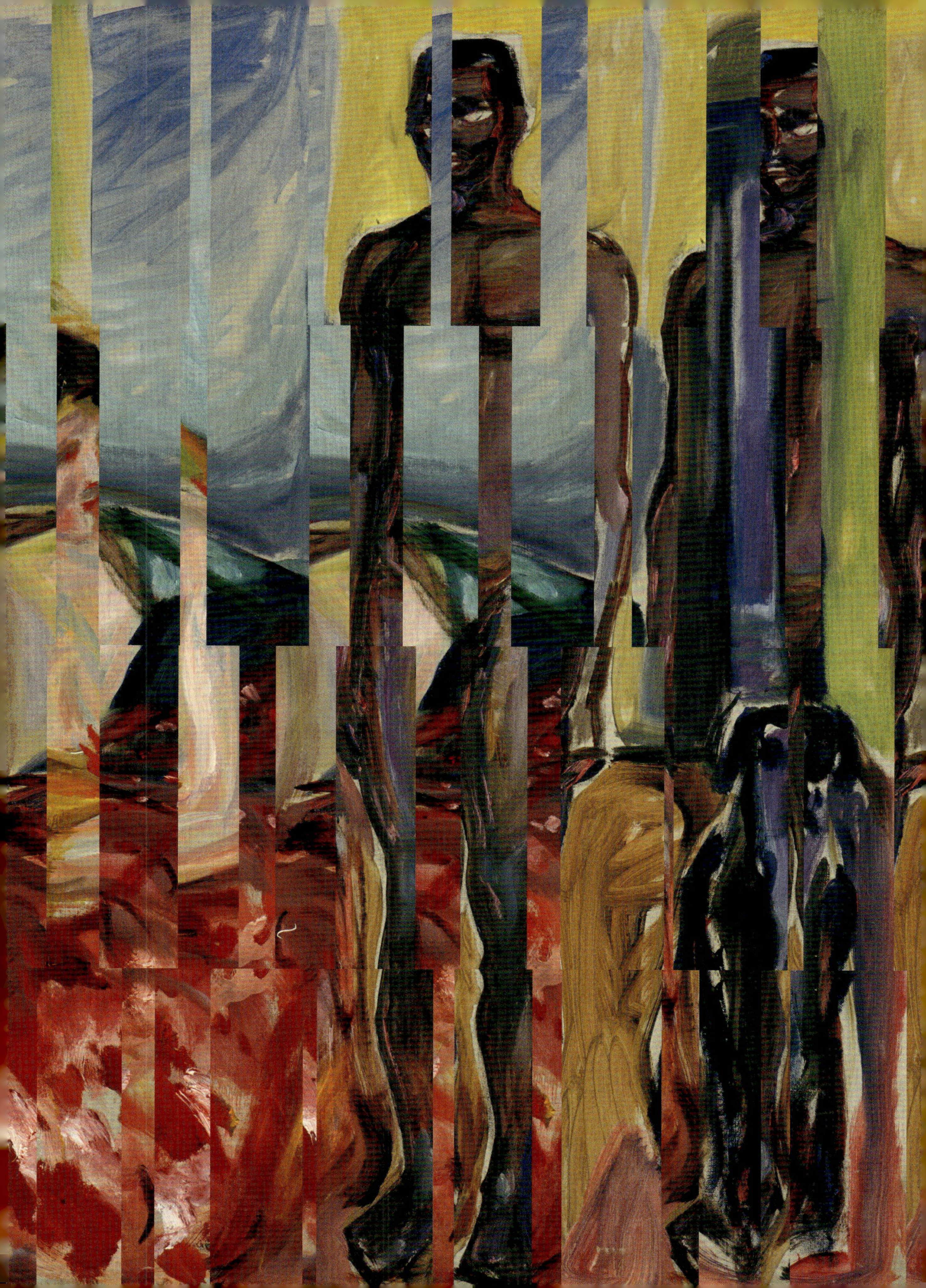

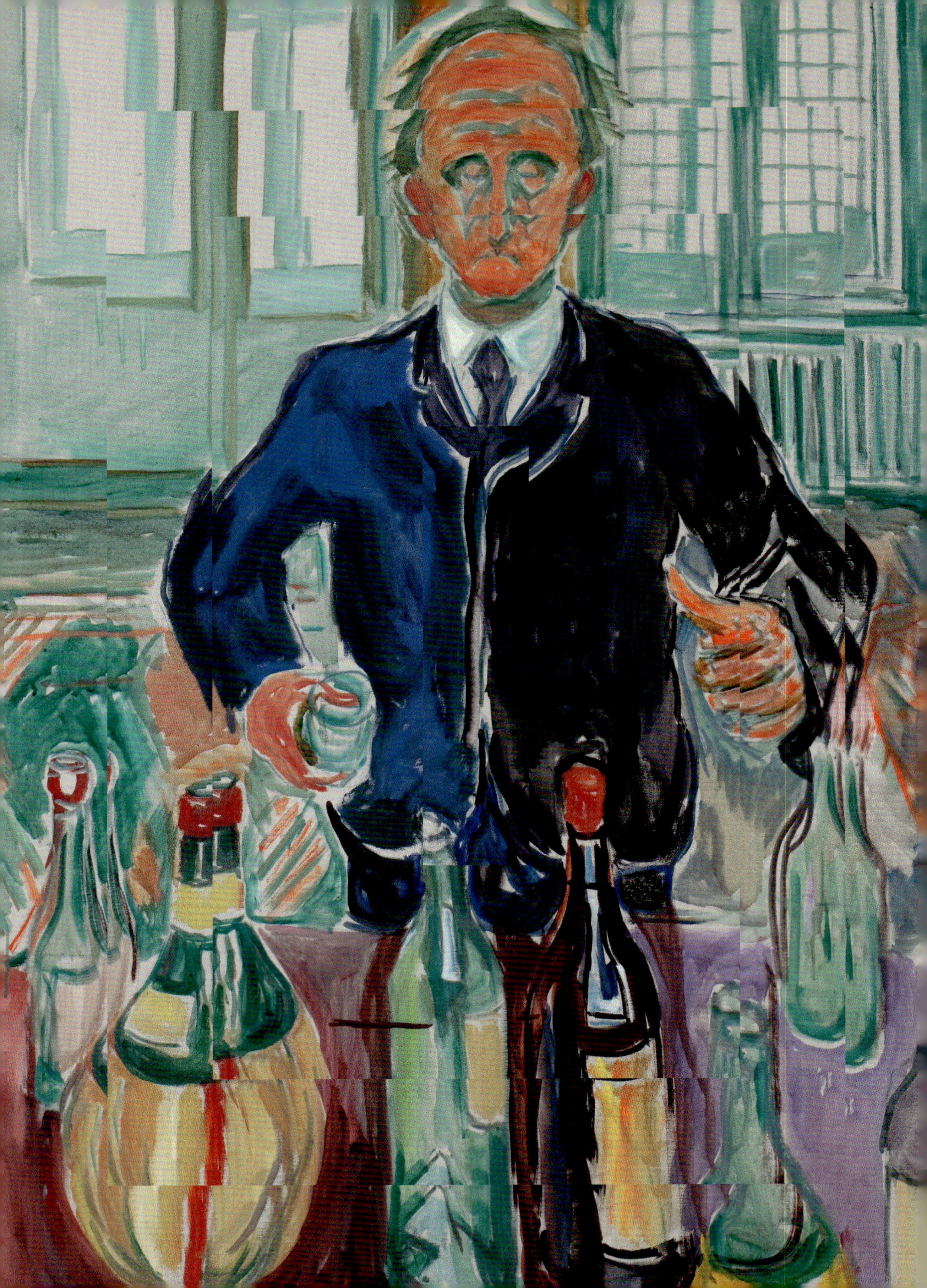

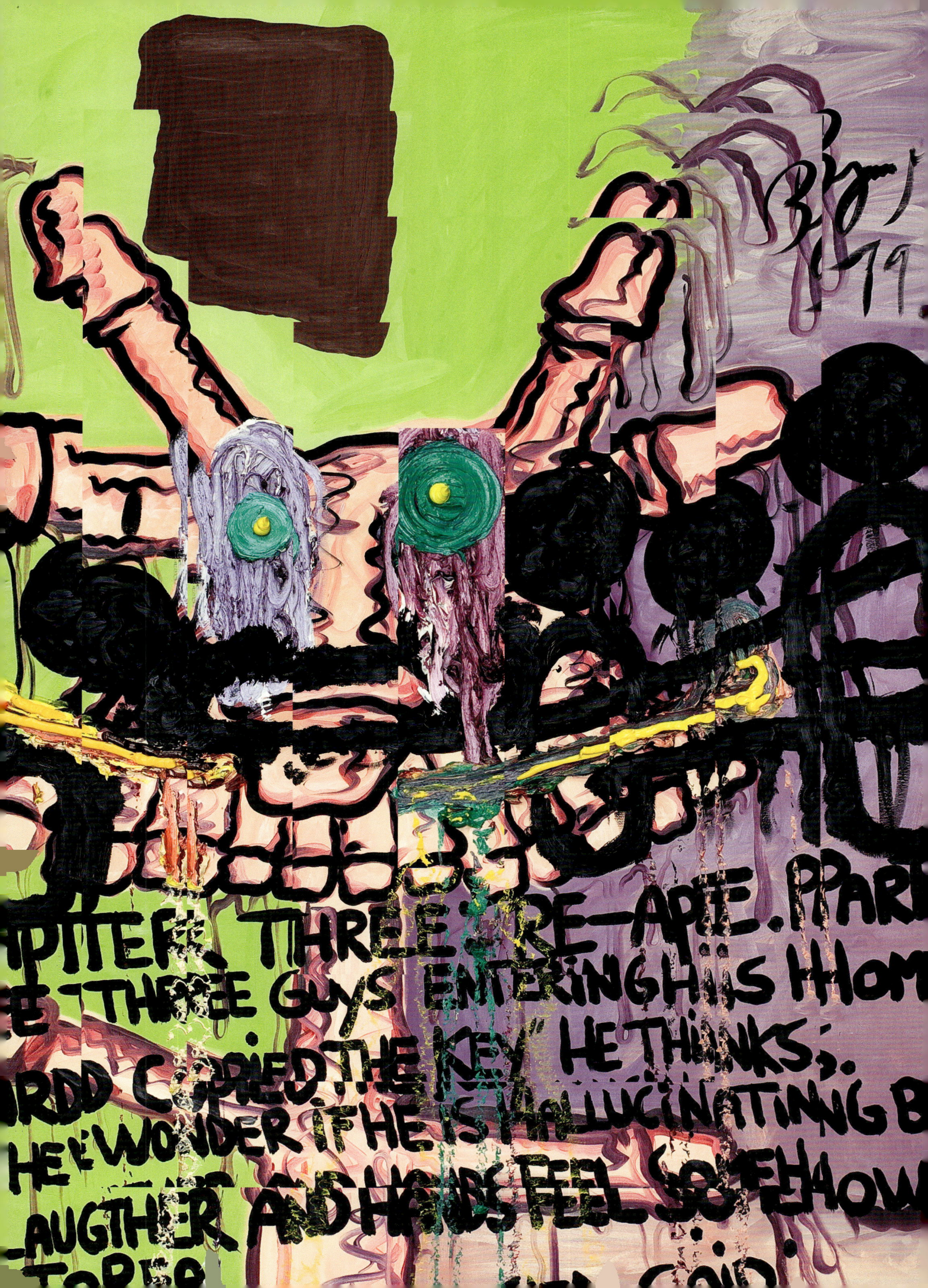
PITER THREE ARE APE. PPART
E THREE GUYS ENTERING HIS HOM
RDD COPIED THE KEY" HE THINKS;
HE WONDER IF HE IS HALUCINATINNG B
AUGTHER AND HANDS FEEL SO EHOW

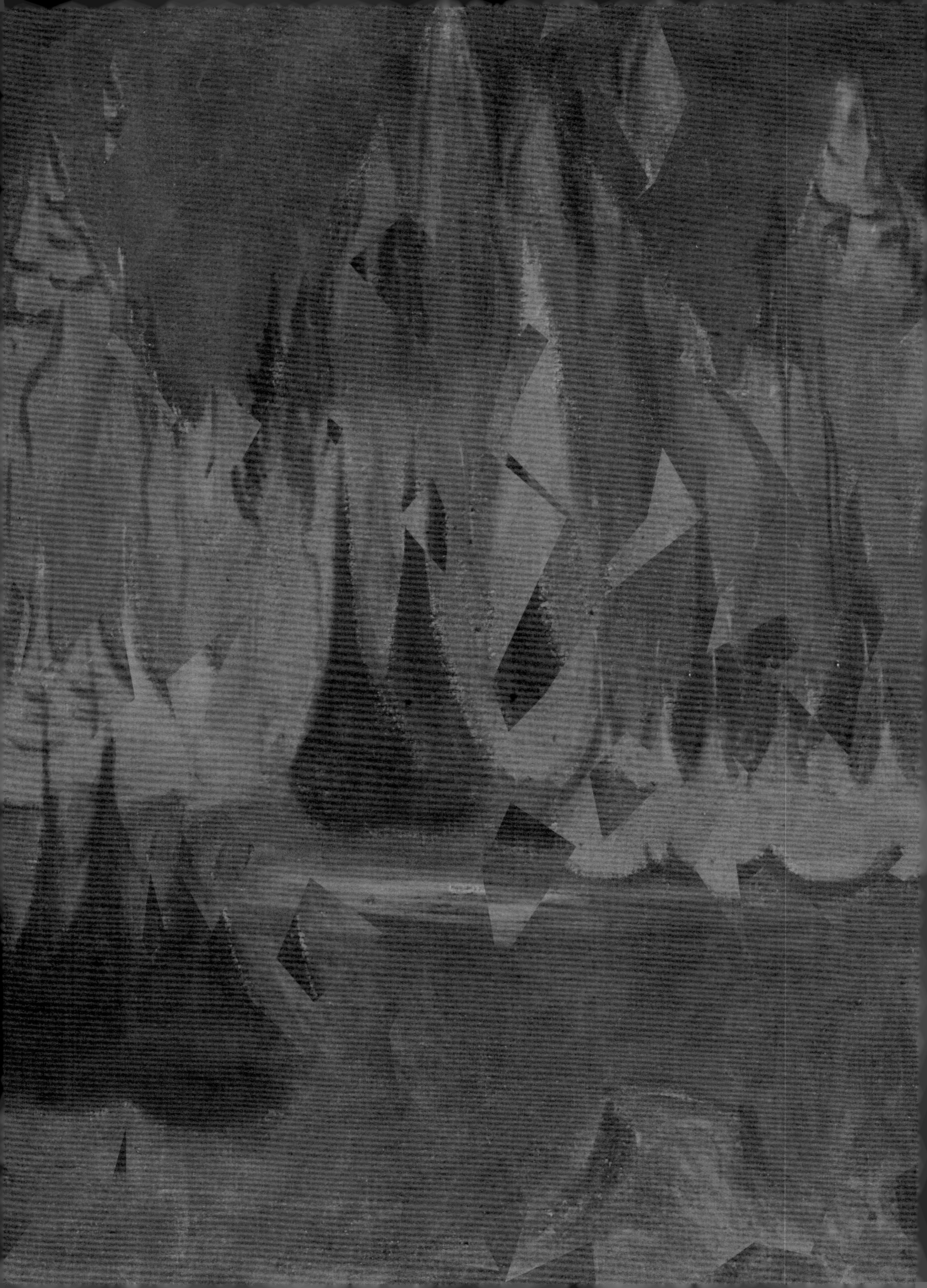

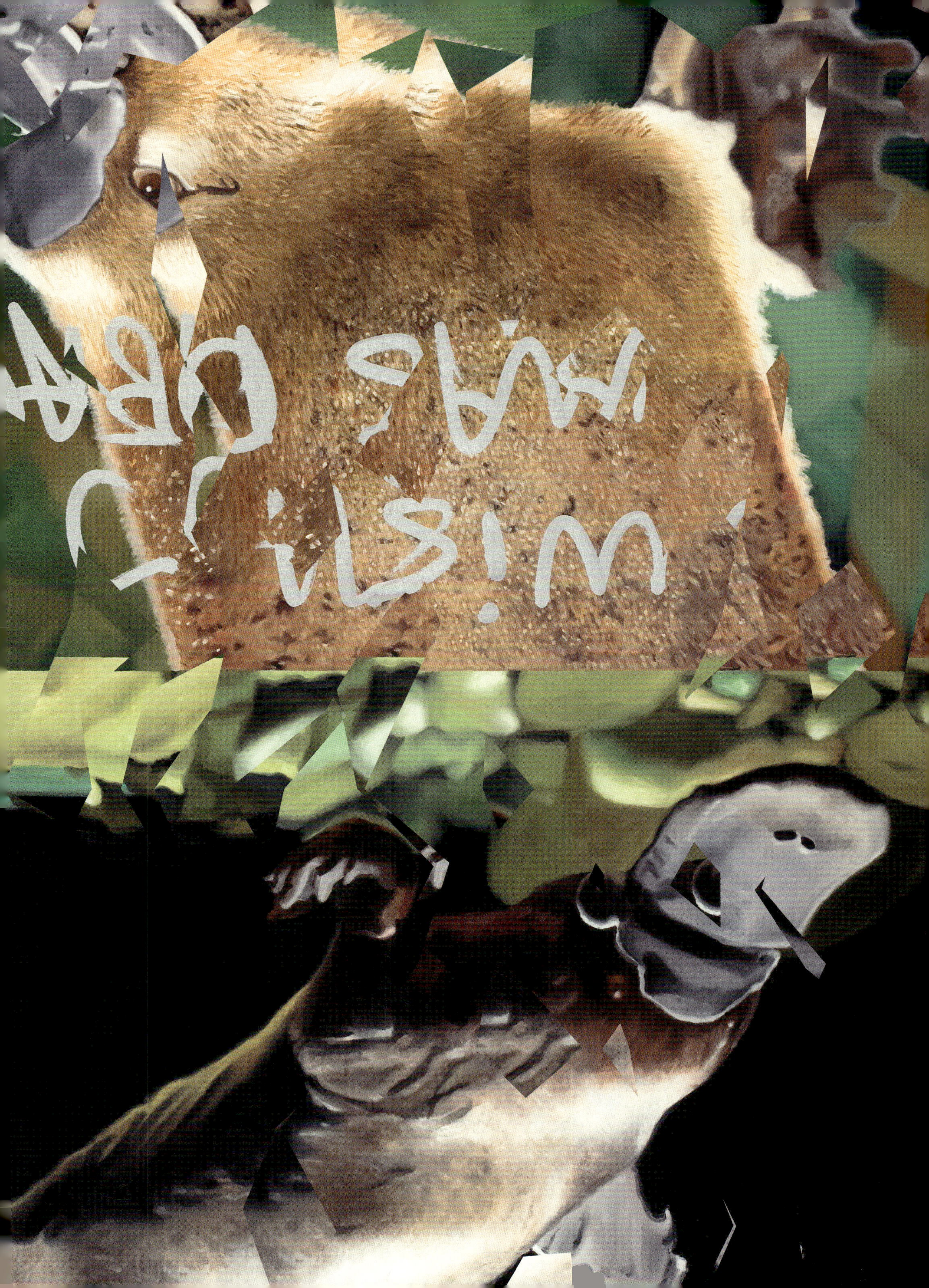

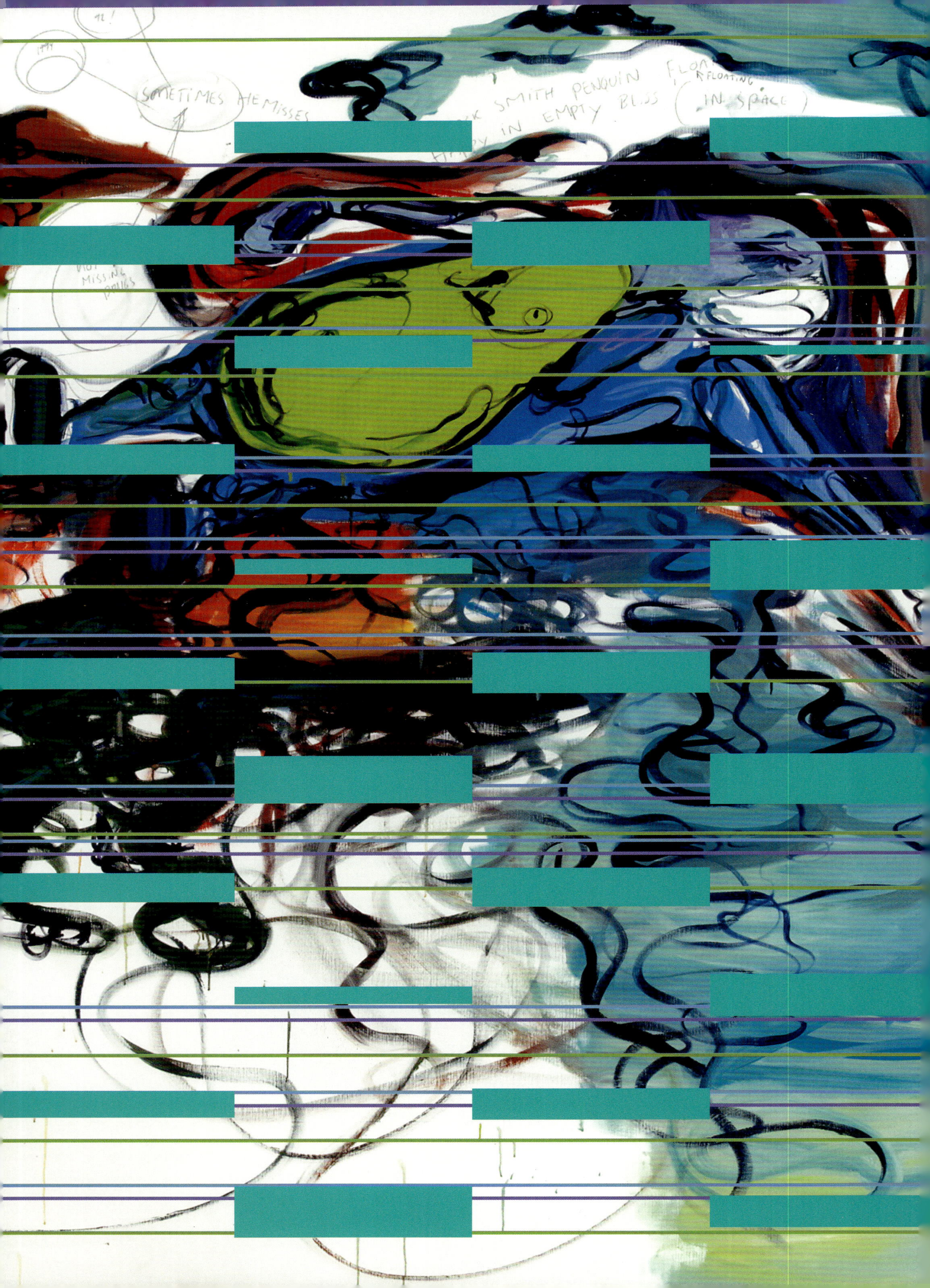
SOMETIMES HE MISSES
SMITH PENGUIN FLOATING
REFLOATING
HAPPY IN EMPTY BLISS
IN SPACE
MISSING DRUGS

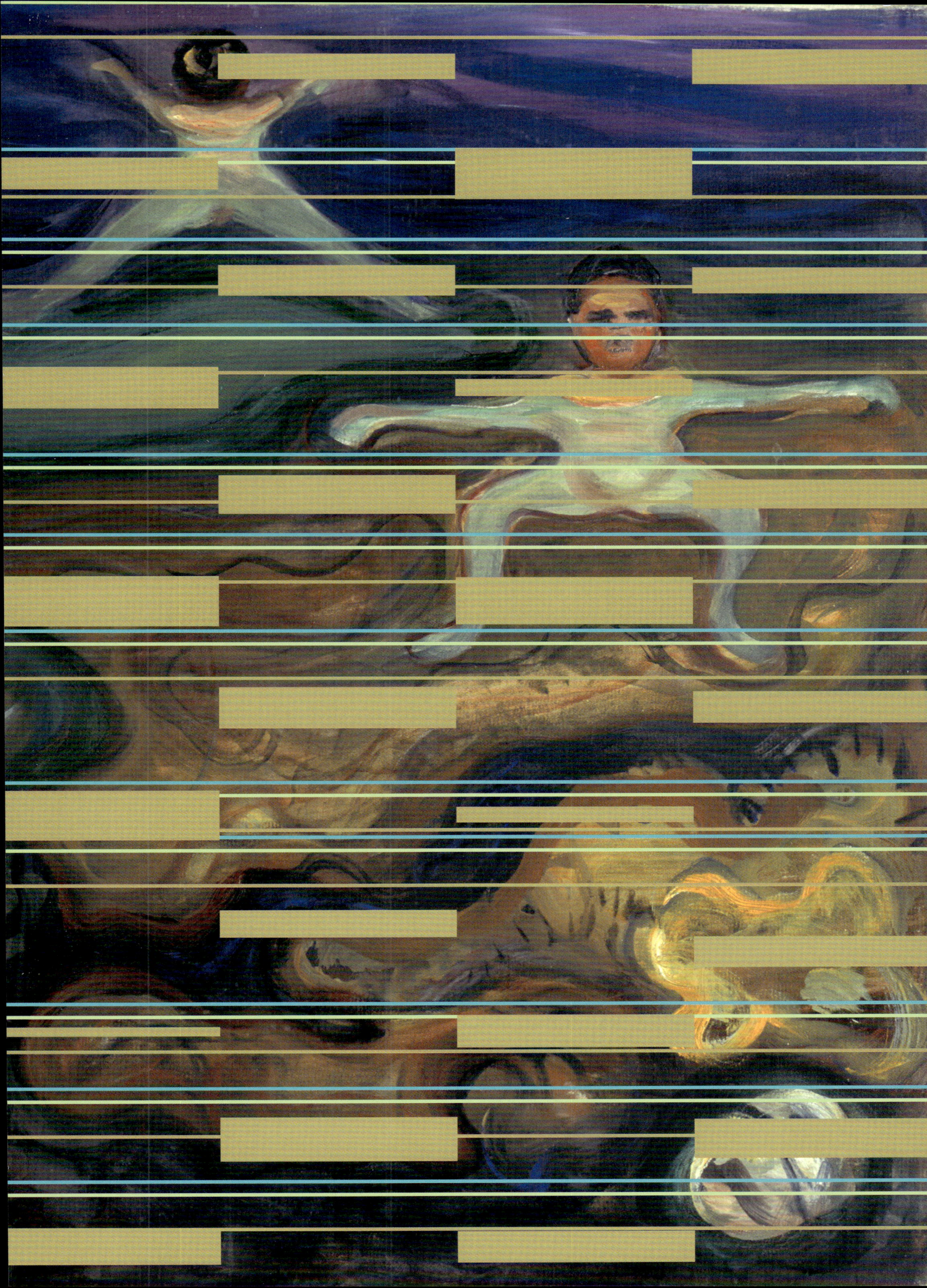

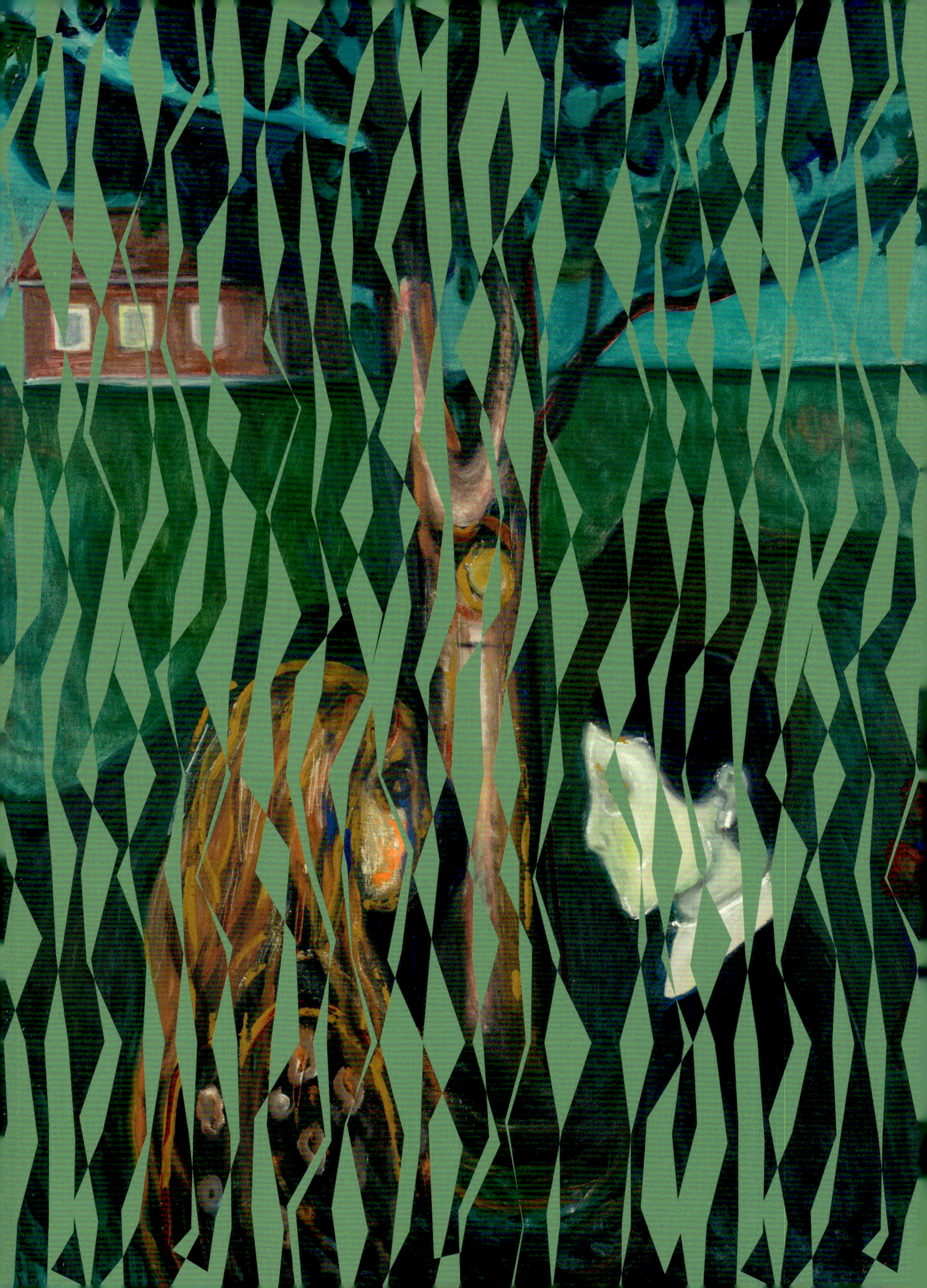

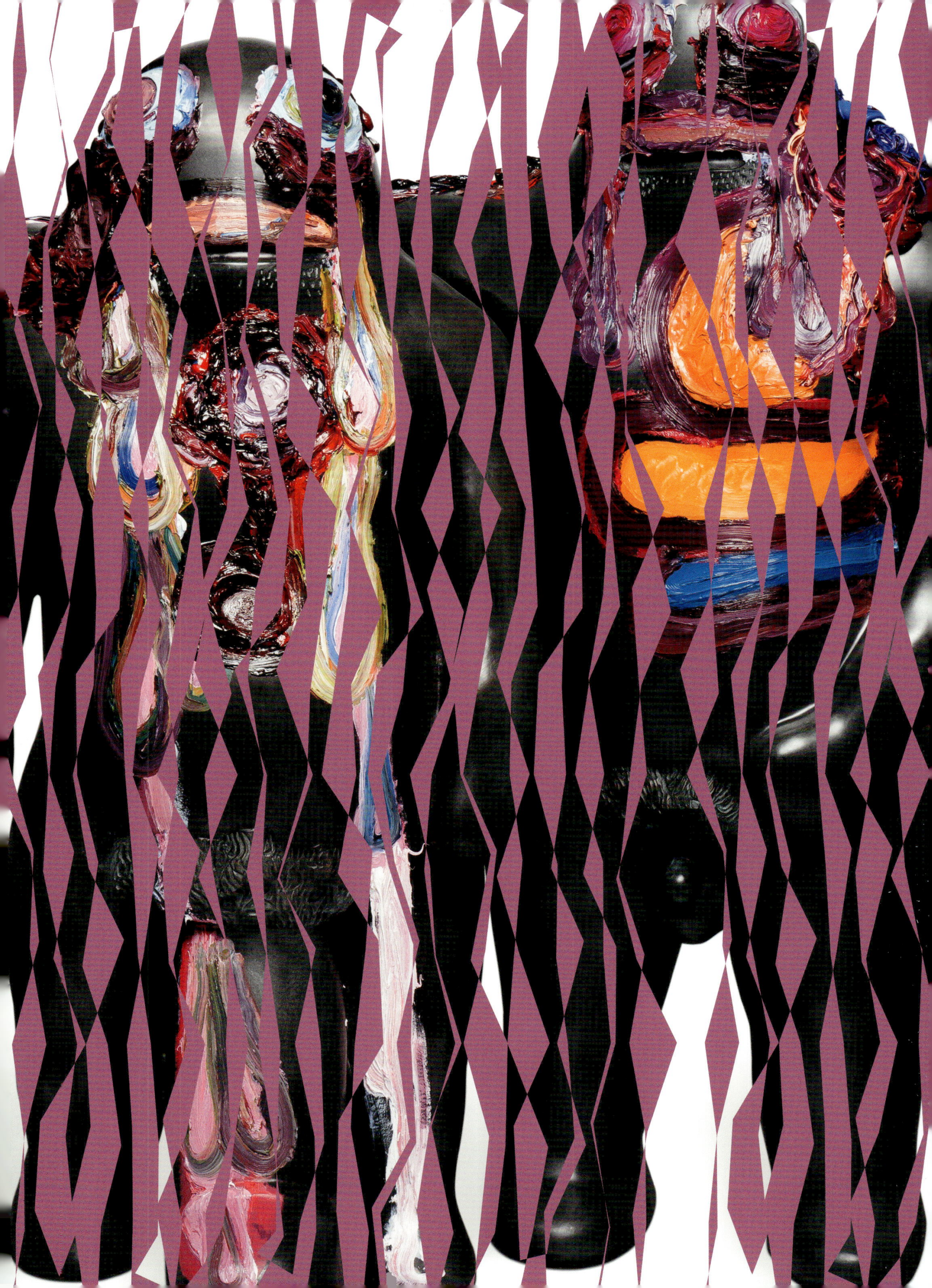

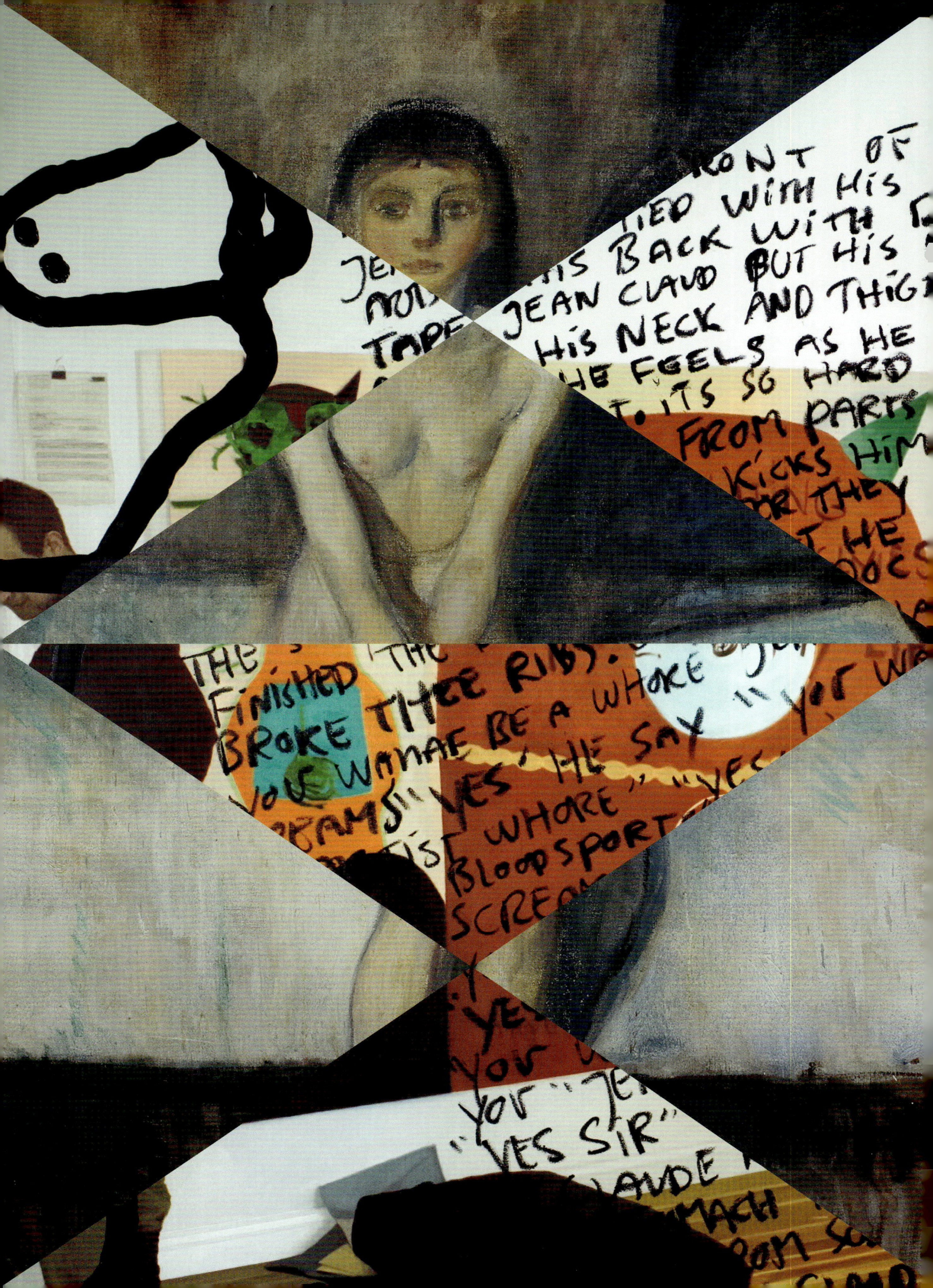
TIED WITH HIS
BACK WITH
JEAN CLAUD BUT HIS
HIS NECK AND THIG
HE FEELS AS HE
ITS SO HARD
FROM PARI
KICKS HIM
THEY
RONT OF
FRONT OF
FINISHED
BROKE THREE RIBS.
YOU WNNAE BE A WHORE
EAMS "YES" HE SAY "YES" YOR W
WHORE
BLOODSPORT
SCREAM
YES
YOR
"YES SIR"
AUDE

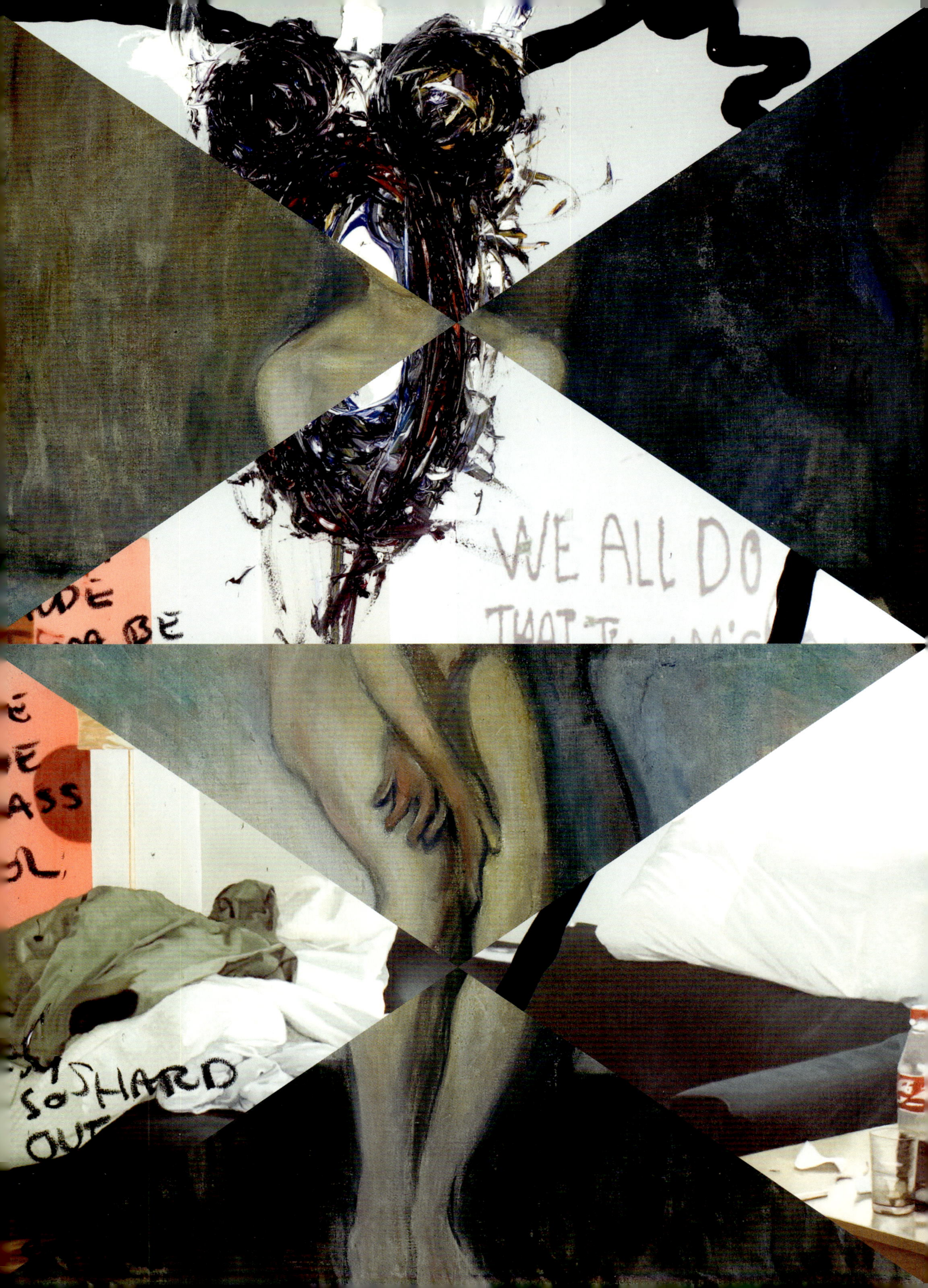
WE ALL DO
THAT
BE
ASS
SO HARD
OUT

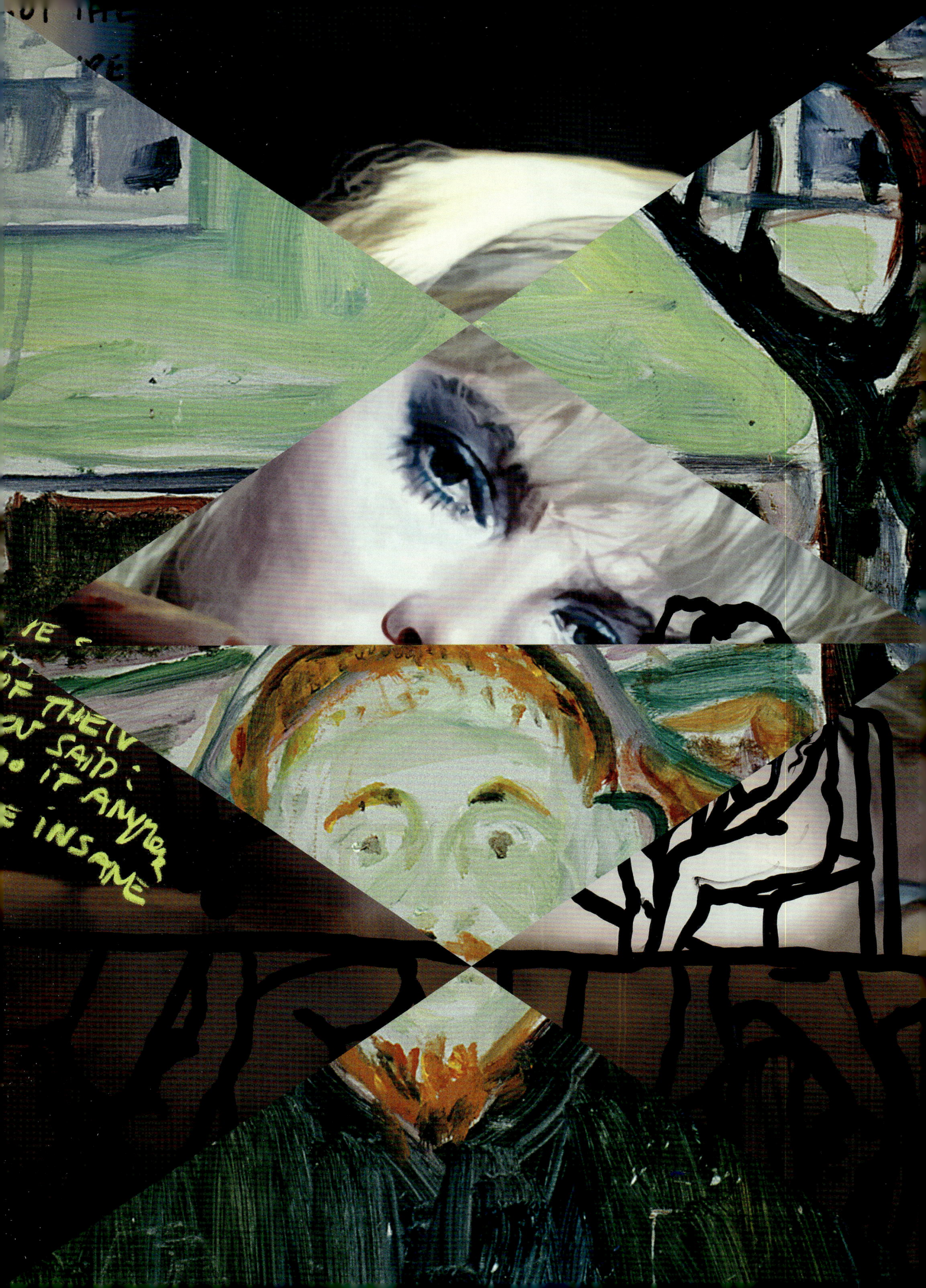
OF THE
SAID:
IT ANYMO
INSANE

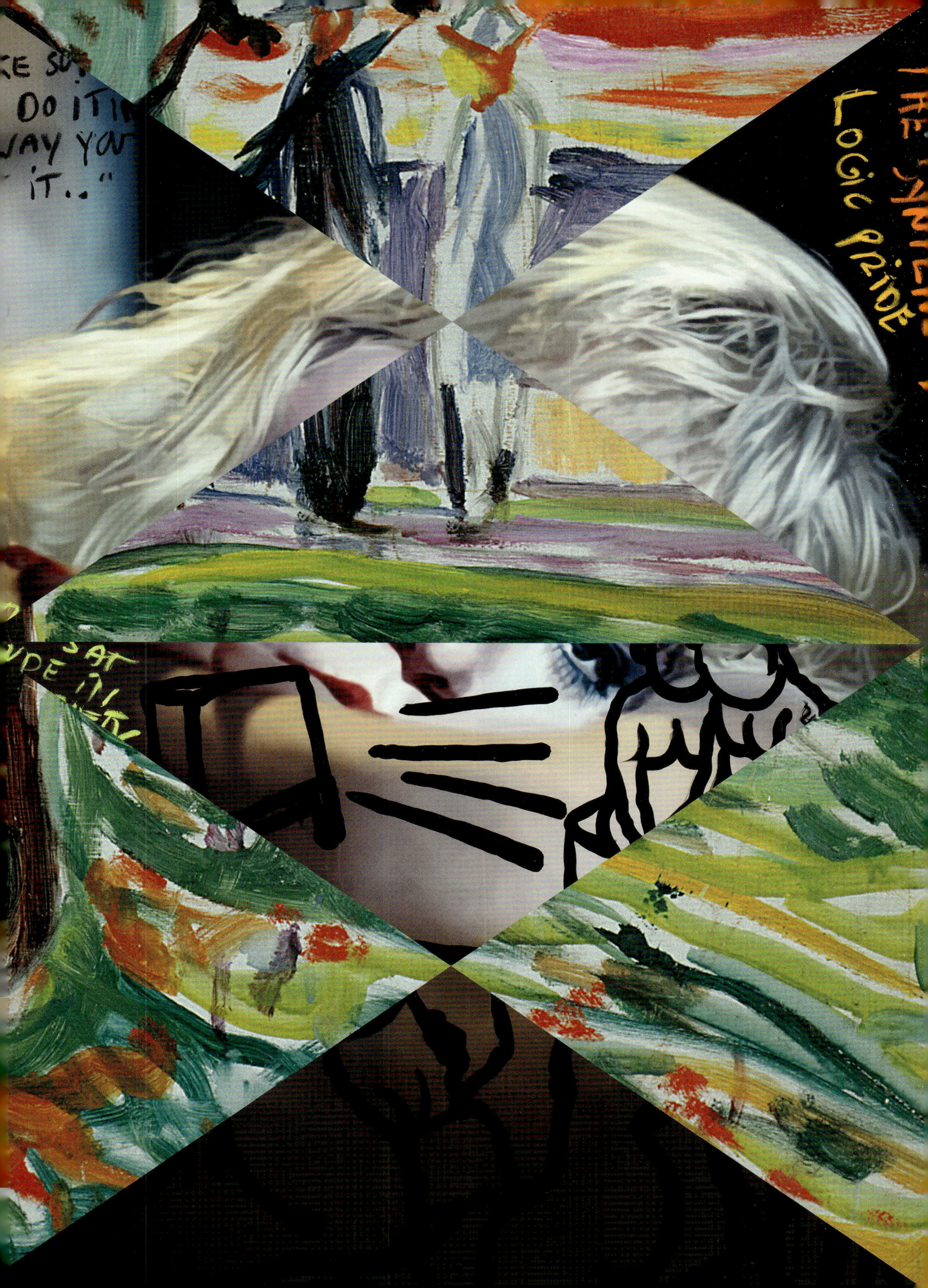
DO IT
AY YO
IT.."
THE SYNTH
LOGiC PRiDE

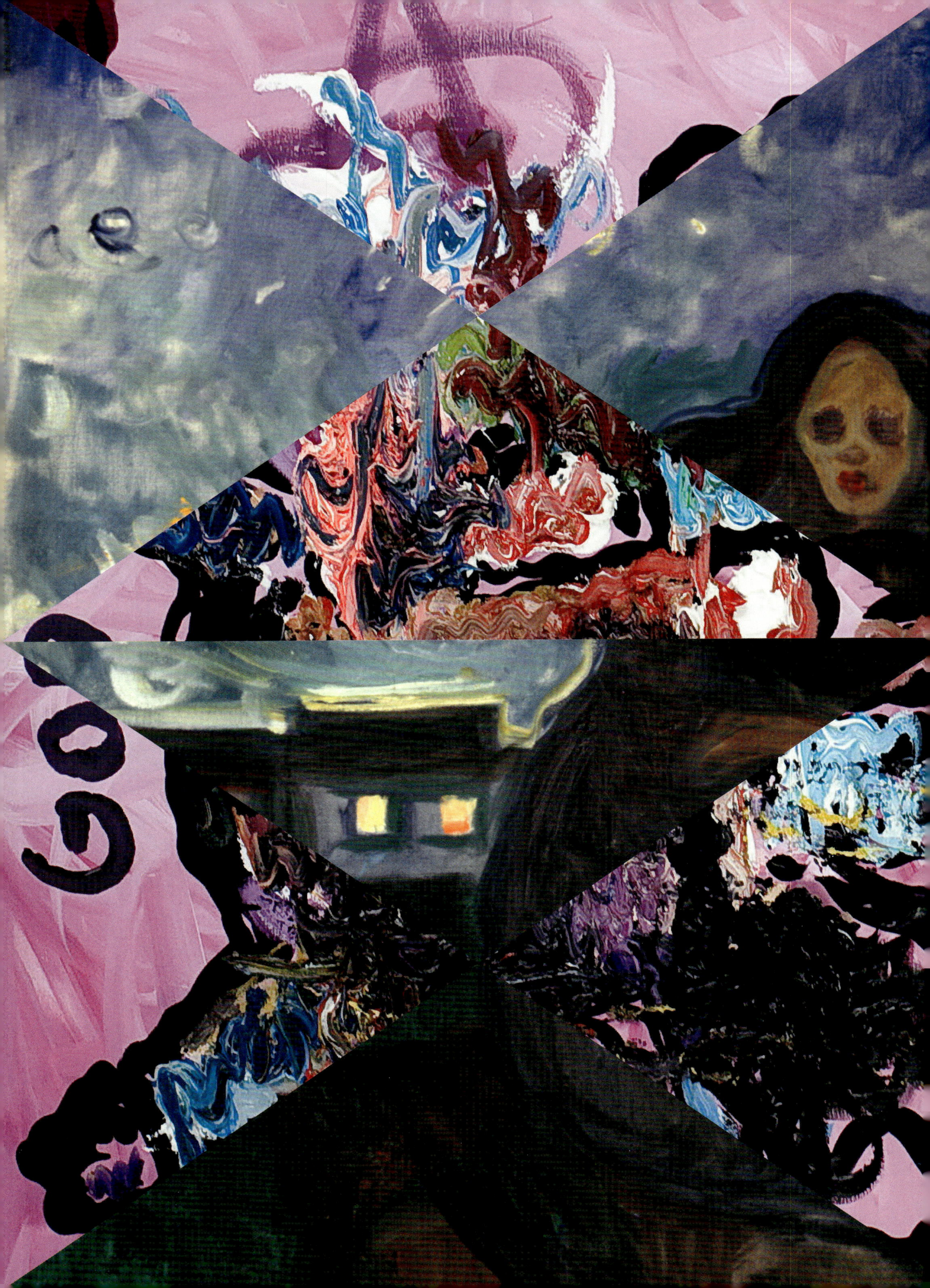

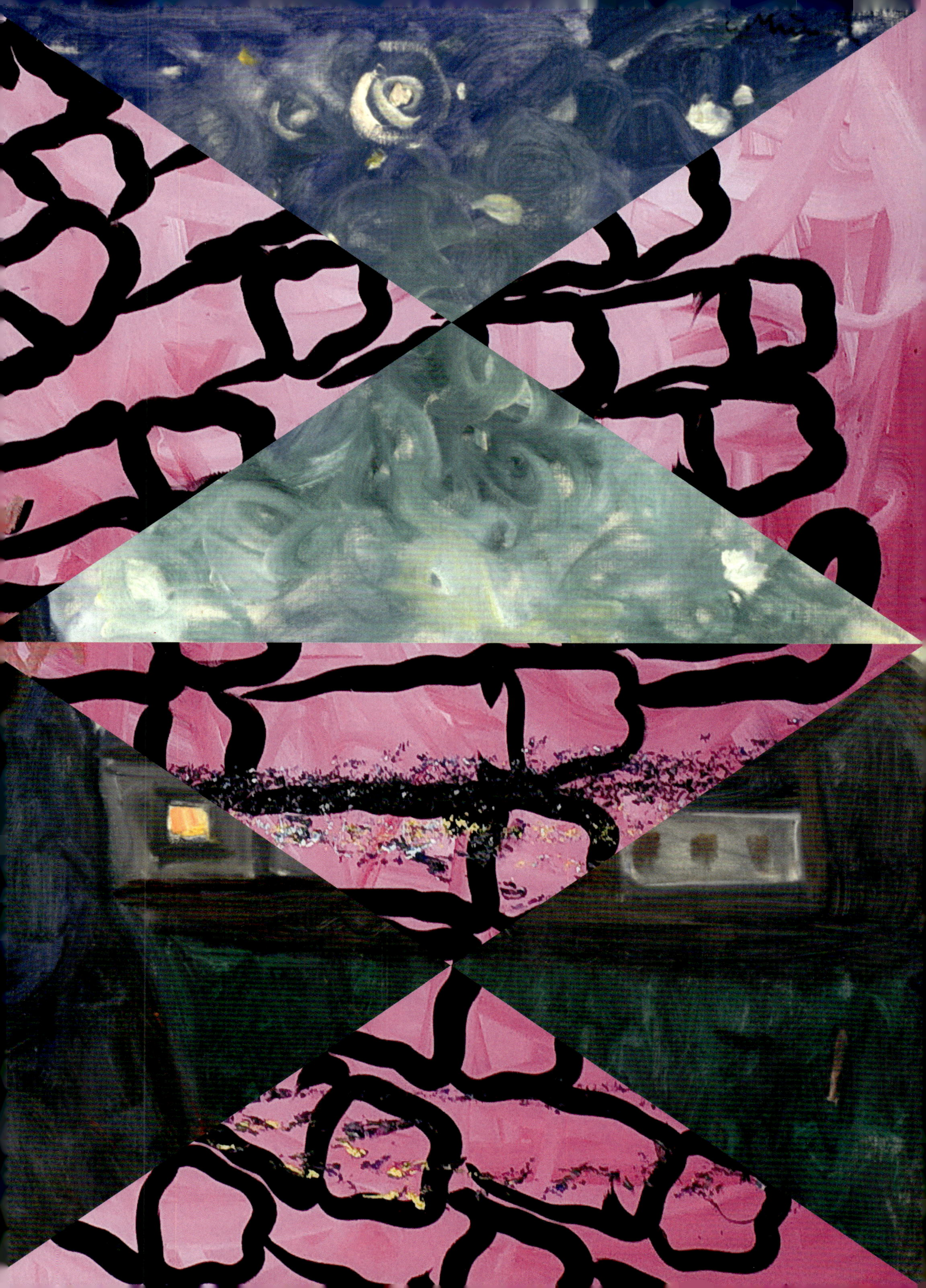

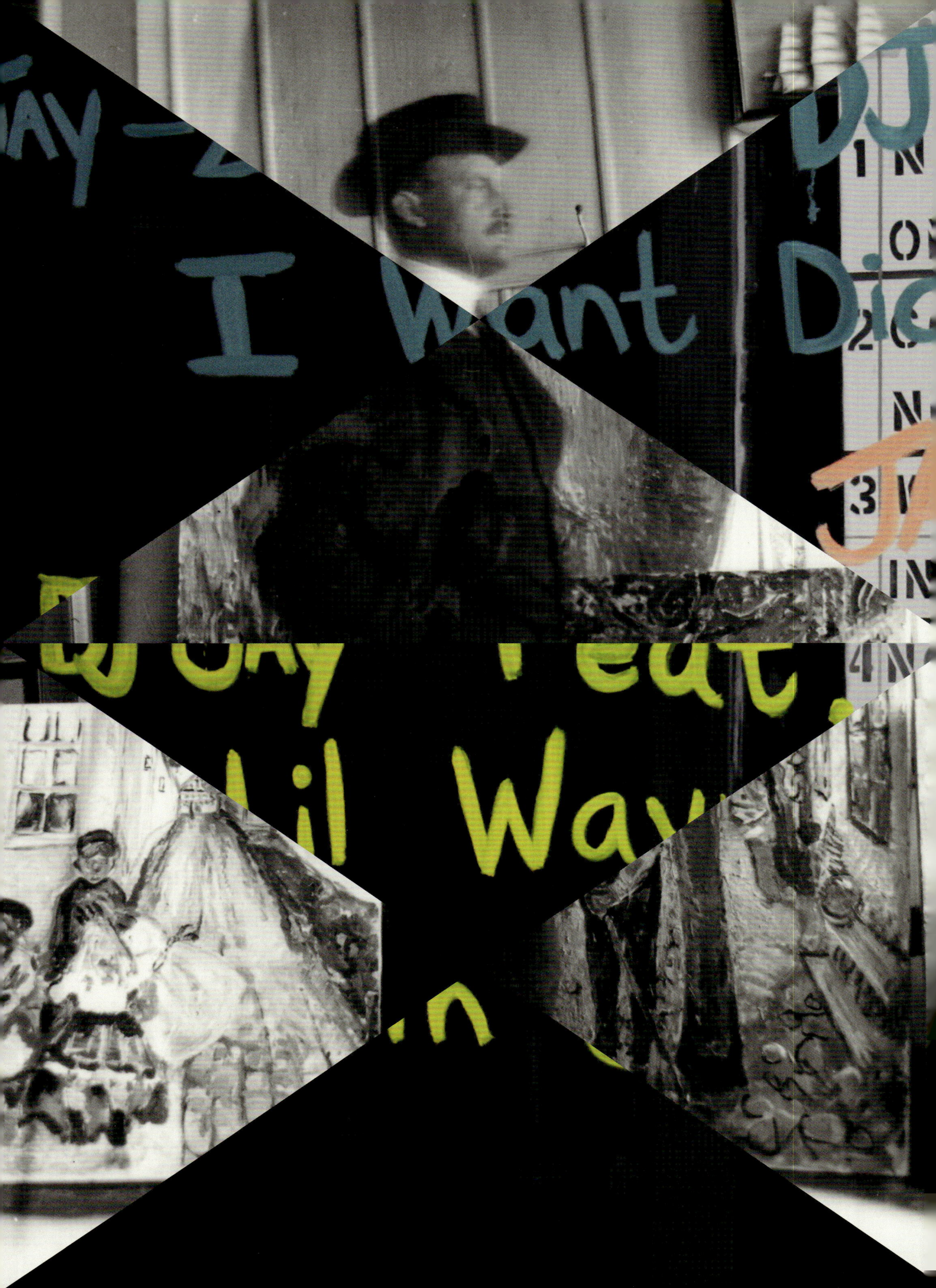
JAY-Z
I want
I want Die
DJ
3
DJ JAY feat.
Lil Way

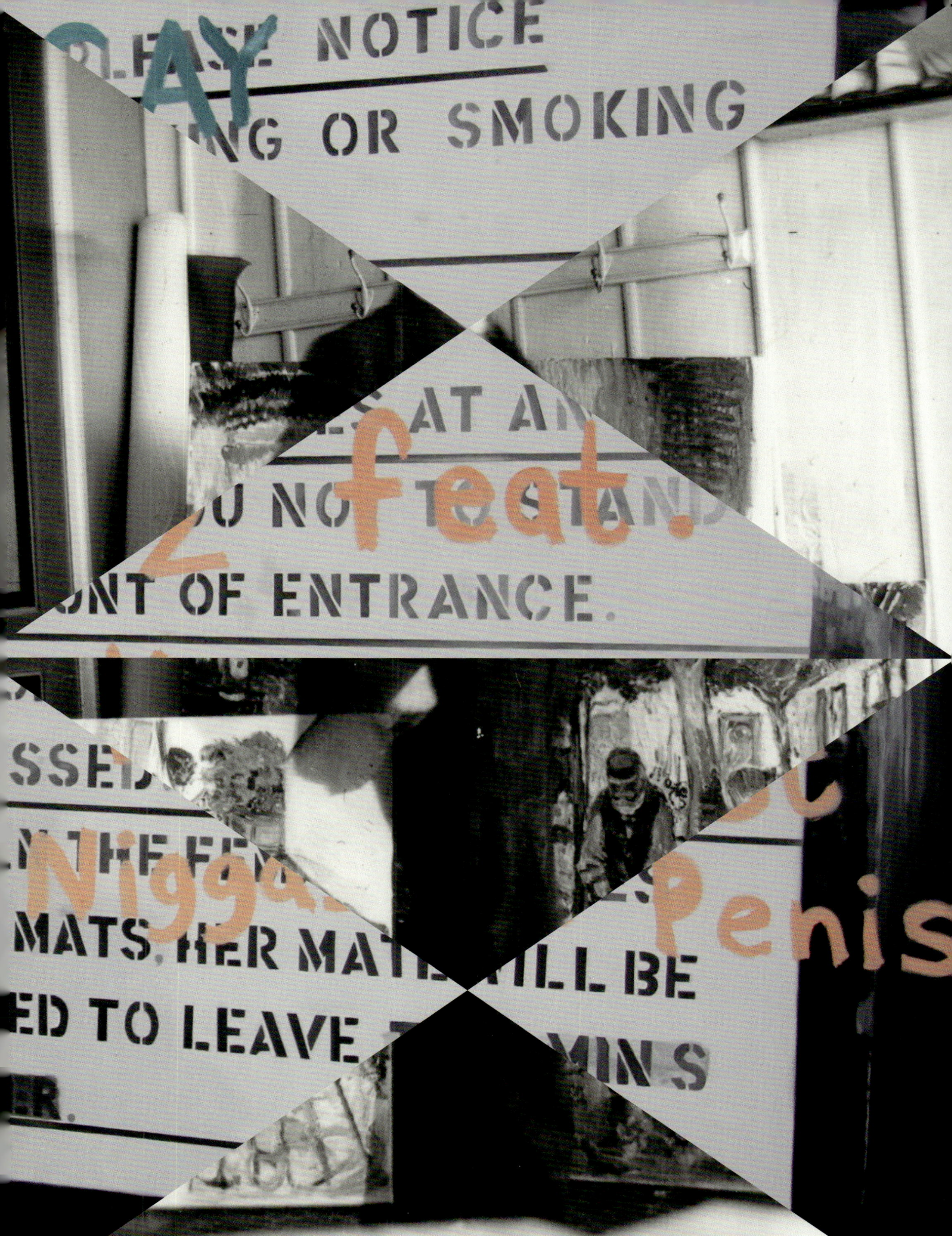
PLEASE NOTICE
NG OR SMOKING
S AT A
U NO STAN
NT OF ENTRANCE.
SSED
N THE
MATS, HER MAT ILL BE
ED TO LEAVE
ER.
AY
feat.
Niggas
Penis

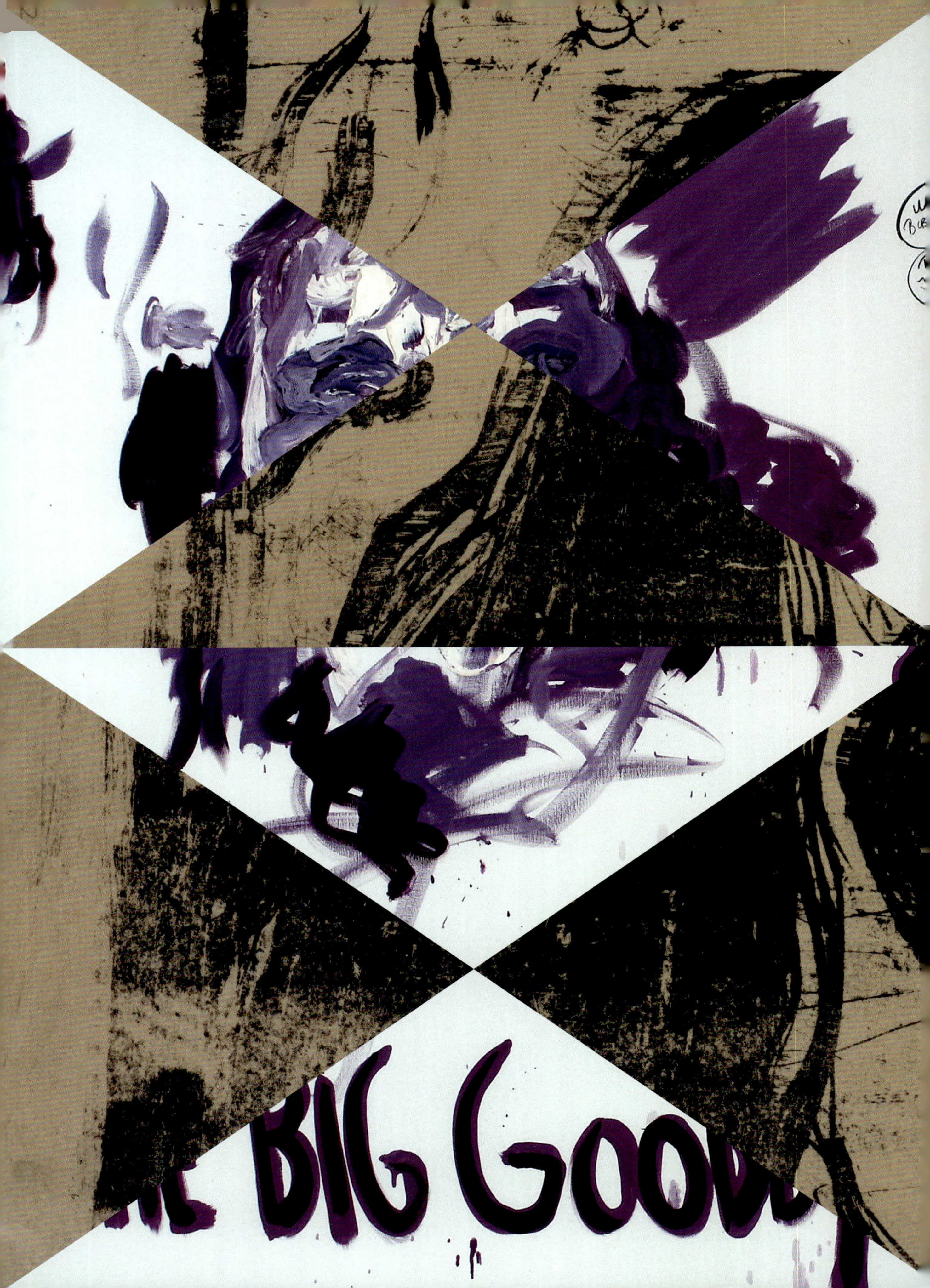
BIG GOOD

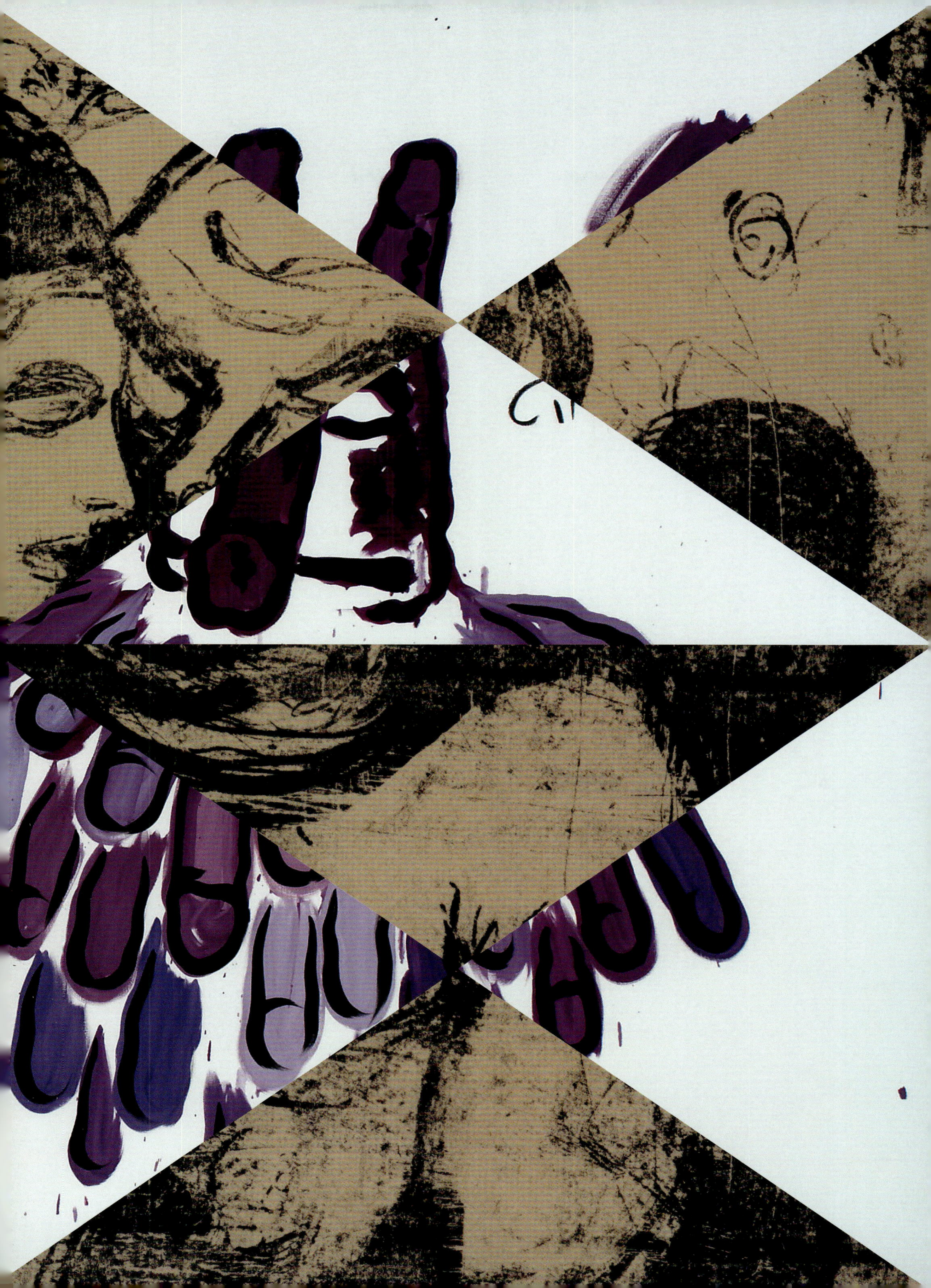

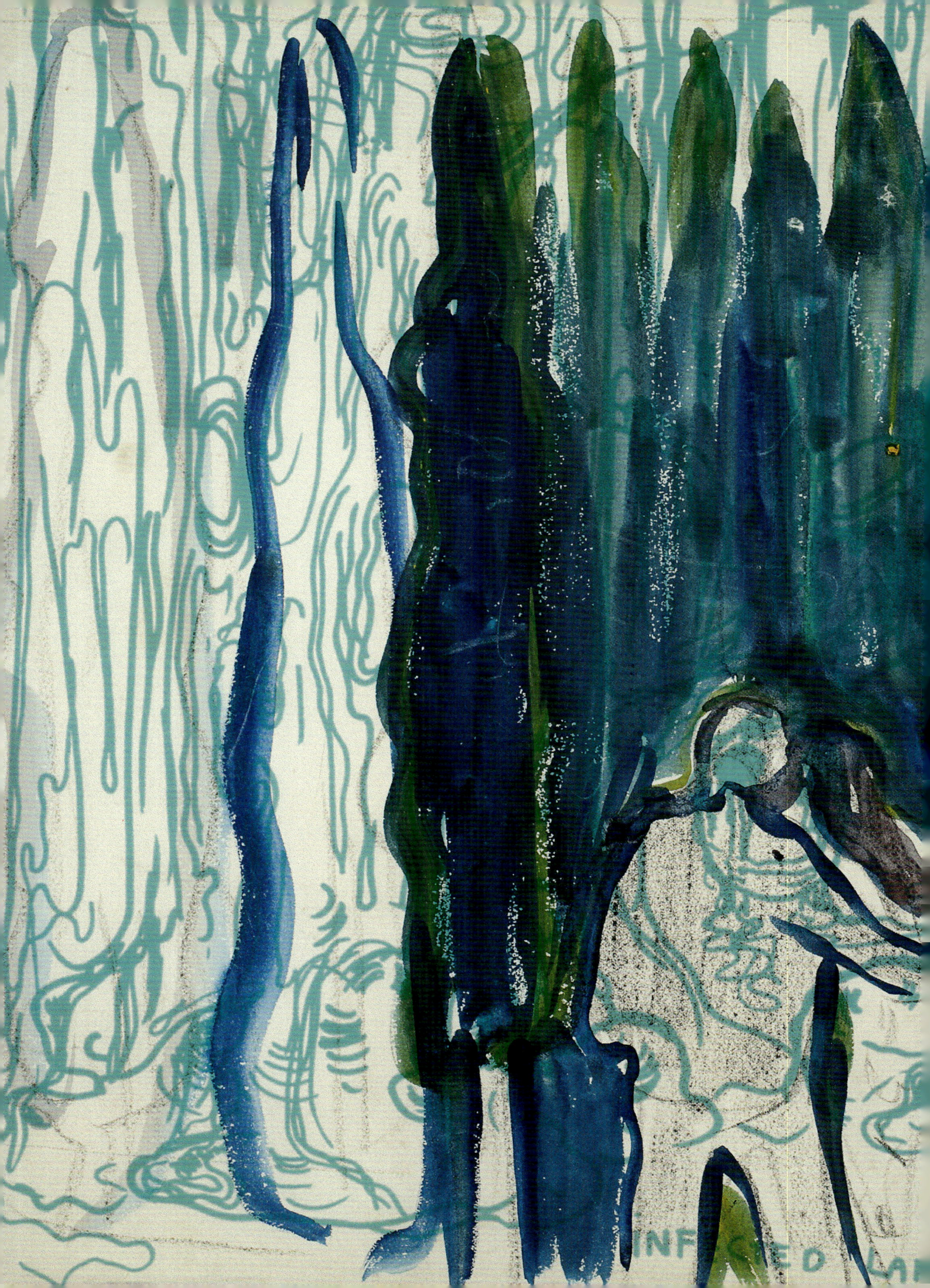
INFECTED LA

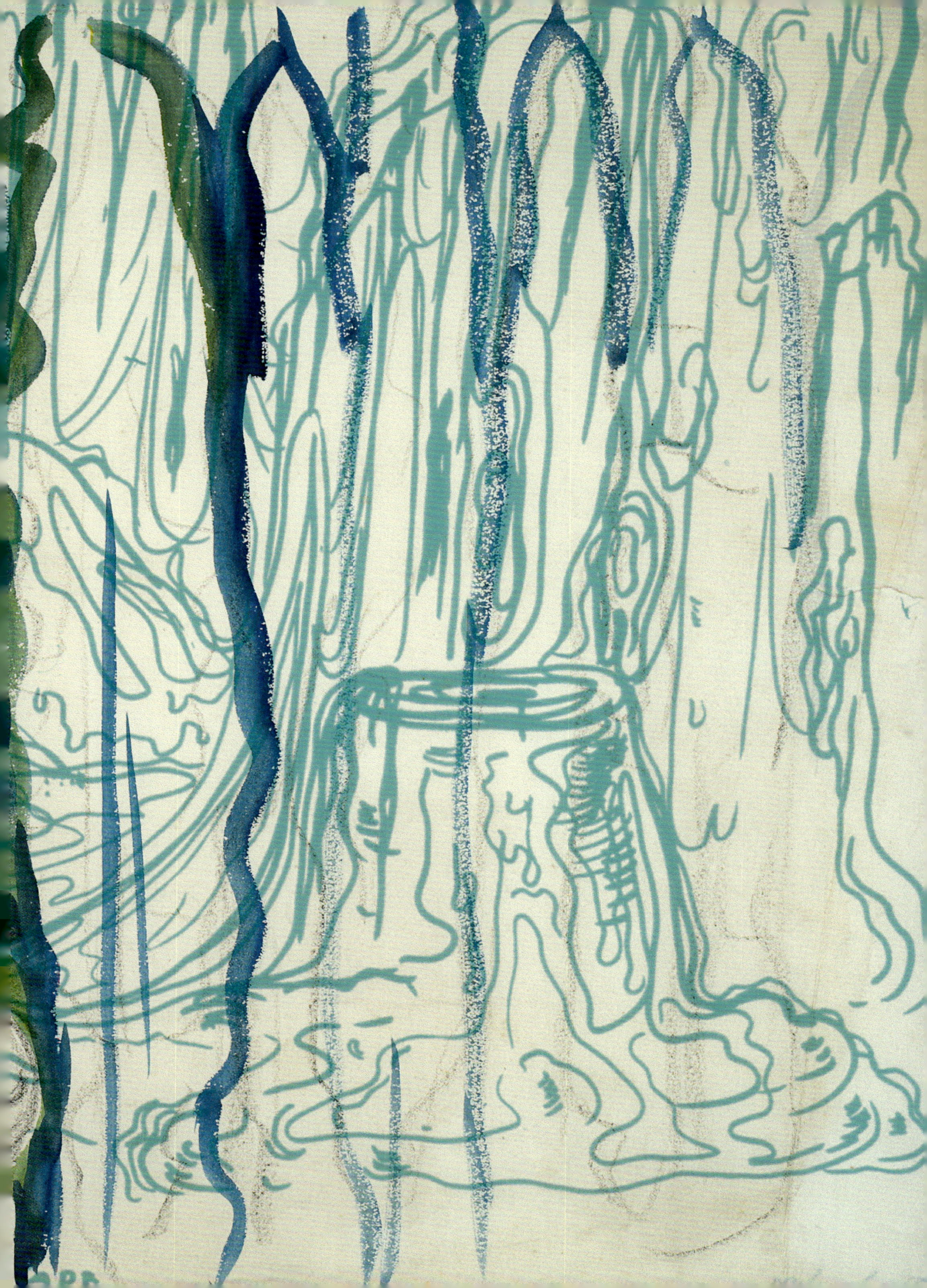

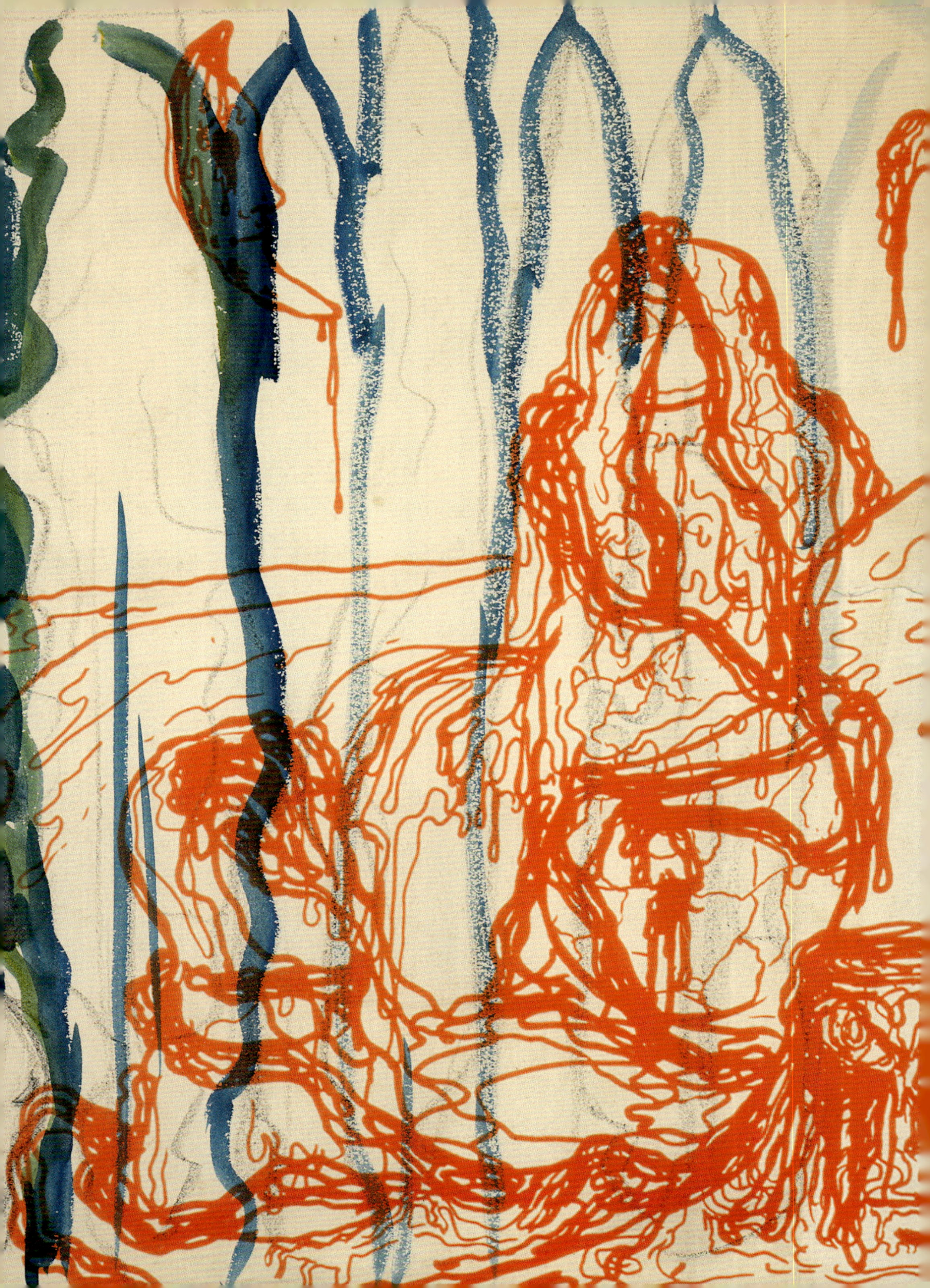

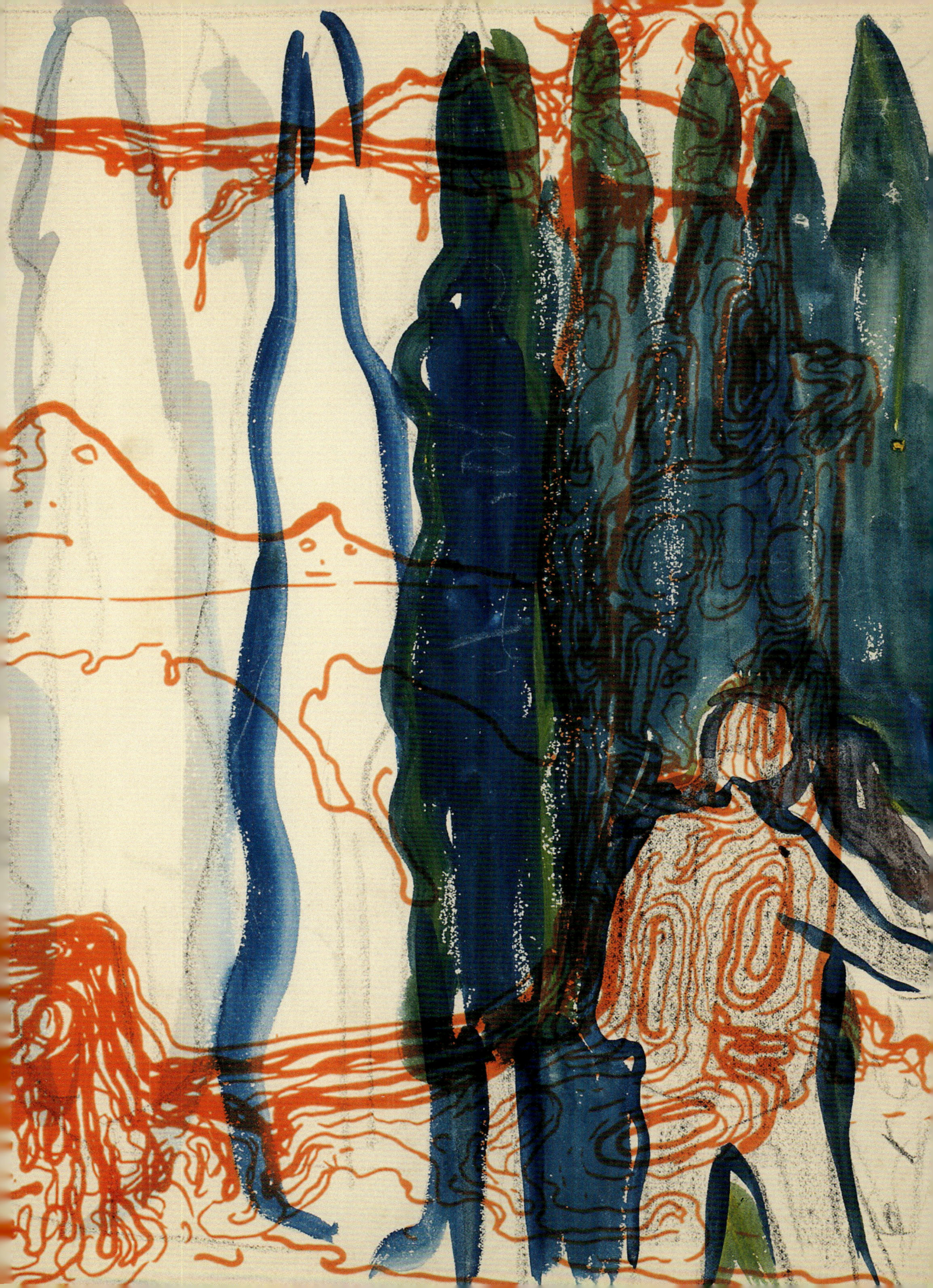

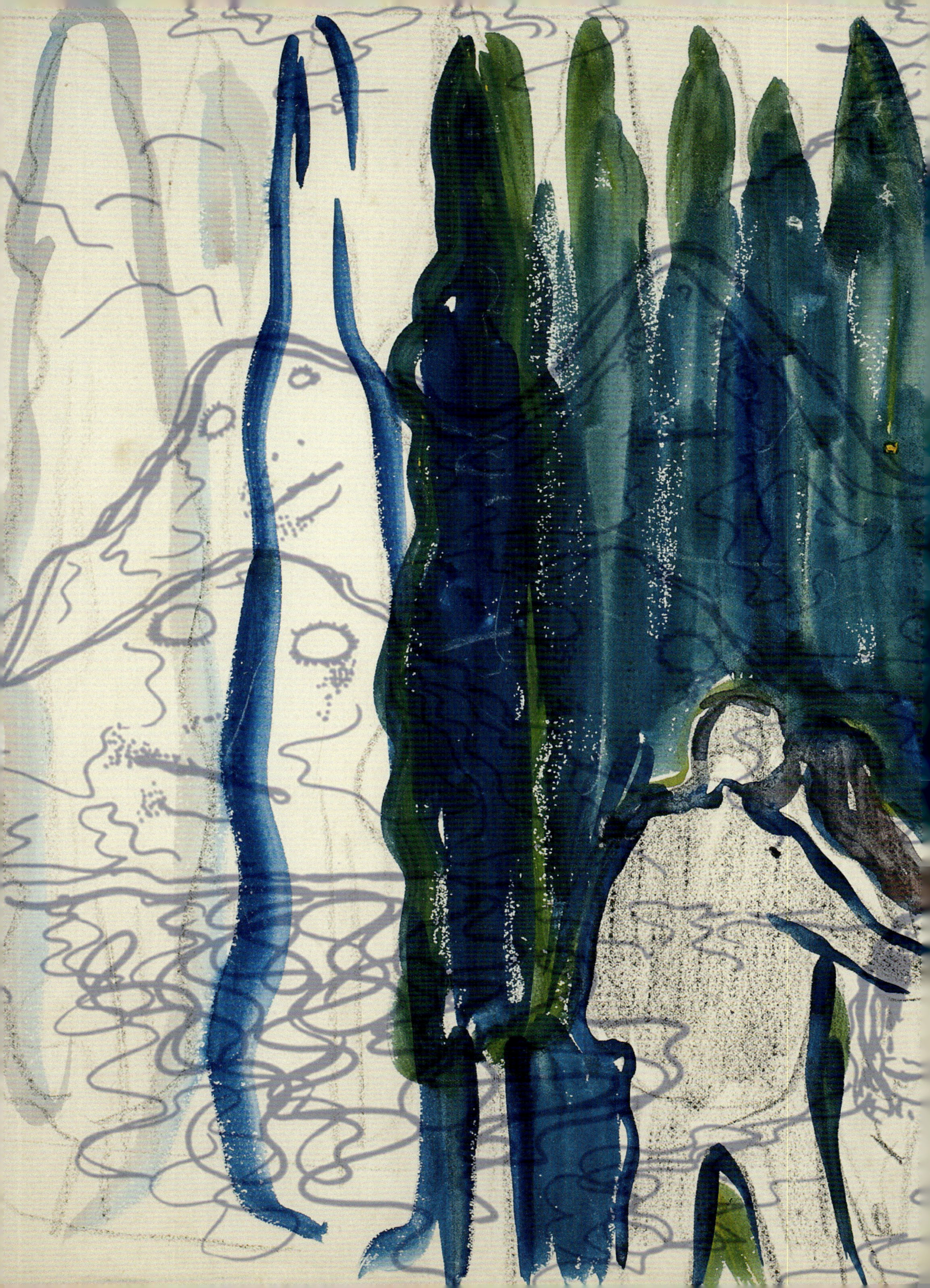

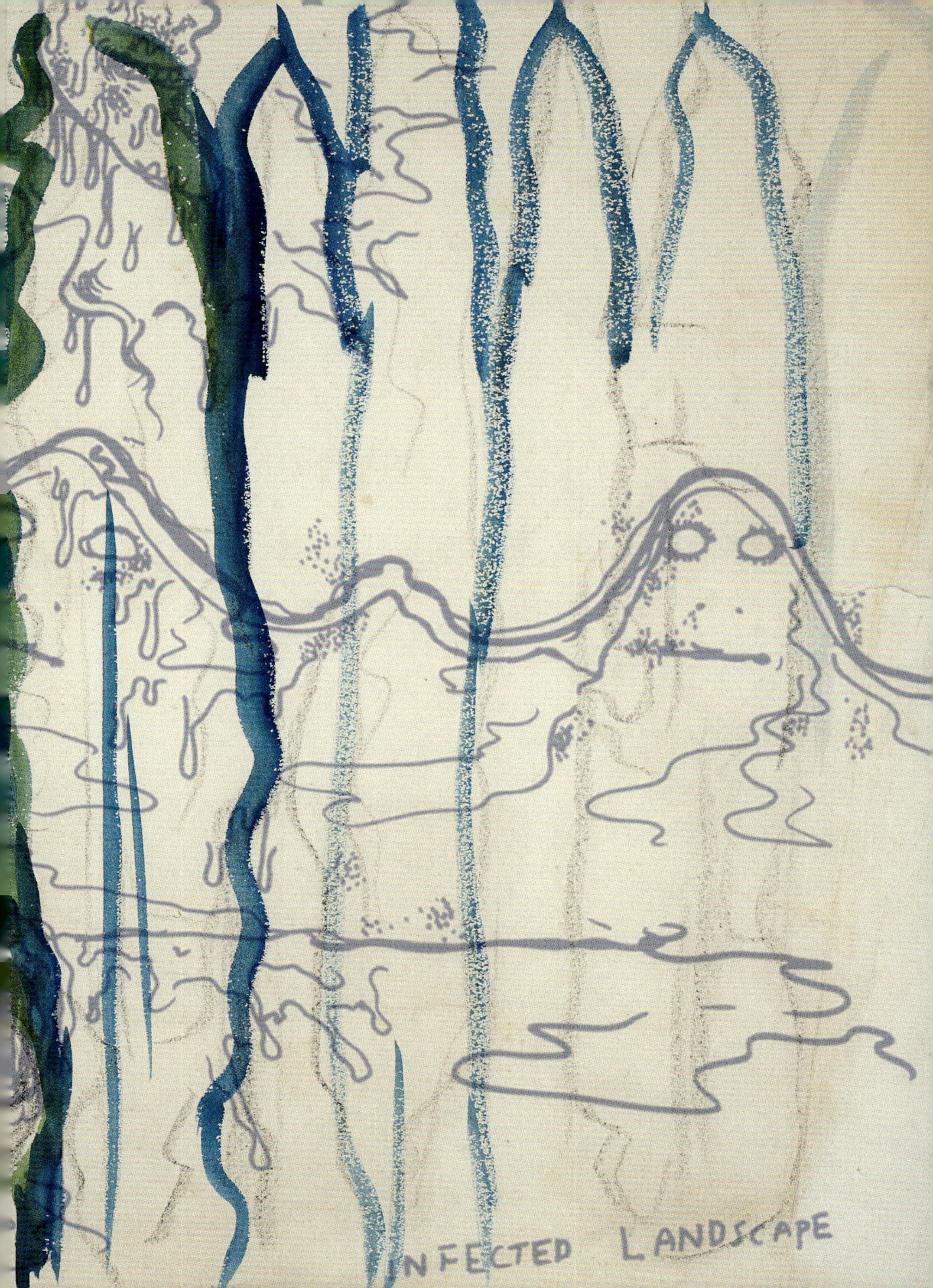

INFECTED LANDSCAPE

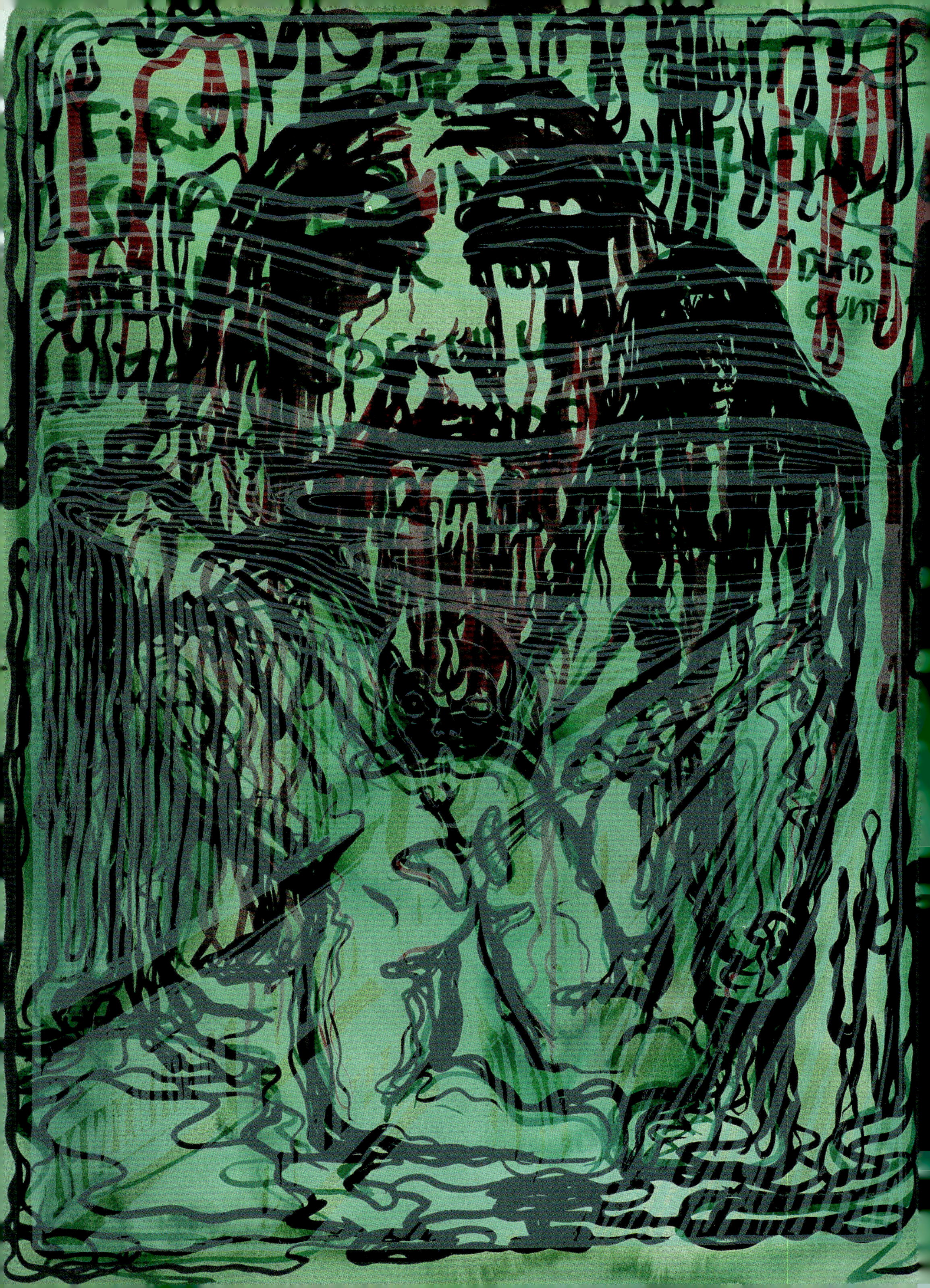
First
David Cunt

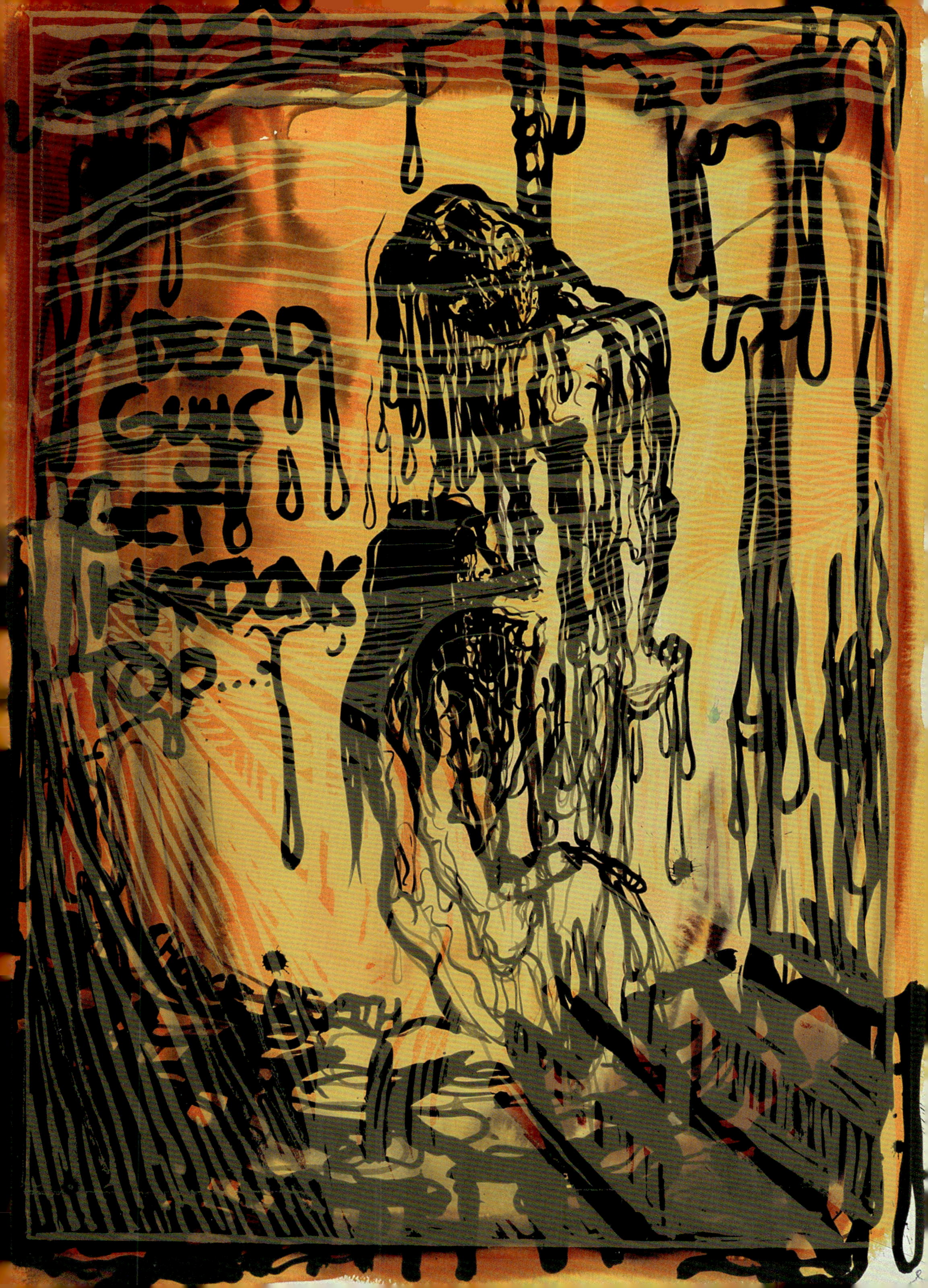

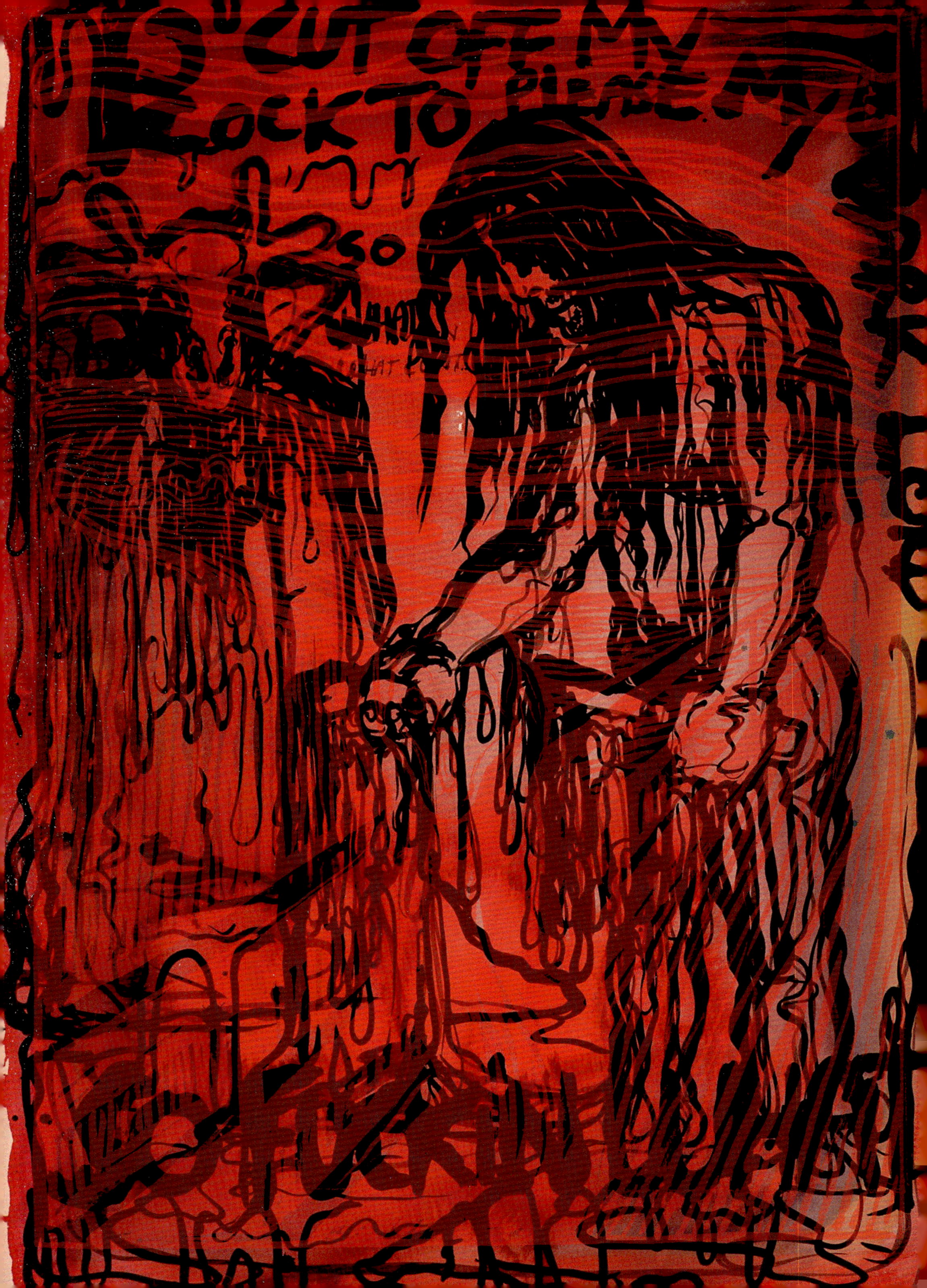
CUT OFF MY
ROCK TO
SO

NICE BITCH...
I CAN'T SEE ANYBODY
ALVE THANK ME CUNT
VIKING METAL
FAN
WE CUT
OUT THE
TOUNGE
OF THE
DOG
KILLED IT
AND HANGED
IT OUSIDE
YOUR
PLACE
I CAN'T SEE
ANYTHING...
KILL ME PLEASE
BLODHEMN

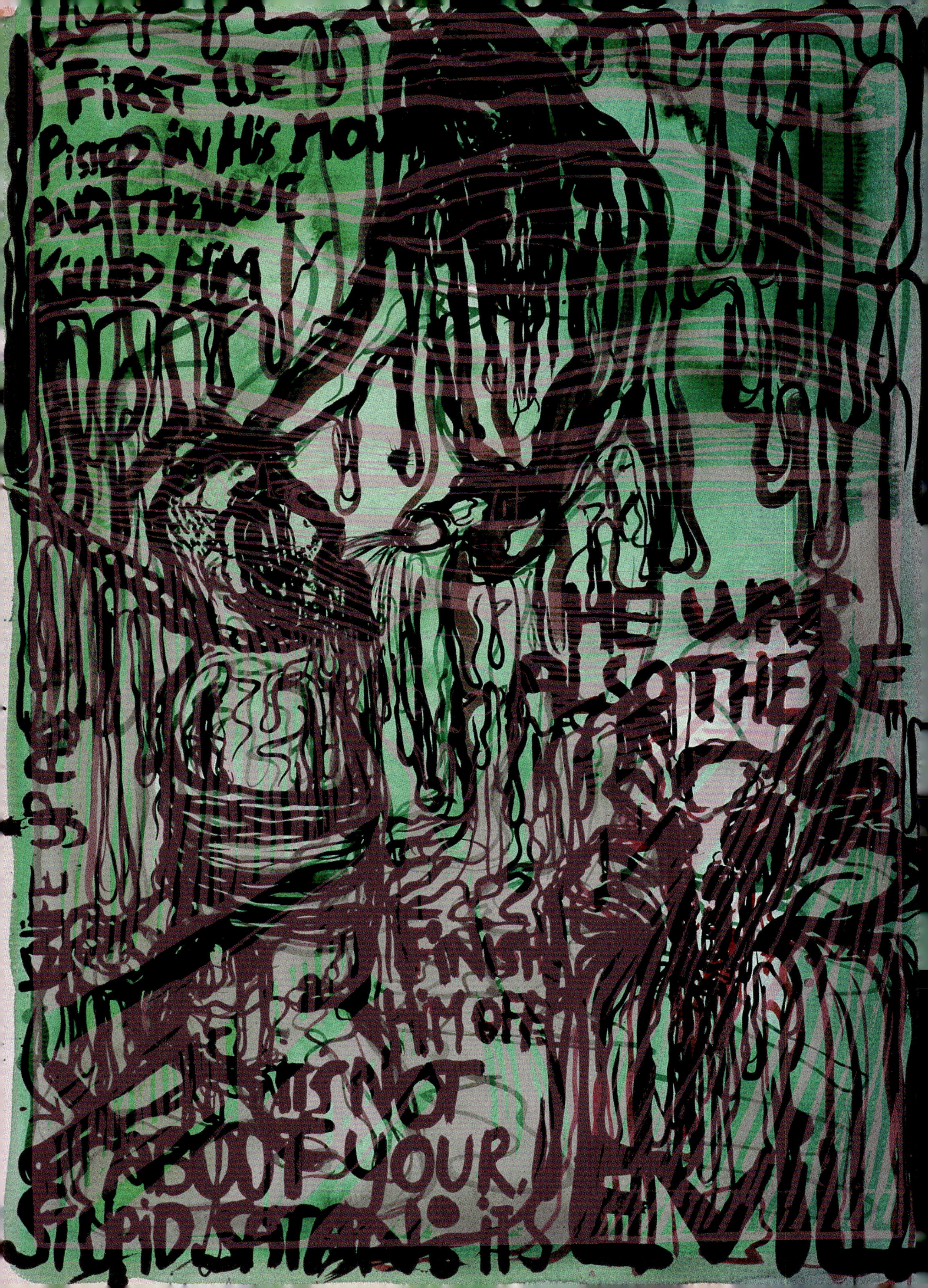

FIRST WE
PISED IN HIS MOU
AND THEN WE
KILED HIM
HE UP
SO THE
FINISH
HIM OFF
IT IS NOT
ABOUT YOUR
STUPID SISTER HIS

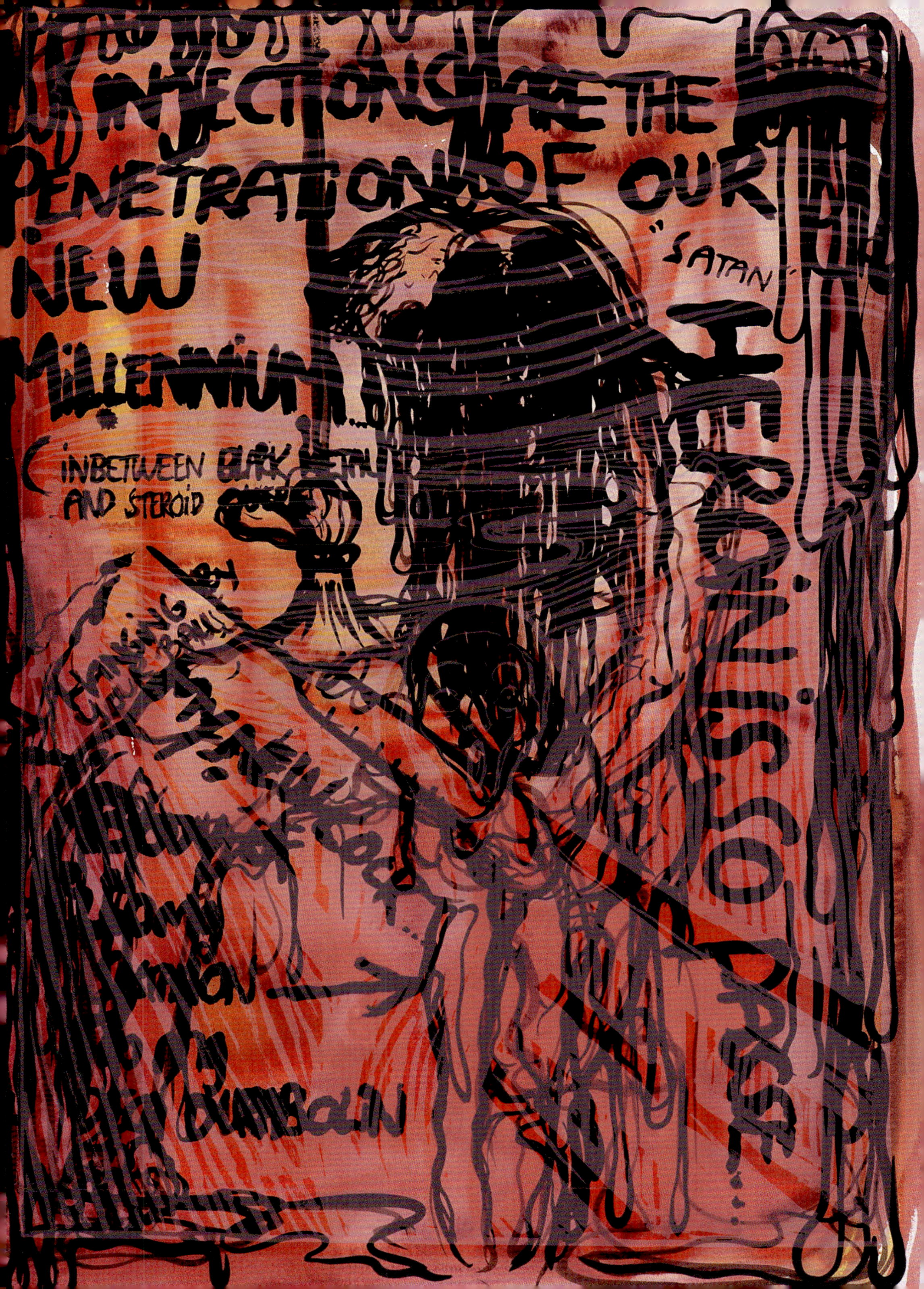
INJECTIONS ARE THE
PENETRATION OF OUR
NEW
MILLENNIUM
(INBETWEEN BLACK METH
AND STEROID
"SATAN"
HEROIN IS COOL

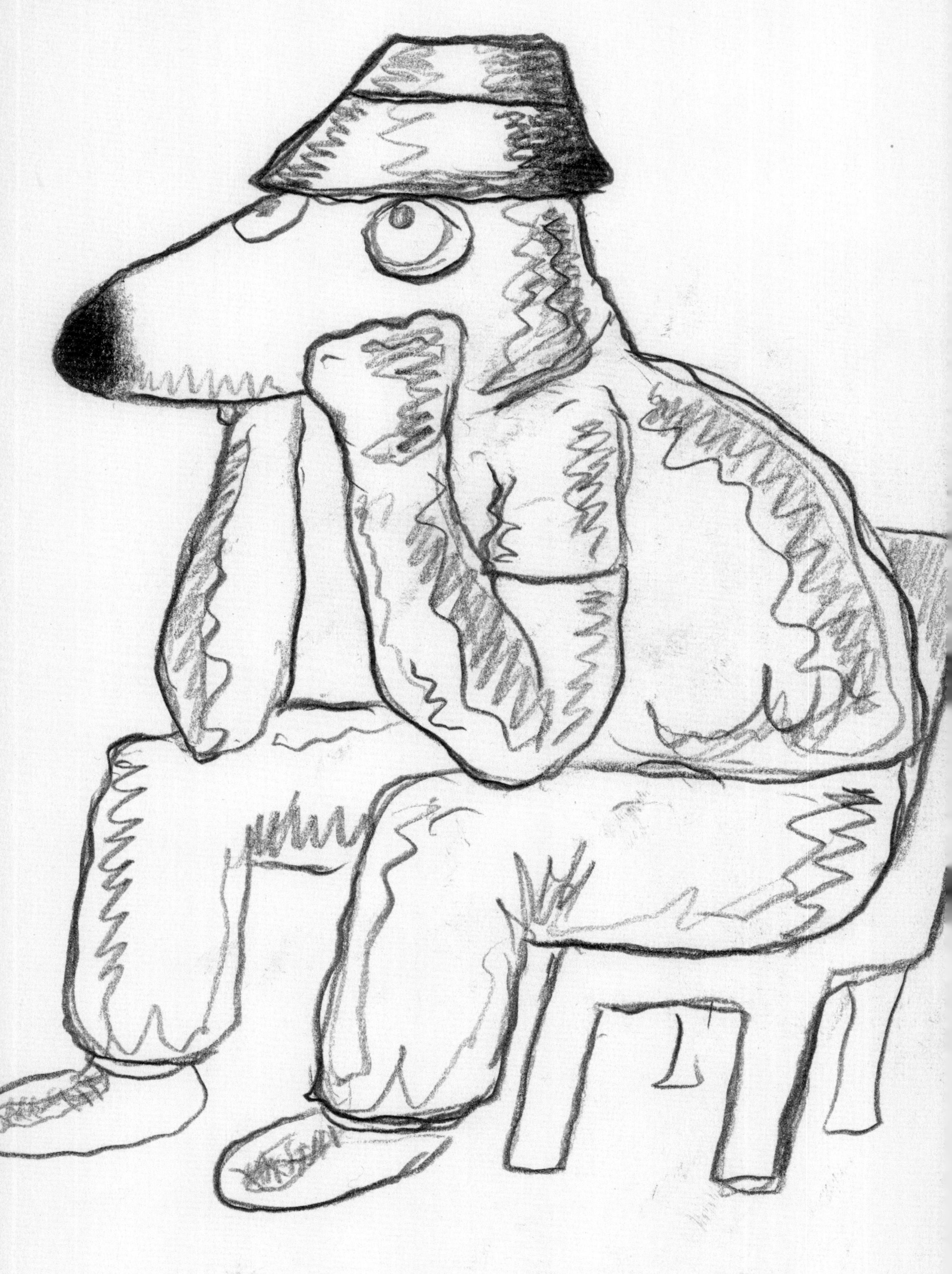

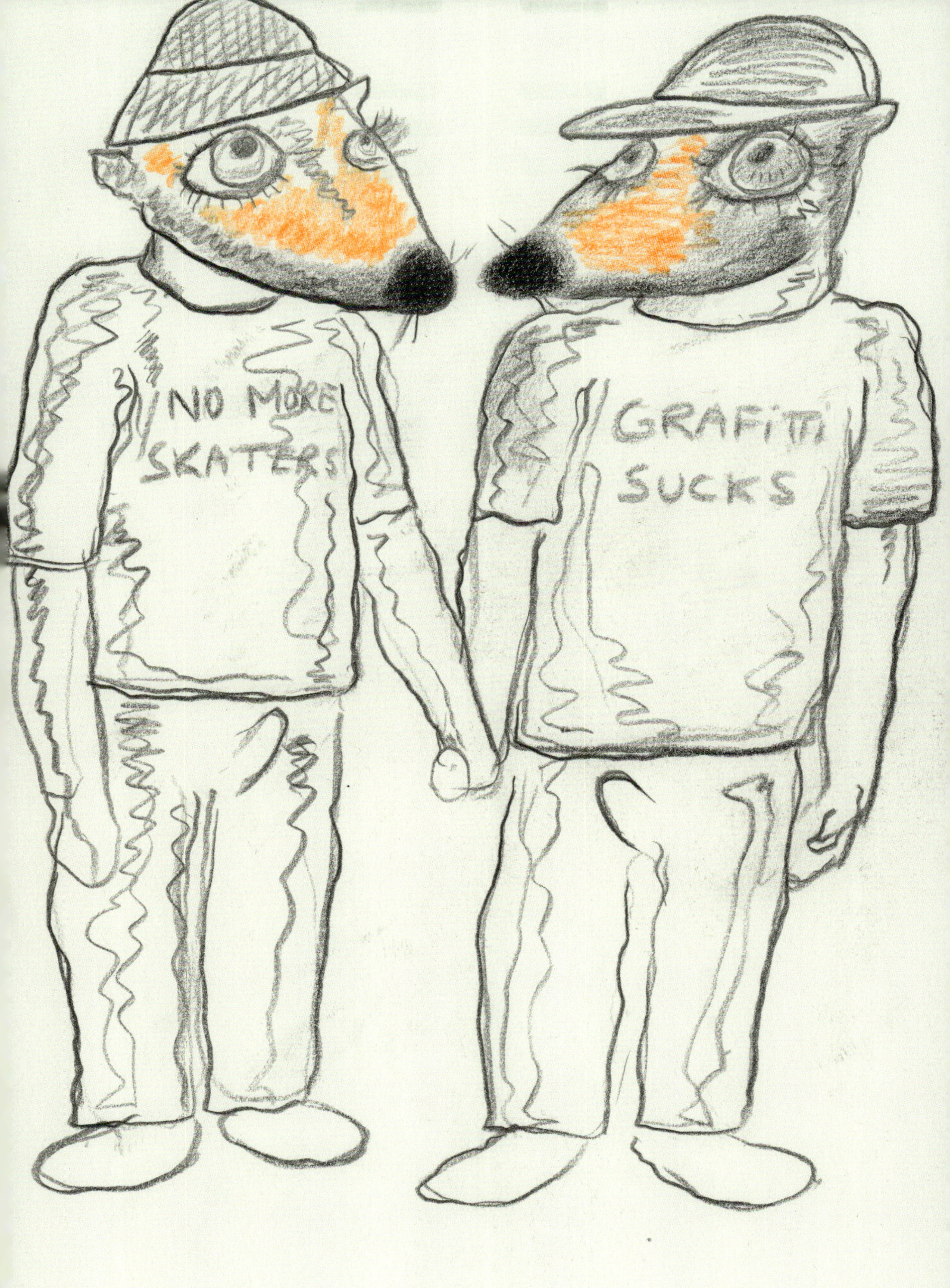
NO MORE SKATERS
GRAFITI SUCKS

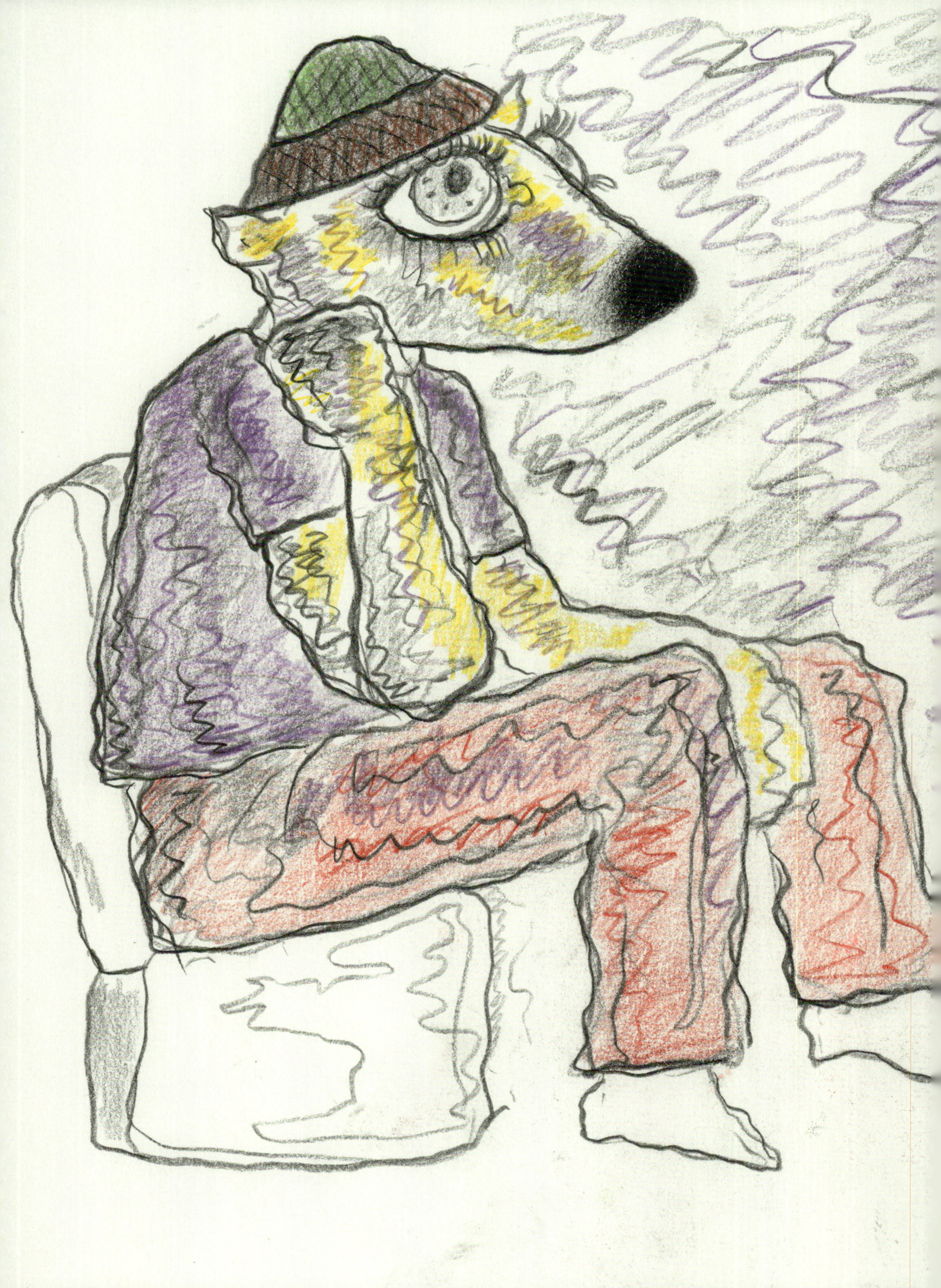

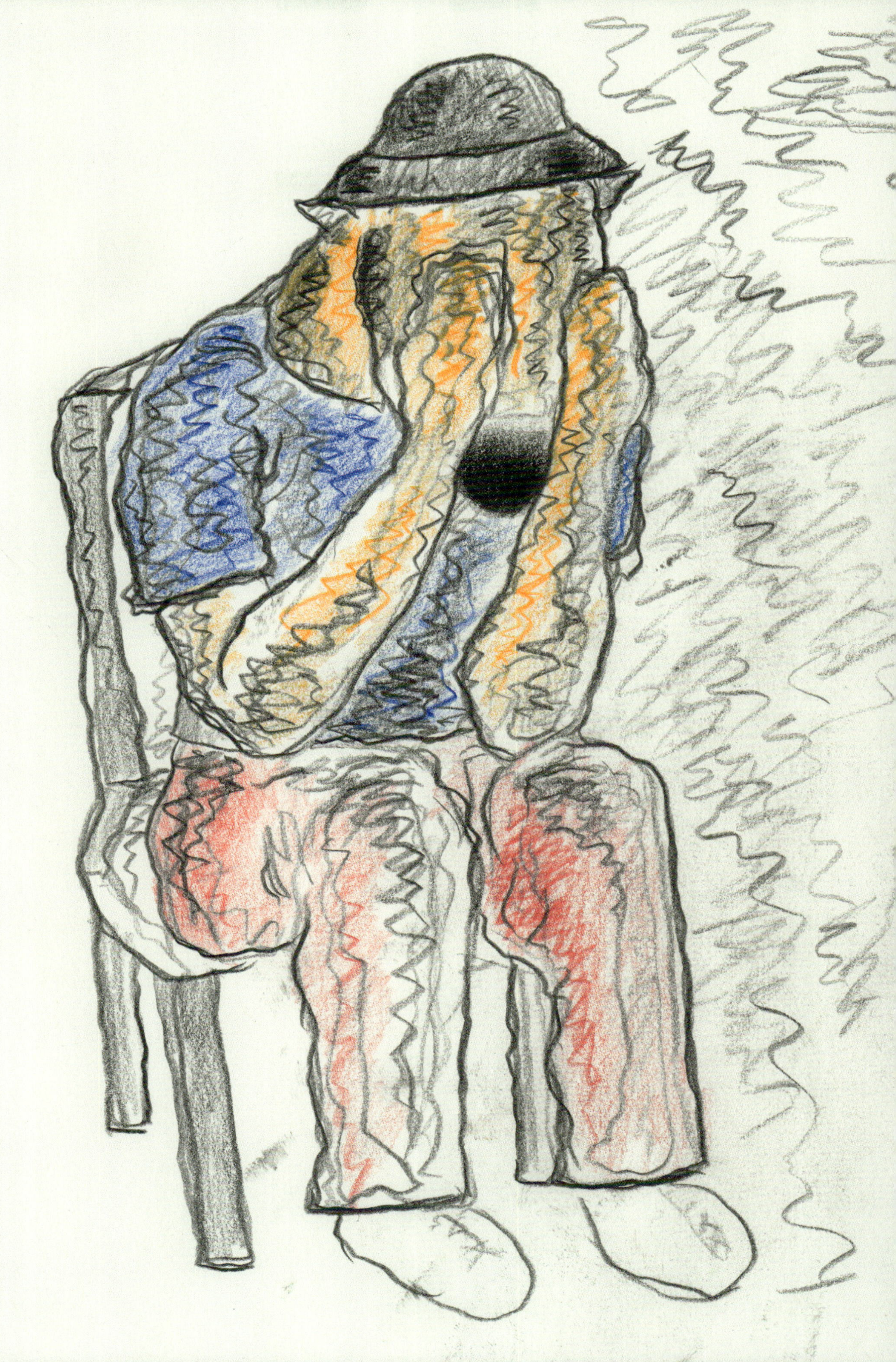

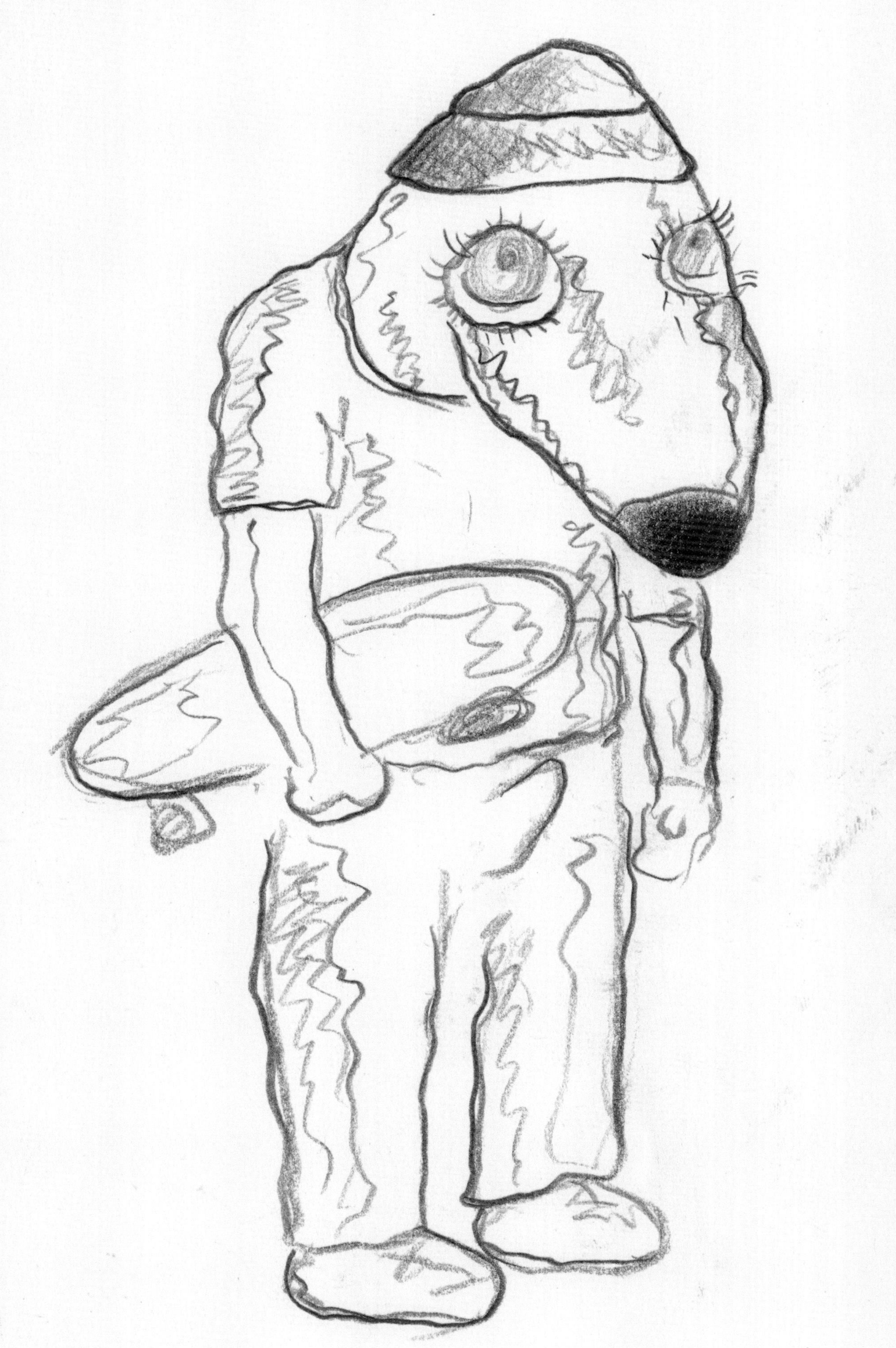

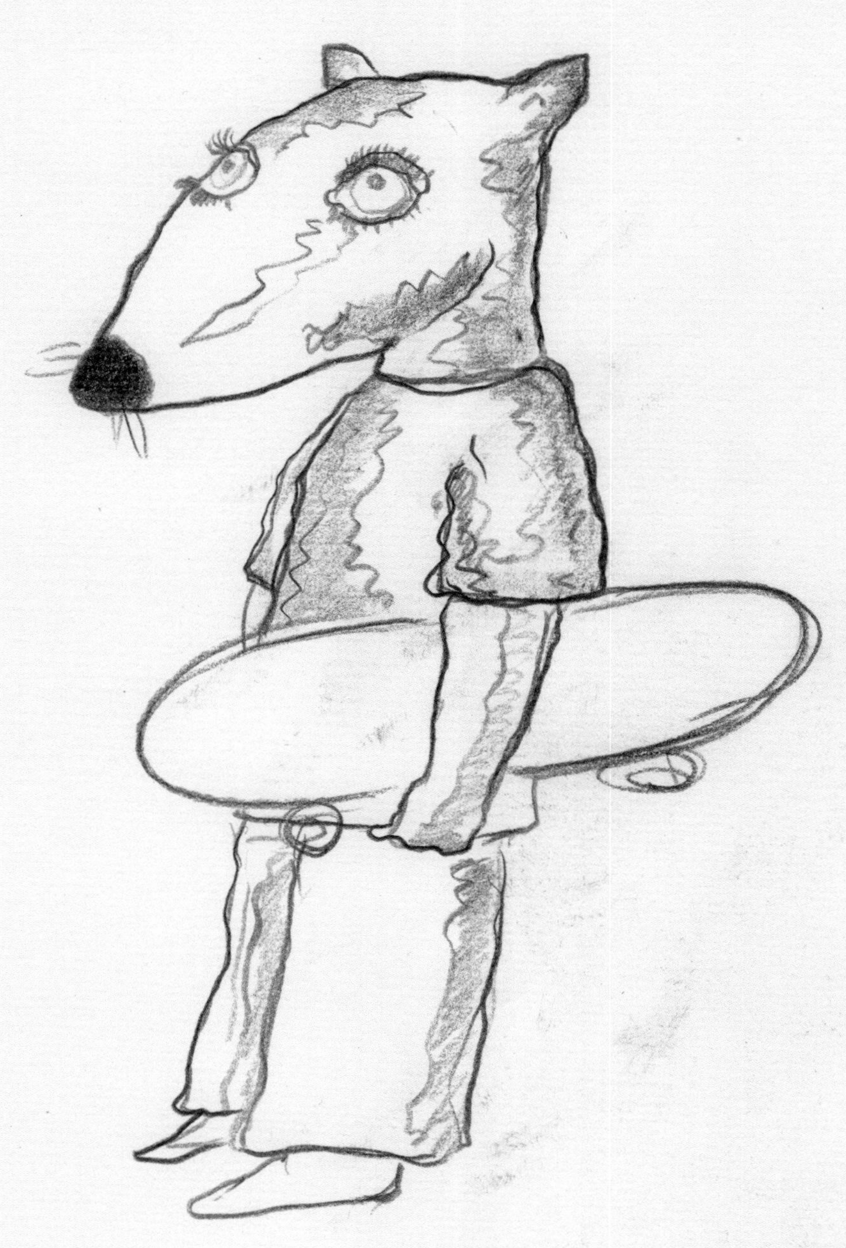

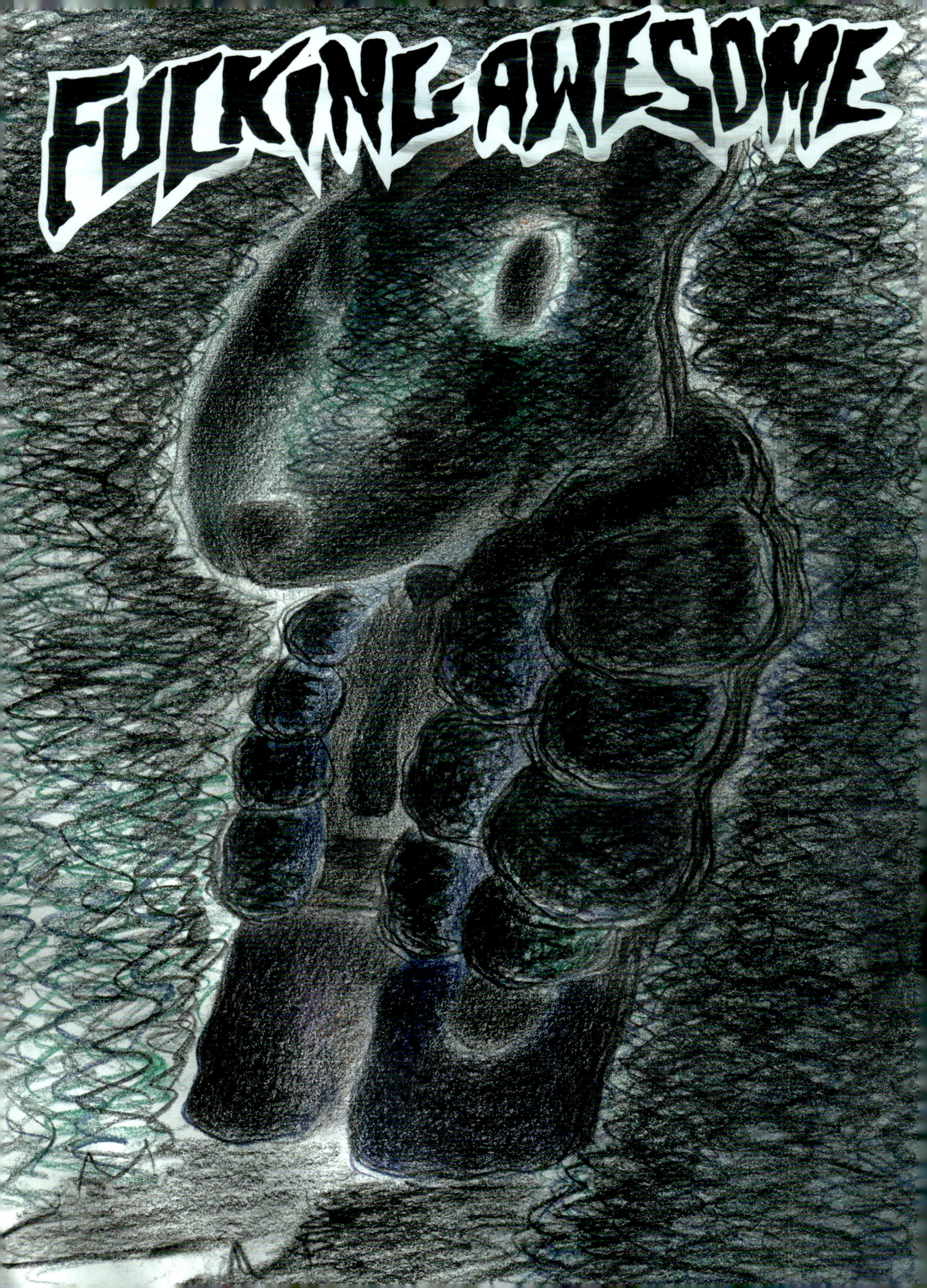

FUCKING AWESOME

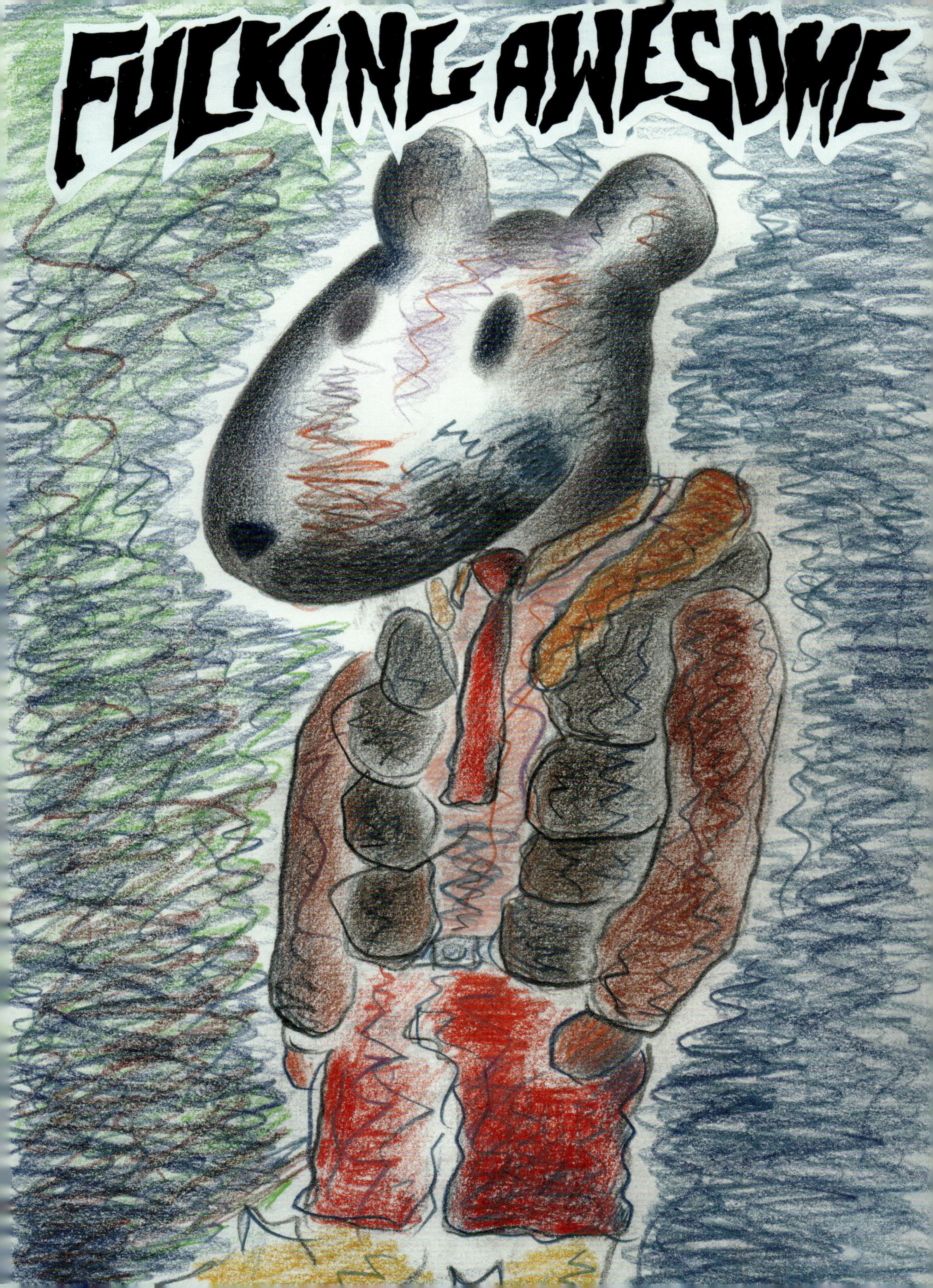
FUCKING AWESOME

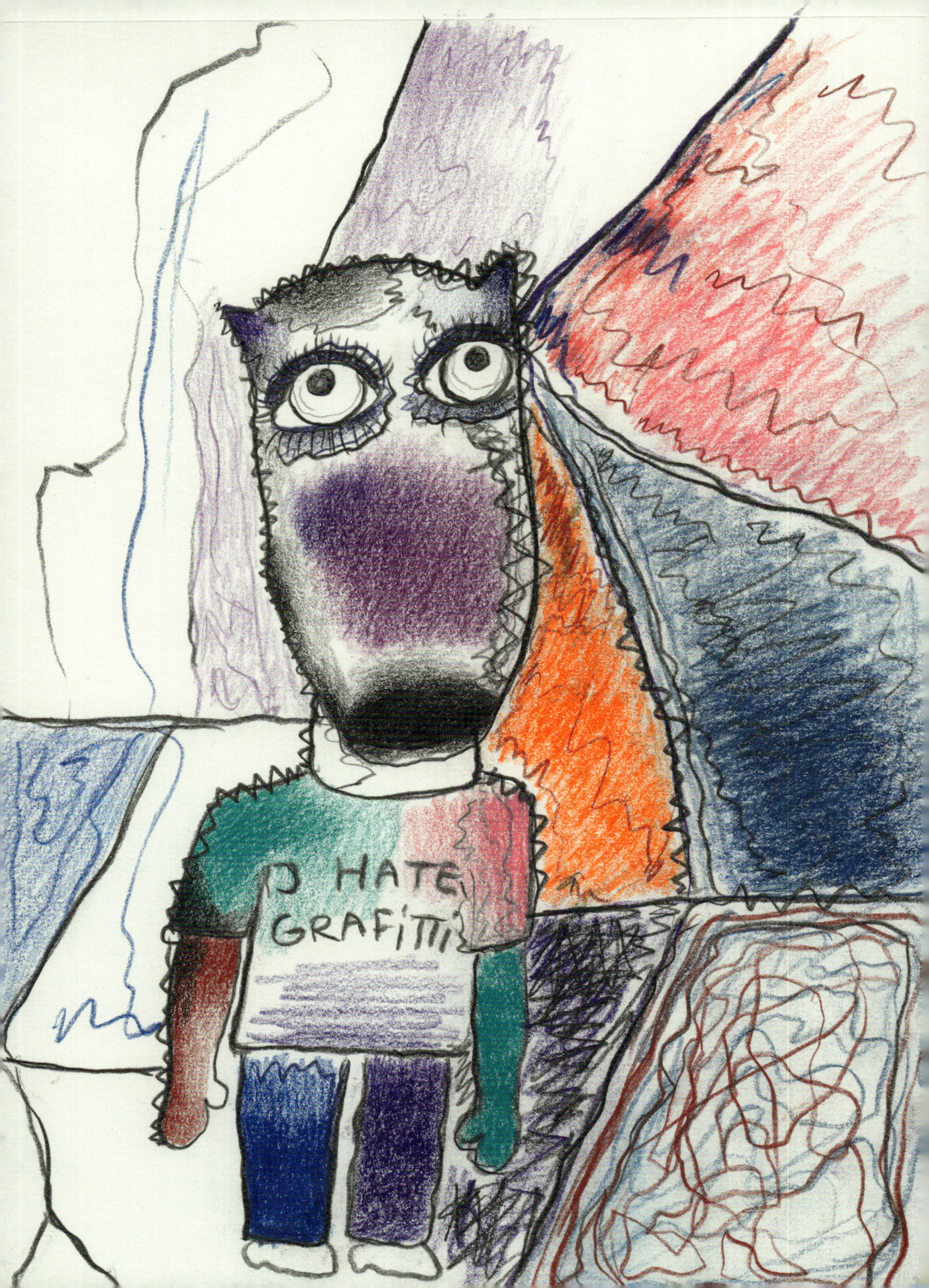

I HATE
GRAFITTI

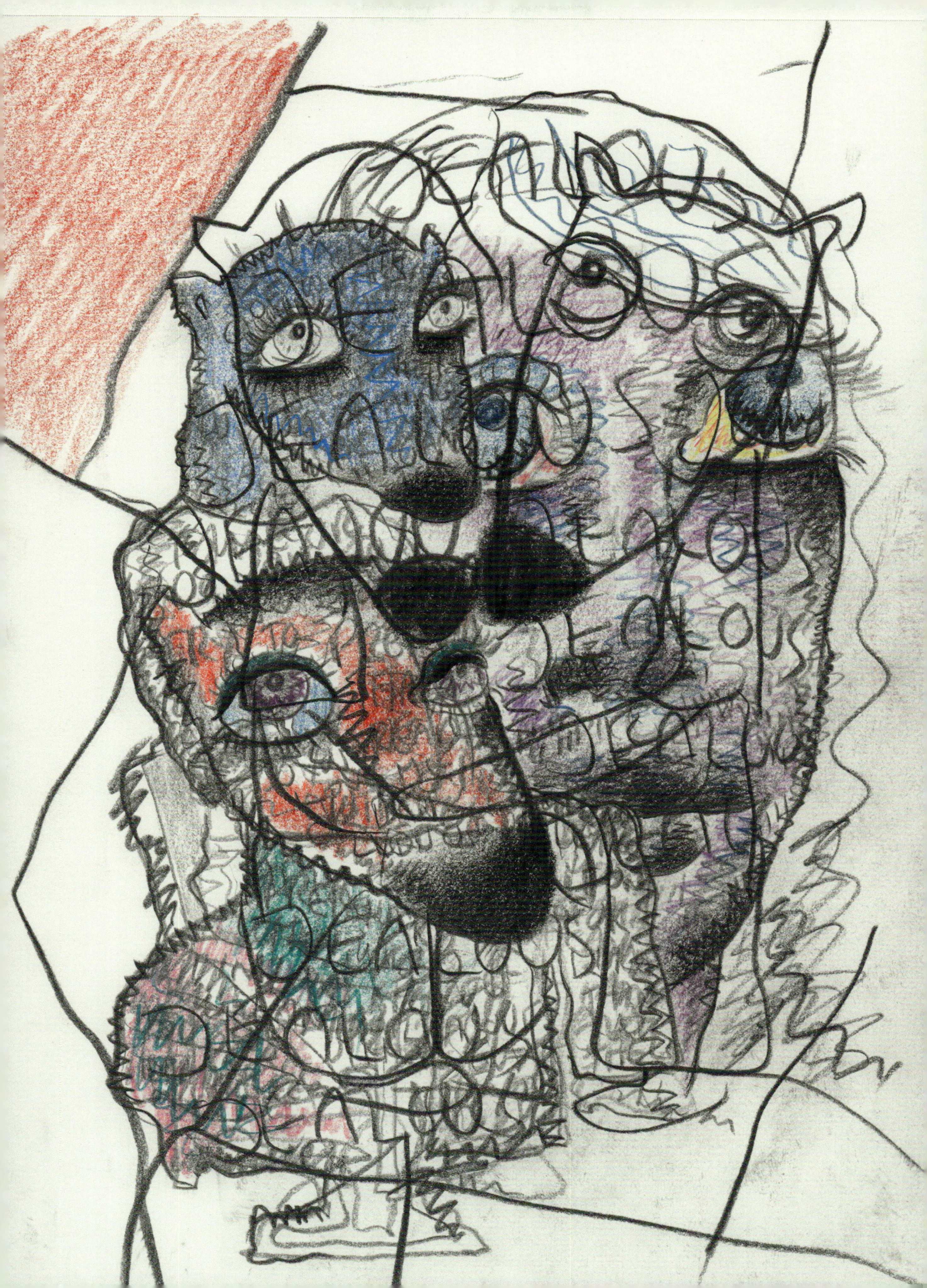

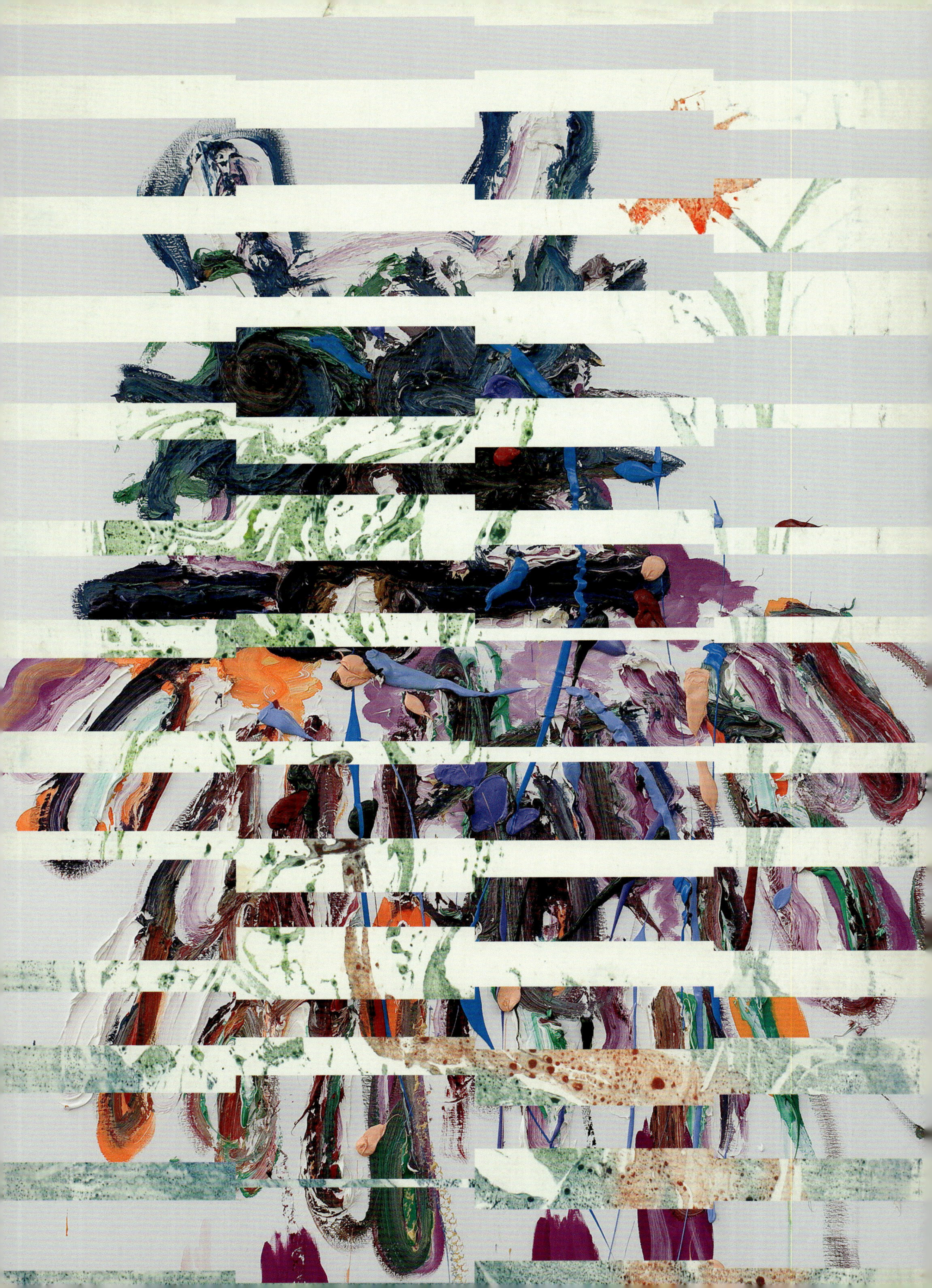

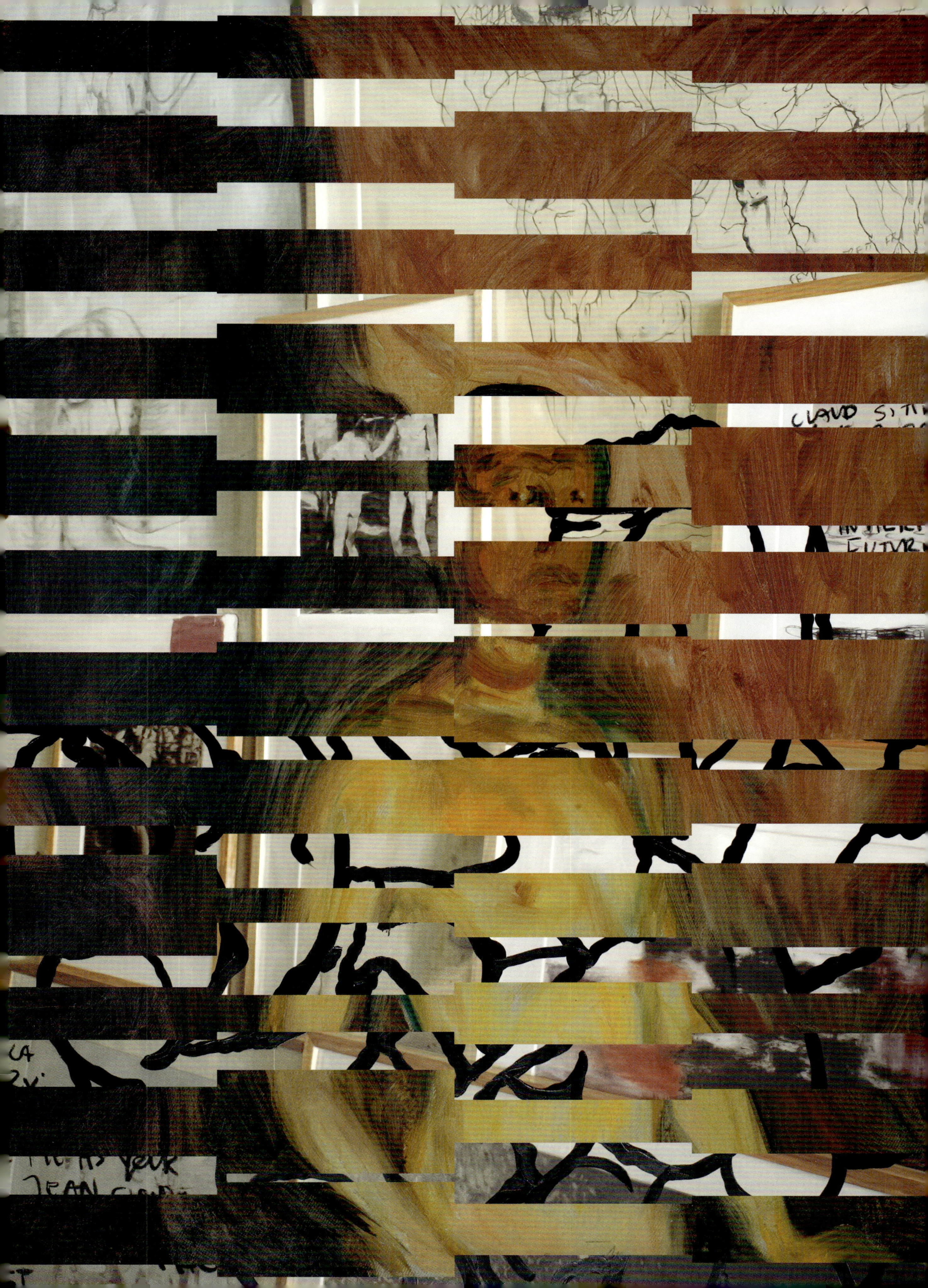

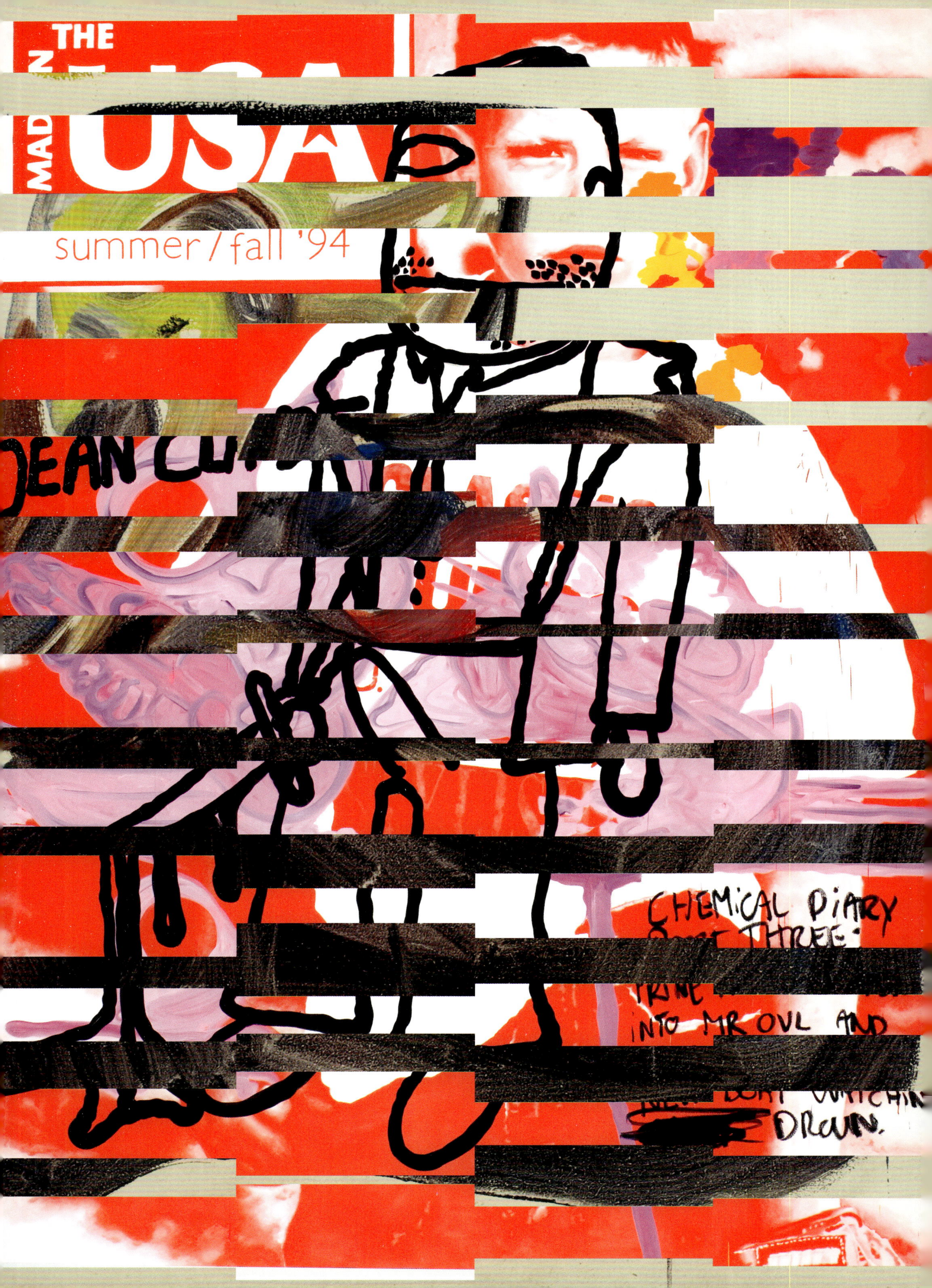

THE
MAD IN USA
summer / fall '94
JEAN CL
CHEMICAL DIARY
THREE
INTO MR OWL AND
DRAIN.

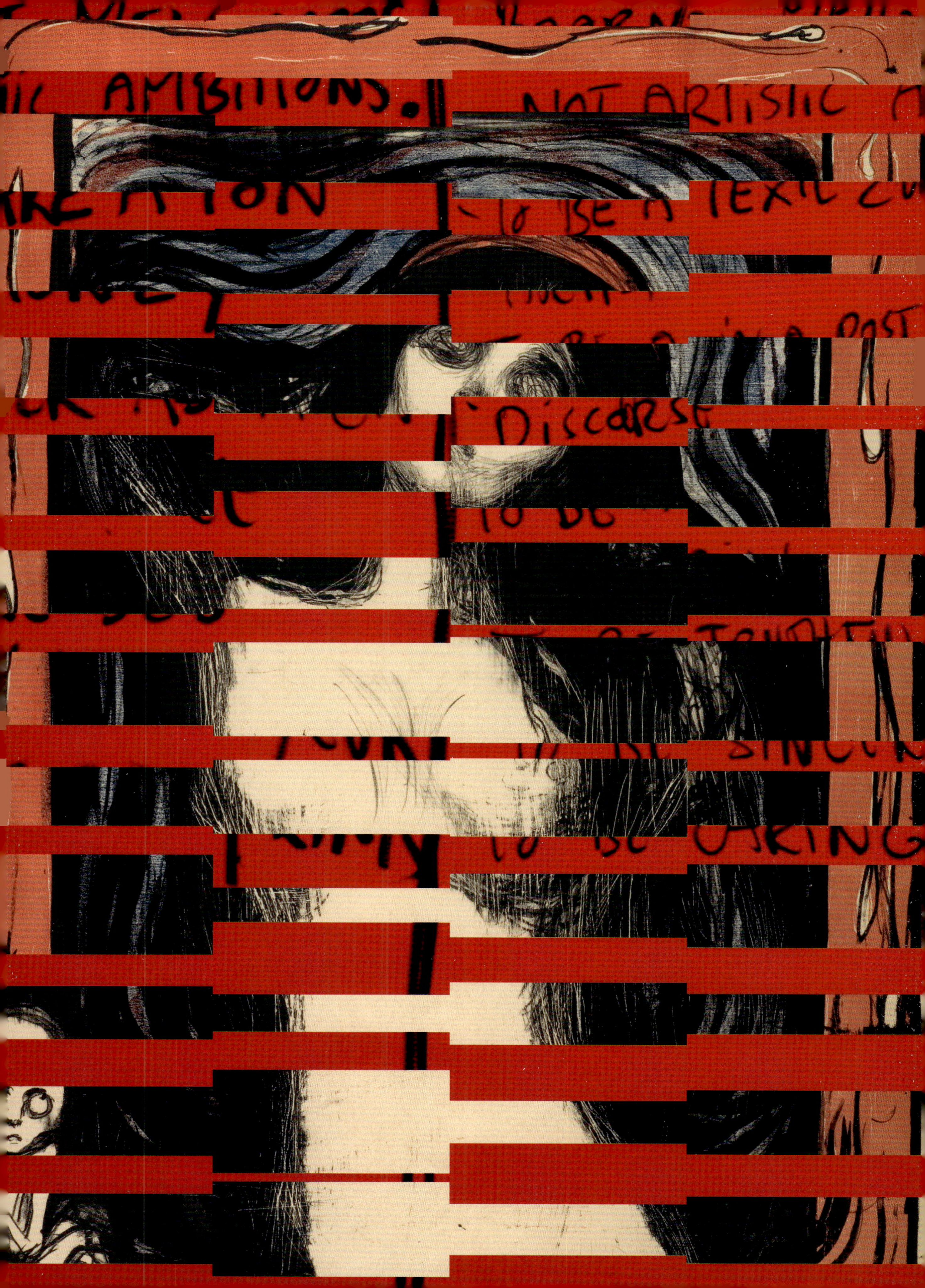
AMBITIONS.
NOT ARTISTIC
CREATION
TO BE A TEXTIL
DISCOURSE
TO BE
SINCER
TO BE WORKING

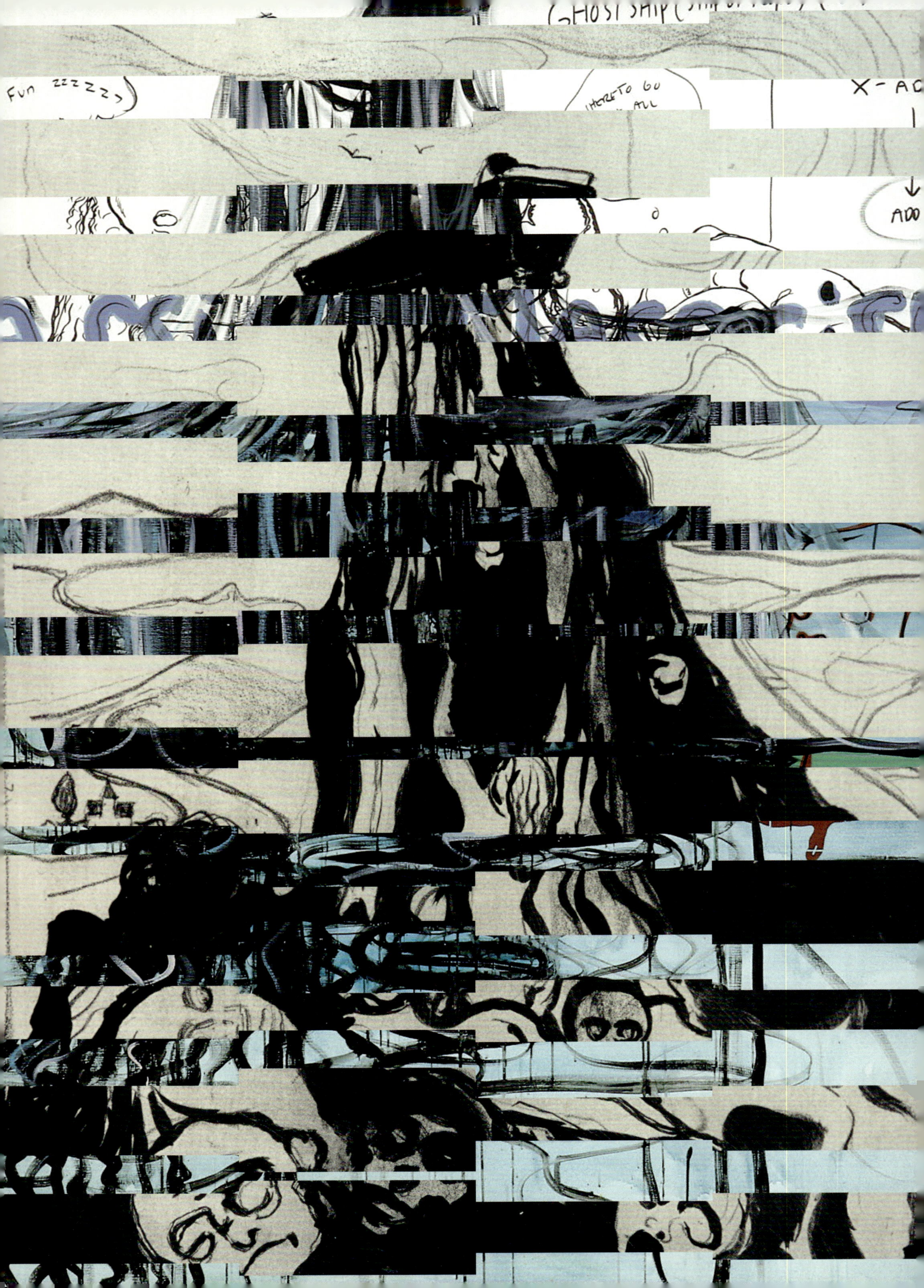
GHOST SHIP
FUN ZZZZZ?
HERE TO GO
ALL
X-A
ADD

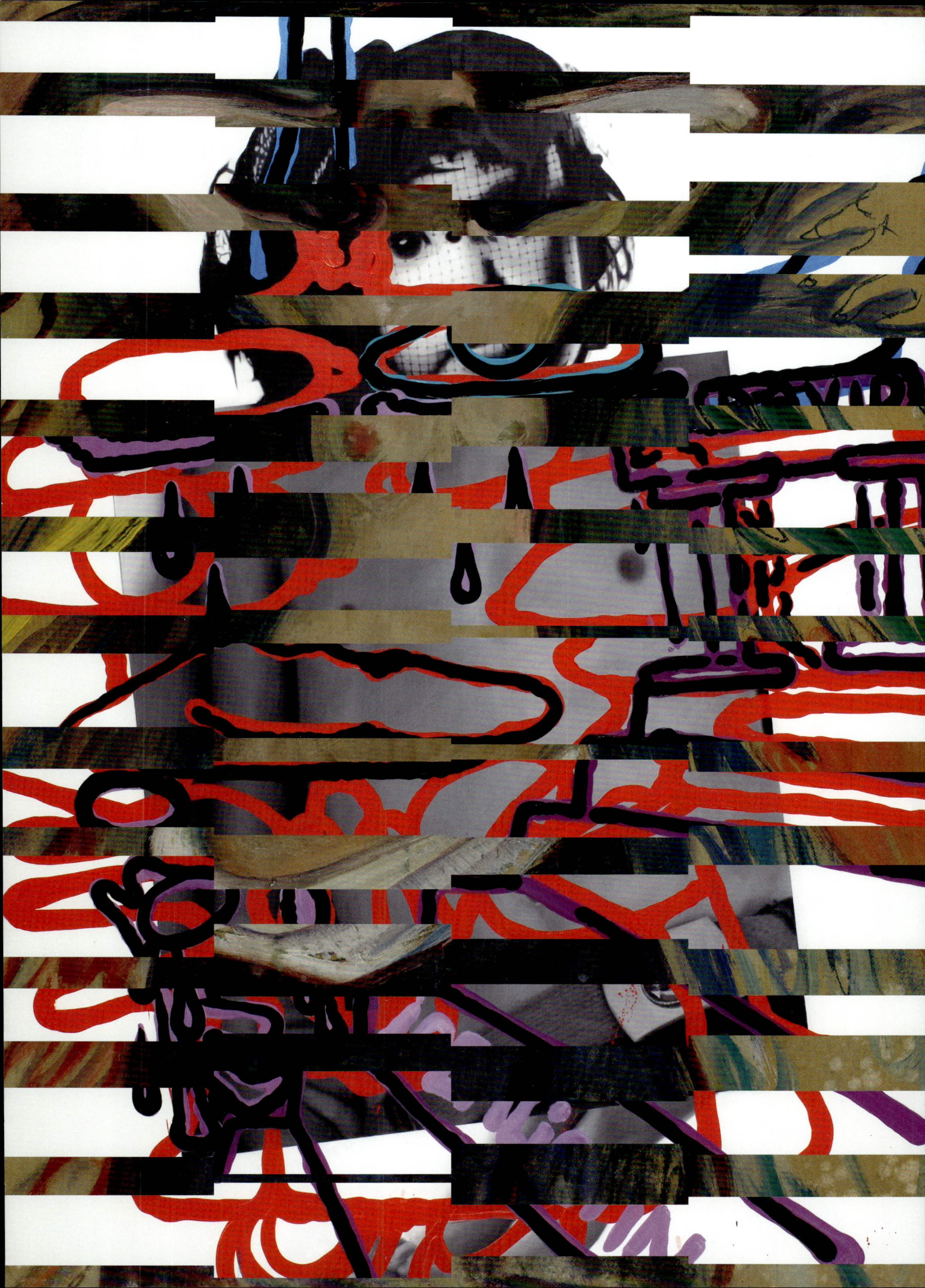

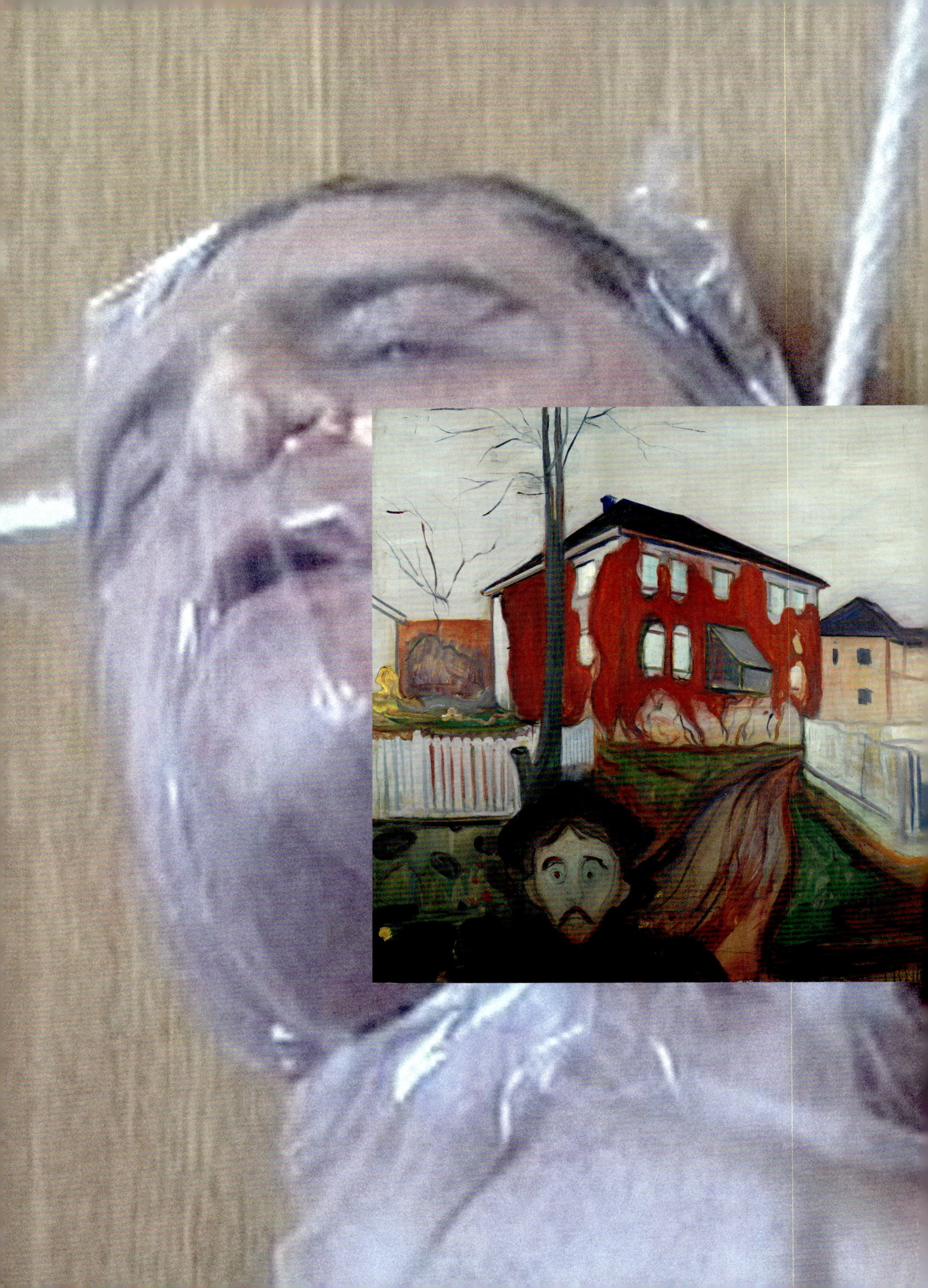

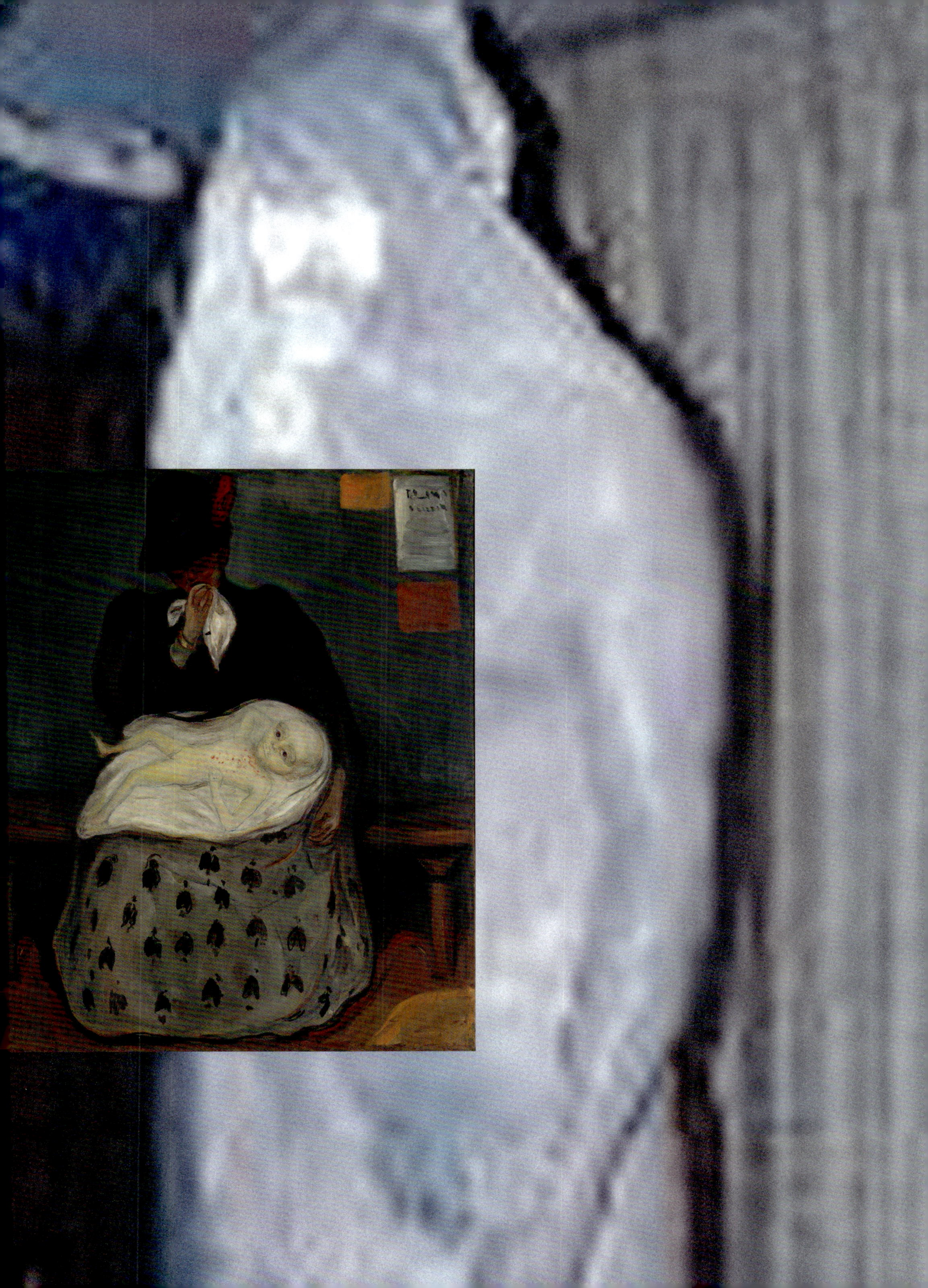

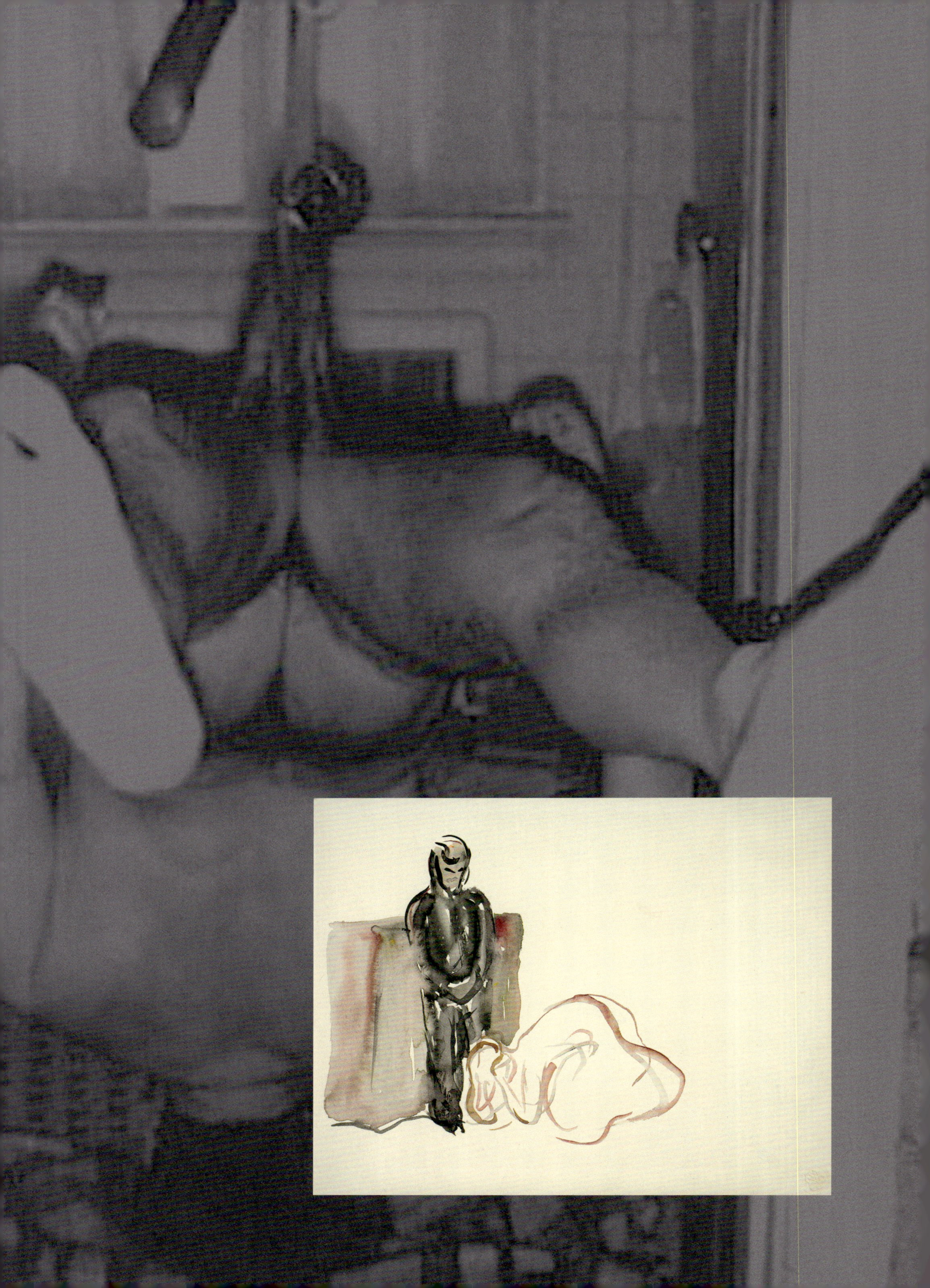

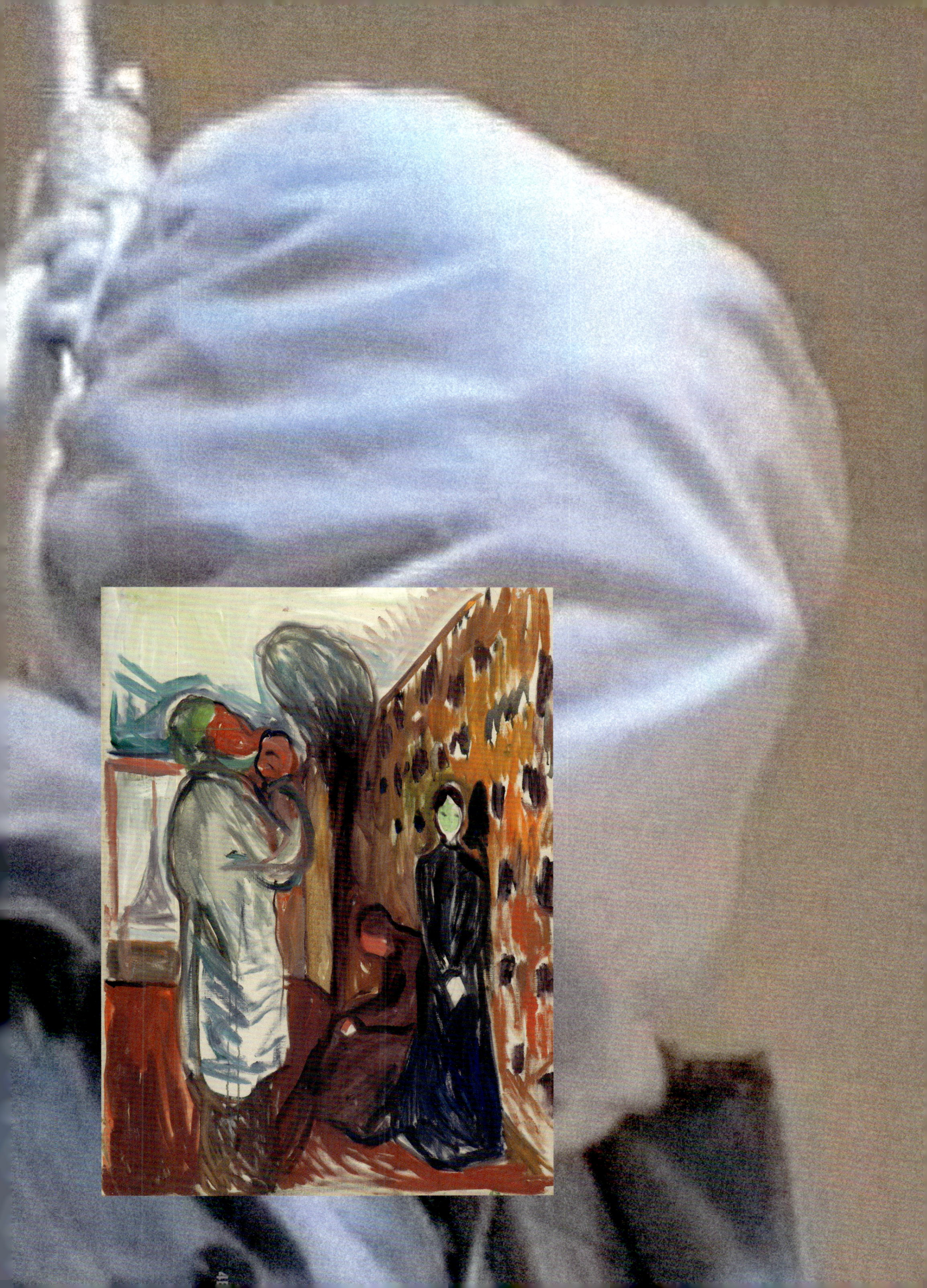

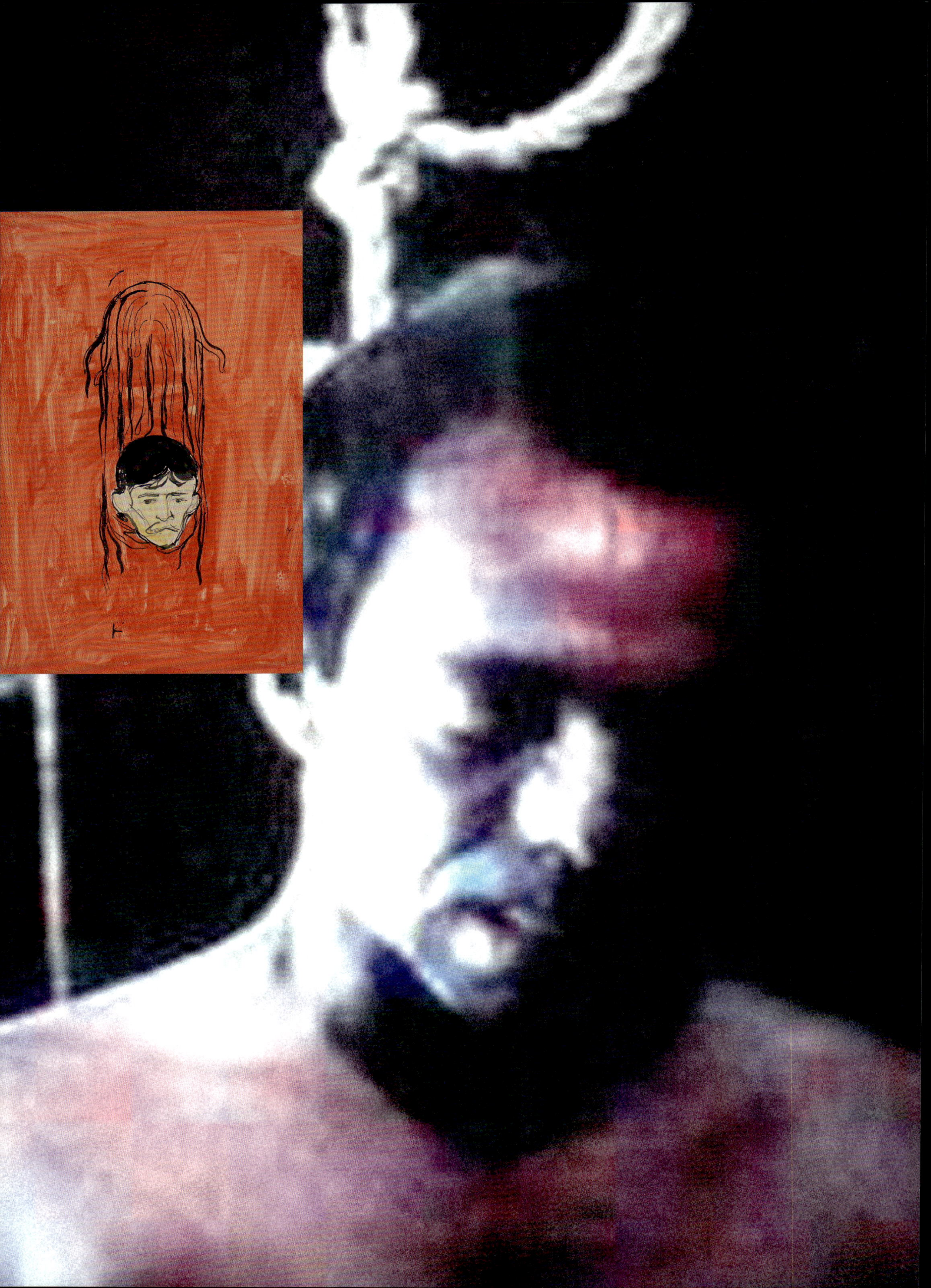

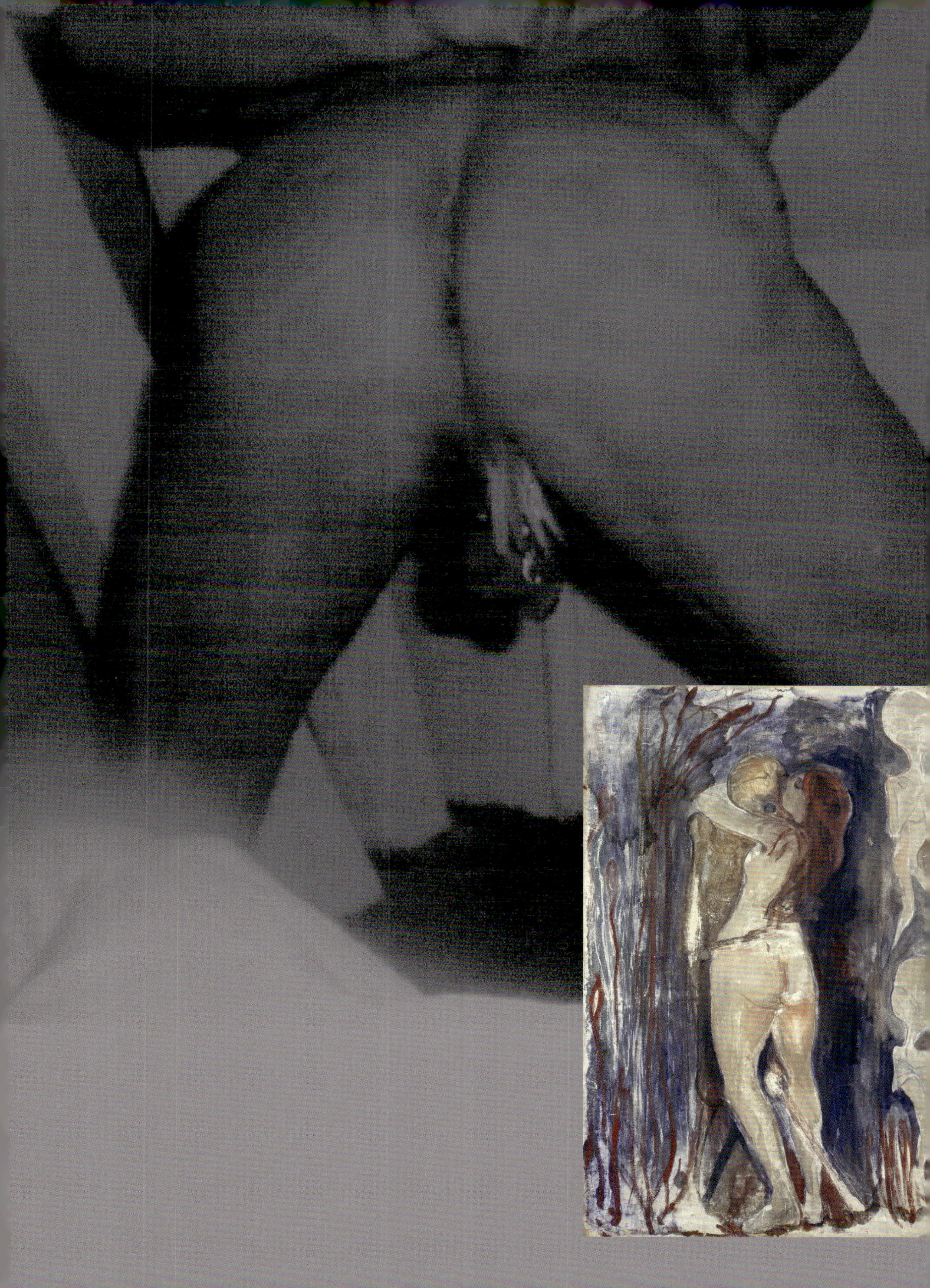

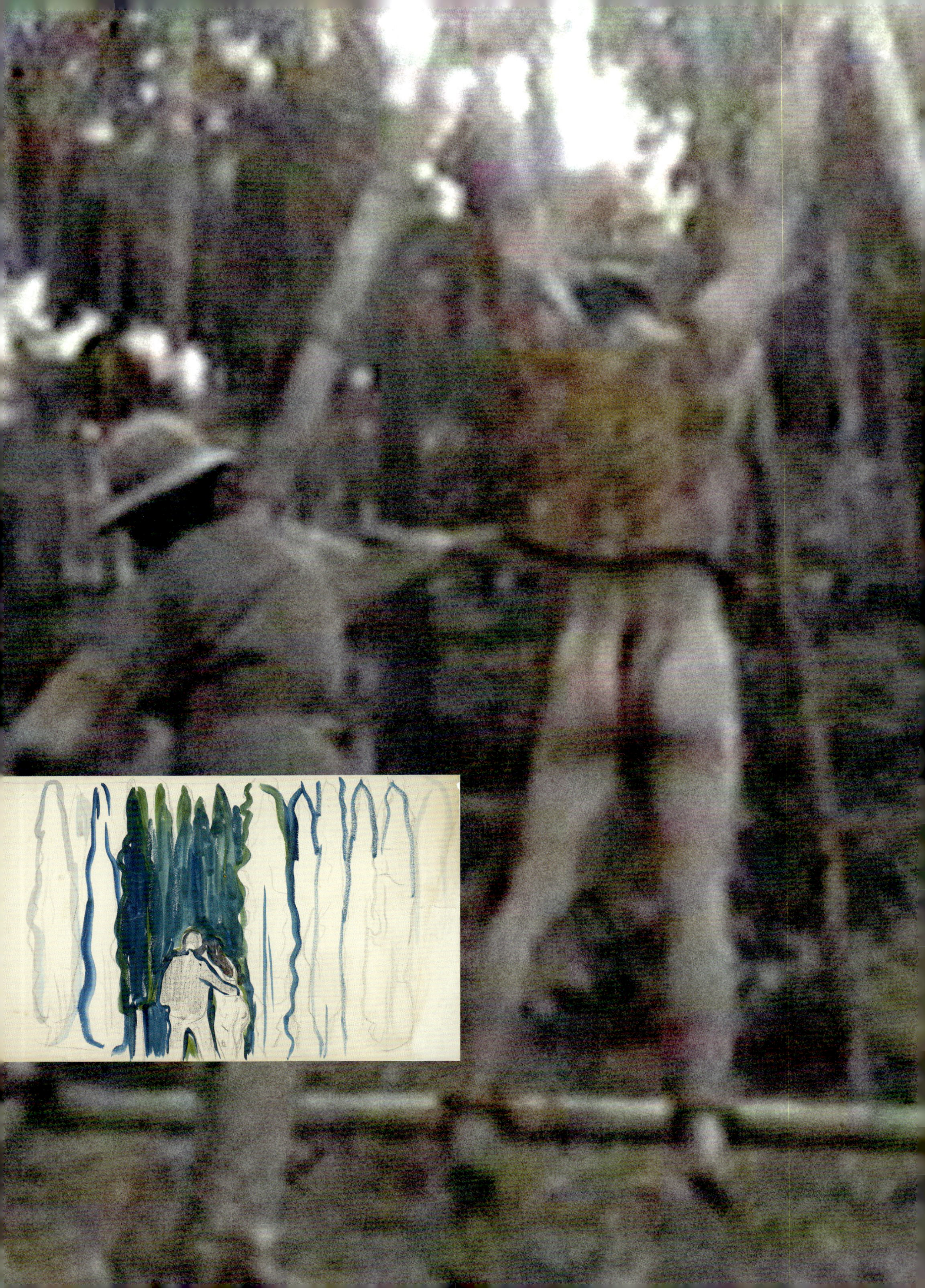

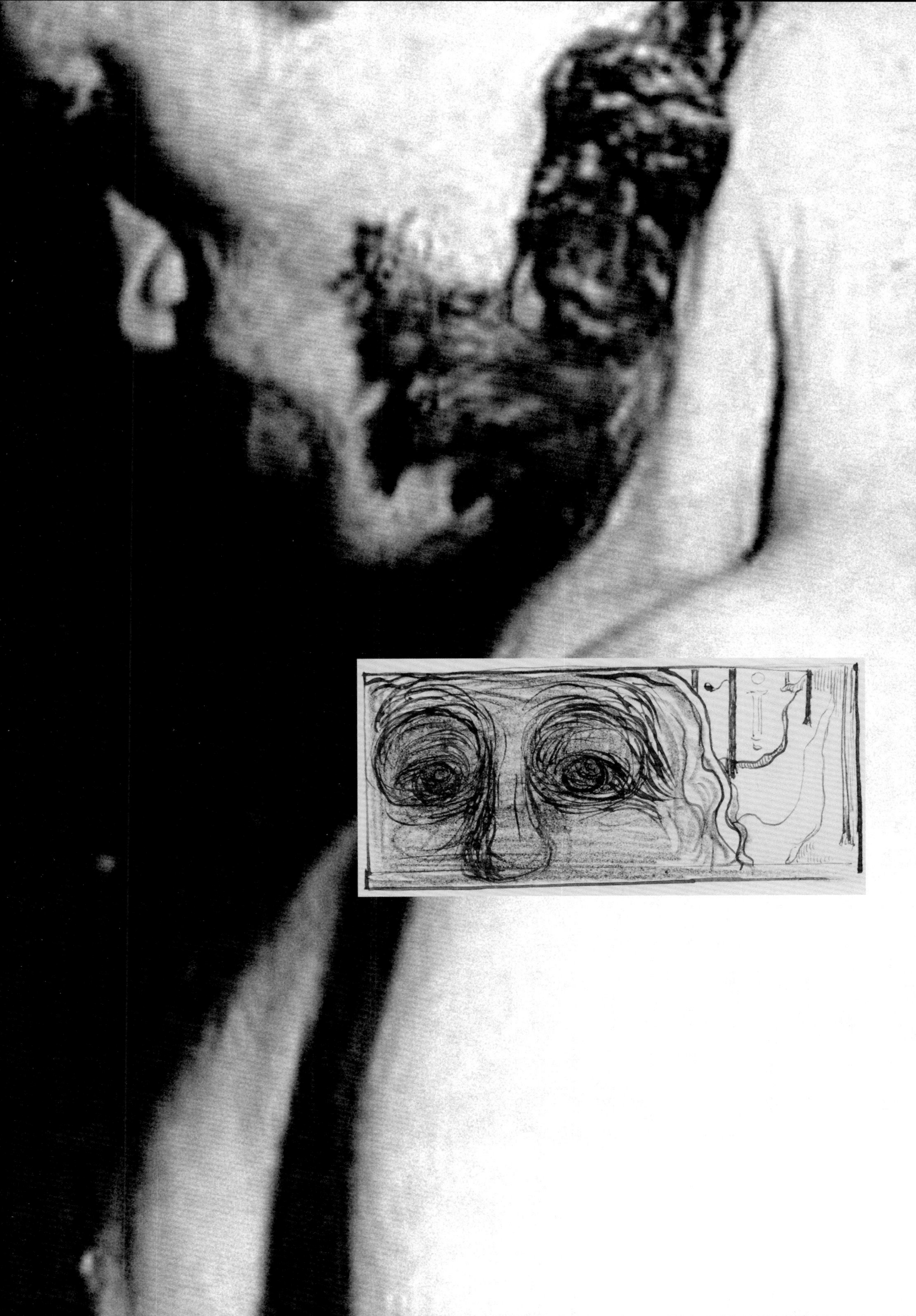

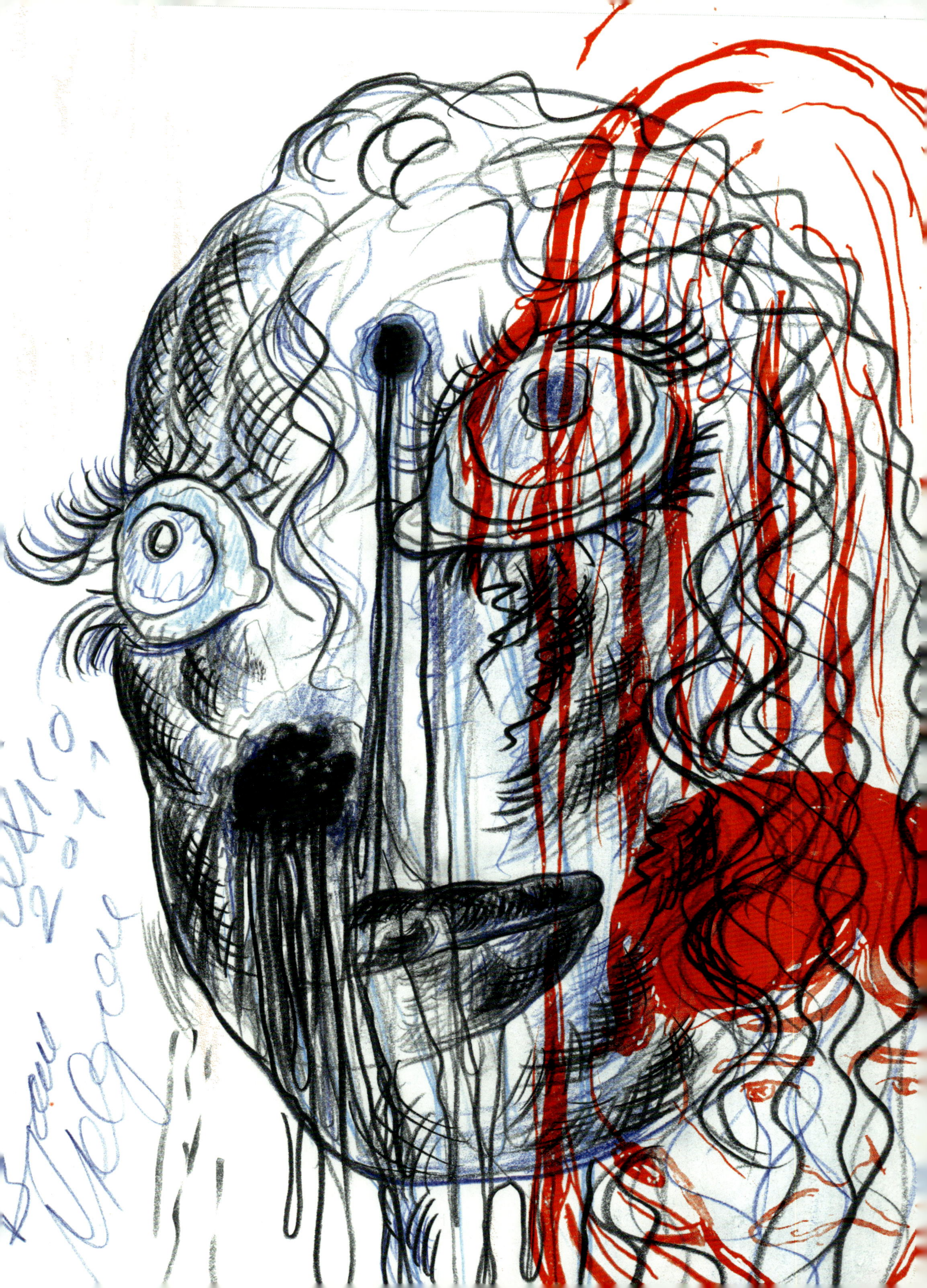

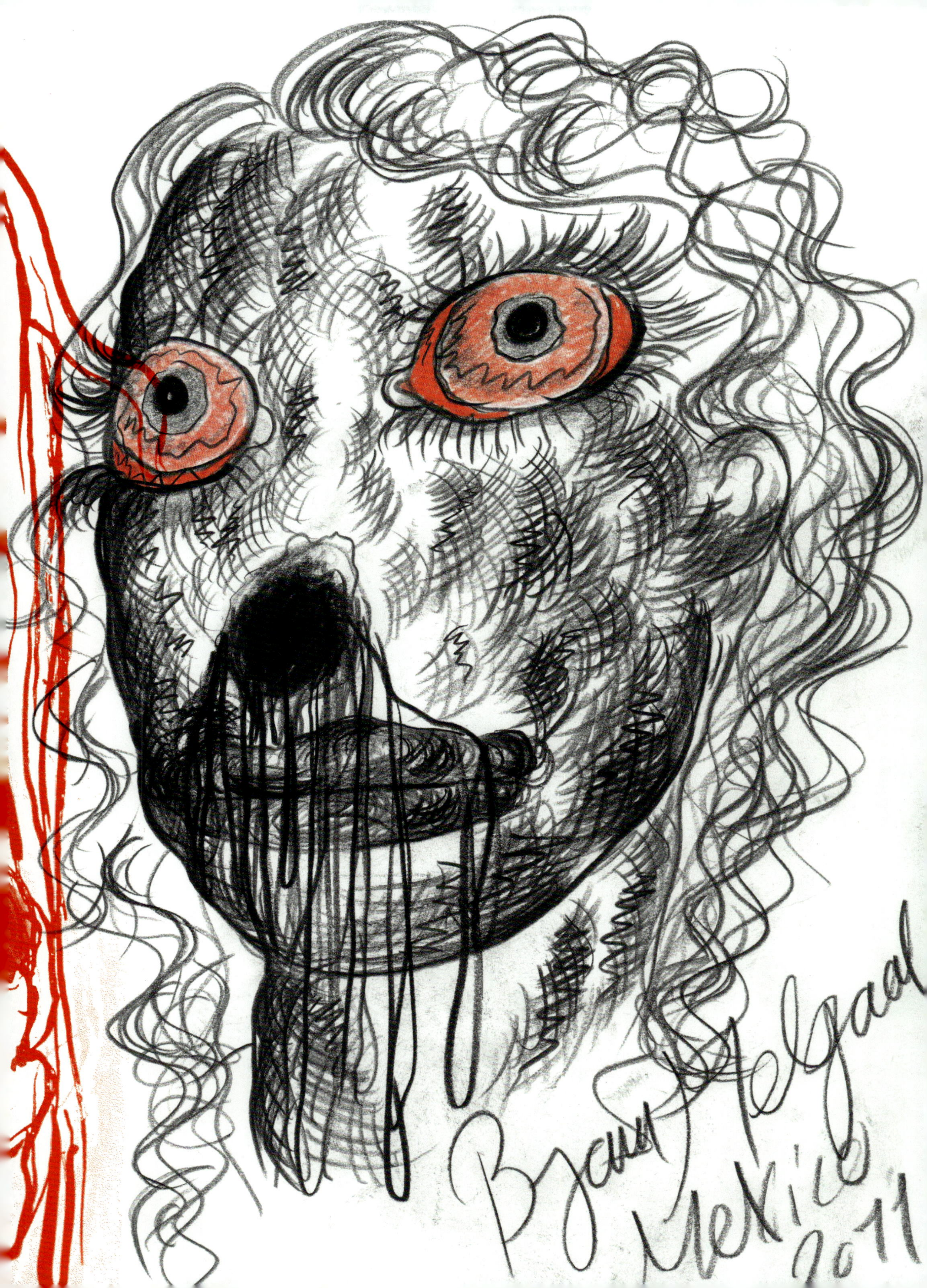

Bjarne Melgaard
Mexico
2011

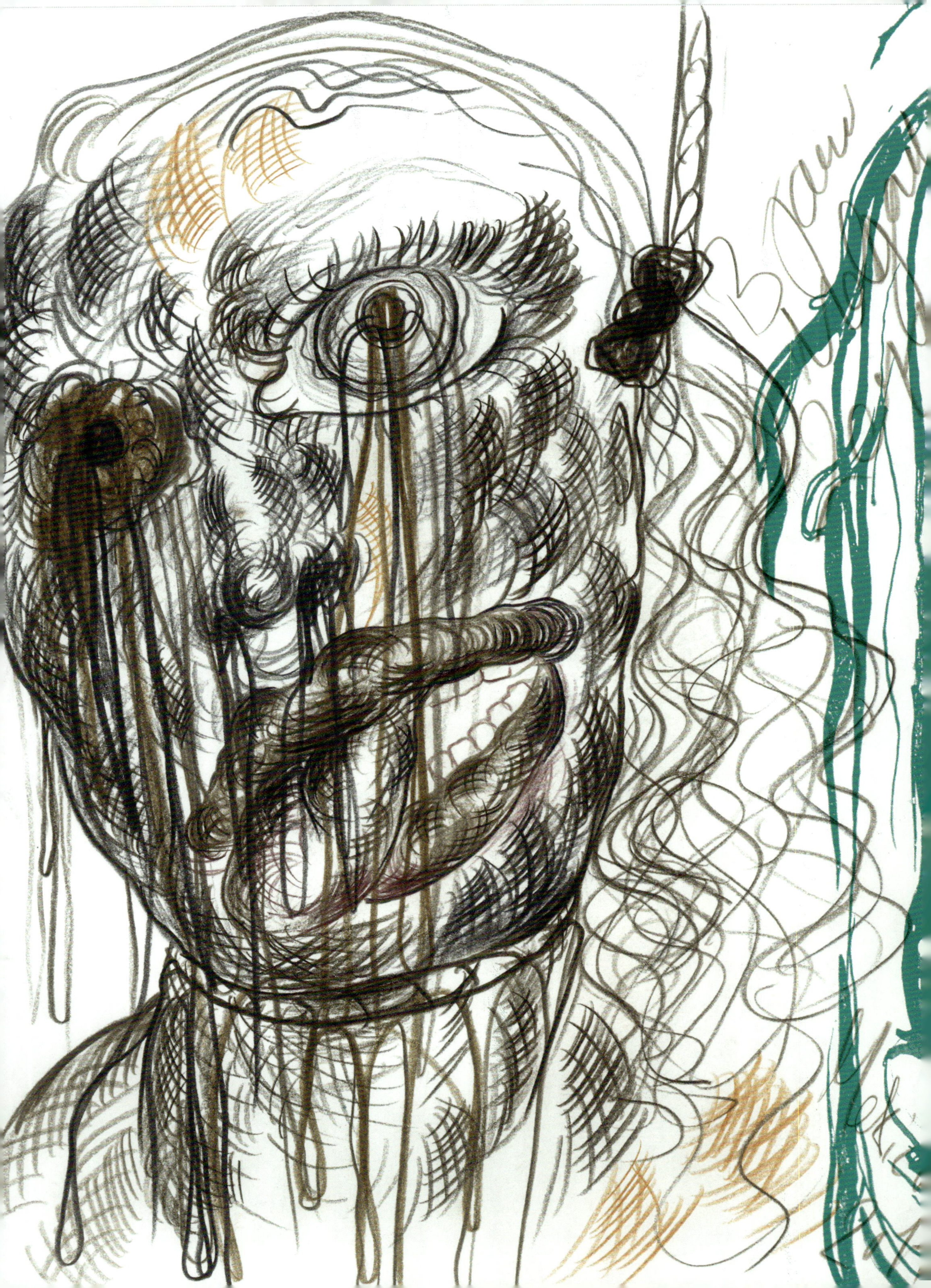

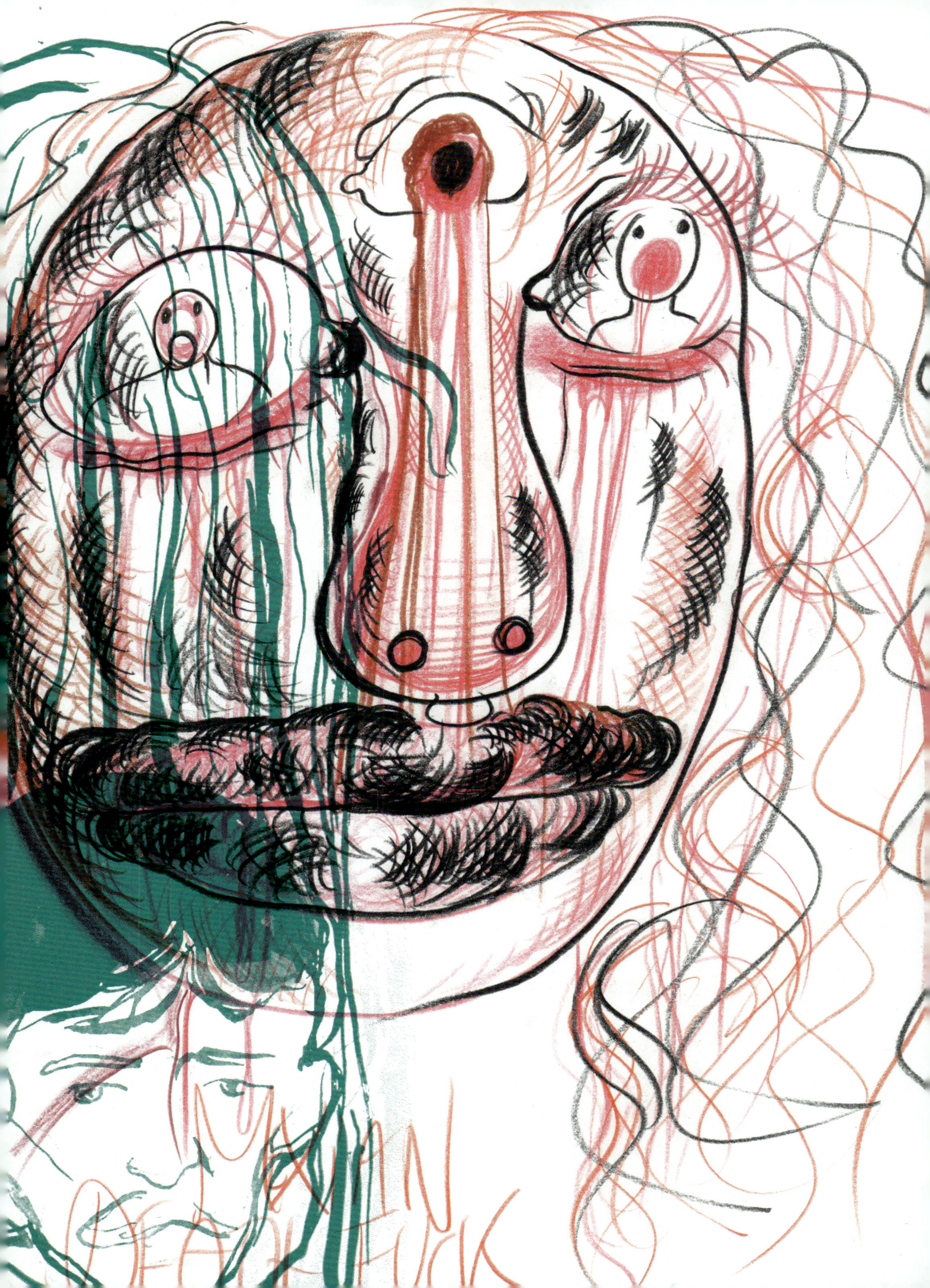

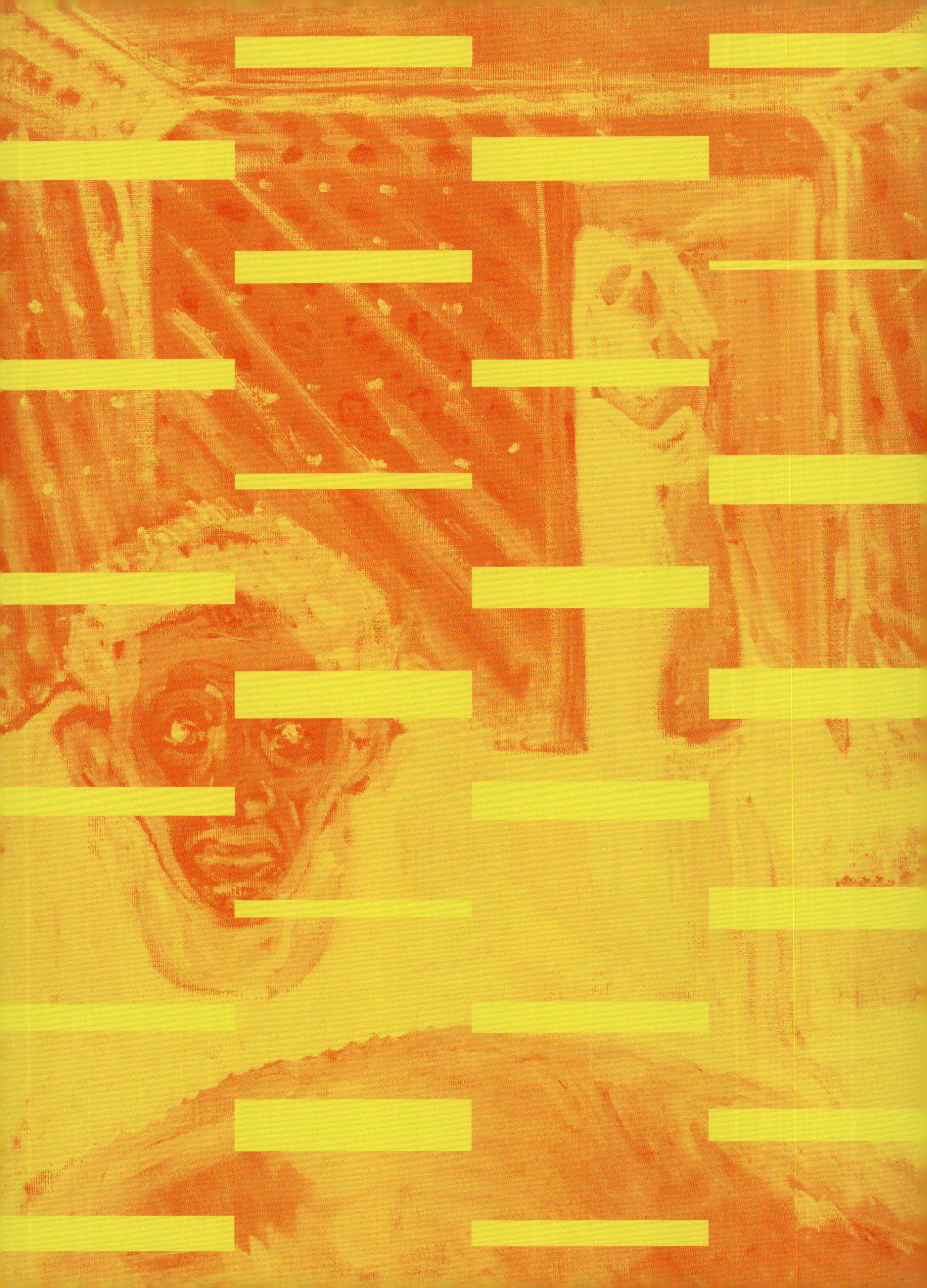

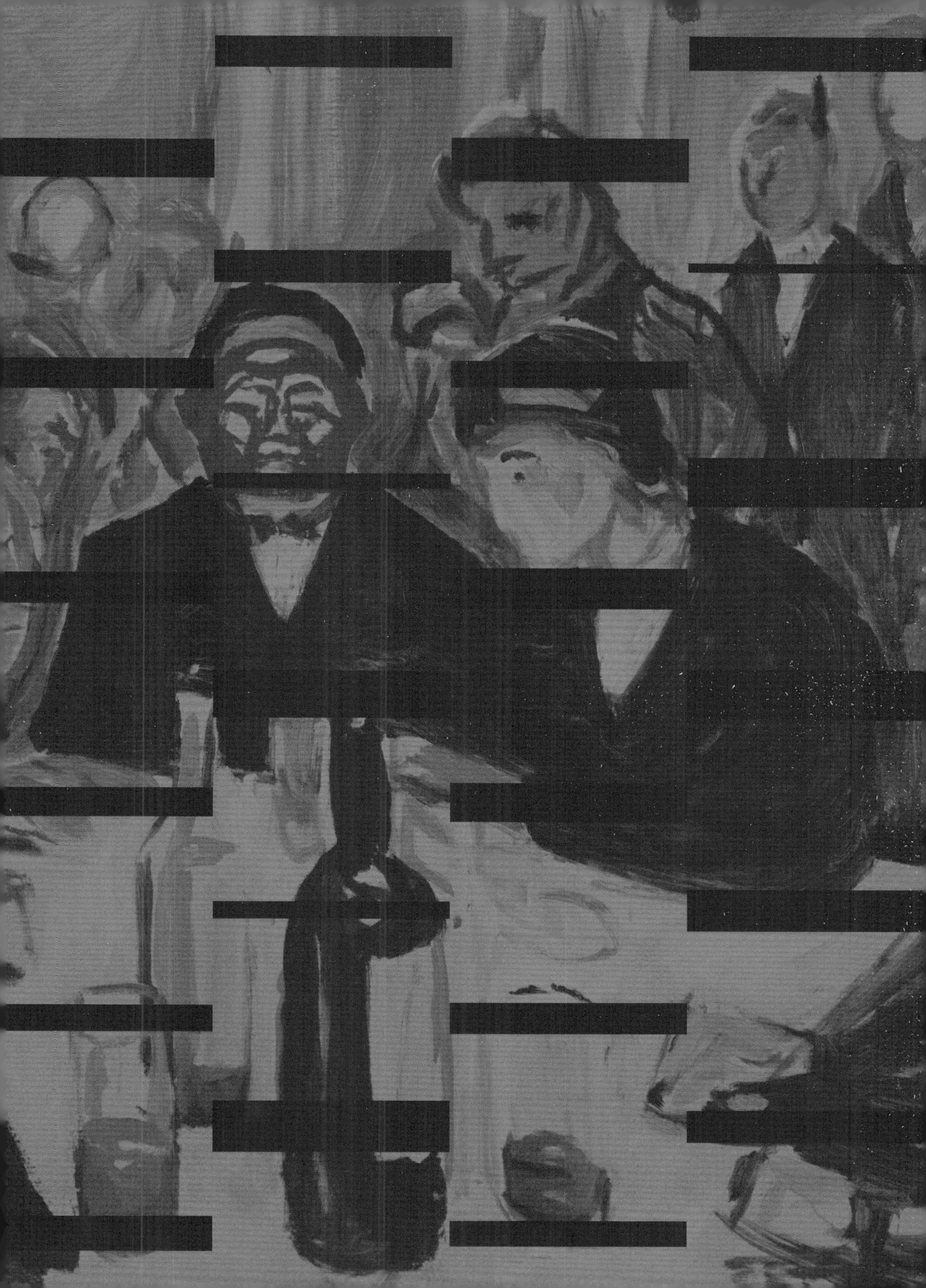

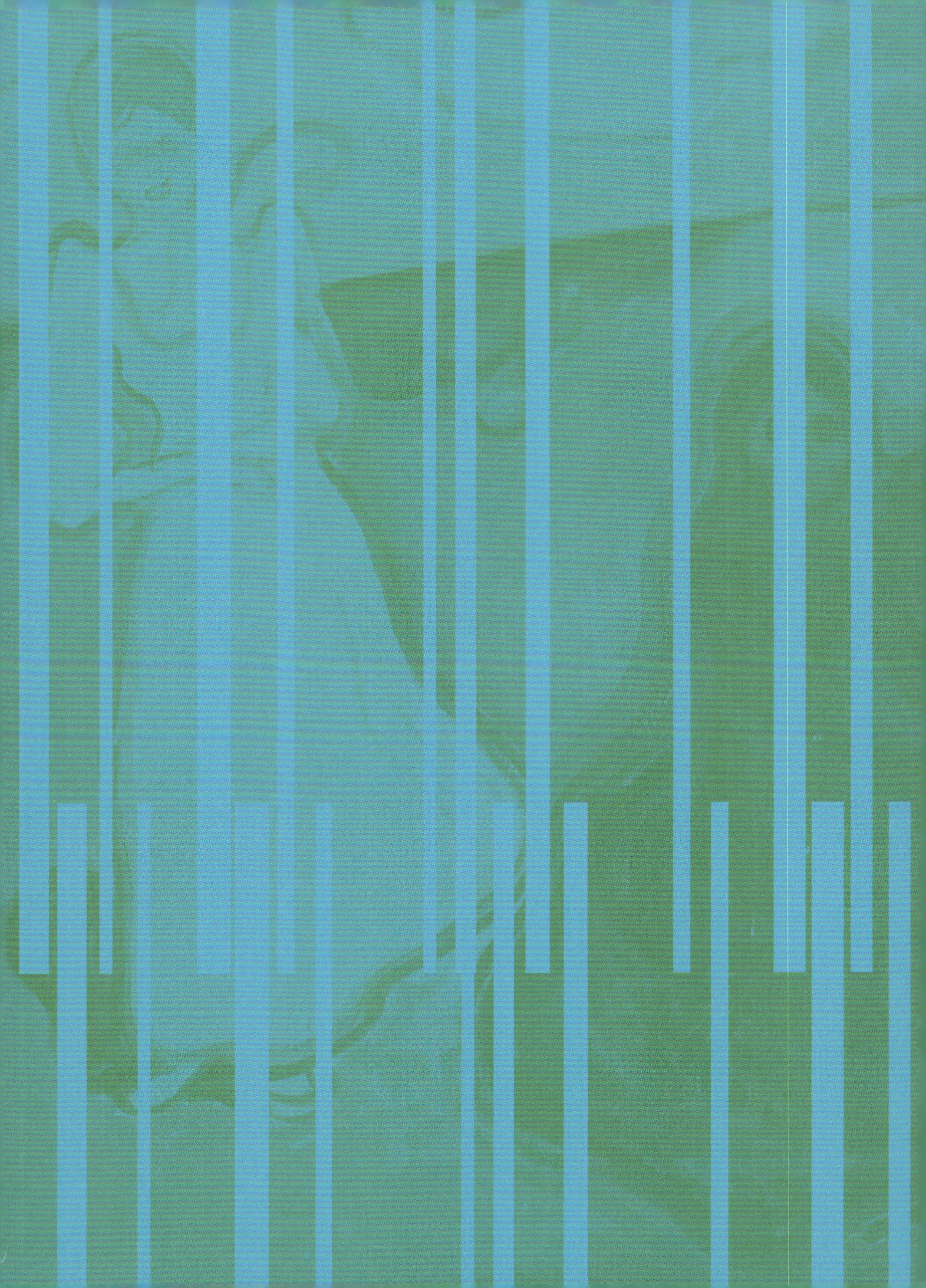

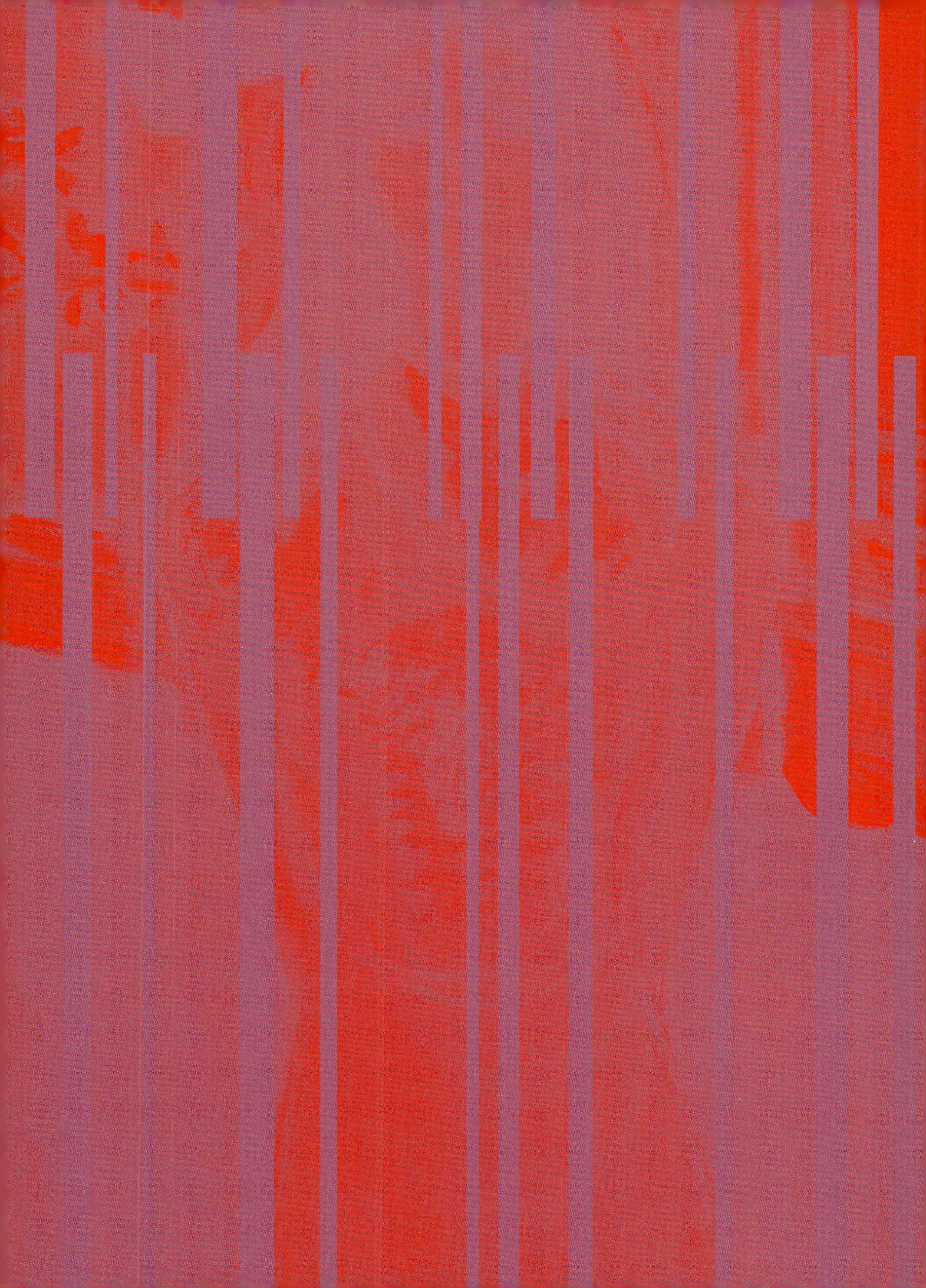

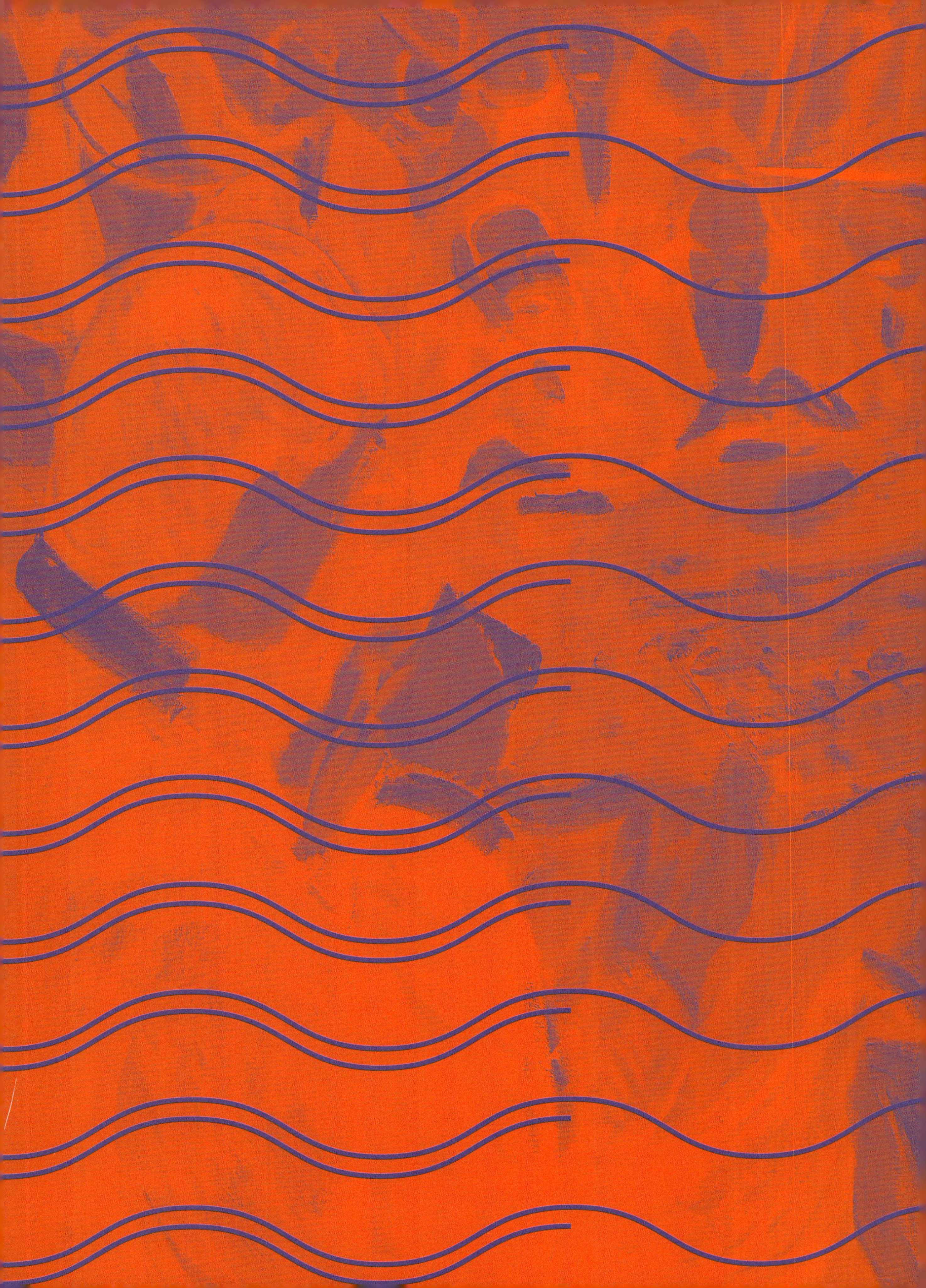

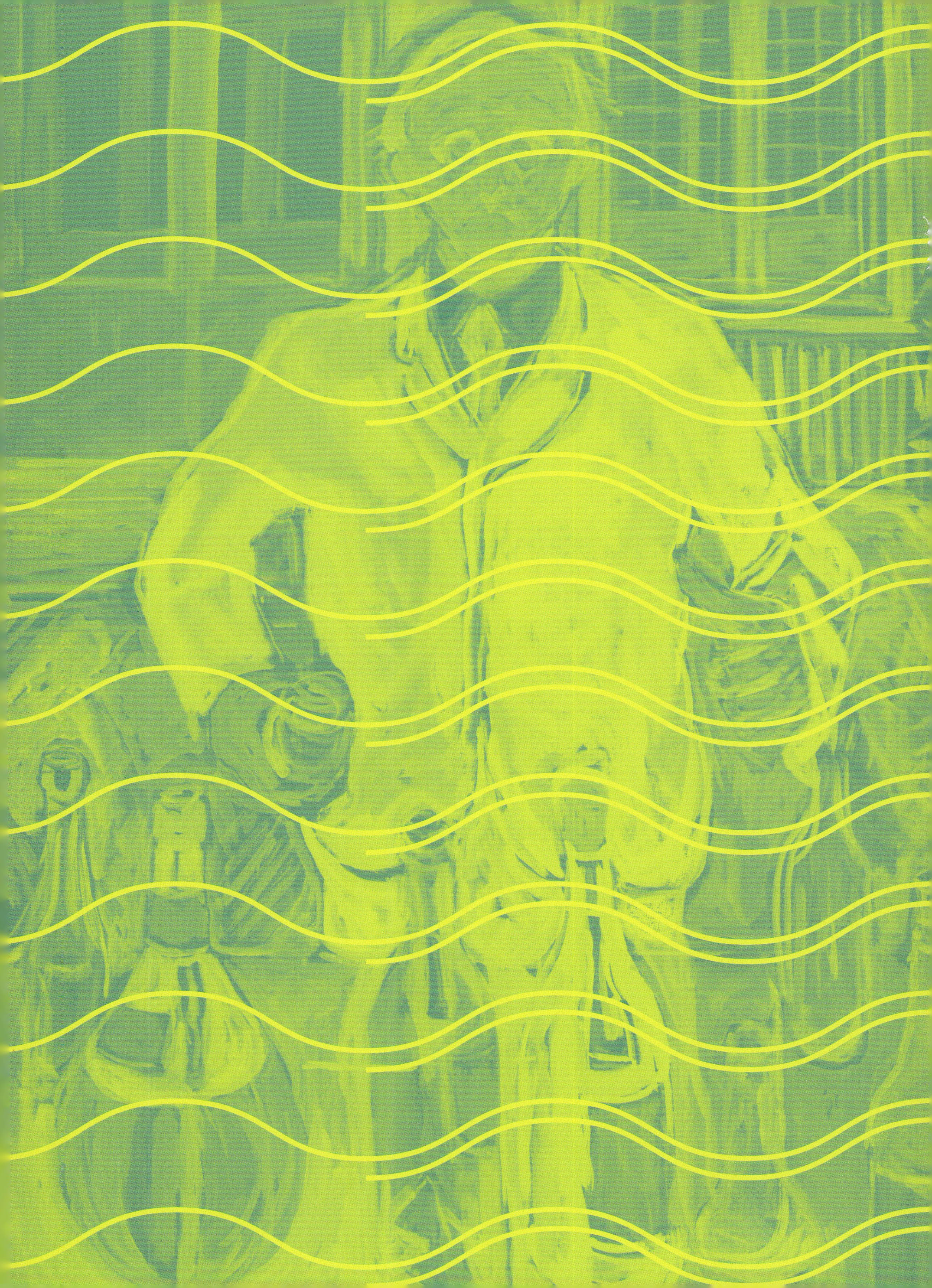

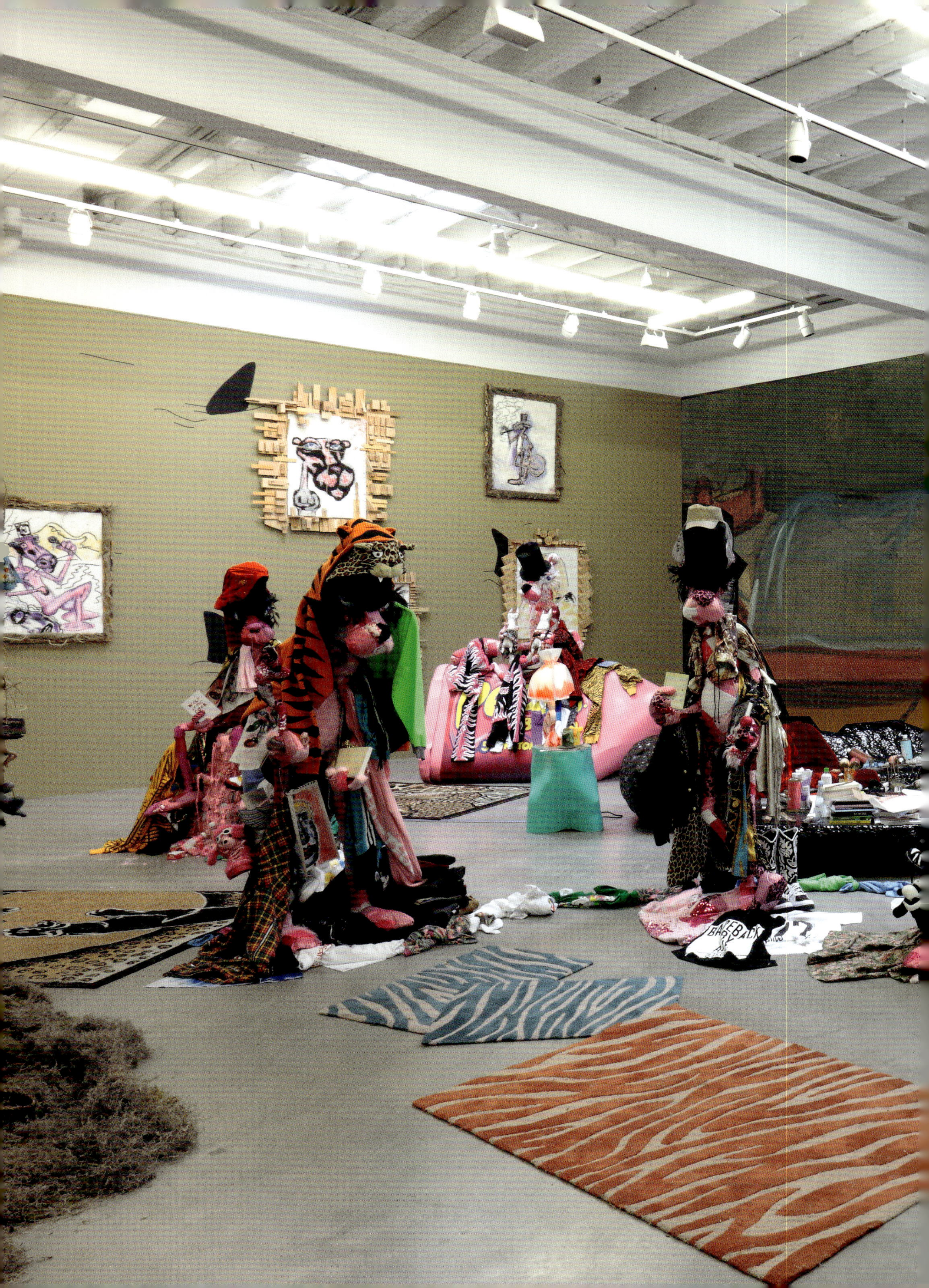

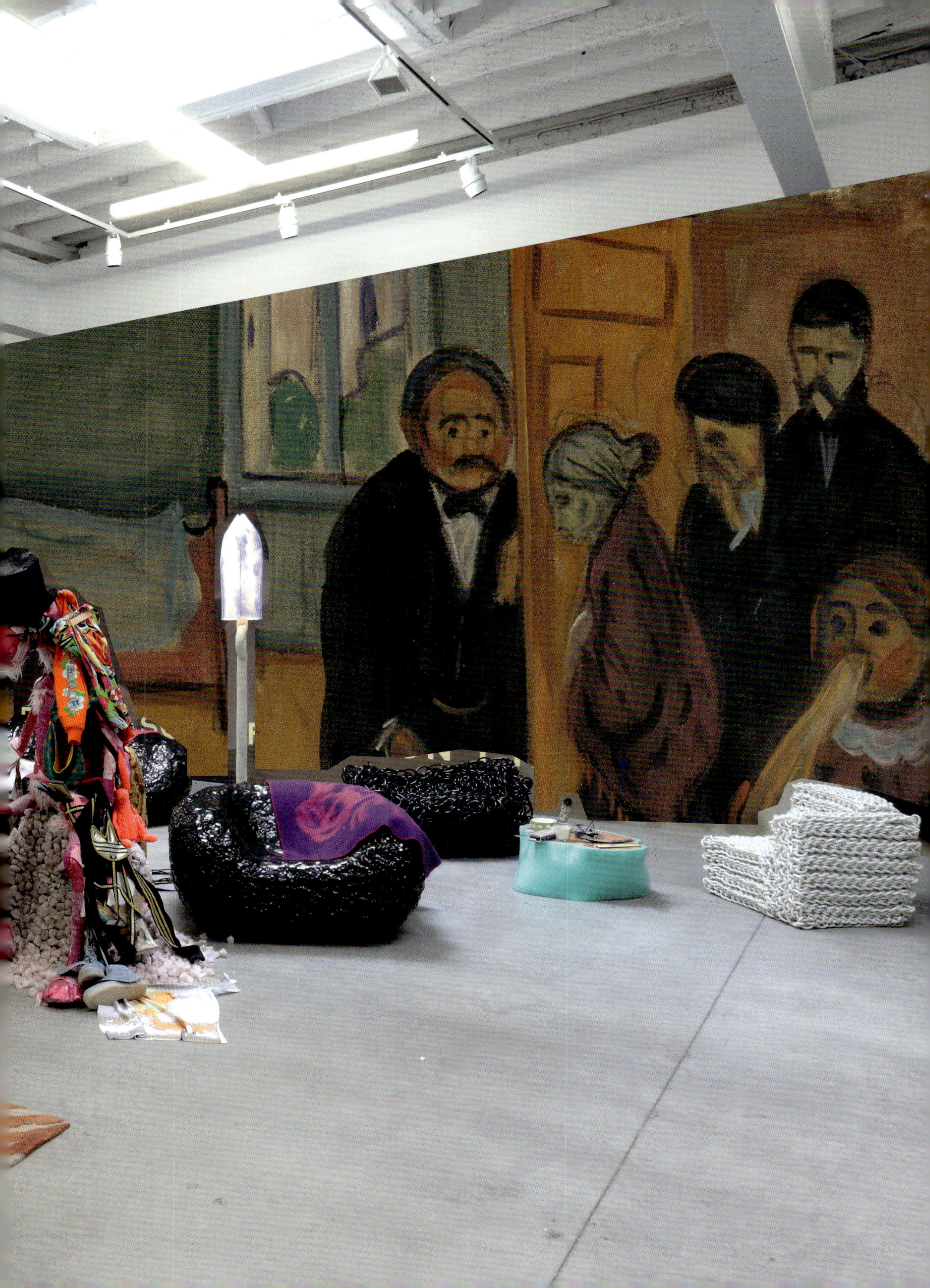

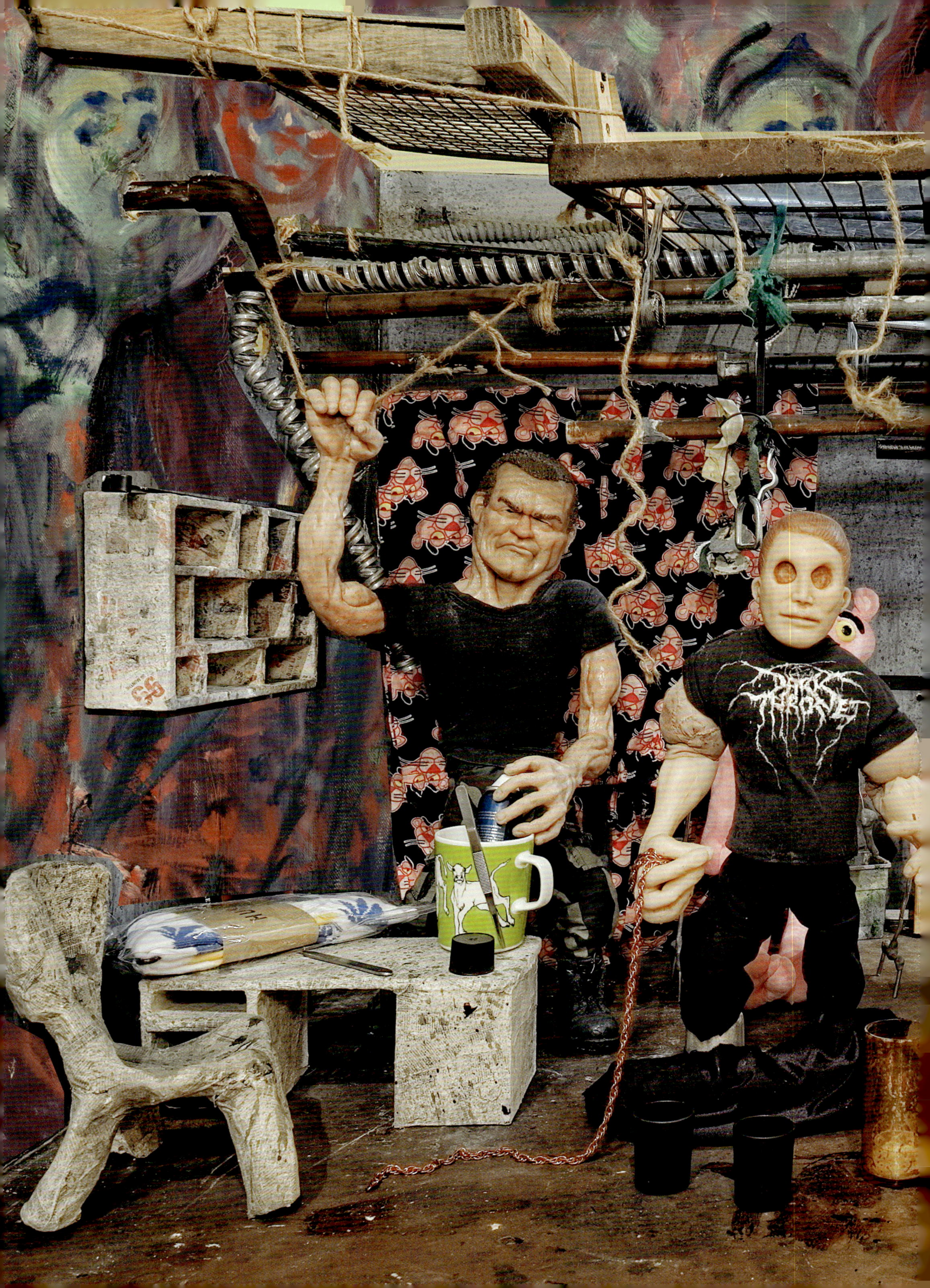

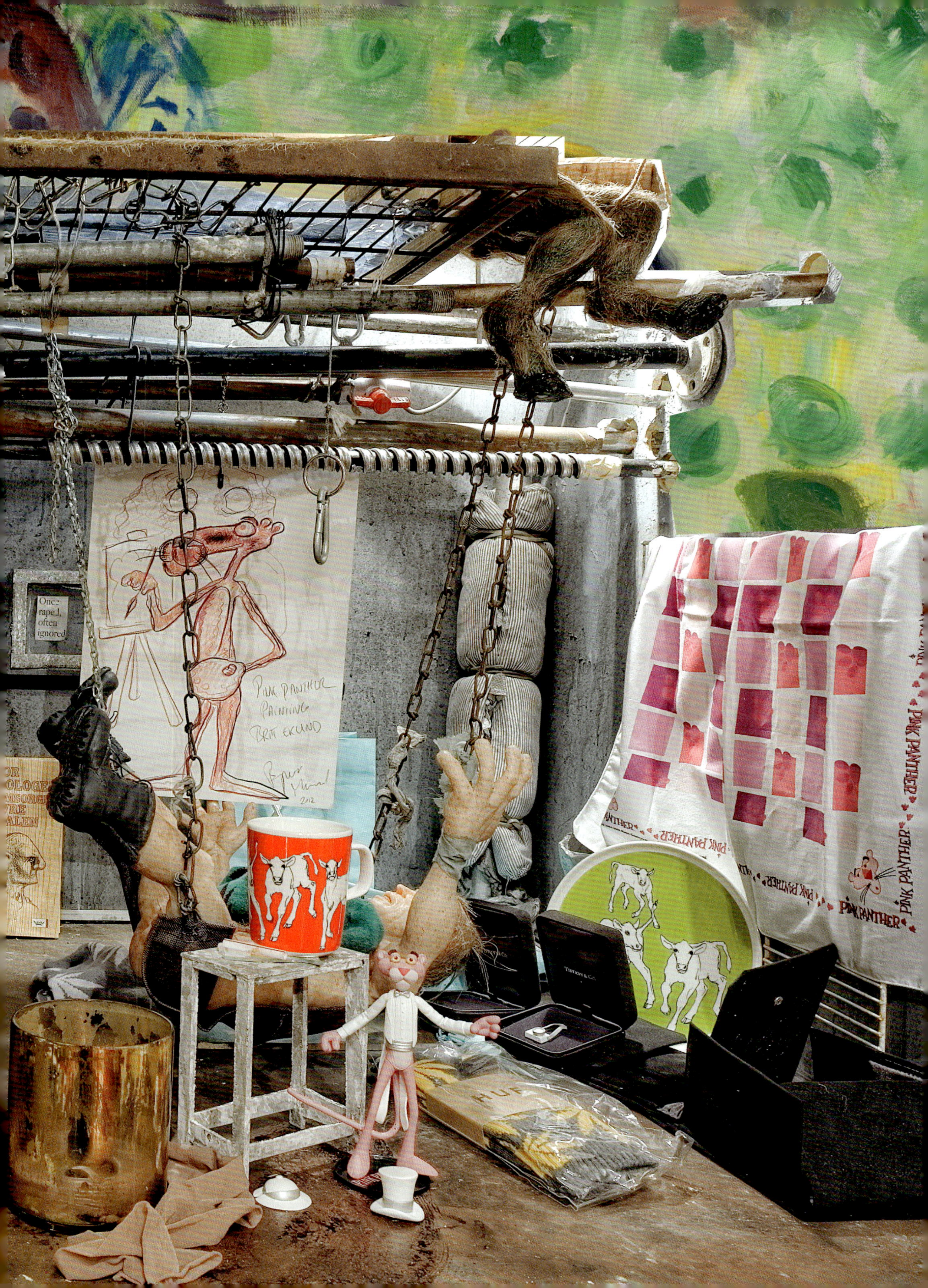

PINK PANTHER
PAINTING
BRITT EKLUND
2012
One-
rape l,
often
ignored
PINK PANTHER
PINK PANTHER
PINK PANTHER
PINK PANTHER

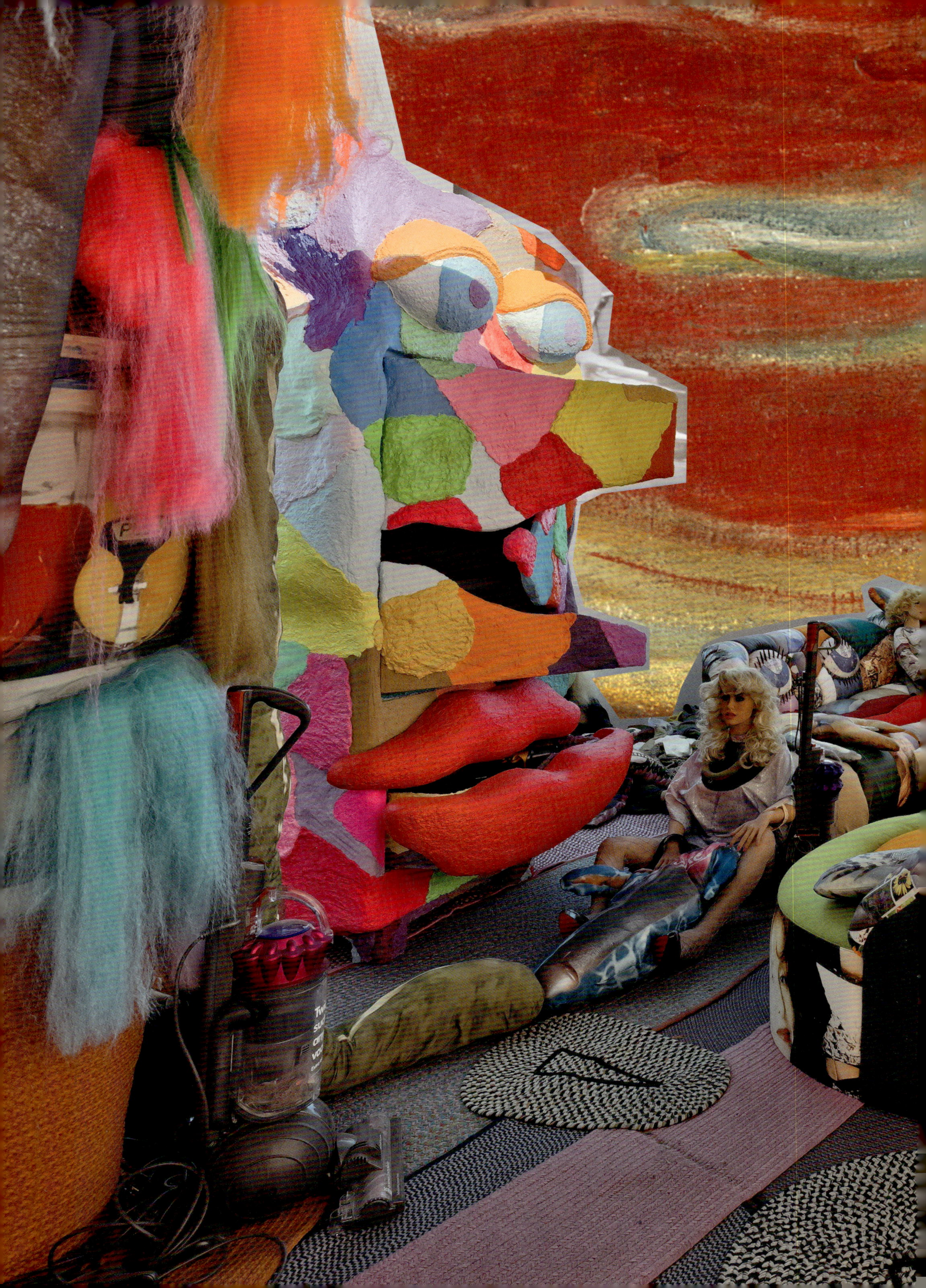

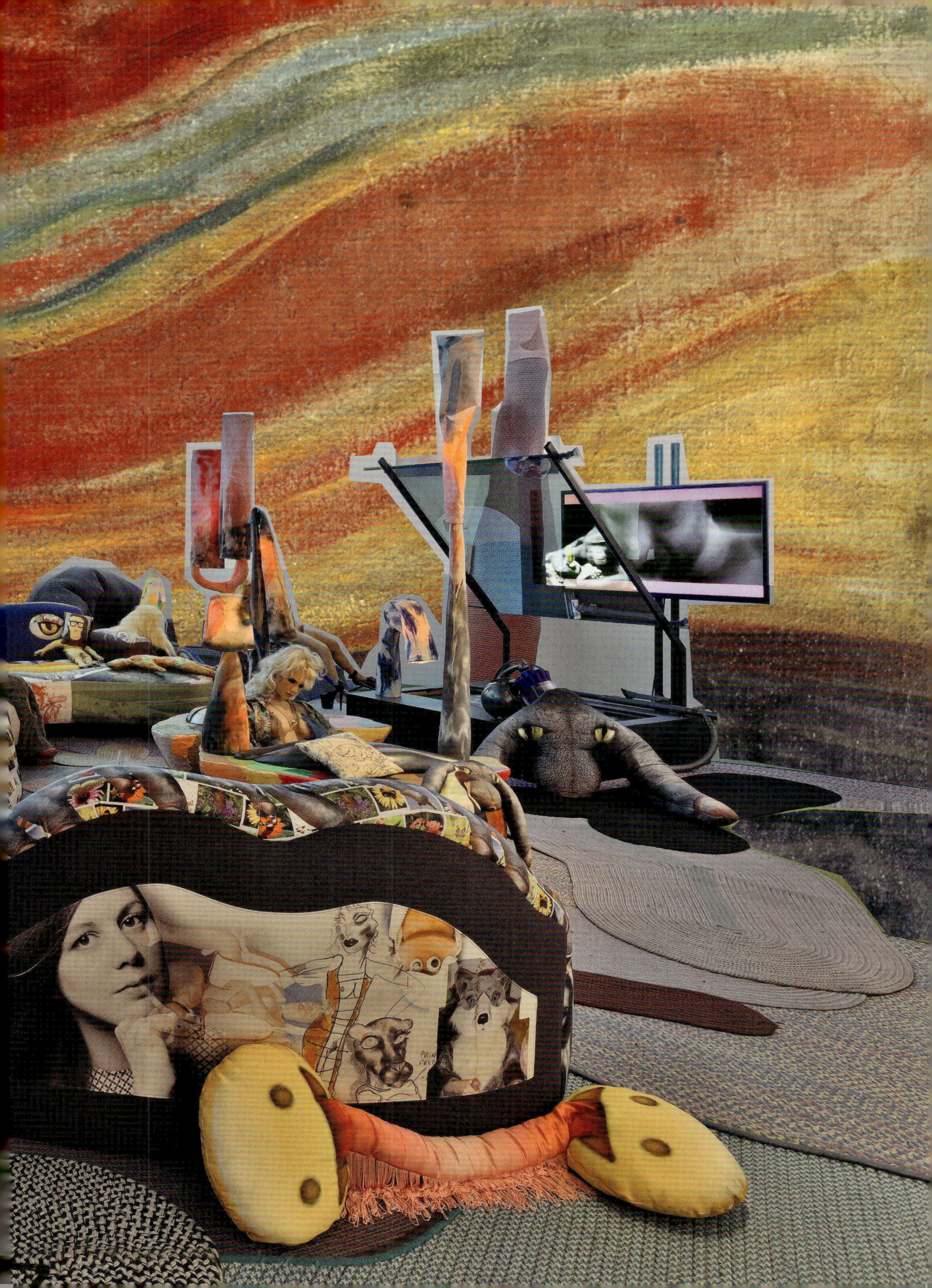

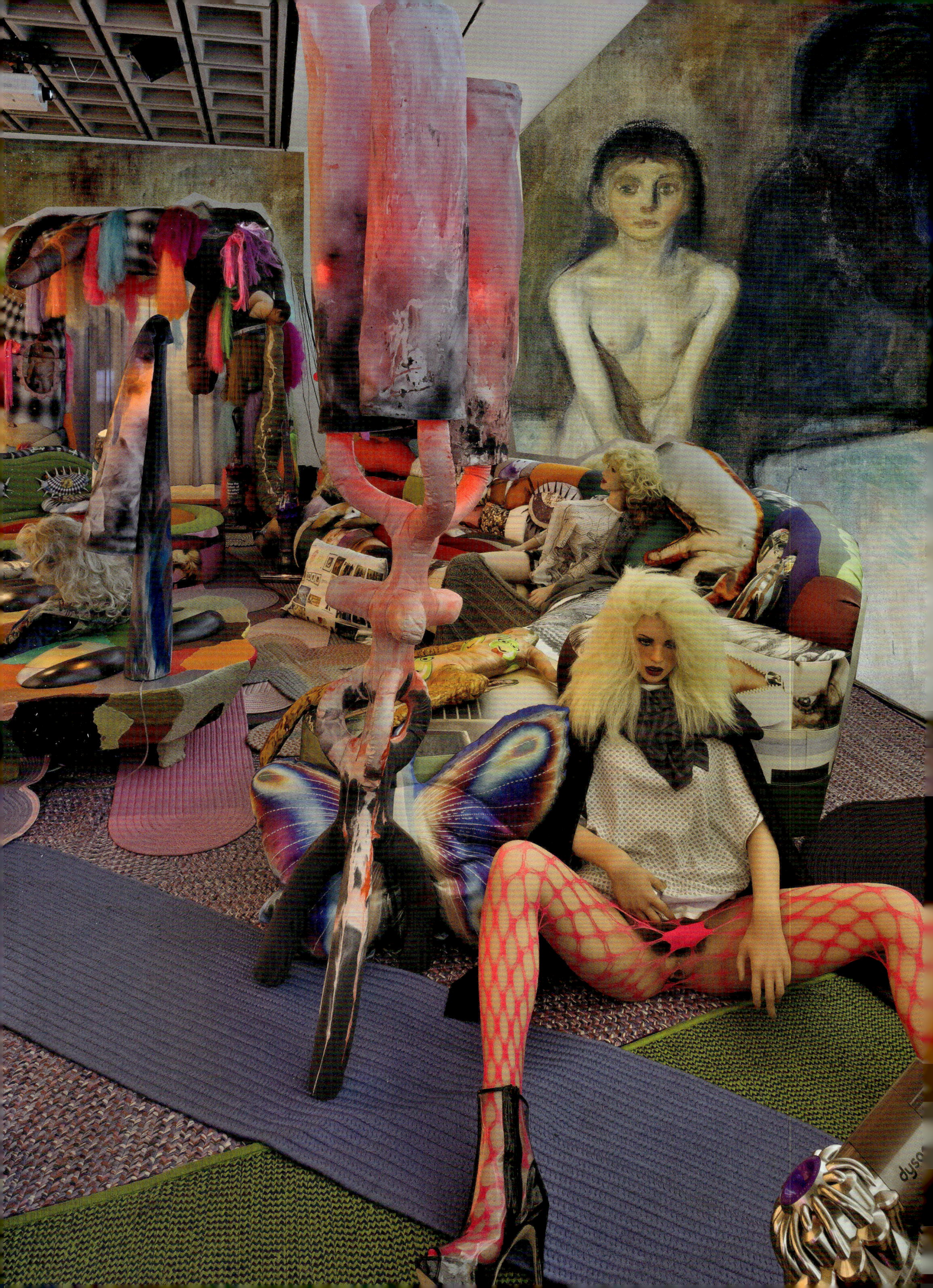

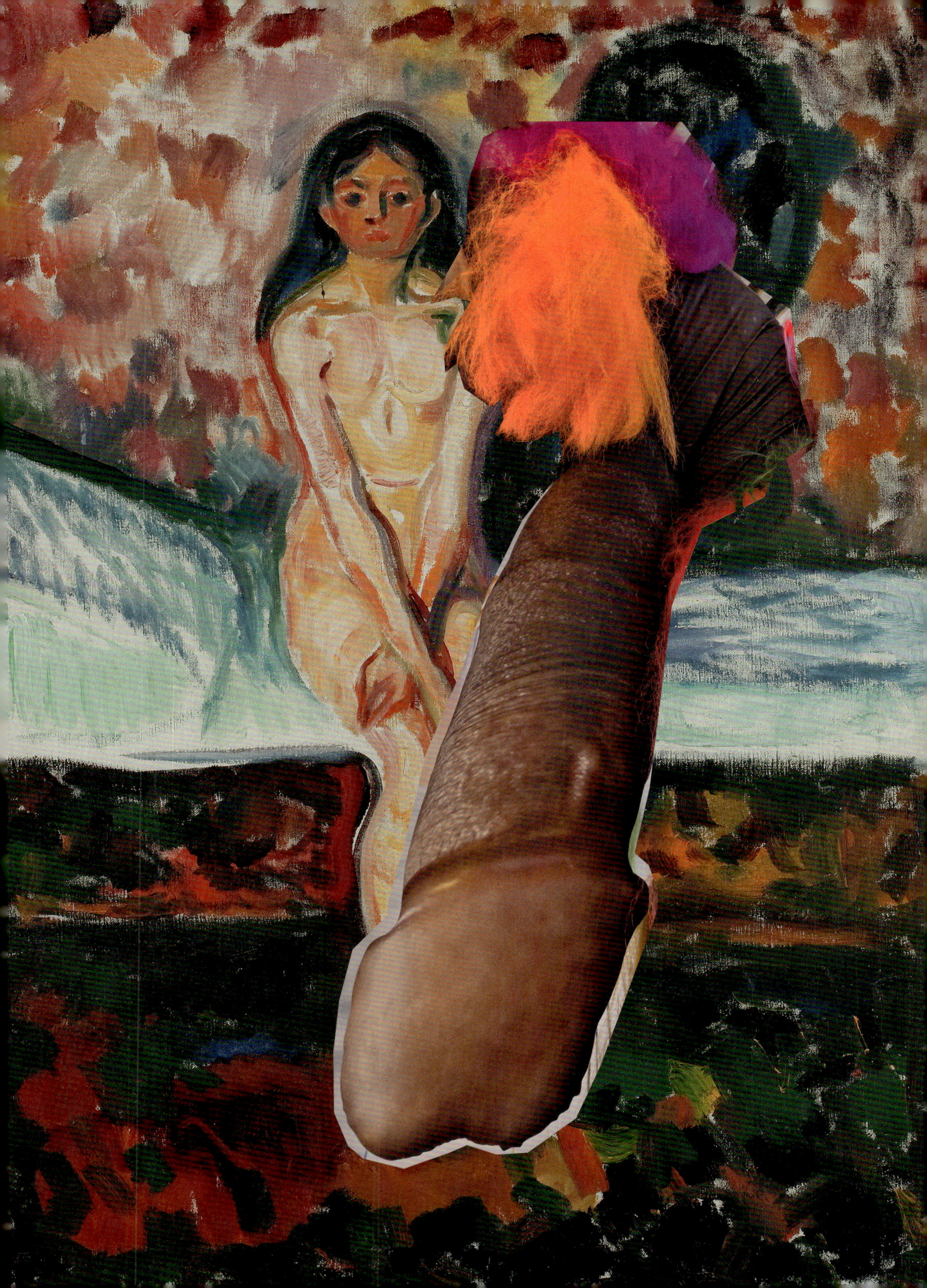

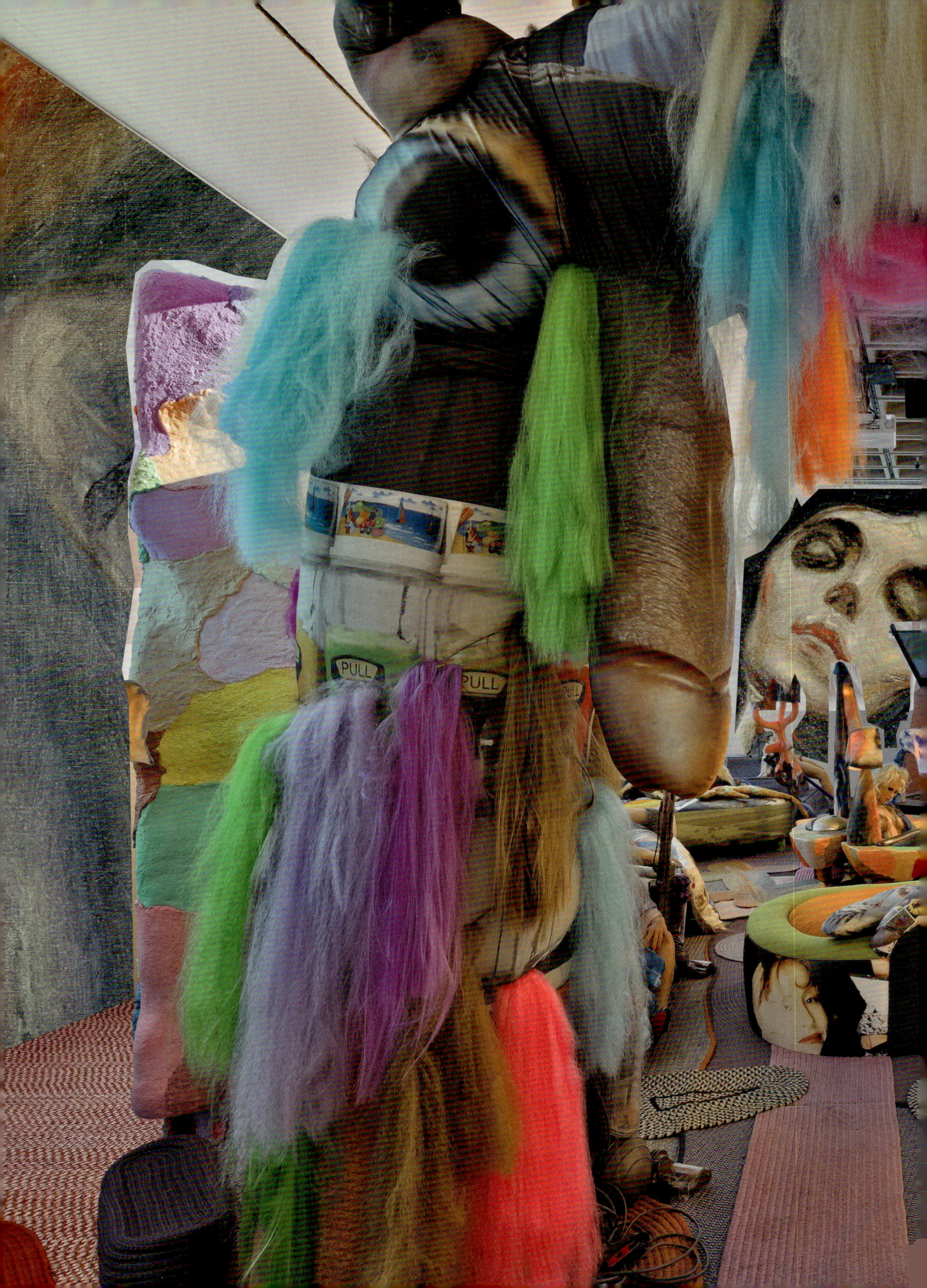

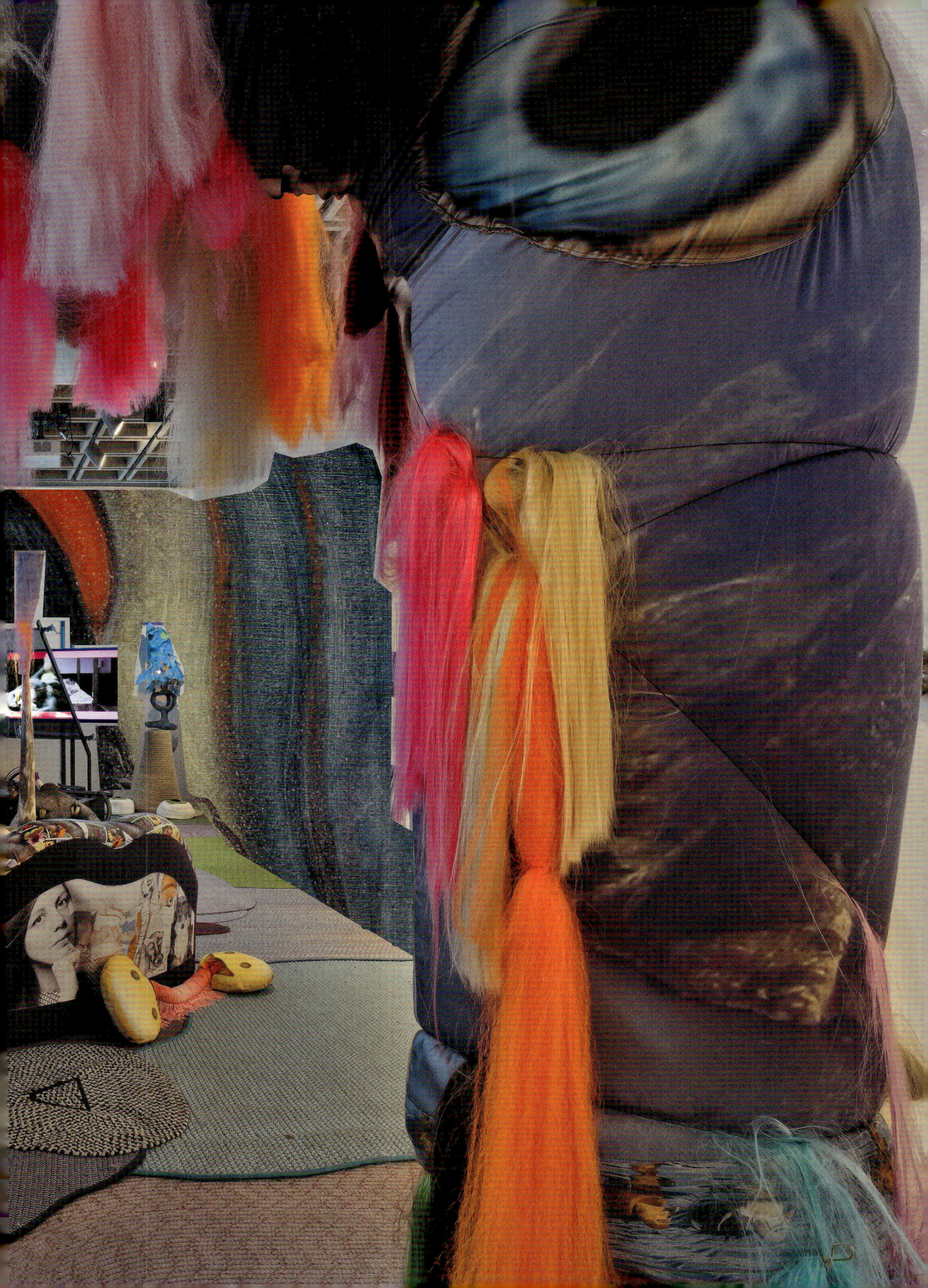

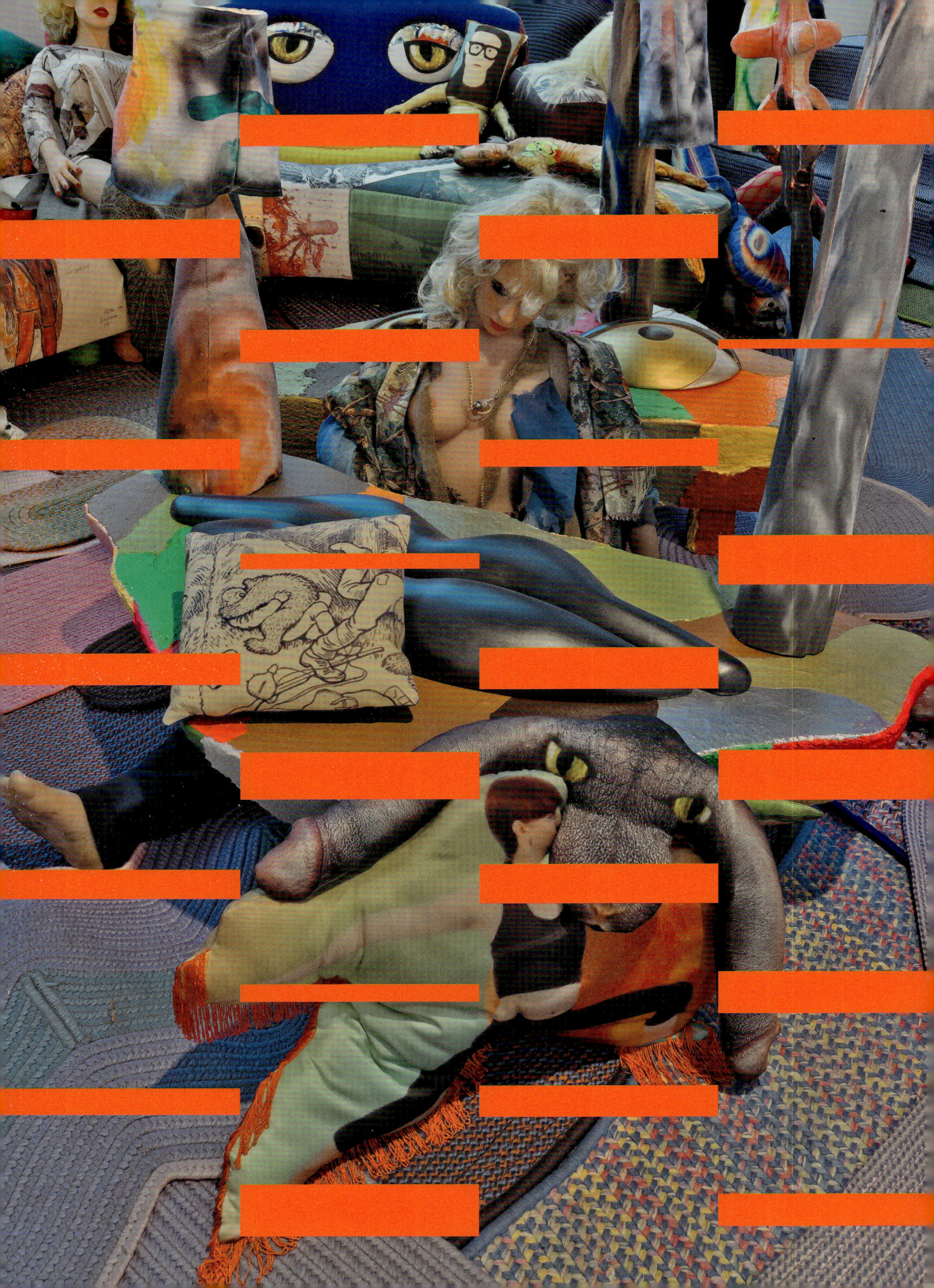

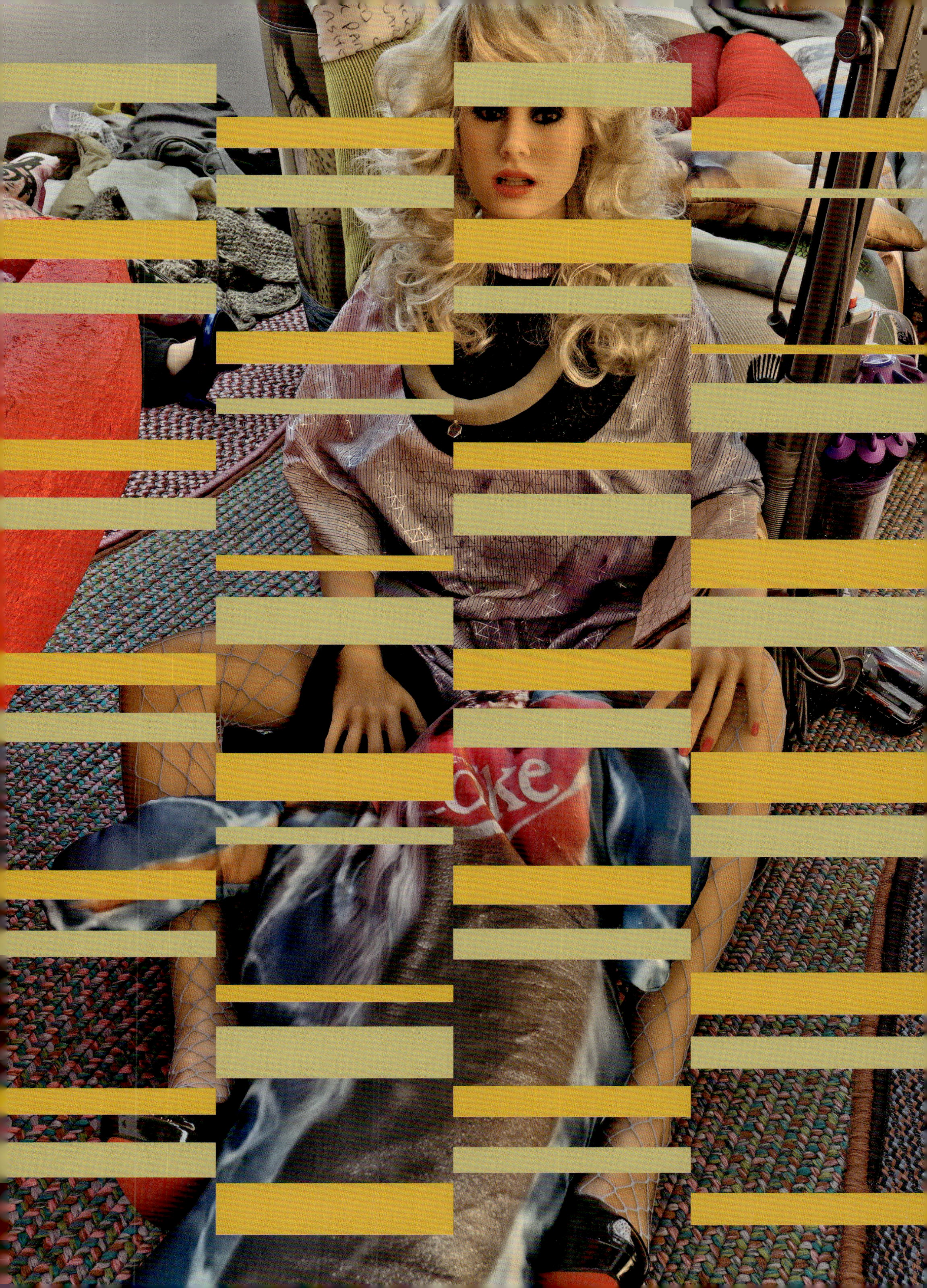

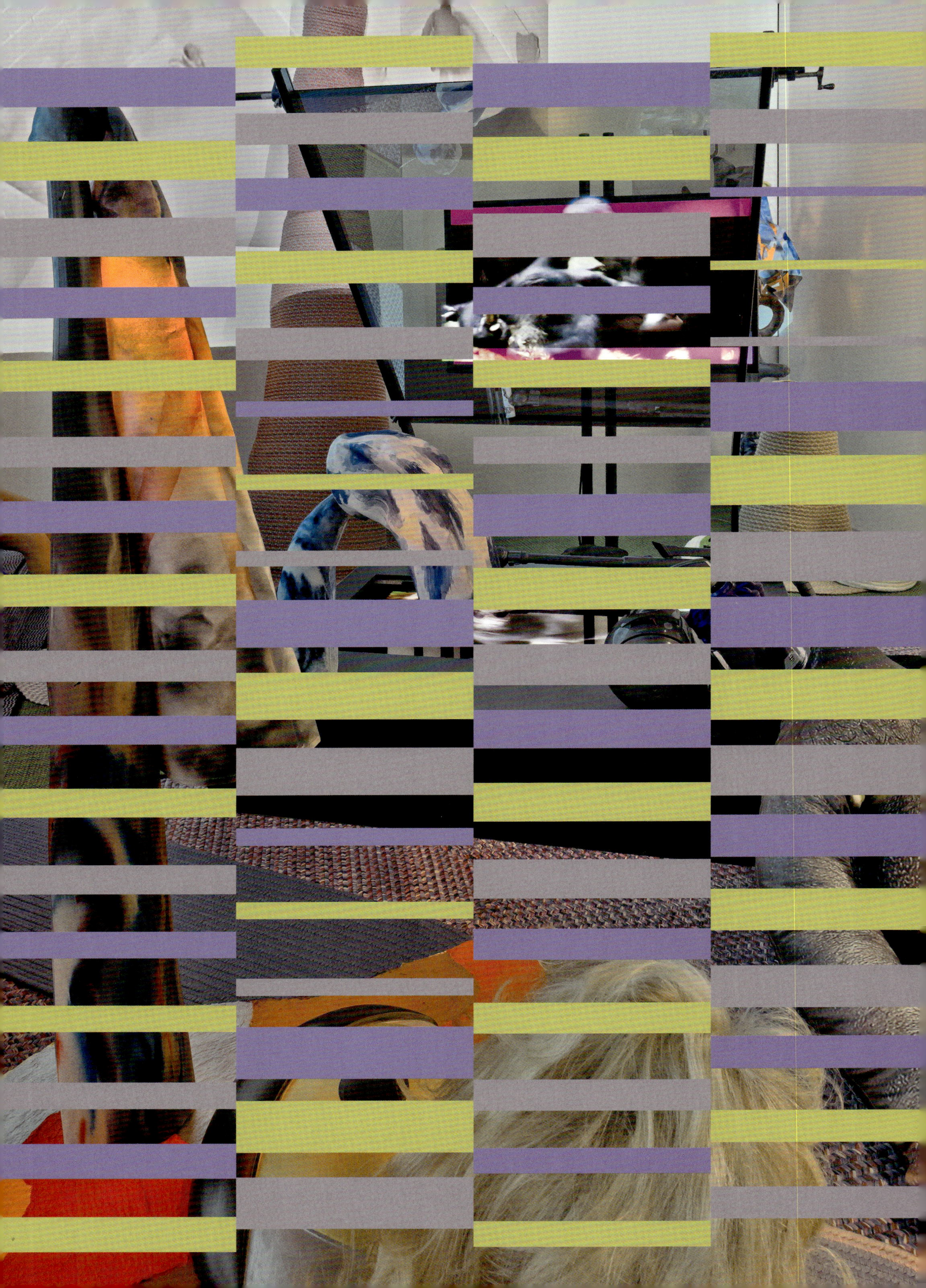

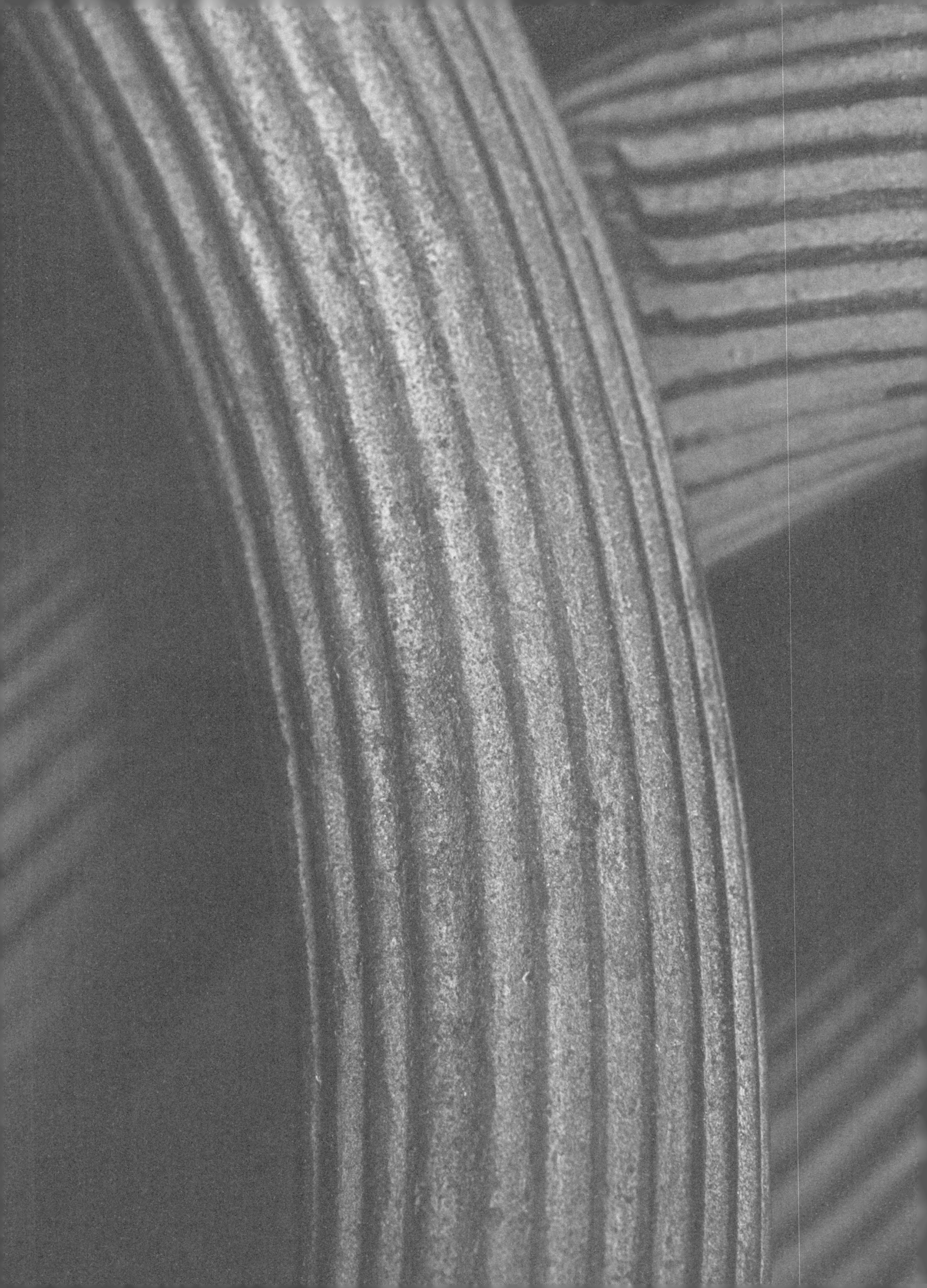

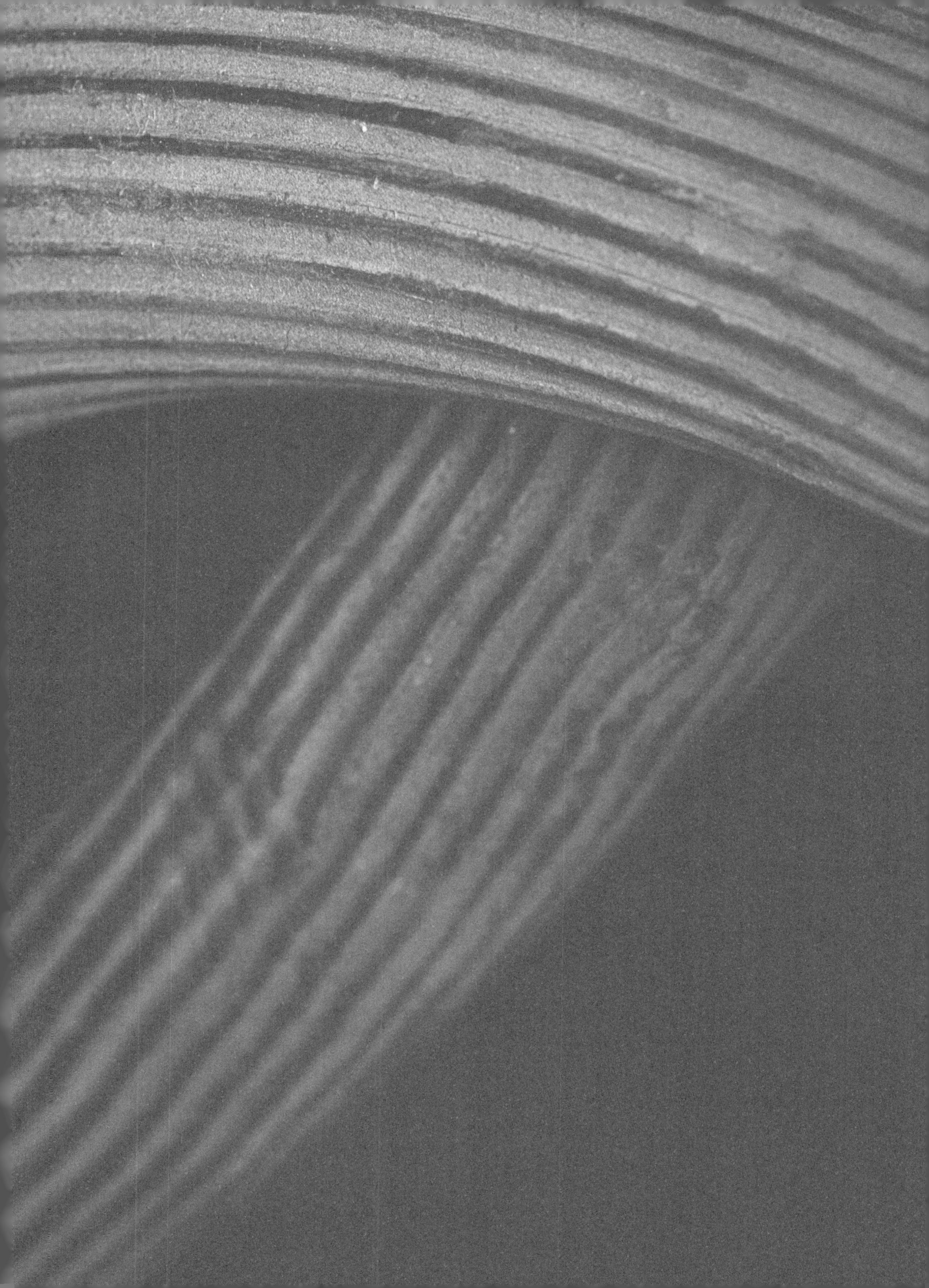

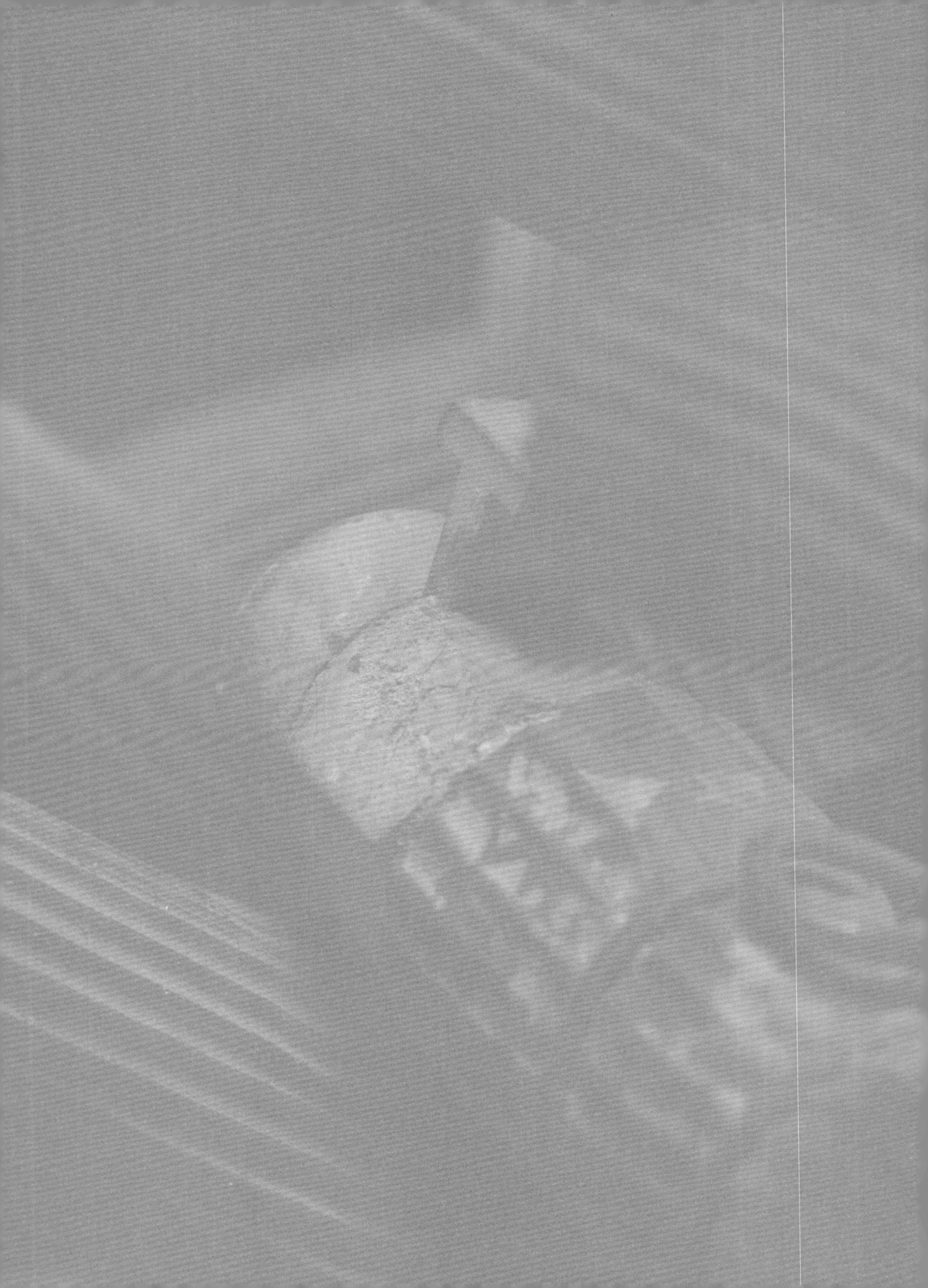

LARS TOFT-ERIKSEN
Curator, the Munch Museum

A Few Thoughts on a Rubber Hose

———

"Sun, sex, sin, divine intervention, death and destruction! Ladies and gentlemen, welcome to the Sodom and Gomorrah Show!"

Pet Shop Boys[1]

"[It is] as if love were 'pure' once the subject absents himself from it, once this love without a subject is settled on its object and is itself absorbed into its object."

François Fénelon, Archbishop of Cambrai[2]

"The only motive that there ever was, was to completely control a person that I found physically attractive, and keep them with me as long as possible."

Jeffrey Dahmer[3]

Amidst the Munch Museum's extensive collection, including approximately 28,000 works of art and a multitude of letters, notes and other museum items which together amount to roughly 45,000 objects, is a peculiar and bizarre object with the registration number MM.I.00325. A rubber hose. It is included in the museum's collection of inventory from Edvard Munch's property at Ekely. The museum has no information about the hose other than that it apparently stems from Munch's property.[4] One might ask oneself why the hose is in the museum's collection at all. An obvious and prosaic answer is that it was simply found among Munch's belongings after his death, and that at some point it was moved to the Munch Museum after the Municipality of Oslo purchased Ekely in 1946. Nonetheless, why in the world is this rubber hose included in the museum's collection? Why does the museum employ space and resources to preserve something so seemingly negligible and insignificant? It was not part of Munch's bequest to the Municipality of Oslo, so there is no legal explanation for its place in the collection. Consequently one might assume that there must be art historical or museological justifications for its inclusion. But this can hardly be the case either. There is nothing to indicate that the hose had any significance for Munch's artistic production, as is the case with his many paintbrushes and paint tubes, which are also included in the museum's collection. Futhermore it is difficult to believe that its presence in the collection might be based on biographical or other documentary motives. From this perspective it is all rather puzzling. And it might seem that the hose is little more than a museum curio, or dare I say a Freudian slip, and that there is no explanation for its inclusion in the collection.

In his book *Rubbish Theory* (1979) anthropologist Michael Thompson discusses how one can categorize objects in relation to a theory of attribution of material value.[5] Briefly summarized he divides all objects into three different categories—objects of lasting value, objects of diminishing value and objects that are considered rubbish. Objects of lasting value are the kinds of objects that are included in museums—such as artworks, archaeological findings and other historic artifacts of significance. Objects of diminishing value are consumer products—such as automobiles, lamps and tomatoes. Rubbish is simply rubbish, i.e. the things a person is no longer interested in—and to which he does not attribute any other term. It is discarded, buried and forgotten. In a museological context, and perhaps in the case of the rubber hose in particular, it is interesting to note that Thompson describes a distinct movement between these three categories, which mainly involves a downgrading. Objects of diminishing value will sooner or later always end up as rubbish. Even objects of lasting value can lose their status and end up as rubbish. But when it comes to the rubbish, under certain circumstances it can rise up from the mud and become an object of lasting value. This might be an archeological find such as a tankard or a bowl, for instance, which is elevated via excavation to becoming a museum object. The object has thereby gone from being displaced, to becoming an object of value and significance. The rubber hose—old, dried out and brittle as it is—no longer has any function, and would be considered rubbish by most people, had it not been included in the Munch Museum's collection. By being registered in the collection, if we follow Thompson's reasoning, the hose has gone from being rubbish to being an object of museological value.

And if we follow museologist Samuel Alberti, the hose, as a museum object, is also ascribed a certain significance or meaning.[6] When an arbitrary object is introduced into a museum collection it is, according to Alberti, placed in relation to a number of other objects through its cataloging and exhibiting, and via this museum practice is ascribed a particular significance and meaning. The rubber hose has gone from being an old and useless garden hose to being *Munch's* rubber hose. Yet, although Thompson's theory in a way explains what has occurred to the rubber hose within a culturally determined value system, there is something grating about it with regard to Alberti's theory. It is still difficult to imagine that the hose can have any biographical, art historical or documentary qualities that are necessary to give it meaning or significance in relation to the other objects in the Munch Museum's collection. As I have mentioned, there is no explicable reason for the rubber hose to be included in the collection. Nor has anyone in the museum ever bothered about this object—until now anyway.

Because, the rubber hose is in fact not without interest. Precisely as a curio it can actually be of critical relevance. The hose opens the door to critical reflection regarding how objects are assigned value in a museum context, and not least how museum objects are included in a scheme in which various artifacts are placed in relation to each other and thereby interpreted and given meaning. More specifically it raises the issue of the Munch Museum's role as a producer of artistic and art historical meaning. For, what does Munch's bedspread actually say about his painting *Between the Clock and the Bed*? The French philosopher Michel Foucault was particularly interested in the unbridgeable distance, or gap, between things and our perception of things—or the order in which things are embedded. For Foucault things have no meaning to begin with. Meaning arises through the culture's interpretation of them. In a lecture in 1967, Foucault introduced the concept of heterotopia.[7] Heterotopias are places that are something completely different from what they seem to be, or as Foucault himself formulated it:

> There [...] exist, and this is probably true for all cultures and all civilizations, real effective spaces which are outlined in the very institution of society, but which constitute a sort of counter arrangement, of effectively realized utopia, in which all the real arrangements, all the other arrangements that can be found within society, are at one and the same time represented, challenged, and overturned: a sort of place that lies outside all places and yet is actually localizable. In contrast to utopias, these places which are absolutely other with respect to all the arrangements that they reflect and of which they speak might be described as heterotopias.[8]

Heterotopias are the places in a culture that open to differences, where the culture's established order cracks and lets in what is outside, what is different and without language. For Foucault the museum is such a place. In the museum, objects that stem from widely differing times and places are positioned together and given significance through the museum's interpretation. Although the museum's function is to interpret, and thereby contribute to our conceptual understanding of the world, the museum is also a place that discloses the impossibility of attaining true knowledge about things. For according to Foucault the museum is a place where things are taken out of their original context, and thereby invites its public to reflect on the gap between things and the order of things. In this perspective the rubber hose becomes a discursive object of reflection that emphasizes the museum's heterotopic role and raises questions about what it means to display specific objects together in a museum context.

For anyone who wonders what in the world this has to do with an exhibition of Bjarne Melgaard's and Edvard Munch's art, at first glance it is as unclear as the rubber hose's inclusion in the Munch Museum's collection. But in its capacity as a discursive object of reflection, the hose can underscore the arbitrariness of this comparison of Melgaard's and Munch's artworks, and thus raise critical questions about the museum's comparison of two artists and a number of artworks, that have moreover been created during different eras and in different contexts. This is an issue one should be aware of when one positions artists in "dialogue" with one another, and maybe in particular when one places highly active and living artists up against grand old masters like Edvard Munch. Such museological comparisons tend to generate not only interpretation and production of meaning, but also promotional prospects and the attribution of both cultural and economical value. Munch's name has not infrequently been used by critics, gallerists, art dealers and curators in order to promote potential international stars from the Norwegian art world. The number of new "Munchs" in Norwegian art are not few: Ludvig Karsten, Arne Ekeland, Kai Fjell, Jakob Weidemann, Odd Nerdrum, Bjørn Carlsen, and Olav Christopher Jenssen, to name just a few. And just as frequently the artists themselves, both Norwegian and foreign, have vegetated on Munch's fame through citation and paraphrasing, as though it would contribute to invigorating their artistic project. We find this in everything from numerous artists' pastiches of Munch's paintings, to Tracy Emin and Marina Abramović's interpretations of *The Scream*—as well as in Andy Warhol's appropriations of Munch's motifs as a critical commentary on the trivialization and leveling of artistic expression through popular consumption. Munch's name has been used, and still continues to be used, in canonizing, branding and promoting other artists, as well as in strengthening the artistic projects of others, both critically and uncritically. In this way Edvard Munch is on the one hand held forth as a towering monument that casts long shadows over the entire Norwegian art world. And in a way he becomes the only model Norwegian artists are measured against. This easily becomes reductive for artists who are compared with Munch. On the other hand, Munch's art is just as easily reduced to trivial evaluation markers in promoting other artists.

These issues are highly relevant when it comes to Bjarne Melgaard. He has been compared to Munch, or proclaimed the greatest thing to happen in the Norwegian art world since Munch, countless times—in everything from art critical essays to spectacular newspaper headlines. This is of course largely associated with the financial circumstances surrounding Melgaard's oeuvre, where the Munch brand is used for all it is worth. By setting Melgaard up against Munch, gallerists, art dealers, and the press contribute to consolidating Melgaard's position as an important artist. But it also testifies to a form of cultural impoverishment or lack of imagination when Munch appears in an almost hackneyed way as the *only* reference to art that one has in Norway. It should be mentioned that Melgaard has greatly contributed to this comparison himself. In many of his pictures there are direct references to Munch's motifs, such as *The Hands* (1893–94), *Kiss* (1897) or *The Woman and the Bear* (1895). These references are often mentioned when Melgaard is compared to Munch. The same applies to Melgaard's painterly style, which is often compared to Munch's expressive and art nouveau-like brushwork. That Munch has had significance for

Melgaard's oeuvre is indisputable, but as Melgaard mentions in the interview in this book, this should not be exaggerated. He is somewhat critical of this comparison and claims that for him it has rather been a question of putting Munch behind him—and to a certain degree even to have a critical attitude toward Munch's art. One should of course be critical to Melgaard's comments, but his opinion is interesting and not without significance in this context. For, with reference to Melgaard's comments, it might be more interesting to look at Melgaard's and Munch's art from a different point of view than that of banal references and citations.

When I came upon the rubber hose in the museum's collection some time ago, I inquired about it to several of the museum's longtime staff. No one could really say much about this mysterious object. But after a few days I received an e-mail from former Chief Curator Arne Eggum. He thought, arguably enough, that he recognized the hose in a photograph Munch took in the winter of 1927. According to Eggum, one could trace the hose in the photograph leading down from the glass porch in Munch's villa at Ekely, and then disappearing in the dark space beneath it. Eggum continues to conjecture that the photograph must have been staged. It was taken in midwinter with the garden full of snow, and it seemed absurd that the hose should still be there at this time of the year, by which time Munch's gardener would in all probability have stored it away for the season. For Eggum's museological interpretative yearning, the rubber hose's inexplicable place in the collection becomes irresistible as it opens up to a heterotopic abyss. Hence Eggum goes on to link the photograph to Munch's painting *Woman by the Veranda Steps* from 1942, in which a female figure is depicted facing the same section of the house and veranda. Instead of snow, the house in the painting is covered with red ivy or possibly licking flames or dripping blood— in Eggum's view an overt expression of desire. As an extension of this, and keeping in mind all of Munch's serpent motifs, to Eggum the rubber hose in the photograph might be interpreted as a symbolic representation of contact with "the underworld, or a dark alter ego."[9] His interpretation is of course highly speculative, subjective and not least humorous. And it probably has very little to do with the museum's rubber hose. Yet as a Munch expert, Eggum's associations are nevertheless not without relevance. For it is precisely this unknown and unspeakable darkness that is lurking in Foucault's notion of heterotopia—and surely for that reason Eggum's associations are also of interest to the relationship between Melgaard's and Munch's art.

For, is it not in this speechless gap between the hose and its place in the museum, in the chasm of cognition's silenced scream, that one can also find a kinship between Melgaard and Munch? Is it not heterotopia that we encounter in Munch's *Red Virginia Creeper* (1898–1900), in the speechless despair immediately following the catastrophe, when everything comes apart, when all illusions are shattered, outside the home, in an alarmingly foreign and claustrophobic landscape—in the "Unheimlich" heterotopia, to paraphrase Sigmund Freud? Something that exists somewhere between the known and the unknown is the definition of Freud's concept of *das Unheimliche*, or the uncanny, precisely that which does not lend itself to being transformed into a conception. Or what about Melgaard's *Bloodsports for all* (2004)—is it not a demonstration of total devastation that we encounter in this pandemonium of sexual drives, desires and neuroses, where the distinction between the subject and object of desire is erased in a sado-masochistic play, and where a totally incomprehensible and speechless self-annihilation strikes us like the uncanny scream of desire?

Eggum's associations lead me, with reference to Foucault's concept of heterotopia, to think of the philosopher Slavoj Žižek's theory of the parallactic gap. In his book entitled *The Parallax View* (2006) Žižek lays the groundwork for an epistemology via a Kantian development and critique of Hegel's dialectics. Simply stated one can say that Žižek's point is that there is no synthesis, in the sense that Hegel, with his dialectics, rescues us out of the Kantian chasm between objects and our perception of them. Or to put it more precisely, Žižek claims that Hegel's concept of synthesis describes precisely this Kantian chasm, and that Hegel therefore does not overcome Kant's antinomies with his dialectics. Hegel's syntheses become, in Žižek's interpretation, an insurmountable gap or void between thesis and antithesis; between Kant's phenomenal realm, understood as our image of the world, and the noumenal realm understood as the world as it actually is—*das Ding an mich* and *das Ding an sich*, in Kantian parlance. It is this abyss that Žižek calls the parallactic gap. Žižek's Hegel thus surpasses Kant by placing cognition as such and the self in this gap. In Žižek's theory there is an incommensurable chasm between all positions—a gap that according to Žižek implies that the self never gains true knowledge about the world of the objects or itself, as there is always another position—or, as Žižek formulates it, another framing of reality, understood as an unredeemable play between reality and its representation. In order to conceptualize the parallactic gap Žižek draws on the modernist discourse of the frame. Not surprisingly, with reference to the motif's integrated frame, Žižek points to Edvard Munch's *Madonna* as a, one might say paradoxical, illustration of the double character of the frame or the parallactic gap:

One of the minimal definitions of a modernist painting concerns the function of its frame. The frame of the painting in front of us is not its true frame; there is another, invisible frame, the frame implied by the structure of the painting, the frame that enframes our perception of the painting, and these two frames by definition never overlap—an invisible gap separates them. The pivotal content of the painting is not communicated in its visible part, but located in this dis-location of the two frames, in the gap that separates them. This dimension in-between-the-two-frames is obvious in [...] Edvard Munch's *Madonna*—the droplets of sperm and the small fetus-like figure from *The Scream* squeezed in between the two frames. The frame is always-already redoubled: the frame within 'reality' is always linked to another frame enframing 'reality' itself. Once introduced, the gap between reality and appearance is thus immediately complicated, reflected-into-itself: once we get a glimpse, through the Frame, of the Other Dimension, *reality itself turns into appearance*. In other words, things do not simply appear, they *appear to appear*.[10]

In other words, the frame in Munch's motif tells us that it is a representation of a representation, and thus emphasizes that *reality* will remain unattainable. The woman making love thus remains fleeting and incomprehensible. So what is it we see, or rather what do we not see, in Munch's deceptive framing of the woman making love in *Madonna*? By referring to this picture by Munch, Žižek turns to the Freudian psychoanalyst Jacques Lacan, and the parallactic gap thereby becomes an interpretation of Lacan's theory of *objet petit a* as a certain aspect of the object of desire. According to Lacan this concept refers to the structural position the object of desire (here: the woman making love) takes in relation to the subject, where *objet petit a* appears as a gap in between subject and the object of desire, as part of the object of desire which desire never manages to grasp—as a kind of *das Ding an sich* of desire. For Žižek desire is precisely an experience in which reality's incomprehensibility discloses itself, and where the parallactic gap reveals itself as a break in the order of symbolic representation. For desire directs itself towards something the subject of desire can never achieve. The chasm between the subject and the object, the parallactic gap, thus always exists there as part of the structure of desire. And as always in Žižek's post-Freudian universe, *the mother* plays a central role in understanding this unobtainable and incomprehensible dimension of the object of desire. For is it not precisely *the mother* who reveals herself in the *Madonna's* frame, as an uncanny reminder of the subject's fleeting and inherent self-annihilation? In this connection it is interesting to note that Munch, and conceivably others as well, has cut out this frame in several editions of the lithographic version of *Madonna*. The Munch Museum's painting with the same title from 1894 at one point even had a similar frame depicting spermatozoa and the dead fetus. This frame was also removed early on, conceivably by Munch himself.[11] The National Gallery's former director and Munch expert Jens Thiis at one time even applauded the removal of "this distasteful frame."[12] It is as though by doing so Munch retreated from the chasm, which the frame represented, and in a desperate attempt at sublimation attempted to reestablish the symbolic order by insisting on the woman's virginity and the mother's purity.

Žižek elaborates on this aspect of Munch's art in his book *Enjoy Your Symptom* (1992). Through a symptomatic reading of *The Scream* (1893), where the figure and the landscape's anamorphic and anthropomorphic distortions reflect and contrast the picture's mute scream, Munch's picture, according to Žižek, opens up for a transgressive and self-destructive desire—or in Lacanian parlance—in *The Scream's jouissance*, understood as desire's true gratification or *objet petit a*, reveals itself in reality. According to Žižek it is essential that the picture portrays a mute scream, which among other things is symbolized by the figure holding its ears and the shape of the figure's head being similar to that of an ear. According to Žižek the silence of the scream is underscored and intensified through the hovering and hallucinatory lines of the figure and the landscape, and the silent scream points to the speechless experience of the abyss between reality and our conception of it—or "the scream through nature," as Munch called it. And this speechless scream obviously refers to desire, and the incommensurable gap between the subject and the object of desire:

> [T]he opposition of silent and vocalized screams coincides with that of enjoyment and Other: the silent scream attests to the subject's clinging to enjoyment, to his/her unreadiness to exchange enjoyment [...] for the Other, for the Law, for the paternal metaphor, whereas the vocalization as such corroborates that the choice is already made and that the subject finds himself/herself within the community.[13]

According to Žižek, then, *The Scream* depicts nothing less than the experience of the parallactic gap, or a desire that exposes the fact that reality is different from how we conceive it. And here one finds the motif's Lacanian angst as well, for in this experience also lies the awareness of the self's own status as object, and thereby also the paradoxical impossibility of true cognition of oneself. One exists *oneself* in the parallactic abyss. For as Žižek writes: "[T]he subject's gaze is always-already inscribed into the perceived object itself, in the guise of its 'blind spot,' that which is 'in the object more than the object itself,' the point from which the object itself returns the gaze."[14] The parallactic gap thus exists always and already in the subject, according to Žižek, and reveals itself in what he calls the experience of *minimal differences* or *blind spots* in the representation of the world of objects. These are spots that open up to the genuinely, i.e. the Lacanian, real or the void between the subject and its objects of desire—and thereby the subject's inherent self-annihilation. In the *minimal difference* lies what, according to Žižek, is a self-negating movement; that is, a cognition of the subject as being other than oneself, which draws on Hegel's concept of dialectical negativity understood as inner contradictions in the categories of cognition. But as opposed to Hegel, the negative is never revoked in Žižek's model. The negative parallactic gap remains insurmountable.

As with Žižek's Munch, it appears that it is this negativity, or the *minimal differences*, that Bjarne Melgaard is seeking, when he refers to the American literary theorist Leo Bersani and claims that the aim of art is to penetrate into the negative spaces of a culture. For—as he states elsewhere in this publication: "There is something fundamentally anti-social about Munch. I feel that it has great relevance today. According to Leo Bersani, there is something to gain from exploring the negative elements in a culture, the things that oppose the social order." Melgaard's characterization of Munch is of course influenced by his own artistic project, but it is not without relevance in this context. In his book *Homos* (1995), Bersani laid the foundation for what has been called the anti-social turn in queer theory.[15] With this book Bersani formulates a

theory concerning homosexuality, but also sexuality more in general, as anti-relational and anti-social. Rather than a hetero-normative, morally and rationally determined sexuality in the form of life, propagation and *futuriority*, Bersani formulates a concept of sexuality that breaks with the idea of a sexuality premised on the personal intimacy of the couple, and instead opens for a notion of sexuality as a radical narcissistic and self-destructive force. With a reference to Jacques Lacan's development of Freud's concept of the death drive as symbolic, sexuality, according to Bersani, opens up to a negative and oppositional force toward what he elsewhere calls "the tyranny of the self."[16] Through readings of Patrice Leconte's film *Confidences trop intimes* (2004), homosexual *barebacking cults* and Jeffery Dahmer's tragic bestialities, as well as the horrors perpetrated by the Bush administration in Iraq, in his book *Intimacies* (2008) Bersani outlines the possibility of an ethics based on his so-called anti-social theory of sexuality. The homosexual figure appears repeatedly throughout Bersani's book, and it can be read to great benefit with Melgaard's oeuvre in mind—whether it has to do with his representation of the *bareback cults* or Dahmer's sexualized violence, both of which have relevance to Melgaard's artistic universe. The point of reference for Bersani's discussion of *barebacking* is Guillaume Dustan's auto-fictive novel *Dans ma chambre* (1996), which has also had great significance for Bjarne Melgaard and his art. This is most strikingly evident in Melgaard's novel *A New Novel* from 2012, which, in its outrageous, all-consuming and self-destructive sexuality is reminiscent of Dustan's novel. But with a significant difference, if one follows Bersani. Melgaard's novel is written in the era of the *bareback cults*, whereas Dustan's story is played out at the height of the AIDS crisis during the 1980s at a time when the germ of this cult was sown—for as Bersani writes: "[...] perhaps AIDS infects sex with a consciousness of death. Death, however, not as a threat, but as temptation, as a lure. [...] The potentially fatal fuck is a powerful aphrodisiac."[17] This might seem absurd. But if one is to take the Lacanian Bersani seriously, there is obviously something behind this apparently insane self-destructive cult. As with archbishop François Fénelon's concept of "pure love," Bersani claims that *barebacking* allows the subject to abandon himself to an unintelligible and unknown otherness:

> The barebacking gang-bang has none of what we usually think of as the humanizing attributes of intimacy within a couple, where the personhood of each partner is presumed to be expanded and enriched by knowledge of the other. The barebacking bottom enters into an impersonal intimacy, not only with those who have pumped their semen into his body, but also with all those unknown partners, perhaps now dead, with whom he has never had any physical contact. His subjecthood is, we might say, absorbed into the nameless and faceless crowd that exists only as viral traces circulating in his blood and perhaps fatally infecting him. For him, their identities are nothing more than these viral remains; his willingness to allow his body to be the site of their persistence and reproduction is not entirely unlike the mystic's surrender to a divine will without any comfortable recognizable attributes whatsoever.[18]

Bersani's discussion of the *barebacking cult* must not be taken as an insensitive and heedless encouragement of potentially fatal behavior or a glorification of destructive human forces. His point is rather, as with the far more extreme case of Jeffery Dahmer, that out of this destructive or negative behavior one can find a motion toward something that is neither life nor death, toward something that transcends inherent human egoism. In Bersani's view *barebacking* is to be understood as a manifestation of a sexualized longing for death, which introduces the possibility of an ascetic communion of impersonal non-egoistic intimacy, where the subject literally allows himself to be penetrated by *the other* in a Lacanian sense. As opposed to Žižek, inherent in this view is a radical motion toward a potential, albeit non-utopian, self-annihilation and reconciliation with *jouissance*—i.e. a Hegelian motion toward *the other*. As Bersani summarizes it:

> Interpreted as a mode of ascetic spirituality, bug-chasing and gift-giving among barebackers are implicit critiques of the multiple forms of ego-driven intimacy: from the most trivial expressions of sexual vanity [...], to the prideful exclusiveness of the family as a socially blessed, closed unit of reproductive intimacy, and even to the at once violently aggressive and self-shattering ego-hyperbolizing of racial, national, ethnic, and gendered identities.[19]

In contrast to Freud, where the subject exists in an endless and indomitable struggle against the splitting of *the self* through *the other*, like the experience of the self which Žižek discusses in his reading of Munch, Bersani introduces an anti-psychoanalytical politics of desire, in which the disparities are a goal in themselves—where the subject resigns himself to the fact that there will always be something *else*, something *foreign* in the self, which he cannot overcome, and where an opportunity exists for a form of intimacy and desire that is indifferent to personal identity and egoistic considerations. On the basis of this, and somewhat in contrast to Žižek, it is tempting to propose that Munch's art, as Melgaard suggests, may not only be read as an exploration of the negative in a Bersanian sense, but also as a potential opening onto an other concept of intimacy. For, doesn't Munch's *Madonna* after all depict the fatal fuck, as Bersani calls it?

Just as the rubber hose, via Arne Eggum's associations, opens up to related readings of Melgaard's and Munch's art, the hose also closes this space. Because, when it comes down to it, this hose is just a random rubber hose, and only first ascribed significance through my interpretive use of it, which to begin with did nothing more than point to the construed relationship between the museum's artifacts and the stories we create around them. And that can be considered the garden hose serpent's final sting. For just as it exposes the museum as a staged scenario, it also points—in this context—to the artist as a staged persona. In Munch as in Melgaard, the concept of the artist's life is interwoven with their art in a nearly impenetrable network of literary figures, which intensifies and supports the subject matter of their art. As Melgaard himself says in the interview in this book: "There is actually not very much autobiography in my art at all. I am more interested in auto-fiction. I think it is more interesting to create different auto-fictive personalities, and make people speculate about what

is true or not true. [...] There is something subversive in it as well, and in a way that intensifies the extreme quality of my pictures." Just as the hose points to the museum as a heterotopia, Melgaard's remark demonstrates that our concept of the artist can also be understood as a heterotopic character—a mythological figure on the margins of society, who through provocation and otherness investigates and discloses the negative spaces of culture.

Translated from Norwegian by Francesca M. Nichols

1　Pet Shop Boys, "Sodom and Gomorrah Show" on Pet Shop Boys: *Fundamental* (Parlophone, 2006).

2　Quoted from: Leo Bersani and Adam Phillips: *Intimacies* (Chicago, 2008), p. 53.

3　Stone Phillips, *Confessions of a Serial Killer,* interview with Jeffrey Dahmer, NBC, 1994.

4　There is no preserved protocol of accession in the museum that documents when the hose arrived at the museum or when it was registered for the first time as part of the collection. The only protocol entry that can possibly confirm that the hose at least stems from Ekely is the valuation protocol of Munch's estate dated 15 April 1944. Listed as part of the inventory is a garden hose measuring 60 meters. But strictly speaking this does not prove anything other than that there was a garden hose at Ekely, and far from it being the same garden hose that exists in the museum's storage.

5　Michael Thompson, *Rubbish Theory: The Creation and Destruction of Value* (Oxford, 1979).

6　Samuel J. M. M. Alberti, "Objects and the Museum" in: *Isis,* no. 96, 2005, pp. 559–571.

7　Michel Foucault, "Of Other Spaces: Utopias and Heterotopias" in: *Rethinking Architecture: A Reader in Cultural Theory,* Niel Leach, ed., (New York, 1997), pp. 330–336.

8　Foucault 1997, p. 302.

9　Arne Eggum in an e-mail to the author, 9 November 2014.

10　Slavoj Žižek, *The Parallax View* (Cambridge, MA, 2006), Kindle edition, location 478–485.

11　Gerd Woll, *Edvard Munch. Complete Paintings* (London, 2009), p. 352.

12　Jens Thiis, *Edvard Munch og hans samtid. Slekten, livet og kunsten: Geniet* (Oslo, 1933), p. 218.

13　Slavoj Žižek, *Enjoy Your Symptom: Jacques Lacan and Hollywood and Out* (New York, 1992), Kindle edition, location 3003.

14　Žižek 2006, location 251.

15　Leo Bersani, *Homos* (Cambridge, MA, 1995).

16　Leo Bersani, *The Culture of Redemption* (Cambridge, MA, 1990), p. 4.

17　Bersani and Phillips 2008, pp. 38–39.

18　Bersani and Phillips 2008, p. 53.

19　Bersani and Phillips 2008, p. 55.

DAVID LOMAS
Professor of Art History, University of Manchester

Sick Art

—

"My subject is not physical illness itself but the uses of illness as a figure or metaphor."

Susan Sontag[1]

Among the points of comparison that emerge from a juxtaposition of Edvard Munch and Bjarne Melgaard, the part played by illness and disease in the art of both of them is perhaps the most salient. Munch, the son of a doctor, took a keen interest in disease. The illnesses that affected him, members of his family, and his circle of acquaintances, and others that were of concern to the wider society, form a vital part of his subject matter. Munch's portrayal of illness was imbued unavoidably by terms that were prevalent and circulating in the fin de siècle culture— meanings and metaphors that also come to inform his aesthetic stance. A century later, the calamity of AIDS, though more selective in its choice of victims, has been no less significant for its impact on visual art. I shall argue in respect of Melgaard that not only is AIDS omnipresent as a "risk" within the gay sub- culture that his work documents, and important to him for this reason, but that (as with Munch) it has also determined in significant ways the form of his art practice.

The other side of the equation is the way that accusations of sickness have been leveled at artists. Munch and Melgaard have each been subject to this charge at one time or another, and both have had exhibitions closed down on this account. By embracing illness and reveling in aberrancy, the fin de siècle avant-garde of which Munch was a part was an easy target—too easy perhaps. Similarly, AIDS reactivated a linkage between homosexuality and abnormality whose origins lay in the final decades of the nineteenth century, fuelling a venomous homophobia that is evident today in quite a few parts of the world. The grisly apotheosis of the atavistic reflex to brand art as sick was the Nazi Degenerate Art exhibition in 1937. That event casts a long shadow, imposing an ethical demand upon us to defend an art of extremity. Inevitably, too, it acts as a prism through which we must view the relation between art of the present and that which the Nazis had sought to suppress.

Edvard Munch
In 1905, Dr. Louis Rénon presented a series of lectures to the Faculty of Medicine in Paris on "trois périls" that were widely regarded as the most

serious threats to health in that period: tuberculosis, syphilis and alcoholism.[2] This unholy trinity of afflictions acted in concert with each other, syphilis and alcoholism uniting to produce enhanced susceptibility to tuberculosis. Not coincidentally, Munch took all three perils as subjects for his painting.

In the era before antibiotics, tuberculosis was often lethal.[3] It claimed the lives of Munch's mother and his sister Sophie. When Munch himself was aged thirteen, he suffered an episode of coughing blood that was severe enough to give rise to fears that he may die. This was thought, probably with good cause, to have been tuberculosis. Munch stated: "The illness followed me all through my childhood and youth—the germ of consumption placed its blood- red banner victoriously on my handkerchief."[4] Two of his best-known images, *The Sick Child* and *Death in the Sickroom*, commemorate the death of his sister. *The Sick Child* (1886) exists in six painted versions and was made into prints in a variety of media, reflecting not only its importance for Munch but also the market for a subject that spoke to a common experience of loss. *The Son* (1904) forms a pendant to the aforementioned works of which it combines elements from both. A sick child depicted in profile, his head resting against a pillow, accords with turn of the century descriptions of tuberculosis as a wasting disease (origin of the term "consumption"), the child's pallid profile melding with the pillow, and the notion that the infectivity of tuberculosis was a function of contagion plus heredity. The latter is evoked by three generations of a family assembled in the room. An unusual blood-red extrusion from the boy casts a shadow across two framed portraits of women on the back wall. Comparable to the magnified shadow that looms ominously behind the figure in *Puberty*, it also recalls the fluidic emanations captured by spirit photographers.[5] Perhaps referring to Munch's near death experience in 1876, it may be that the child's soul is about to join those of his two lost female relatives—though Sophie was still alive at that point, the picture reflects the benefit of hindsight. While containing elements of autobiographical material, imaginatively reworked, this picture is illustrative of a tendency by Munch to draw upon his past but to place it at arm's length, and by speaking about himself in the third person to fictionalize autobiography to an extent.

The second peril identified by Dr. Rénon was venerian excess. Beyond menacing an afflicted individual, syphilis was an insidious threat to "the family, the child, the species, and the nation." A not unusual pattern of spread noted by doctors was from a husband who had contracted syphilis before marriage, then going on to infect his wife, and from her being passed to the offspring. In medical parlance, the term hereditary syphilis used for vertical transmission perpetuated belief that syphilis was an inherited condition. In *Inheritance* (1897–99), Munch's most startling treatment of this subject, the "sins of the father' are visited upon the child. A woman sitting on a bench as she waits to see a doctor cradles a sickly infant with a skin rash, the certainty of the impending diagnosis evident from her tearful countenance. The institutional setting enables us to view this appalling *maternité* with a degree of detached, even cynical, equanimity. In a letter to Dr. Max Linde (1903), Munch proudly referred to the picture as an example of his "syphilis art [*Mein Syphilis Kunst*]," implying that it comprised a definable genre. It would appear to be cognate with a group of works showing women in a hospital ward based on firsthand observation of prostitutes who were forcibly detained for treatment if they were found to carry venereal disease.[6] The moralizing discourse that surrounded a sexually transmitted infection, where blame was ascribed to certain of its victims, notably the female prostitute, can account for Munch's revival of a traditional theme of the "Dance of Death," treated famously by Hans Holbein the Younger in a series of woodcut engravings of 1538, as seen in his etching *Death and the Woman* (1894).

The third of Rénon's perils was alcoholism whose epidemic proportions made it a source of major concern for campaigners. Attention came to be focused on the café and music hall as causes of insobriety, and the illnesses, including venereal disease, which ensued from it. Such campaigners would not have disagreed with Van Gogh's observation on his picture *The Night Café* (1888)

that: "the café is a place where one can ruin oneself, go mad, commit a crime." Munch's *Self-portrait with a Bottle of Wine* (1906) is a work of a similar ilk, confessing not only to its author's alcohol dependence but also his precarious mental state. From Van Gogh, Munch might have adopted the idea of color as evocative of extreme emotions bordering on mental derangement. He witnessed and recorded the depths of depression and jealous hatred to which two of his companions fell prey, emotions of such a fever pitch that they might easily have gone mad or committed a crime. Both men were casualties of the free love ethos that existed in the avant-garde milieu, a homosocial network where women by and large were not cultural producers but mere exchange tokens. Of interest to the subject of jealousy that Munch portrays with forensic acuity in the haggard face of the Polish poet Stanislaw Przybyszewski (Munch was its cause as he was conducting an affair with the poet's wife) is Freud's contention that delusional jealousy is a defense against an unconscious wish of a homosexual nature. Freud writes: "As an attempt at defense against an unduly strong homosexual impulse it may, in a man, be described in the formula: '*I do not love him, she loves him!*'"[7] Freud's schema shows the propensity for the intense bonds of friendship that operated between men to spill over into more dangerous and forbidden territories.

In tandem with the discovery of causal agents for diseases such as cholera and tuberculosis, the extension of ideas of contagion beyond infection *per se* was a striking feature of commentary on a range of pressing social issues. The crowd psychologist, Gustave Le Bon, asserted that: "Ideas, sentiments, emotions, and beliefs possess in crowds a contagious power as intense as that of microbes."[8] Le Bon made comparisons with the herd behavior of animals such as sheep and horses in support of his thesis of an inherent tendency for ideas to spread by contagion. A copycat phenomenon was held responsible for certain crimes that were thought to be on the increase. In *La Contagion du meurtre* (1890), the physician Dr. Paul Aubry blamed an epidemic of female crimes of passion, the court trials of which often garnered saturation coverage in the press, on several factors operating in unison: "suggestion, imitation, heredity and contagion." A perceived rising tide of suicides provoked a spate of medical and sociological studies, beginning with Moreau de Tour's *De la contagion du suicide* (1875). The incident in which Munch injured his hand with a pistol during an altercation with his mistress Tulla Larsen, which inevitably recalls Van Gogh's self-mutilation, has something of a copycat character to it. As he found himself becoming more and more addicted to gambling, which he made the subject of several pictures in the years 1891 to 1893, Munch was caused to reflect: "It is a sickness like others—is it contagious? Are there bacteria in the rooms of Monte Carlo?"[9]

The diversity of themes connoting illness and disease in Munch's oeuvre would be bewildering without reference to the overarching concept of degeneration. The theory of degeneration was widespread and entrenched in medical thinking in the second half of the nineteenth century. It was often invoked to explain nervous and mental disease following the publication in 1857 of Bénédict Morel's *Traité des dégénérescences*, though by the end of the century it had come to encompass almost any and every ill besetting the individual and social body.[10] Although presented by its partisans as scientific in nature, it was bound up with the ambient pessimism of the era, and especially the general concerns about progress and decline in social, political and national terms. Its adherents promoted the view that degeneration was not only hereditary but also cumulative in its gravity from one generation to the next. What was mere over-excitability in one generation might become insanity in the next. In certain families madness was deemed inevitable and snowballing. One prominent physician, Dr. Jules Dejerine, affirmed that neurasthenia was the basis for all other nervous diseases as its effects were accumulated and transmuted across time.[11] Ultimately, it was believed to result in sterility among the descendants, and thus it was held responsible for declining birth rates across Europe. Degeneration theory also supported the annexation to psychiatry of aspects of criminology. Although Lombroso's influential notion of the "born criminal"

was disputed, there was a general tendency to consider certain wrongdoers in terms of hereditary disease. The murderers and other criminals depicted by Munch would have been examined by doctors looking for physical clues or "stigmata" of degeneracy: such things as cranial abnormalities, a misshapen ear, or facial asymmetry.

The discovery by Robert Koch in 1882 of the tubercle bacillus did not displace heredity as a factor in the causation of disease. An infectious agent, the "seed" (*germe*), required a predisposed host, the "soil" (*terrain*), in order for disease to take root. Munch was utterly convinced of his flawed heredity, stating that: "I inherited two of mankind's most frightful enemies—the heritage of consumption and insanity—illness and madness and death were the black angels that stood at my cradle." A drawing entitled *Family Tree* portrays his ancestry on his father's side as a sickly vine clinging to a wall of what appears to be a tomb in a churchyard. One of the most obscure pictures possibly relating to this theme is titled *Blood Waterfall* (1915–16). Painted during the Great War, it may refer to the war as a bloodbath, though it seems more plausible that it references ideas of heredity—of "blood," or more precisely "bad blood,' coursing through the veins of generations. The subject of a waterfall in a landscape was popular in Norwegian painting of the century before Munch. Streams, essential for the logging industry, were the economic lifeblood of the country and as such were often depicted by artists such as Johan Christian Dahl. Munch overturns the connotations of the motif with individual health and national wellbeing: what he represents instead is the bad blood of a tainted heredity. He deliberately chose to portray the sky as blood red in a lithographic version of his iconic image of *The Scream* (1895), an equivalent spillage from the body to landscape.

The issue of a blighted inheritance is pertinent to the lithographic version of *Madonna* (1895), a work that reverses expectations for an image of the mother of Christ. Syphilis, a recognized cause of abortion, may account for the presence of a sickly fetus huddled in one corner. Unhinging sexual pleasure from the process of procreation, which is relegated to the framing device, we can see *Madonna* as reflecting Munch's concerns about his heredity—elsewhere he implies that this deterred him from ever marrying. More radically, though, I believe one can discern a stance that is actively *against* procreative sexuality, or what more recent queer theory has termed reproductive futurity, in Munch's work.[12] Declining birthrates in many European countries led to campaigns to promote marriage and childbirth. Libertinism and free love as preached by Hans Jæger, a spokesperson for the Norwegian avant-garde, were at odds with the natalist ideology. The presence of spermatozoa but no egg perhaps reflects an Aristotelian view of reproduction, according to which the female contribution was simply to provide the matter ("soil") for implantation of the male seed. Nor should we forget that in painting the ground refers to the support, paper or canvas, upon which the artist applies his paint. Some commentators have suggested that Munch's *Madonna* figure is supine and viewed from above which would reinforce this analogy of the picture plane with the horizontal ground. What this allegorical image represents, therefore, is also a process of artistic conception—that, by extension, is permeated with or contaminated by ideas of disease.

"Seed" and "soil" resonate beyond their literal sense in Munch's illustrations for a re-edition of Baudelaire's *Fleurs du mal* (1857), a project that was not realized. Baudelaire was a seminal figure for the Symbolist generation of artists and poets. "Une charogne [A Carcass]" is one of the poems for which Munch completed a sketch. The poet and his lover are strolling along a country lane when they come upon a rotting carcass. In a ghastly parody, its legs stuck in the air are "like a lubricious woman' displaying "in a shameless, nonchalant way" a belly swollen with decomposition. The poetic description dwells unduly upon the processes of putrefaction going on in the rank body.[13] "And the sky was watching that superb cadaver blossom like a flower" the poet declares. Turning back to his lovely companion, he reflects: "And yet you will be like this corruption, like this horrible infection." In Munch's suite of drawings, the dead animal is replaced with a human corpse occupying the foreground of an image dominated by a naked embracing couple

adapted from *The Kiss*. Munch was clearly still thinking of Baudelaire when he stated: "From my rotting body flowers will grow and I am in them and this is eternity."

In Decadent writing, the *locus classicus* for a linkage of flowers and disease is J.-K. Huysmans' novel *Against Nature* (1884). Des Esseintes, the dandyish hero, is excessively fond of flowers. In order to satisfy his penchant, he has a hothouse filled with exotic species of plants. But such is his appetite for the macabre that the sickly blooms he amasses more resemble patients in a ward or sanatorium. Huysmans writes:

> [...] the gardeners brought in still more varieties, this time affecting the appearance of factitious skin covered with a network of counterfeit veins. Most of them, as if ravaged by syphilis or leprosy, displayed livid patches of flesh mottled with roseola.[14]

Declaring that horticulturalists are the only true artists remaining, Des Esseintes insists that Nature would be incapable of producing "such depraved, unhealthy species"—positive terms of approval in this reverse, wilfully perverse aesthetic discourse. Leaf patterns resembling the skin lesions of syphilis provoke in Des Esseintes a nightmarish vision of unceasing torment passed down generations of men by "the virus of distant ages." "It all comes down to syphilis in the end" he remarks fatalistically. No less than the painter of *"Syphilis Kunst,"* Huysmans' lurid evocation of "the inexhaustible heritage, the everlasting disease" was formed out of ideas of a disease-ridden heritage that haunted the fin de siècle imaginary.

Death, the counterpart to this cultural pessimism as an aesthetic, stalks Munch's image world. His pale, disembodied head shrouded in blackness stares out from a self-portrait lithograph of 1895. Beneath it lie the bones of the artist's forearm stretched out at the lower border. One cannot fail to be reminded by this of the first ever X-ray of a human hand taken by Wilhelm Röntgen in December 1895.[15] For this to have been a source for Munch, he would have to have completed the lithograph some time after the date assigned to it. Whatever the case, we readily surmise that the skeletal forearm is a metonym for the body as a whole.[16] Within a Western visual tradition, the male body when it is recumbent, as opposed to upright and in active movement, is generally dead. This conditions our reading of Munch's body draped with sheets on an operating table, one of the pictures he made after his hand injury. Images of dead bodies stretched out on the ground are so numerous in Munch's oeuvre as to comprise a distinct sub-category of his visual production. Within medical and social commentary, the step was often made from this individual body to the ailing social body.

In 1919, Munch fell ill with Spanish flu. In one of the self-portraits he made whilst convalescing, he slumps dejectedly in the armchair where his sister Sophie had spent her final days, as though resigned to the eventuality of his own demise. It is estimated that the influenza pandemic that swept the world in 1918 killed as many people in six months as died from AIDS in three decades. Then, too, many artists fell victim to the disease. Gustav Klimt produced some intensely moving drawings of his wife as she died from it; three days later he was dead too. Munch was luckier. Indeed, having also recovered from active tuberculosis as a child, it may be that he had inherited a more robust constitution than he thought. How different his art would look had he recognized that.

Interlude: On Degenerate Art
Decadence in art and literature was premised on a metaphorisation of illness. The adulation of aberrancy by radical artists and poets gave vent to feelings of alienation from the bourgeoisie and disillusionment with the nineteenth century mantras of modernity and progress. But this made them a ready target for their detractors.

Leading the charge against the avant-garde was Max Nordau, a medically trained journalist and author of an infamous text, *Degeneration* (1892). In Nordau's eyes, these disciples of Baudelaire who professed abnormality had already condemned themselves. Nordau is an example of the growing readiness by physicians in the late nineteenth century to fill a vacuum left by the declining

authority of religion. They dressed up moralized judgments about culture in the medicalized terms of health and disease. Nordau wields many fashionable notions from the medical and psychiatric discourse of the day, which confer a spurious objectivity upon his judgments. His account of how literary and artistic schools are formed conveys the flavor of his prose:

> This is the natural history of the aesthetic schools. Under the influence of an obsession, a degenerate mind promulgates some doctrine or other—realism, pornography, mysticism, symbolism, diabolism. He does this with vehement penetrating eloquence, with eagerness and fiery heedlessness. Other degenerate, hysterical, neurasthenical minds flock around him, receive from his lips the new doctrine, and live thenceforth only to propagate it.[17]

A language of contagion, of the infection of weak and suggestible minds with the germs of crazy ideas, are recruited from Le Bon but here directed specifically against the avant-garde. Excessive emotionalism is one of the attributes of the degenerate that he purports to find in avant-garde writing; ego mania is another. The distortions of modern artists are attributed to defective vision, while anti-naturalistic color is an index of a diseased mind. Munch was spared *ad hominem* attack unlike many of his peers and predecessors, though one can see that he would have amply fulfilled Nordau's criteria for a degenerate artist. Nordau accuses the degenerate of apocalypticism yet is oblivious to the fact that the picture he paints of an effete and degenerate culture on the brink of collapse makes him most susceptible to the charge.

The 1937 Degenerate Art exhibition mounted by the Nazis has retrospectively assured Nordau's notoriety. Not the least irony is that Nordau was Jewish and would later become one of the ideological founders of Zionism. His pessimism and resentment was in part a reaction to the deeply entrenched anti-semitism of French society that was laid bare by the Dreyfus Affair. Be that as it may, it did not prevent his book serving as a bedrock for Nazi cultural ideology in the visual arts. Aping Nordau, a brochure explained to visitors what the Degenerate Art exhibition was intended to show:

> It means to show, too, how these symptoms
> of degeneracy spread from the deliberate
> troublemakers to infect those more or
> less unwitting acolytes who, in spite
> of previous—and in some cases also
> subsequent—evidence of artistic talent, were
> so lacking in scruple, character or common
> sense as to join in the general Jewish and
> Bolshevik furor.[18]

German Expressionism was the prime target of this attack, together with the museum directors who had supported this art form, many of whom were purged from their jobs. The predilection of modern artists for the child, the "primitive," and the insane was cynically turned against them. To manifest their contempt, the Nazis displayed works in the exhibition in a crowded and haphazard fashion, with derogatory slogans scrawled over adjacent walls. It is not known with certainty whether any pictures by Munch were included, but as an acknowledged precursor for Expressionist art with links to movements branded degenerate by Nordau, 82 works by him were confiscated from German public collections at this time and many of them sold. Fearing the same fate might befall the extensive collection he had formed of his own work, four days after the Nazi occupation of Norway Munch took steps to sign over ownership of it to the Municipality of Oslo; that subsequently became the collection of the Munch Museum.

Kranke Kunst (*Sick Art*) (1975) is a small-scale work on paper by the German postwar artist Anselm Kiefer. A painter allied with Neo-Expressionism, Kiefer is known for his monumental canvases dealing with German history. Kiefer cites a reluctance to confront the Nazi era in post-war Germany as one of the factors that drove him to become an artist. *Kranke Kunst* has an underlying image of a mountainous landscape with a lake, a clichéd scene familiar from

Expressionist painting as well as in works by artists approved of by the Nazis, that has been covered over with festering sores. Kiefer has revisited this subject periodically since 1975, when this version was produced, most recently in a picture shown earlier this year (2014) at the annual Royal Academy summer exhibition. These latter-day examples of "*Syphilis Kunst*" bring to mind the deranged diatribe about syphilis that fills a dozen pages of *Mein Kampf* (1925) and the toxic language of infection that drove the cleansing of Expressionist art from German museums. *Kranke Kunst* is a shockingly visceral "return of the repressed" and a warning of the heavy price exacted upon the avant-garde by its keeping common cause with disease.

Bjarne Melgaard

"Beyond Death: Viral Discontents and Contemporary Notions about AIDS" was the title of a program of seminars delivered at a local university by Bjarne Melgaard as Norway's representative at the 2011 Venice biennale. A separate installation produced by Melgaard with students who took the course titled *Baton Sinister* occupied the Palazzo Contarini Corfù from 2–31 June.[19] The project, a unique artistic undertaking, posed questions about the relationship of disease to the art practice of an artist widely regarded as Munch's successor.

The eruption of AIDS in the early 1980s ushered in a new fin de siècle with the apocalyptic specter of a disease at least as lethal as those that ravaged Europe in Munch's time. Though much has changed since, for the first decade there was no effective treatment to halt the depredations produced by the HIV virus on the body's immune system. A diagnosis of HIV was akin to a death sentence. Diseases that had been thought vanquished by antibiotics, such as tuberculosis, returned as opportunistic infections in bodies whose capacity to fight off other invaders had been destroyed. The potent cocktail of sex and death presented by AIDS is not dissimilar to syphilis a century before, though AIDS is more discriminating in its choice of victims.[20] Dubbed the "gay plague" to begin with, AIDS reinforced a link between homosexuality and disease that was a vestige of the late nineteenth century. It fuelled a rise in homophobia and anti-gay violence that is still evident in many parts of the world today. As with syphilis in the nineteenth century, the moralizing of disease and the blaming of its victims was rampant. In the US it helped precipitate the culture wars that pitched a fundamentalist religious right, for whom AIDS was "god's wrath" for immoral behavior, against a supposedly godless avant-garde. To an extent, everyone, though especially gay men who are deemed "at risk," has been living with AIDS since it was identified. Within popular culture, a deluge of disaster movies with titles like *Epidemic* (1987) and *Contagion* (2011) reflect a mood of pessimism and foreboding for which AIDS is at least in part responsible. More benignly, metaphors of viral contagion have permeated thinking in the three decades since the appearance of AIDS. The fashionable term "gone viral" to describe contagion in the social media is an illustration of how culturally we have been immunized with the virus.[21]

AIDS was the cause of a profound crisis in and of representation. This was not only because of the invisibility of the virus, its long latency period and the fact that it is only secondary illnesses such as Kaposi's sarcoma that make it visible, but also on account of its sublime un-representability. AIDS was both infinitely large—in terms of the potential numbers infected—and infinitely small. AIDS took a heavy toll on artists. For those infected or at risk because of their sexuality, it was no longer business as usual. ACT UP, an activist group that was formed at this time to agitate against the political inaction of the Reagan administration, appropriated the pink triangle from the Nazi Holocaust which appeared above the slogan SILENCE = DEATH. "ACT UP is impolite, abrasive, rude—like the virus that is killing us," wrote one of its members. The question of what has become of activist art was a central concern of "Beyond Death: Viral Discontents and Contemporary Notions about AIDS" to which we will return below.[22]

Despite all of this, it seems that "cool" was the watchword for mainstream contemporary art in the 1980s and 1990s. In New York, post-minimal, post-conceptual art was the only show in town as far as critics who called the shots were concerned. At this time, the Neo-Expressionism of European artists Georg Baselitz, Anselm Kiefer, and others, and their US equivalents, artists like Julian Schnabel and Jean-Michel Basquiat, was lambasted as a reactionary return to painting by influential critics Benjamin Buchloh and Hal Foster.[23] But, as Pierre Bourdieu reminds us,

> Detachment, disinterestedness, indifference—aesthetic theory has so often presented these as the only way to recognize the work of art for what it is, autonomous, *selbstandig*, that one ends up forgetting that they really mean disinvestment, detachment, indifference, in other words, the refusal to invest oneself and take things seriously.[24]

Such a pose of *hauteur* and ironic indifference was inimical to an artist deeply affected by the AIDS epidemic. Affirming his relation to an expressionist tradition that includes Emil Nolde, Oskar Kokoschka, and groups like CoBrA and the Viennese Actionists, Melgaard states that "art is to express emotions that somehow are both universal and marginal."[25] Melgaard is *not* cool. His art exudes a surplus of affect. He works rapidly: one can see this haste, as a manic turning around of mourning possibly, in artworks that flaunt their provisionality and ephemerality. He paints not for posterity but with the expectation that it may all just vaporize and disappear. His working process is one that tries to capture the immediacy of an idea and leaves no time for revision. It is raw, uncensored, and defiantly not politically correct.

The AIDS epidemic gave rise to a body of literature that has been an important influence for Melgaard who sees his paintings as akin to novels. One response was the emergence of a testamentary form of writing by authors who were themselves diagnosed with AIDS. In the era before HAART transformed life expectancies, these autobiographic narratives "plotted" in diaristic fashion the inevitable physical decline that accompanied falling T-cell counts, tracking a literal "death of the author." Within the field of AIDS literature, Monica Pearl describes a second, hybrid form of "autobiographical fiction" that she designates as queer. Pearl points to an analogy between the impurity of genre, where the truth-telling imperative of autobiography is contaminated by fiction, and AIDS itself. The hybrid nature of the texts marks them as impure or infected, she writes.[26] *To the Friend Who Did Not Save My Life* (1991), a novel by the French author Hervé Guibert, is an example of this genre. Though a novel, it so happens that the narrator is also called Hervé Guibert. He is ill with AIDS from which his friend Muzil dies in the course of the novel. The latter turns out to be a truthful portrait of Michel Foucault who died from AIDS in 1984. Guibert's writing adopts the format of a diary, but avails itself of the extra resources of fiction. Melgaard cites as an important influence on him novelist Guillaume Dustan's *In My Room* [*Dans ma chambre*] (1995), described as a work of "auto-fiction."[27] Dustan was a Parisian magistrate who spent his nights cruising the gay bars and clubs. The novel, which has also been dubbed "autopornobiographie" gives a "blow by blow" account, related in drily matter of fact language, of his sexual exploits with the men he picked up. *In My Room* reveals how "the band played on," so to speak, notwithstanding the ubiquitous presence of AIDS in the background.

Melgaard has written more than a dozen novels. These generally consist of fairly rudimentary scenarios that are amenable to translation into the visual format of painting and installation. They are comparable in this respect with a Freudian definition of phantasy as "still scripts (*scénarios*) of organized scenes which are capable of dramatization—usually in visual form." Phantasies are a "sequence in which the subject has his own part to play and in which permutations of roles and attributions are possible"—like auto-fiction, they are neither purely biographical nor fictional.[28] The indeterminacy of auto-fiction enables Melgaard to vacillate between a neutral observer and a participant in the sub-cultures he documents. Ann Demeester astutely remarks: "[Melgaard] himself never specifies how far he is involved in the scene, if he really shares their obscure preferences and beliefs or if he is just an interested 'outsider' who solely observes the

phenomenon from a distance."[29] Once again, this is not dissimilar to phantasy where the subject typically is both an observer and a participant. A form of self-presentation that hovers somewhere between truth and fiction and where phantasy has a large part to play is common experience in web-based chatrooms, catering to interests ranging from vanilla to the more extreme. The images that Melgaard downloads from the internet, ostensibly shocking, of practices like auto-asphyxiation, turn out quite often—though exactly which ones it is not always possible to say—to demand a "suspension of disbelief."

"Auto-fiction" sets aside the obligation of autobiography to tell the whole truth and nothing but the truth. The assumption that the author and the narrator are one and the same is also thrown into disarray. For the gay artist or writer, this can represent a liberation from an imprisoning stricture that goes with being gay, namely the expectation that absolutely everything about one follows from one's sexuality. It returns one to the happy limbo of a non-identity. For this reason, Pearl is right to designate the hybrid form of AIDS literature, which stages a "death of the author" in this more metaphorical sense, as queer.[30] The sheer eclecticism and heterogeneity of Melgaard's art practice entails a similar queer disruption of identity. A paradigmatic postmodernist, he ranges adeptly across a bewildering multiplicity of forms of expression: painting, filmmaking, the novel, installation, curating, etc. "I don't see myself as a painter but view equally all my artistic output as similar and just as one continuous big work" he states.

With Melgaard, the naïve faith in art as the direct expression of an authorial subject is thwarted. The source of an enunciation—a provocative statement daubed on a canvas—is routinely left vacant, as an open question to the viewer. Melgaard speaks of using language to "recontextualize the most banal references and somehow make them almost transcendental by just letting them exist." The work is an arena in which Melgaard orchestrates competing, often contradictory, voices. It is similar to an epistolary genre such as the mail art of Ray Johnson where the work is formed of an accumulation of utterances by different authors.

Melgaard's familiar technique of graffiti-like overpainting creates a dialogue with the underlying image or artwork. It is instructive to refer to Mikhail Bakhtin's notion of heteroglossia in seeking to account for this cacophonous mixture of voices within the space of the visual image. In a paper on "Discourse in the Novel" (1935), Bakhtin defined heteroglossia as a coexistence of, and conflict between, different varieties of speech, each of which implies its own distinct point of view. Bakhtin argues that the novelistic form derives its power from the relativizing force of the collision and hybridization of linguistic utterances.[31] Melgaard speaks pertinently of "taking on voices that are not necessarily your own and inhabit[ing] those words with [new] content and meaning." Once again, hybrid impurity might be thought analogous to a virus that overruns the body's immune system, infecting it with alterity.

The potential conflict between theory and the need for urgent action in the face of official inaction has been a thorny issue since the outset of the AIDS epidemic. More overtly political than his previous installations, *Baton Sinister* borrowed an *agitprop* format from the historical avant-garde. Pictures hung awry on walls had slogans daubed upon them, some of which questioned the exclusion of various figures from the Venice biennale. Adjacent walls were covered with screeds of text. An entire room was covered with the words "Capital," "Power," "War," "Die," "Live," "Sex," "HIV," "God" densely packed in random permutations. There were also piles of posters printed with the same slogans for visitors to take away with them, a visual homage to Félix Gonzáles-Torres, the Cuban born gay artist whose work publicly addressed AIDS before he himself succumbed to it in 1996. At the same time, Melgaard recognizes that queer theory had more of a presence in this work than had been the case before. A lengthy passage from Lee Edelman's *No Future: Queer Theory and the Death Drive* (2004) was copied onto a wall. Melgaard also conducted an interview with Leo Bersani, an eminent academic and one of the pioneers of queer theory, which was made into a film and played on a screen within the installation. For all that, Melgaard did not mean to grant any kind of epistemological privilege to theory. It was just one voice amongst several. Indeed, in the interview with Bersani, his questioning sometimes seems irreverent and skeptical.

"Beyond Death," the overall title of Melgaard's project, points to a main bone of contention with these queer theorists, namely the status that they ascribe to the psychoanalytic death drive and negativity. This could be seen as a legacy of the AIDS epidemic in the first decade when homosexual desire became synonymous with death. Bersani's essay, "Is the rectum a grave?," one of the founding texts of queer theory, was written at the height of the epidemic when anal sex was an absolute taboo, a sort of abjected, phobic object.[32] The approach of these writers has been to endorse the negativity that queerness is taken to represent. "Rather than rejecting, with liberal discourse, this ascription of negativity to the queer, we might," Edelman argues, "do better to consider accepting and even embracing it." Edelman links this queer negativity in a passage copied verbatim on a wall in Melgaard's installation "to the 'aberrant or atypical,' to what chafes against 'normalization.'"[33]

Melgaard's main objection is that these theories are no longer relevant to a situation where HIV/AIDS is not the death sentence that it once was. That seems to be what is implied by the notion of "beyond death". Placing the death drive at the heart of queer subjectivity, Bersani seems to endorse the stereotype of the death-bound gay and could be accused of harking back, in a vein of nostalgia, to the early days of the epidemic. Bersani readily admits the difficulty of translating his views into any form of recipe for political action. Be that as it may, one wonders in what sense, if any, we are now truly beyond death? The imagery reproduced in *Black Low* (2002), one of the darkest and most transgressive of Melgaard's projects to date, suggests that we have not reached that point quite yet. The eroticization of pain and suffocation, whether it is real or mere pretense, could be viewed as a case of traumatic repetition, i.e. of the trauma of AIDS, and thus as needing something like the death drive in order to explain it.

Barebacking, the name given to "unsafe" sex without protection of a condom, which has been blamed for a rise in new HIV infections, has been the object of controversy and theoretical reflection. The majority of individuals engaging in unsafe sex do not actively wish to seroconvert. More baffling are those known as "bugchasers" who deliberately seek to become infected. For Tim Dean, who has devoted a book to theorizing this subject, seroconversion gains the individual access to a community bound through sharing the virus.[34] Once again, Melgaard is very impatient with these explanations. His argument that unsafe sex is on the comeback because people don't like using condoms has a fair amount of common sense on its side. But one wonders if a single person will have been swayed by the summary advice doled out in the Venice installation: "Don't get fucked up the ass. Period." I am inclined to think the solution to our viral discontents may be harder to find.

One area where queer theory and an activist practice coexist more harmoniously is over the need to analyze and confront homophobia, which Melgaard has done fearlessly. Most recently, he strategically repurposed Munch's *The Kiss* in a video of himself and his ex-boyfriend released to coincide with the Sochi Winter Olympics in February 2014 as part of an international protest against laws enacted by Russia that discriminate against homosexuality. The blithe homophobia of Rap and Hip Hop may be one reason for the slogan declaring "Rap Sucks" in *Baton Sinister*, but Melgaard also recognizes that such homophobia exists in the Black Metal groups that are a major source of inspiration for him.[35] Analyzing the causes of homophobia has been one of the tasks of queer theory. Freud's schema for delusional jealousy, discussed above in relation to Munch's treatment of this subject, according to which jealousy represents the disavowal of a homoerotic wish, forces one to consider that jealousy towards homosexuals—of their relative freedom from conventional mores— may be a factor producing homophobic hatred. Freud even compares it in this respect to paranoia. With this in mind, "Jealous," the provocative title of an exhibition by Melgaard in 2010, may have been an accusation directed at the straight audience of the show. At times, Melgaard has advocated more violent resistance based on the example of the Black Panthers in the 1960s, though so far these calls to action remain as gestures. Melgaard's interrogation of the violence, symbolic and actual, that is part of gay lived experience, not just in parts of the world where virulent homophobia is on the increase, makes his art an exemplary instance of a task that Didier Eribon has defined as: "to create spaces— practical spaces as well as literary and theoretical ones—in which to resist subjection and in which to reformulate oneself."[36]

The earnestness of Melgaard's intervention must have struck a discordant note amidst the general frivolity and self-congratulation of the Venice biennale. It is ironic that many of the collectors who are behind the boom in contemporary art, for whom the biennale is a party not to be missed, come from parts of the world that are least tolerant to homosexuality. As a further irony, the art market thrives on risk-taking by contrast with the risk reduction strategies of AIDS prevention. It may be because of the controversy generated by his work, rather than in spite of it, that the artworld—including the art market—has been so hospitable to Melgaard. Is this tolerance because art changes nothing, as he observes? Still, that his art provokes such questions shows that, thankfully, we are a long way from 1937 and the Degenerate Art exhibition.

I wish to thank Lars Toft-Eriksen for providing me with sources that were indispensable for writing this essay, and Bjarne Melgaard for patiently responding to my questions.

—

1   Susan Sontag, *Illness as Metaphor* and *AIDS and its Metaphors* (London, 1991), p. 3.

2   Dr. Louis Rénon, *Maladies populaires: maladies vénériennes, alcoolisme, tuberculose* (Paris, 1905). See also David Barnes, *The Making of a Social Disease: Tuberculosis in Nineteenth-Century France* (Berkeley, CA, 1995).

3   Rénon points out that the annual death rate due to tuberculosis in France alone was equal to the population of a city the size of Toulouse.

4   Quoted in Sue Prideaux, *Edvard Munch: Behind the Scream* (New Haven and London, 2005), pp. 24–5.

5   On spirit photography, see *Le Troisième oeil: La photographie et l'occulte*, exh. cat., Maison européenne de la photographie (Paris, 2004).

6   Among them, *Women in Hospital* (1897) in the Munch Museum's collection (MM M 28).

7   Sigmund Freud, "Some Neurotic mechanisms in Jealousy, Paranoia and Homosexuality' (1922 [1921]), *The Pelican Freud Library*, vol. 10 (London, 1979), p. 199. We shall return to the question of jealousy and homophobia below.

8   Gustave Le Bon, *Psychologie des foules* (Paris, 1991 [1895]), p. 74.

9   Cited in Alison Morehead, "'Are there Bacteria in the Rooms of Monte Carlo?': The Roulette Paintings, 1891–93,' in Mai Britt Guleng and Ingebjørg Ydstie, eds., *Munch Becoming 'Munch'. Artistic Strategies 1880–1892*, exh. cat., Munch Museum (Oslo, 2008).

10   Robert Nye remarks that a "medical model of cultural crisis' arose in this period. Robert Nye, *Crime, Madness and Politics in Modern France: The Medical Concept of National Decline* (New Jersey, 1984). See also Daniel Pick, *Faces of Degeneration. A European Disorder, c.1848–c.1918* (Cambridge, 1989).

11   Susan Sontag (op cit., p. 31) notes that degeneracy arrogated to itself symptoms that had been hallmarks of tuberculosis: weakness, exhaustion, and a gradual ebbing away of life force.

12   See Lee Edelman, *No Future: Queer Theory and the Death Drive* (Durham and London, 2004).

13   Of interest here is Barnes's analysis of *déchéance* or "decay' as a term in medical discourse to describe the effects of disease and alcoholism upon the body. Barnes 1995, p. 151.

14   Joris-Karl Huysmans, *Against Nature* (London, 1959 [1884]), p. 98.

15   Röntgen's wife, on seeing the X-ray of her hand, reputedly said: "I have seen my own death.'

16   The formal homology with a drawing titled *Harpy* (1898) in which a creature hovers above the longitudinally oriented dead body of a man is most telling.

17   Max Nordau, *Degeneration* (Lincoln and London, 1993 [1895]), p. 31.

18   *'Degenerate Art': The Fate of the Avant-Garde in Nazi Germany*, exh. cat., Los Angeles County Museum of Art (1991), p. 360.

19   The installation was recreated in 2012 for an exhibition at the Haugar Art Museum, Tønsberg, Norway. A catalogue with extensive visual documentation of the original installation was published on this occasion.

20   See Sander Gilman, "AIDS and Syphilis: The Iconography of Disease' in *October* 43 (winter 1987), pp. 87–107.

21   See Tony Sampson, *Virality: Contagion Theory in the Age of Networks* (Minneapolis, 2012).

22   A number of focused historical exhibitions in the past couple of years have revisited AIDS activism in the first decade of the epidemic. One explanation for what became of such activism is that it mutated into such things as the campaign for gay marriage rights—for the normalization of gayness, in other words.

23   Hal Foster, *Recodings: Art, Spectacle and Cultural Politics* (New York, 1998).

24   Pierre Bourdieu, *Distinction: A Social Critique of the Judgment of Taste* (Boston, MA, 1984), p. 34.

25   E-mail correspondence with the author, 18 October 2014. All direct quotations of Melgaard in my text are from this source.

26   Monica Pearl, *AIDS Literature and Gay Identity* (New York & London, 2013), pp. 71–75. Rosalind Krauss, in an essay on the "post-medium condition," proposes that fiction operates as an over-arching medium for Marcel Broodthaers' art practice, which like Melgaard's is very heterogeneous. Similar to Melgaard, statements by Broodthaers point to the form of the novel as having been a model for his visual practice. Rosalind Krauss, *"A Voyage on the North Sea": Art in the Age of the Post-Medium Condition* (London, 2000), pp. 46–47.

27 Guillaume Dustan, *In My Room* (London, 1998).

28   J. Laplanche and J.B. Pontalis, *The Language of Psychoanalysis* (London, 1988), p. 318.

29 *Black Low: The Punk Movement was Just Hippies with Short Hair*, exh. cat., MARTa Hertford, 2002

30 Lee Edelman writes, for instance, that: "queerness can never define an identity; it can only ever disturb one.' Lee Edelman, *No Future: Queer Theory and the Death Drive* (Durham, NC, 2004) p. 17.

31 Mikhail Bakhtin, "Discourse in the Novel.' *The Dialogic Imagination: Four Essays* (Austin, TX, 1981), pp. 259–422.

32 Leo Bersani, "Is the Rectum a Grave?" in *October* 43 (winter 1987), pp. 197–222.

33 Edelman 2004, p. 4 and p. 6. Edelman's book could be read as an argument for the ethical and political necessity of sick art.

34 See Tim Dean, *Unlimited Intimacy: Reflections on the Subculture of Barebacking* (Chicago, 2009). The rehabilitation of Guy Hocquenghem in queer theory circles lately reflects a desire for a return to the *status quo ante*.

35 See Zoe Williams, "Hiphopophobia,' *The Guardian* (29 April 2003).

36 Didier Eribon, *Insult and the Making of the Gay Self* (Durham and London, 2004), p. 9.

LARS TOFT-ERIKSEN
New York, 7 October 2014

The Art of Penetrating the Negative

—

An interview with Bjarne Melgaard

LTE: We are working together on an exhibition at the Munch Museum, which opens in a few months. It will be the first in a series of exhibitions in which Edvard Munch's art is shown side by side with the work of another artist. Some of them are contemporaries of Munch, while others come chronologically after him. One of these artists is Asger Jorn, who in his artistic endeavours was very preoccupied with Munch and quite clearly inspired by him. It is not that we are necessarily of the opinion that all of the artists in the series are inspired by Munch, but rather that there is some form of kinship between them. And in this particular exhibition I contribute a curatorial project, where I assert that there is a relationship between Munch's art and yours. But before we come to that, I wonder how you relate to Munch? And what has Munch meant to you with regard to your own artwork?

—

BM: For me—when you are from Norway, you cannot avoid Munch. He's a kind of centrifugal force that is very difficult to resist, and which is very dominating in a way. When I was studying to become an artist in Norway I experienced it as almost oppressive. But it wasn't until I left Norway and matured that I began to look at Munch and beame interested in him. And then in particular with regard to how he worked with untouched surfaces, how he left some of the canvas white, and didn't cover the entire surface with paint. I think it's interesting how Munch's mode of expression is created very quickly. There are stories about how when people sat for him to have their portraits painted, it would take maybe twenty minutes, and then he was done. There's a kind of hasty and disrespectful attitude to painting, at the same time that it's very sure-handed. Munch has been very important to me in the sense that he was an artist who had a kind of quick and sketch-like immediacy, and who accepted the first result he achieved. It all happened instantaneously. At one point this

was important for me as a painter. And then there is the interest in Munch as a personality, of course …

—

LTE: You sometimes refer to Munch's motifs, such as *The Hands* and *Kiss,* in your artworks. What was it you actually intended with these references? What do think about them today?

—

BM: I did that in the 90s, yes. At that time I experienced Munch's presence as so overpowering, and so difficult to penetrate into that I thought I might just as well make use of it. In order to get past Munch's overwhelming position in Norwegian art I thought that I shouldn't be afraid of taking hold of his art and recirculating it in a way, or contextualising it in relation to my own time. Today I think that Munch was just something I as a painter had to relate to and work through. It was a part of the process I was in as an artist at that time.

—

LTE: Your point about Munch's enormous position in the Norwegian art world is interesting. But it is not about his art alone. It also has to do with his reception, with the position we give him in Norwegian art history, as the single great master. Munch is often presented like this, as a monument in Norwegian art, as a standard that all other artists are measured by. If you were to compare this with French art history, which is far more internationally oriented and has a long list of great names—Poussin, Ingres, Courbet, Manet, Cézanne, Picasso, Duchamp, just to name a few of the greatest— it is almost impossible to place someone in such a monumental position and thereby lay the foundation for a uniform standard for all artists. If one looks at Norwegian art history of the past one hundred years, there is a long line of artists who are compared to Munch in one way or another, but apparently always in such a way that their oeuvres remain in the shadow of Munch—as though it is something they are expected to live up to. This applies to a large degree to your work as well. You are often compared to Munch in various ways, whether it has to do with mode of expression or the references to Munch in your pictures, and it applies in particular to the press, which loves to pull out the "Munch card" whenever they discuss your artistic project. Phrases such as "the new Munch" or "the greatest since Munch" appear regularly when you are mentioned in the papers. In my view there is something rather provincial and reductive in this approach to art, where the art of the other artist is virtually reduced to a pale copy of Munch. What do you think about this comparison?

—

BM: I think it is unimaginative and simplistic. It reveals an apparent lack of critical thinking with respect to visual art in general. I also think it seriously diminishes the quality of the discourse surrounding Munch's oeuvre. One should rather pose the question of why one is interested in a new Munch at all. It is a little pathetic and unenlightened, if you ask me. It's as though the Norwegian cultural scene cannot come up with anything new. Do we really need a new Munch? Furthermore, I do not feel any particular kinship with Munch. I have been just as preoccupied with other artists, such as Matisse and Gauguin and Monet. But also the entire classical French tradition: Géricault, Poussin, Millet, Fragonard, Watteau—the whole Rococo period per se. I have also been interested in the expressive school, which Munch is of course a part of. But here artists such as Emil Nolde and Asger Jorn have been just as important to me. I am also very interested in Jean Dubuffet. In other words, I do not feel that Munch has been a pivotal point in my art, someone who I constantly compare myself to. As an artist one is supposed to liberate oneself from the old idols.

—

LTE: In light of what you are saying now, what do you think about exhibiting together with Munch? Just the two of you together, that is? Isn't it a little difficult, a risk that you might be in danger of confirming Munch's significance for you as an artist, and not least the concept of "Melgaard as the new Munch"?

—

BM: I think it is very interesting, actually. The way we have worked on the exhibition, we haven't exactly set the tone for such comparisons. It seems to me rather that you problematize this theme. And then again, I have had free rein with respect to my contribution to the exhibition. In my opinion it has had very little at all to do with Munch. I also think it is interesting how we have organised it so that my contribution is presented as an isolated section within the exhibition, while you curate the remainder of the exhibition with Munch's and my work around this. This gives me the possibility of commenting on the exhibition, of almost sabotaging it in a way.

—

LTE: Sabotage—what do you mean by that?

—

BM: Well, one might expect that if you participate in an exhibition of this kind, as an artist you might take Munch's works as the point of departure and re-work them, instead of insisting on your own universe in the midst of his. For me that would be wrong. I think it is important that as an artist you develop your own project; that you succeed in distancing yourself from your models and don't suffer under a kind of "bad daddy" complex. Perhaps Munch plays this role of "bad daddy" for many. I'm thinking of artists like Martin Kippenberger and Georg Baselitz, and others who have some "bad daddy" or other that they follow and hump after. It's like so retro-garde. For me it's more interesting to see how Munch might have relevance today. I feel that he is on some level very current and socially relevant.

—

LTE: What do you have in mind? Can you give us some examples?

—

BM: For instance his dystopian worldview. How he failed to believe that an interpersonal relationship was possible. There is something fundamentally anti-social about Munch. I feel that it has great relevance today. According to Leo Bersani, there is something to gain from exploring the negative elements in a culture, the things that oppose the social order. Through an exploration of this kind one can contribute to changing society. I feel that Munch occupies such a position. That as an artist he positioned himself as an outsider and entered into the negative side of the social contract and the psychological mechanisms that resulted from it. This is very similar to Freud and the development of psychoanalysis during this period. On one level I don't think that very much has changed since Munch's time. And that is why I feel that his art continues to be very relevant.

—

LTE: Do you see a relationship between your artistic project and Munch's oeuvre in this context?

—

BM: Well—when I was working on my contribution for the Whitney Biennial, I was very preoccupied with the idea of the Antropocene epoch in geology, about how humans in the course of a few hundred years have transformed the earth's geology. Human beings have changed the most fundamental aspect of nature. There is something post-apocalyptic about this. To me this is interesting. On a metaphorical level it says something about human beings, how we exist together. There is a kind of innate self-destructive and catastrophic force in humans. We are driven towards our own demise. The catastrophe awaits and there is no way back. I feel that Munch touches on this in his art. In a way he depicts an acknowledgement of the catastrophic and inhuman aspects of society. One can see this for instance in pictures like *The Death of Marat* or *Red Virginia Creeper*— or *The Scream*, for that matter.

—

LTE: I can see that. But at the same time I feel there is a great distance between your artistic project

and Munch's. Although there are points in common on a fundamental level, I would claim that your work is almost in opposition to Munch's when it come to social and interpersonal issues. While Munch, through his art, appears introverted and isolated, you appear rather extroverted and explorative. More open in a way. I am thinking of how you explore subcultures and make use of this material in your art. In this sense you identify with *the other*—you embrace and incorporate the negative, to quote Bersani. With Munch I experience rather the opposite, that he distances himself from the negative, even though he deals with it in his art. I am thinking for instance of his view of women. How he approaches woman with fear and contempt. Munch expresses fear in an encounter with the negative, in the sense that women represent the negative in a Freudian understanding—as representatives of the irrational in opposition to the rational order of society.

—

BM: Right, in a way it's a kind of twisted tribute to man, and all the problems and neuroses connected to heterosexuality in his work, you might say, which one can experience as very claustrophobic and repressive. I think this eternal female focus of his can be rather oppressive. All of these affairs with women, one gets sort of tired of them.

—

LTE: Yes, perhaps. Art historian Patricia Berman has discussed how Munch's representation of men can appear destabilising in relation to the normative discourse about gender and sexuality during the 1890s. She goes as far as interpreting artworks like *Ashes* from 1894, where Munch depicts a specific "crisis" in the male sexual identity, as a form of rebellion against contemporary normalising and moralising masculine ideals. She links this to the developments in psychiatry during that period with references to thinkers like Richard von Krafft-Ebing and Max Nordau, in which the binary gender model is challenged by their studies of sexuality. In his findings Krafft-Ebing claims that homosexuality represents a kind of deviating and unnatural third gender, which is situated somewhere between the two healthy gender poles. According to Berman, Munch enters into this discourse with his representations that subvert the normative ideas about gender and sexuality. It strikes me that there is a parallel between Berman's point and your reference to Leo Bersani's concept of the negative. One can perhaps view Berman's reading of Munch's representations of gender in relation to your concept of penetrating the negative, and using it subversively in relation to normative perceptions of gender and sexuality?

—

BM: Well—I think the so-called subversive culture that is described in some of my works is a part of the common culture. It's just that it is not visible. I believe that very many people do very strange things in their private lives, which they don't necessarily talk about. But when I depict some of this in my art, and put it out there in public space, there is suddenly a tremendous fuss around it. And then there is something about the innate power of art. Things that people surround themselves with on a daily basis in the media suddenly become much more provoking when they are treated in art.

—

LTE: Yet there are representations in your art that quite obviously transcend what is considered "normal." I'm thinking among other things of your representations of *snuff* and that sort of thing. In many of your pictures you portray rather extreme and violent forms of sexuality, which I would venture to say transcend normal notions about sex. But I guess that through these representations you touch upon more common and normative notions of gender and sexuality, by delving into extreme images that stand in stark contrast to what is normative. As you say, you wish to delve into the negative aspects of the culture. And these forces that you deal with in this way are of course universal, even though they take on extreme forms in your art.

—

BM: When I made the exhibition *Shame* for the Bergen International Festival in 2003, *barebacking* and a certain fetishizing of HIV within homosexual subcultures was an important topic to my work. Yet, no one talked about it. It was totally ignored. I think what this implies is that, on a fundamental level, sexuality is a form of neurosis. And that immediately causes difficulties. One enters the realm of the abnormal and unhealthy, then, and perhaps I even enter into mental experiences that there is no language for. By illustrating violent and self-destructive sexuality, perhaps I touch upon painful human experiences that don't lend themselves to being verbalized. Elaine Scarry writes that pain is just pain, and cannot be verbalized. For me it has been important to delve into this subject matter. I have been interested in exploring the extent to which someone is willing to subject their own body and the destructive experience that this implies. I have done research on pretty heavy subjects. I was on a website talking with men who scrubbed their asses with toothbrushes before they went out to get laid. They wanted to be sure to bleed, so that they could absorb HIV infected semen. There was even one guy I came in touch with on the internet who not only wanted to become HIV infected, he wanted to have sex with someone with *full blown* AIDS, so that he was certain to contract the disease. And then he wanted to go on meds afterwards. We are talking about very extreme conditions for what you are willing to allow your body to go through. It is an extreme form of sexual neurosis, where the body becomes a war zone in a way. I don't really know how this can be explained psychologically, but I don't think it has to do with a death wish, as Jean Laplanche has suggested. I think it's more a form of emotional alienation.

—

LTE: In a sense you are describing the outsider position. And I am not just thinking of alienation in relation to one's own emotions, but just as much of the condition where an individual stands in opposition to the normative society and culture.

—

BM: Yes, it has been very important for me to explore the places where abnormality exists in society. For me it has to do with being homosexual. In many ways I don't think there has been any real homosexual liberation, because this fight for freedom has in some strange way excluded what is different and divergent. The struggle to marry and have children has a reverse side, which shoves everything that doesn't fit into the hetero-normative category into the dark. It creates a sort of quasi hetero-normative situation. I feel that certain aspects of the homosexual culture, which continue to be oppressed, are important. They represent an opportunity or space to explore what is negative in our culture. That which is difficult, painful and possibly without language. One can say that in a way I have been preoccupied with depicting homosexuality as a state of illness, which says something about human beings. For instance my pictures from the exhibition in Herford, where a homosexual male in a sex scene cuts off his own nipple and then takes a drill and bores it into the wound afterwards. Of course it is extreme, but it is also a sick form of sexuality. It's not that I think all homosexuality is that extreme, but I think it is interesting to explore homosexuality as an illness. It is something that opposes the hetero-normative standard, but which also has a more universal relevance. Sexuality also encompasses a kind of sorrow and loneliness. If you think about the whole cruising culture, there is like a great deal of melancholy and a lot of loneliness and enormous existential emptiness in that culture. I have been pre-occupied with depicting this, because I feel

that it has to do with mental states that exist in all of us.

—

LTE: The biographical or diary-like element is an important part of your oeuvre on some level. I am thinking in particular of the novels you have written, but also the written fragments you include in your paintings and drawings. In this way your art—paintings, sculptures as well as drawings—somehow has the feel of having been marked by real life. How do you relate to biography in art? What do you think about its role, and how does it contribute to the mode of expression of your art?

—

BM: There is actually not very much autobiography in my art at all. I am much more interested in auto-fiction. I think it is interesting to create different auto-fictive personalities, and make people speculate about what is true or not true. To me it is an important point that people wonder whether what they see is possible or not. There is something subversive in it as well, and in a way that intensifies the extreme quality of my pictures.

—

LTE: I see. That is something that I also find in Munch, where there is an unclear separation between the biographical and the fictive. And perhaps not unlike you, I think that the biographical or auto-fictive is an operational aspect of Munch's art in the sense that it underscores and intensifies the motif and the subject matter.

—

BM: Right, if you use biographical elements, or something you pretend to be biographical, you achieve enormous energy and an effective way of drawing the viewer into the picture. It is as though you entice him by insinuating that the key to the artist's own life experience can be found here, which very many are actually quite curious about. I believe a form of visual dynamism can arise out of this energy field, which opens the artwork to the viewer. I have painted numerous abstract paintings, but I don't think anyone has ever actually noticed them.

—

LTE: That brings me to think of provocation in art, which of course is another type of energy that draws the viewer into the work via other mechanisms. How to you relate to provocation as an artistic strategy? And how do you view it with respect to your own oeuvre?

—

BM: Well, you know it's somewhat true that something that is seen as very provoking in the art field is not always perceived that way in other areas of society. And I think this has a lot to do with the expectations one has to art as something that serves beauty and goodness. I find it interesting to challenge this. It is a little bit like what we spoke about earlier, that art should be subversive. It is part of my artistic project.

—

LTE: Well, now we seem to have moved on to the predictable question of what art is.

—

BM: To me art is interesting when it moves me, when it changes the image and understanding I have of myself, and helps me to move on. You know, when I lived in Australia I had given up making art. I had quit the Van Eyck Academy in Maastricht and moved to Sydney. I was fed up. But then I caught a performance by Meg Cranston, which was called *God Love the Tragic Artist*, where she explained the drawings she had made of Marvin Gaye. Eventually I understood that it was not about the life of Marvin Gaye; she was explaining her own life through the life and art of another person. It made such a great impression on me that I regained my belief that art can move human beings and change them and open up to new mental states. It changed something in me. So I began to make art again. Had it not been for Meg Cranston, I'm sure I would still be a beach bum in Sydney.

—

Translated from Norwegian by Francesca M. Nichols

ØYSTEIN SJÅSTAD
Ph.D., Art History

Phallosophy: Draft for an Art Theory Based on Munch and Melgaard

———

Phallus, an image of the (usually erect) penis, esp. as a symbol of the generative power in nature, venerated in various religions; *esp.* one carried in the Dionysiac festivals of ancient Greece.

Oxford English Dictionary

"I saw your show last year in New York. Very gay. A lot of cocks."

Janice in Melgaard's novel *A New Novel* (2012)[1]

In April 2009 the Norwegian public broadcasting company NRK aired a piece on Bjarne Melgaard in the cultural program *Safari* in connection with preparations for his solo exhibition *Jealous* at the Astrup Fearnley Museum of Modern Art in Oslo the following year. There was a fuss about a planned series of paintings that was intended to revolve around old photographs from the magazine NAMBLA (North American Man/Boy Love Association). The magazine is published by an association that wants to legalize sexual relations between young boys and older men. Melgaard's paintings contained depictions of boys who were anonymous, yet who might have been victims of sexual abuse. This led to a long line of articles and commentaries being published in the Norwegian press.[2] "Bjarne Melgaard Shocks" was the common refrain in the newspaper articles. Melgaard commented in *Dagbladet*: "I view this as a homo-political issue. For me it is important to present an aspect of the homosexual identity that is not so mainstream, where it is not enough to just get married and behave and have a great time. I believe you can arrive at the core by investigating marginal phenomena."[3] The director of the museum, Gunnar Kvaran, promised that the exhibition would not include works that might be considered illegal. As a result there were no shocking pictures to be seen when the exhibition finally opened.

The reason I mention this is that in the summer of 2009 I was on an outing with the Art Historical Society to the Kistefos Museum north of Oslo, which included a tour of the sculpture park. The guide, a young girl who most likely was a student and worked here during the summer, showed us around with great enthusiasm, but when we arrived at Melgaard's *Octopus* (1997) her manner changed. She bluntly informed us—presumably in light of Melgaard's statements in the media—that she had no desire to say anything about the sculpture and asked us to ignore it. Why did she not want us to observe and discuss the sculpture? *Octopus* is partially hidden in the landscape, and we could see the creature's head sticking up out of the ground, while its tentacles grew up through the grass around it. The sculpture is frightening but at the same time alluring—*unheimlich*, to use Sigmund Freud's term. The sweet-looking head, with its ambiguously scary expression, pops up as though to lure little children to come closer, while the tentacles appear to move about like eight randy slimy phalluses ready to seize the unsuspecting children. It is a monster with sinister intentions hiding behind an innocent mask. This is how one might interpret the work in light of the guide's reaction.

The fuss in 2009 was neither the first nor last time Melgaard created a sensation in the media. Moderna Museet in Stockholm exhibited a work by Melgaard in 2000 that is perhaps even more disturbing than the paintings of more recent years. The video *All Gym Queens Deserve to Die* (1999) portrays an adult male sucking on the arm of an infant. Because it is shot close-up, to begin with you cannot be sure what you are looking at, and it is almost impossible not to mistake the arm for a phallus. This is why it is so disturbing when you realize that the arm belongs to a little child. The video was reported to the police for its paedophile tendencies and the museum management decided to stop the exhibit.

Melgaard is interesting in a historical perspective in these works; in the way he tests how far he can go before he is reported to the police, for instance. Not that it is necessarily the artist's intention, but the works can be perceived as a test of this kind. Art historians such as Whitney Davis, Christopher Reed and Richard Meyer have demonstrated in their work how homosexuality is an area where art can explore and challenge society's moral boundaries when it comes to the limits of freedom of speech. Melgaard's art from 2009 is particularly challenging because he includes paedophile tendencies in the realm of homosexuality. By using this strategy Melgaard emphasised the point made by Davis, Reed and Meyer, in an era when homosexuality has lost much of its provocative power. Although this particular work was an appropriation of existing photographs, and as such does not imply breaking the law, the works nevertheless challenge the moral boundaries of society. Melgaard's art is what Meyer calls "outlaw representation"—a type of art that society wishes to censure based on a form of sexual morality.[4]

Melgaard's works obviously do not represent a romanticising of paedophilia, just as they do not equate homosexuality with paedophilia. But they challenge common standards for how we talk about sexuality, as well as the framework within which society handles the disturbing sides of sexuality.

According to Whitney Davis homoeroticism is a fundamental factor in theories regarding both sexuality and art, and in the work of major theoreticians such as Johann Winckelmann, Sigmund Freud and Michel Foucault, aesthetics and homosexuality coincide in decisive ways. In his studies Richard Meyer emphasizes that both art and homosexuality are "marginal domains,"[5] and that this is something that binds them together. Art and homosexuality are two marginal social orders, which have historically been drawn to each other.

Freud recounts how the artist genius Leonardo da Vinci, as the result of a complicated and traumatic sexual relationship with his stepmother, developed into a narcissist and a homosexual.[6] According to Freud, the narcissistic and homosexual Leonardo exaggerated the aesthetic beauty of the penis and experienced a libidinal desire for it—both his own, but not least that of others. Normally you can only desire what you are not, or do not have, but according to Freud, something goes wrong in the homosexual, which turns him into an immature penis-hungry narcissist. Leonardo was *excessively* interested in penises, and Freud was of the opinion that the homosexual and the narcissist are one and the same, or in other words an onanist. Homosexual artist types like Oscar Wilde, and later Andy Warhol, and not least Bjarne Melgaard, can from a Freudian perspective thus be seen as narcissists and onanists with an unhealthy libidinal interest in penises.

Michel Foucault and others have demonstrated how the concept of the homosexual male was formed around 1870.[7] Interesting to note, this coincides with the emergence of the idea about the avant-garde artist. At this time both the fact of being homosexual and being an avant-garde artist became ideological and psychological categories for identity in the modern sexual and class society. Homosexuality was one of the many new categories that thinkers of the nineteenth century established in order to explain and systematize human behaviour, and homosexuality was often associated with art and aesthetics. In the English vernacular to call someone "artistic" or "arty" was a euphemism for homosexuality, and well into the twentieth century calling someone an "artist" was a nice way of insinuating between the lines that the person in question was gay.[8] There is also a widespread conception that homosexual males, due to their unique combination of masculine and feminine traits, have an exceptional sense of aesthetics, not only as artists, but also as interior decorators, designers, stylists and hairdressers. To have good taste and be artistically inclined could, and still can, be taken as a symptom of being gay. Interestingly enough, Freud's early homosexual patients were aesthetes, and thereby shaped Freud's view of homosexuals. The categories thus overlapped in Freud's mind. To be an "aesthete" might mean that one was gay, as well as that one was an artist. The dandy is an interesting category in this sense, where the artist and the homosexual merge together into one category. Oscar Wilde was more or less an archetypical example of the dandy, on the borderline between artist and homosexual as categories of identity. As Meyer writes about Wilde: "The category of art here serves as both a stand-in for love between men and an aesthetic justification for it."[9] Wilde defended his homoerotic preferences by pointing to his well-developed sense of aesthetics. The homosexual and the artist are, to use Wilde's words, people from whom one expects a distinctive sensitivity and sense of aesthetics. Or as Melgaard says, "Gay men are tender."[10]

In other words, there is convincing evidence that points to a strong connection between homosexuality and the art world in the history of ideas. Perhaps it was precisely because of Wilde that the connection between the two categories has become so strong in our consciousness. He was the first famous homosexual male, and it seems that the concept of aesthetics of that time linked modern art and homosexuality together in such a way that heterosexual artists have since had to fight against it.[11] To be an artist had, and still has, something feminine and homosexual about it. In recent times the connection between art and homosexuality has been designated by expressions such as *camp* and *queer*. These expressions are used today to describe homosexual types and homosexual subcultures, as well as being central expressions in contemporary art. This occurs quite independently of the artist's supposed sexual orientation, with the presumably heterosexual Jeff Koons as contemporary art's most *camp* example. The list of artists who combine an ambiguous sexual identity with artistic abilities is long. During the 1960s Marcel Duchamp was held forth as a *grand old drag-dandy* for a long line of artists who worked with conceptual art, in addition to the Neo-Dadaists Robert Rauschenberg and Jasper Johns. Andy Warhol became a contemporary version of Oscar Wilde himself. Homosexuality became a power influence in its own right in art. To be an artist was to be *queer*. To be *queer* was to criticize the establishment through one's life, the equivalent of being avant-garde. The oppression of homosexuality over time has laid the foundation for a strong and characteristic underground culture, which in turn has made homosexuality a fascinating and effective theme for many artists who are specifically in search of a transgressive idiom.

There is perhaps something exclusive and secretive about the homosexual culture, as well as with the seemingly shocking aspect of its transgressive sexual activity, which appears to be irresistible to the art world—for artists and the public alike. Melgaard plays on this in his art; he draws the viewer into the artworks via a titillating gay subculture, to then shock by appearing transgressive in relation to normative heterosexuality. As Reed writes, "Homosexuality, inscribed by sexology as the secret status of the artist as a 'type,' became the paradigmatic secret of avant-garde art. Its status as an 'open secret'—constantly suspected and hinted at, but never frankly acknowledged—is among the defining characteristics of the modernist avant-garde."[12]

To be gay or *queer* has since the nineteenth century been seen as a way of challenging society's moral codes, as well as legal and social restrictions. To quote Michel Foucault: "To be 'gay' isn't to identify oneself with homosexuality but to seek to

develop a mode of living … an historic occasion for reopening relational and affective virtualities."[13] It has to do with borderline experiences that shatter the self when doing the unthinkable. Melgaard has referred to this himself when, in connection with the Whitney Biennial in 2014, he explained his artistic project as being a radical exploration of human experiences: "I just wanted to experience anything. I wanted to try anything."[14] These are the same ambitions, which the avant-garde and bohemians had during Edvard Munch's time. Munch voluntarily moved about an investigative identity landscape. Munch scholar Patricia G. Berman has demonstrated in her research how Munch portrayed himself as part of a decadent aesthetic, and how he was interested in the contemporary topic that revolved around the decadent artist and ideas regarding morbid and failed masculinity.[15] In some of his pictures Munch reverses the gender roles, and the man, including Munch himself, is often depicted as overly sensitive and weak, almost "feminine." As Christopher Reed writes about this period: "Where some sexologists classed behaviors, including sexual behaviors, into binaries modeled on the two genders, the Aesthetes and Decadents sought to open themselves to the widest possible range of sensations, experiencing everything for its aesthetic potential and transforming it into art."[16] Not surprisingly, this was at about the same time that Freud classified sensitive artist geniuses like Michelangelo and Leonardo as homosexuals, and that Wilde defended homosexuality as a distinctive sense of aesthetics.

In connection with Melgaard's 2012 exhibition *A House to Die In*, the magazine *Dazed & Confused* wrote: "If you just looked at Bjarne Melgaard's paintings without context, you'd still assume him to be a wild, transgressive bad-boy artist, with *a penchant for penises*, violence and tigers."[17] Phalluses and penises, both deflated and in a state of erection, have appeared throughout the entire history of art, from vessels and vases from antiquity to Melgaard's drawings and paintings. Not surprisingly, they are often motifs that have been characterised as homosexual. When an archaeologist came upon a 2500 year old drawing of a phallus on a rock in Greece in 2014, a British newspaper typically came up with the following headline: "The first gay graffiti in history?"[18] Phallicism is a fundamental part of human culture, and the phallus symbol has followed mankind since we began creating objects.[19] In his book *Phallic Worship* (1966) British writer George Ryley Scott maintains that the study of phallicism can be equated with the study of religion: "... it may safely be stated that no one who neglects the study of phallic worship can hope to secure any adequate understanding of the origin of religion."[20] And in this way one enters what one may call a phallicratic culture, which is largely the case in the history of Western Civilization.[21] Those with a penis have the right to dictate how those without a penis should live and what they should believe.

Literally speaking the phallus is drawings or objects, whether natural objects or objects shaped by humans, that resemble an erect penis or are reminiscent of an erect penis. From a semiotic perspective the phallus is thereby symbolic. It is something that points to something that is more than itself. The phallus is thus something more than the anatomical organ of the penis. A phallus can for instance be a weapon, like a spear or an arrow in cave drawings, which through their form and function resemble a penis. Other typical phalluses are flowers and trees, different types of bird and animal figures, not least serpents, fingers and hands—as for example in Edvard Munch's painting *The Hands* (1893–94), or the obscene gesture of giving someone the finger. It is easy to understand how the penis goes from being an organ of the body, via a symbol to being a phallus object, which, as Norwegian writer Solveig Aareskjold writes: "It [the penis] must resign itself to being perceived as an organ made of muscles and bone, controlled by will, like an arm."[22] In all of these cases the phallus symbols can mean different things that are culturally and contextually defined.

The phallus is traditionally associated with fertility and rights of passage rituals and myths related to masculinity, but an important shift occurs in the study of the phallus with the emergence of Freud's theories regarding castration and phalluses. In Freud the penis gains a new significance, which occurs at the expense of the traditional fertility symbolism of the phallus. Central Freudian

concepts such as penis envy and castration angst are related precisely to the penis. Freud used the term "castration" when referring to cutting off the penis itself, while castration in a purely medical sense has to do with the testicles. It is the testicles that are important for fertility and virility, and not the penis.[23] That the scientist Freud's phallus fundamentally referred more directly to the penis, and not the testicles, led to modern phallicism becoming more a symbol of lust and pleasure than of fertility. The homosexual male, who through his behaviour is infertile, becomes the perfect penis user in a Freudian sense.

To expand on the above I would like to conclude by drawing a few theoretical Freudian parallels between Munch and Melgaard. Taking into consideration the myriad fertility motifs in Munch's oeuvre, at first glance it might appear that Munch exists in a pre-Freudian phallicracy, where the phallus exists in the sign of fertility. In works such as *Fertility* (1899–1900) and *Metabolism* (1898–99) the tree looms like a phallic symbol of fertility. On each side of the tree a man and a woman stand as universal images of procreation, as well as of nature and a moral social order. But in *Metabolism* a phallic unease reveals itself. The tree, the very symbol of fertility, gains its nourishment from a human corpse, from death itself. In a Freudian sense it is tempting to interpret this as castration. And if one takes a closer look at another motif by Munch, *Eye in Eye* (1899–1900) the castration is complete. The motif is the same as in *Fertility*, a man and a woman stand on either side of a tree—they are even equipped with symbols of fertility, such as the basket of fruit and a scythe for reaping with—another phallus symbol but with an ominous undertone. At closer inspection, one can see that a branch has been cut from the tree, leaving a scar which stares at the viewer like a blind eye. The tree, a primeval symbol of the phallus in itself, is thus castrated, and accepts this in the perfect Freudian crisis, where the phallicracy's foundation of fertility quivers. To put it simply, one can say that Munch's phalluses have fallen into a Freudian crisis, where the male sexual identity and gender are put to the test. And one sees this perhaps also in Munch's many phallic shadows that threaten or are threatened by woman. In these pictures the phalluses resemble fleeting yet threatening ghosts that afflict women, who themselves appear to still exist in the sign of fertility. In the sign of a Freudian phallus man is in danger of losing himself, in the sense that the phallus is on the verge of losing its *raison d'être* in fertility's reproductive rationale. Munch's castrated phalluses thus exist in the sign of death and extinction. In this phallus lies the kernel of a phallus in the sign of pleasure, a phallus beyond the fertility phallus's moral phallicracy.

In Freud the phallus is no longer primarily associated with fertility, and thus loses its phallicratic power. And it is in this post-Freudian phallicracy that Melgaard's art is found. In Melgaard one encounters only pleasure seeking phalluses, which exist for the purpose of narcissistic lust, but which also risk the self-destruction of castration. The phallus has become a destructive weapon where pleasure and death meet. In Melgaard the tree is exchanged for knives, revolvers and injections.

Phalluses that warn of the potentially catastrophic outcome of an all-consuming and limitless pleasure. In the sign of the pleasure phallus illness and death are an everyday occurrence. For as Melgaard writes in his novel *A New Novel* (2012), which is about the homosexual penis-obsessed Jean Claude: "*You've got a very advanced case of AIDS. You've got Hepatitis A, B, C, and D, you have gonorrhoea in your anus and mouth and hair, and you have syphilis and crabs ...*"[24] In Melgaard's work there are no vestiges of the phallus's pre-Freudian fertility symbolism. But rather a post-Freudian phallicracy that points towards death and destruction. Sexuality is no longer primarily about fertility, but has to do with the transgressive complexity of lust, which opens up to experiences of pleasure and pain that have no language—or what the psychoanalyst Jacques Lacan would call true experiences.

Translated from Norwegian by Francesca M. Nichols

1   Bjarne Melgaard, *A New Novel* (Oslo, 2012), p. 212.

2   For a summary of the debate in the media, see Mariann Enge, "Bjarne Melgaard og etikken," *Kunstkritikk.no*, (24 April, 2009): http://www.kunstkritikk.no/kommentar/bjarne-melgaard-og-etikken/?d=no (read 8 October 2014). See also texts by John Kelsey and Hanne Beate Ueland in *Bjarne Melgaard. Jealous*, exh. cat. Astrup Fearnley Museum of Modern Art (Milan, 2010).

3   Quoted in Randi Fuglehaug Kristensen, "Lager kunst av pedofili-bilder. Bjarne Melgaard sjokkerer," (*Dagbladet* 14 April 2009). http://www.dagbladet.no/2009/04/14/kultur/bjarne_melgaard/kunst/5733896/ (read 8 October 2014).

4   Richard Meyer, *Outlaw Representation. Censorship and Homosexuality in Twentieth-Century American Art* (Boston, 2002).

5   Richard Meyer, "At Home in Marginal Domains (2000)," in Eds. *Catherine Lord and Richard Meyer, Art & Queer Culture* (London and New York, 2013), p. 358.

6   Whitney Davis, *Queer Beauty. Sexuality and Aesthetics from Winckelmann to Freud and Beyond* (New York, 2010), pp. 53–54 and 200–203; Sigmund Freud, "Leonardo da Vinci and a Memory of his Childhood (1910)," in

Ed. *James Strachey, The Standard Edition of the Complete Psychological Works of Sigmund Freud. Volume XI* (London, 2001 [1957]).

7   Christopher Reed, *Art and Homosexuality. A History of Ideas* (Oxford, 2011), p. 70; Davis, *Queer Beauty*, p. 244.

8   Reed 2011, p. 106.

9   Richard Meyer, "Inverted Histories: 1885-1979," in Ed. *Lord og Meyer, Art & Queer Culture*, p. 19.

10   Quoted in Baran, "Gay Porn At The Whitney Biennial."

11   Reed 2011, p. 94–95.

12   Reed 2011, p. 137.

13   Quoted in Davis 2010, p. 247.

14   Quoted in Adam Baran, "Gay Porn At The Whitney Biennial." http://thesword.com/gay-porn-at-the-whitney-biennial-part-1-bjarne-melgaard-gets-fucked-up.html.

15   See e.g. Patricia G. Berman, "Body and body politic in Edvard Munch's *Bathing Men*," in eds. *Kathleen Adler and Marcia Pointon, The body imaged. The human form and visual culture since the Renaissance* (Cambridge, 1993) and Patricia G. Berman, "Edvard Munch's Self-Portrait with

Cigarette: Smoking and the Bohemian Persona," in *The Art Bulletin* 75 (4) (1993): pp. 627–646.

16 Reed 2011, p. 103.

17 Francesca Gavin, "Q&A/Art: Bjarne Melgaard," in *Dazed* (2012). http://www.dazeddigital.com/artsandculture/article/14265/1/qa-art-bjarne-melgaard (read 17 October 2014). (My highlighting).The journalist also uttered the following play on words: "... he [Melgaard] is proving himself to be one of the most interesting artists of his generation, with a hard-on for beauty."

18 http://www.dailymail.co.uk/sciencetech/article-2683692/The-gay-graffiti-history-Researchers-reveal-large-phalluses-carved-rocks-Greece.html (read 14 October 2014).

19 For a historical summary of the phallus in art and culture, see Johan J. Mattelaer, *Le phallus dans l'art et la culture* (Kortrijk, 2000). See also Lee Alexander Stone, *The Story of Phallicism* (New York, 1976 [1927]); George Ryley Scott, *Phallic Worship. A History of Sex and Sex Rites in Relation to the Religions of all Races from Antiquity to the Present Day* (New Delhi, 1975); and Solveig Aareskjold, *Fallos. Det mangfaldige i det mannlege* (Oslo, 1997).

20 Scott 1975. p. V.

21 Eva C. Keuls, *The Reign of the Phallus. Sexual Politics in Ancient Athens* (Berkeley, 1993 [1985]), p. 2.

22 Aareskjold 1997, p. 11.

23 Mels van Driel, *Manhood. The Rise and Fall of the Penis* (London, 2011 [2009]), p. 8.

24 Melgaard 2012, p. 237 (italics used in the original).

PATRICIA G. BERMAN
Professor of Art, Wellesley College
Professor II, University of Oslo

Melgaard, Munch, and Scriptophilia

___

In 1929, Virginia Woolf commented on the seductions of cinema, noting that "[t]he eye licks it all up instantaneously, and the brain, agreeably titillated, settles down to watch things happening without bestirring itself to think."[1] What appears flickering on the surface is so immediate and distracting that the deeper resonance dissolves. In the works of both Edvard Munch and Bjarne Melgaard, there are echo chambers of resonance secreted behind the obvious motifs emblemizing sex, violence, death, and sentimentality. In Melgaard's creations in particular, the surface of things—which includes texts, film, paintings, photographs, drawings, objects, textiles, and animals—invites speculation about the artist in unusually direct ways. When the two artists are superimposed, as in a group of Melgaard's works from the late 1990s, the surface "licks the eye" and repels easy consumption.

Among the very prescient things written about Edvard Munch is the opening line of a recent article by art historian Magne Bruteig: "This is probably not how it happened."[2] So much of Munch's reputation, as it developed and was crafted during his own lifetime, was premised on a notion that Munch's art was a record of his experiences and feelings, a form of a diary. Munch seemed to live his life in public, offering images, and the occasional published text, to an increasingly appreciative audience. Thanks to the platform provided by his self-staging and the writings of his intimate circle, the private and the public converged. Munch's early biographers, who were among his closest friends, read the artist's works as testimonies of lived experience.[3] In an article published in 1894, entitled "Psychic Naturalism," the Polish writer Stanislaw Przybyszewski articulated the way in which memory and experience materialized, unfiltered, in Munch's work: "Edvard Munch is the first one who has ever undertaken to represent the most subtle and inconspicuous of psychological processes just as they appear spontaneously in the pure consciousness of individuality, and quite independently of any mental activity on our part."[4] So powerful is the motif of Munch as the testifying agent to his lived experience that even his most meticulous historians and critics confuse his motifs with his daily life. In

his *Woman* (1894) and its various permutations, for example, the women remain abstractions, but the man in the motif is "Munch."

Art historian Mai Britt Guleng and others have explored the very intricate relationship between testimonial and representation in Munch's work, revealing an artist who mined his experience, but in an exploratory, rather than expository, manner. Munch's visual production was intertwined with literary experimentation and ambition, from his "Frieze of Life" sequences to his lithographic series *Alpha and Omega* (1908–09). Within Munch's narratives, intimate first-person narrative is a literary conceit.[5]

Bjarne Melgaard has likewise seen some light shining through the almost imperceptible fissure between Munch and his representations: "I became more preoccupied with Munch when I traveled away from Norway. He is a fascinating figure and a fascinating artist. Both are equally interesting."[6] He also offered, *inter alia* Munch, a coded strategy for thinking about the self in relation to representation: "It is important for me to be honest about how I have lived and such—and I am often confronted with it—but when I was in Norway last I found that one was primarily interested in the arts. Norway has a very strong tradition of self-portraiture, and I grew up with Munch's self-portraits. What is interesting is that this artist, who looks at himself, is a portrait by other people."[7]

Inevitably, both in Norway and internationally, Munch is invoked as a kind of father figure to Bjarne Melgaard, his "stylistic and spiritual mentor,"[8] securing Melgaard's national identity, his "expressionism," his perceived transgressions, and even his censored exhibitions.[9] In 1892, when Munch displayed his work with the Verein Berliner Künstler in Berlin, the exhibition was prematurely closed after it occasioned a press scandal over the artist's cursory treatment of form and his lack of finish. As noted by Øivind Storm Bjerke and Dieter Buchhart, such a "lack" provided some of the terms of a "material-based" modernism in which the visible traces of accidents, the rapidity of execution, and a lack of anticipated academic finish, signaled authenticity, the bodily traces that give form to intuition.[10] The event also gave rise to one of the formative stories about Munch—that he was a provocateur. Munch's biographers also conferred upon him the status of sexual and psychic agonist. His friend and confidant Rolf Stenersen, for example, characterized Munch as pursuing "a constant quest for a non-existent happiness, [which] was nothing but turmoil and need, sex, sorrow, and anguish."[11] Sex and sorrow always claim more attention than an artist's discipline and method. In Munch's work, they were explored in the service of a greater engagement with the ambitious project of what it means to be human.

Melgaard's referential work—visual, acoustic, and textual—with its images and sounds drawn from Black Metal music and culture, NAMBLA (the North American Man/Boy Love Association), and other referents, all woven into a deep web, have triggered responses that ranged from the closure of his exhibitions, to the indignation of child protection advocates, to a global calumny regarding race and power. Those who admire his creations imagine his representations as proxies: "Melgaard's art comes across as something much closer to need itself, something manically important he's trying to get at—even if he knows that in our oversaturated, defensively cynical moment that this is almost impossible ... [the result is] death drive and life force in collision," writes critic Jerry Saltz of the artist's 2013 installation *Ignorant Transparencies* at Gavin Brown's Enterprise. "[His] characters are simultaneously surrogates for the artist and creatures trying to avoid extinction, engaging their appetites, and surviving in the cracks. They emit a psychological bioluminescence that makes me feel like I'm seeing what they're like and what they do in the dark. They may inhabit this psychically scorching hypothermal Babel, but they live. And they aren't easy clichés."[12]

Melgaard's installations are frequently described as "chaotic." Yet they are highly reasoned and rigorous site-specific works that are both topical and timely. One installation does not necessarily predict the specific dynamics or visual syntax of the next. He moves from one "idea space" to another, each exhibition probing a different set of problems as his images and "characters" transmogrify from one site to the next—be they certain personae, animals, or the Pink Panther. As Melgaard stated, "You need to reinvent yourself all the time—that's where you get your energy from. If you just sit through the same thing over and over again you don't get any energy ... It's important for me to move between different areas of professionalism, from very low-key galleries to an upper-class [Manhattan] gallery ... I don't want to communicate to the same audience all the time. You want to know what strangers think of your work."[13] Because Melgaard deploys representations of bodies, violence, and sexual commerce; because he produces texts that deal with desire and sex; because his images appear to be simultaneously by and of the artist; and because of his seeming spontaneity in execution and installation, the artist and his work are, as in the case of Munch, often seen as inseparable. Within such a convergence, representation itself slips into the realm of the "real."

For the Whitney Biennial Melgaard created an installation that was repeatedly termed a "funhouse" (in many reviews, "Pee-wee's Playhouse"), and into which the spectator entered through a diaphanous curtain, and then a freestanding archway padded with clusters of day-glo yarn and wigs, fabrics, and immense upholstered penises. In this hectic, candy-colored patterning, and the unnaturally static population of "RealDolls" that simulated female figures, the eye had much to "lick." The room beyond was a multi-layered projection hall, with various videos screened on its walls in overlapping configurations. Additional semi-opaque, freestanding screens populated one corner of the room, masking the view to the wall projections, and to each other. Anthropomorphic sofas and chairs, specially fabricated for the exhibition with photo-transfer fabric, sported images of faces, bodies, and body fragments, as did pillows and soft forms throughout the room. Anatomically enhanced mannequins were placed around the space in gestures of sexual presentation and masturbation and set amidst soft-form pillows and hybridized dolls imprinted with photographic images. Biomorphic forms with projecting parts, covered in fabric to produce lamps, and a large wardrobe-like object with projecting drawers, were painted in keyed-up neon colors. Everywhere the eye traveled, more and more representations could be seen—photo-upholstered bodies embedded in the entry arch, pictures within pictures throughout, newspapers, vacuum cleaners, and other objects. Louche and fantastic, it was a scene enacting the surfeit of excess—excess of materialism, of sexuality (of men, women, and animals), of violence (in video clips drawn from the web, from the Boston marathon bombing, from Melgaard's own production), of color, line, and stimuli. Everything was exquisite. And the composite, overlapping, multiplying excess of it all transformed the exquisite into the Sublime, in the sense of Edmund Burke. The more closely you looked, the more infernally turbulent was the view. The accumulation, and not the objects per se, became the story.

A didactic panel signaled that the excess was a materialization of the "Anthropocene," the term characterizing a new geological epoch created by human behavior—an age of self-extinction. It also provided a literary and moral platform for the artwork by explaining that an eighteenth-century satirical novel, *The Sofa: A Moral Tale*, by Claude Prosper Jolyot de Crébillon, was a point of reference.[14] In a deft gesture of deflection, what was on the surface of the "funhouse" was impossible to inhabit and digest. The resistance to easy consumption was the gambit.

Melgaard's physical spaces, his paintings and drawings, and other objects interact with his extensive writings, including his many novels, which themselves refract back into the spaces of exhibition. His 2012–13 exhibition at Luxembourg & Dayan, *A New Novel by Bjarne Melgaard*, elided space, place, and text into an experience in which the narrative was accreted by the viewer's body moving through the installation, coming across stacks of the published book, and carrying away a copy to read it elsewhere. The book itself did not conform to orthodox typography or structure, as multiple narrators appeared and disappeared on its pages and chapters were labeled out of numerical sequence. One chapter was reproduced in the catalogue of the Biennale de Lyon (published in 2013): in it the text interacted with photographs and with skeins of atomized

paint that nearly masked sections of writing.[15] In its episodic effacements, the text became a visual trap that initiated a circuit of desire precisely because of its borderline legibility.[16] The conventional programmatic ways in which reading is premised on legibility were sidetracked by such a stratagem, calling attention to the text itself, and therefore to its graphic violations of the body contained in the text. Art historian Ina Blom has written eloquently about the complexity of such a venture, identifying the design-environment "novels" and the episodic writing form as a path of somaticizing narrative:

> The extreme conditions of physical pain that subtend the strange novelistic universe of Bjarne Melgaard ... alert us to a new and different type of focus. It might exemplify a more contemporary tendency to place physical bodies at the center of the real, as seen in the new political landscapes of genetic engineering and bodybuilding (in the broad sense of the word), or in the horrible ubiquity of torture as a technology of 'information,' despite the official strictures of international law ... the novel, here, is not a dignified cultural format and not a token for the benefits of reading. It is a name that stands for the resurrection of a specific fictional site—a site where bad ideas are allowed to proliferate freely, where thinking and attention follows the wacky logic of what actually takes place rather than what should ideally happen. It is a site where one event connects to the next in a rhythm more reminiscent of contingency than of meter. For this reason it is also one of the few places where it is possible to articulate not just the abjection but also the strange and expensive resources of the body in pain.[17]

Elsewhere, Blom offers that through excess, repetition, and approaches to narrative as itself a referent, Melgaard's representations constitute a form of abstraction, not an abstraction that is depoliticized or devoid of the violence and sexuality that the representations carry, but one that constitutes a screen for projection and reflection, the "'non-ground' or 'unground' in Melgaard's work—a highly strategic lack of grounding in the figure of the self or the subject around whom either representations or forms would gather."[18] The visual, material, spatial, and auditory excess in the Whitney installation, and its intertwining Nabokovian narratives, provides such a state of abstraction.

Much writing about Melgaard produces a slippage between the artist and his work, as though his narratives are self-confessions without aestheticization. As noted by Hanne Beate Ueland, members of the Norwegian press have from early on focused on the spectacle of the "enfant terrible," the censored and provocative.[19] The physicality and urgency of Melgaard's narratives attract others' self-confession. As one critic wrote, "Bjarne Melgaard and I have something in common: we both love dick. In fact, writing on Melgaard is a very convenient excuse to write about my favorite male member as well as one of my favorite pastimes, gay sex."[20] And then there is Melgaard himself, as portrayed in interviews, which he patiently gives, answering repeatedly identical questions with gentle variation, always bringing the conversation back to process, but masking his deeper sources and ways of thinking. One gets the sense of a very still and contemplative force at the center of all the bioluminescence, the "chaos," and the *terribilità*:

> [...] I use the first person a lot. But I'm probably more concerned that there should be some sort of narrative short story feature in the works than the work should operate so much about me and my life. I think that when it comes to all art, one is curious about the artist behind the work. You cannot say that the two do not hang together, and there will of course be speculation around it. I do not see my art as confessional or autobiographical.[21]

Regarding the critical confusion between autobiography, disclosure, fiction, convention, and spectatorial puerility, Melgaard has said, "We haven't killed anyone or anything like that, but the things that seem most likely to be fictional are the ones that are not."[22] Melgaard's films, often created in relation to or embedded within his installations, offer further expansions of narrative potential. For a project featured at the 54th Venice Biennale in 2011, *Beyond Death: Viral Discontents and Contemporary Notions about AIDS*—accompanied by a seminar held at the University of Venice and resulting in an installation entitled *Baton Sinister*—the artist filmed "a fictitious interview" with the queer literary theorist Leo Barsani.[23] Their wide-ranging discussion of gay identities was interrupted by overlays, repetitions, enhancements, and intercutting, creating glosses on the conversation through Brechtian interludes. A still image excised from the film and published by Melgaard in *Art in America* displayed a simple red line drawing of two large ejaculating penises superimposed on the two men, angled as though in a sword fight. The drawing was hilariously vulgar in its hypertrophic subtext of desire and its kinship with Wassily Kandinsky's early *Improvisations*. Other animations and montages were more directly political. Stills and segments from David Wojnarowicz's film *A Fire in My Belly* (1986–87) were among the media interposed in the film, and an image of Wojnarowicz with his lips sewn shut, from *Silence=Death* (1990), provided a visual shorthand to the theme of political activism. The conversation with Barsani revolved around radical queer activism, and Melgaard's articulation of "gay terrorism" staked a position and a rhetoric that resisted consumption.

"If you're from Norway, Munch is inescapable," Melgaard said in a recent interview, "I almost felt claustrophobic."[24] Yet when Melgaard has overtly regarded Munch, given his own intricate and layered approach to narrative as art and art as narrative, he displayed a profound connoisseurial intimacy. It is often difficult, if not impossible, to discern the delicacy of Melgaard's antennae, so packed and layered are his installations, and so distracting is the critical focus on violence. However, a close reading of Melgaard's works reveals his sympathy. In the painting *Untitled (Tahiti)* (1998), Melgaard enlisted the affirmative language of Munch's touch, his drippings and leavings on his canvas surfaces, and his motifs, using a process of sublation: two seated men replace the male and female figures in Munch's *Moonrise*, an image from his lithographic suite *Alpha and Omega* from 1908–09. Melgaard substituted Munch's moon with the image of the sun, sliced into a small wedge by a blue horizon and discharging rays of light reminiscent of Munch's *Sun* in the University of Oslo Festival Hall, but more directly recalling the allied lithograph, *Towards the Light* (1914). Melgaard rendered the male bodies in linear configurations that repeat the patterns of that lithographic representation of male musculature, as well as the flipper-like hands. He pigmented them in a manner that calls to mind Munch's suntanned *Bathing Men* (1904) and other sunbathing figures of the 1910s, thus creating "Munchs" as pastiche and homage.

In Melgaard's painting, both men are viewed from behind and represented in *profil perdu*. The figure to the right in Melgaard's painting repeats the posture and physiognomy of the one pictured in his 1998 work *Untitled (Sperm on the Grave of Paul Gauguin)* and the figure beset by penises from every direction in his *Untitled* from 1998—itself an interpretation of Munch's *The Hands* (1893–94). The particular figure forms a strongly valenced narrative element in Melgaard's work in the 1990s. The face of the man to the left, viewed from behind, is reduced to a thick J-shaped contour line, replicating the many images of anonymous men that populate Munch's paintings and are often seen as self-portraits. Art historian Signe Endresen has counted 70 such figures in Munch's work and has called attention to their ambiguous presence as witness-participants, signs for the artist himself who is, at the same time, not "Munch."[25] Allison Morehead has similarly focused on the man turned away from the viewer in light of Munch's narration of gambling addiction and dysphoria in Monte Carlo (*At the Roulette Table in Monte Carlo*, 1892), noting that such representations might productively be understood in terms of the artist's analytical strategies.[26] This is not a matter of such figures serving as "proxies," but of some version of the Self as Other. Munch wrote of his period in Monte Carlo: "It is important for me to study the various inherited phenomena that form the life and destiny of a human being, especially

the most common forms of madness. I am making a study of the soul, as I can observe myself closely and use myself as an anatomical soul preparation."[27] Morehead made the observation that:

> Writing implement in hand, a piece of paper held up, his gesture might be interpreted in three by no means exclusive ways. Is he taking notes for the purposes of his [gambling] system ... Or should we understand him to be sketching the players round the table, recording in visible form what he sees? Or is he in the process of observing himself ... the symptomatic proof of using himself as an "anatomical soul preparation" to investigate the psychological experience of gambling mania? These three readings together—method, observation, experimentation on the self's altered states—suggest the depth of Munch's commitment to developing a workable method for transforming pathological subject matter into universally legible form.[28]

In *Untitled (Tahiti)*, Melgaard's transformation of the gendered identities of "Alpha" and "Omega," and his subtle shifts in the figures' postures and gestures, occasions a subtextual reading of Munch's bodily representations. Painting techniques deployed here similarly adapt Munch's "hand" with its characteristically resolute lack of "finish"—dripped paint, long, pirouetting linear gestures, and broad and braided brushstrokes—while the uneven horizon line brilliantly extends Munch's episodic approach to landscape representation in paintings such as *Moonlight* (1895). Melgaard's scrawled words, doodles, and caricatures to the right of the unpainted canvas surface relocates the invented island in Munch's *Alpha and Omega* to "Tahiti," which in itself is not a place but an idea of a place (Gauguin's place). Melgaard's brilliant discernment of "signature" touches by Munch add up to a painting of homage, yearning, and mythologizing.

Melgaard's "Munch" is in part predicated on mark making. The mark of the hand in motion seemingly locates what Henri Matisse once termed "the moment of the artist,"[29] transmitting an immediacy of touch that we quickly translate into the immediacy of experience, of self-confession as interpolated through the spontaneous-seeming act of making. Melgaard recognizes the discipline inherent in the effect of immediacy, both in Munch's control over his medium and also over the problem of "authentic" biography: "[Munch] worked hard to make things unfinished, he worked quickly and very sketchily. It was important for me. Being able to let things remain unfinished, leave areas of canvas uncovered by paint."[30] In *Untitled (Tahiti)*, the hand that is and is not "Munch's" hand, making marks that are and are not "Munch's" marks, opens the question of authenticity and technique on which so much interpretation and speculation about the two artists is founded.

The spontaneous line work, which seemingly short-circuits mediation and training, became a signifier of freedom, a "totem of modernity," in the years when Munch matured as an artist.[31] He testified to the liberating aspect of such rapid execution: "it is purely the type of movement and its speed [energy] ... it determines the 'being set free' aspect ['airiness'] of painting."[32] Reductive, seismographic lines signifying models' bodies rapidly become eroticized, transferring the experience of the bodies themselves onto the artists' eyes that "caressed" them and the hands that registered their contours.[33] So secured was the connection between the hand, the eye, and the models' bodies that the motifs created with such gestural lines were increasingly "real" in direct proportion to the ways in which their flesh disappeared into free linearity. Whether, Ann Wagner noted, female models actually masturbated in Rodin's presence—as some of his drawings show—or later, in the presence of Klimt, the gestural drawings that illustrated such activity made the actions authentic. This technique, with its attendant immanence of bodies that have been seen and gestures that were enacted, reified the "free line" as sexual. Such a convergence of the artist's body with his (or her) imaginary—encompassing things seen and things invented—offers, in the words of Patrick Maynard, "haptic linearity," that is gestures that offer touch as well as optical experience, serving as both

an event and its trace.[34] The condition of the "haptic" refers to the sensation of touch, temperature, and pain, and to the recognition of one's own body as a perceiving instrument.[35] Film critic Laura U. Marks reads into it the convergence of subject and object: "In haptic seeing, all of our self rushes up to the surface to interact with another surface. When this happens there is a concomitant loss of depth [...] We give up believing that meaning is formed after the fact, in our minds, and attribute power to create meaning to the interaction itself [...] Our loss of center and subjectivity is thus a gain in subjectivity for the object."[36] It is this spectatorial position, in which the optical and the haptic experience of the surface converge with the artist/producer that gives rise to a kind of "scriptophilia," the love of the line, or gesture, of excess. Within this formulation, the artist's authentic presence, as marked by the seeming rapidity and randomness of mark making, seems to be witnessed. Munch's gloriously eccentric uses of paint and graphic medium, his thick, liquid, responsive lines rendered in ink and in lithographic tusche, are echoed in Melgaard's works. The touch that reads as directly as an "autograph," in concert with Munch's seeming self-confessional motifs themselves, seems to conjure the "real Munch." For the spectator, the process of looking at a static work becomes the act of witnessing process. The "chaos" and excess, the violent imagery and the obfuscations in Melgaard's work also operate as traces, in a manner similar to Ina Blom's characterization of Melgaard's viscerally present texts. In an article in *Art in America*, Melgaard signaled painterly technique as a conduit:

> The idea that painting is an innocent and inactive process is foreign to me. I have always seen paintings as capable of potentially lethal acts of violation ... Though it is nearly always linked to the formal, for me the act of painting begins and ends with sensuality. I have always envied Watteau for the way that his paintings broadcast the pleasure he found in every brushstroke ... Dubuffet's abandonment of canonical language in favor of emotionality and

unmediated creativity is particularly relevant now. His rejection of tyrannical beauty, and his proposition that a celebration of vulgarity is the most direct means of accessing psychological complexity within the practice of art-making, are vital and crucial ideas within my own practice.[37]

Seemingly inhabiting Munch's hands and motifs, constructing webs of narrative and referentiality, and pouring out image and text, Melgaard opens up the question of Munch's own "unmediated creativity."

He suggests a kind of identity for the older artist that is otherwise hard to reckon: one that resists easy consumption, despite the commodification of Munch's motifs in blow-up dolls and t-shirts. While one's eye licks in one direction, narratives of both artists emerge on the periphery, buried in an excess of material or, as Melgaard suggests of Munch, in the "self-portraits" painted by others.

"I am more interested in telling a good story than a boring truth,"[38] says Melgaard. But still, this is probably not how it all together happened …

1   Virginia Woolf, *The Cinema*, (1926), full text available at http://www.woolfonline.com/timepasses/?q=essays/cinema/full (accessed 1 October 2014).

2   Magne Bruteig, "'How art was originally created'—Munch's sketchbooks," in *Edvard Munch. Works on Paper*, Magne Bruteig and Ute Kuhlemann Falck, eds. (Oslo, 2013), p. 20.

3   See Patricia G. Berman, "(Re-)Reading Edvard Munch: Trends in the Current Literature, 1982–1993," *Scandinavian Studies* 66 (Winter 1994): pp. 45–67; Patricia G. Berman, "The Many Lives of Edvard Munch," in Gerd Woll et. al., *Edvard Munch: Complete Paintings* (Oslo, 2008), pp. 1277–93; and Jay A. Clark, "Art Equals Life? Munch and the Problem of Biography," in *Edvard Munch 1863–1944*, Mai Britt Guleng, Birgitte Sauge, and Jon-Ove Steihaug, eds., exh. cat., Munch Museum and National Museum of Art, Architecture and Design (Oslo, 2013), pp. 50–61.

4   Stanislaw Przybyszewski, "Psychischer Naturalismus," in *Freie Bühne. Neue deutsche Rundschau* V, no. 2, (1894), p. 150, excerpted and translated in Charles Harrison, Paul Wood, and Jason Gaiger, eds., *Art in Theory, 1815–1900: An Anthology of Changing Ideas* (Oxford, 1998), p. 1045, and quoted in Øivind Storm Bjerke, "Meaning and Physicality in the Art of Edvard Munch," in *Edvard Munch: Signs of Modern Art*, Dieter Buchhart, ed., exh. cat., Fondation Beyeler and Kunsthalle Würth (Ostfildern, 2007), p. 27.

5   See Mai Britt Guleng, "Edvard Munch—The Narrator," in *eMunch.no—Text and Image*, exh. cat., Munch Museum (Oslo, 2011), esp. pp. 219, 229.

6   Kjetil Lyche, "-Vi hater mennesker, begge to," *Dagens Næringsliv* (5 October 2014). http://www.dn.no/etterBors/2014/10/05/2052/Kunst/-vi-hater-mennesker-begge-to (accessed 23 October 2014). Author's translation.

7   Maria Torkilsen Horvei, "INTERVJU | Bjarne Melgaard," *Smug #2*, 27 (August 2011), http://smug.no/post.aspx?ID=6412 (accessed October 19, 2014). Author's translation.

8   Gunnar B. Kvaran, "Bjarne Melgaard—Jealous," in Gunnar B. Kvaran, Hanne Beate Ueland, and Grete Årbu, eds., *Bjarne Melgaard—Jealous*, exh. cat., Astrup Fearnley Museum of Modern Art (Oslo, 2010), p. 9.

9   Both artists were profligate producers of works in word and image. There is an uncountable number of drawings, paintings, texts, and objects by Melgaard. They are catalogued with near precision in the case of Munch. The Munch Museum website makes reference to 28 000 items in its collections alone. Ute Kuhlemann Falck reminds us that Munch participated in 573 exhibitions in his lifetime (an average of 8.8 per year), exhibiting, among other media, 10 662 prints in 148 of those exhibitions. Ute Kuhlemann Falck, "Edvard Munch's works on paper," in Bruteig and Falck 2013, pp. 10–11.

10   See Øivind Storm Bjerke, "Meaning and Physicality in the Art of Edvard Munch," in *Edvard Munch: Signs of Modern Art*, ed. Dieter Buchhart, exh. cat., Fondation Beyeler and Kunsthalle Würth (Ostfildern, 2007), esp. p. 27.

11   Rolf Stenersen, *Edvard Munch: Close-Up of a Genius* (Oslo, [1944] 1994), p. 15.

12   Jerry Saltz, "The Guy Can't Help It; Safe, Fake Transgression is All Over Chelsea These Days. And Then There's Bjarne Melgaard." *New York Magazine*, 7 October 2013, http://www.vulture.com/2013/10/

saltz-on-bjarne-melgaard-ignorant-transparencies.html (accessed 18 October 2014).

13 Francesca Gavin, "Q&A / Art: Bjarne Melgaard," *Dazed*, (September 2012), http://www.dazeddigital.com/artsandculture/article/14265/1/qa-art-bjarne-melgaard (accessed 28 October 2014).

14 The novel was circulated in 1740, despite a royal decree that forbade its publication. In Melgaard's layered referentiality, its appearance despite censorship offers contemporary reflexivity. The text of the book may be found at http://www.yorku.ca/inpar/crebillon_sofa.pdf (accessed 20 October 2014).

15 Bjarne Melgaard, "Listen. How Many Guys do you Think Wanna do this? ...," in *12ᵉ Biennale de Lyon, Entre-temps ... Brusquement, et ensuite*, exh.cat., Le Musée d'art contemporain (Lyon, 2013), pp. 316–35.

16 Susan Stewart, *On Longing: Narratives of the Miniature, the Gigantic, the Souvenir, and the Collection* (Durham and London, 1993), pp. ix–xiv.

17 Ina Blom, "Many Novels: An Afterword" in Bjarne Melgaard, *A New Novel* (Oslo, 2012), unpaginated.

18 Ina Blom, "Working Class Abstractions," *Afterall*, Spring 2008, p. 42.

19 See Hanne Beate Ueland, "Disgust and Admiration. Bjarne Melgaard in the Norwegian Media 1994–2009," in Kvaran, Ueland and Årbu, eds. 2010, p. 21–27.

20 David Everitt Hoew, "Bjarne Melgaard," in *Art Review*, 62 (October 2012), p. 76.

21 Maria Torkilsen Horvei, "INTERVJU | Bjarne Melgaard," *Smug #2*, (27 August 2011), http://smug.no/post.aspx?ID=6412 (accessed 19 October 2014). Author's translation.

22 Andrew Russeth, "'After Shelley Duvall': Bjarne Melgaard on Curating at Maccarone," *New York Observer* (21 October, 2011), http://observer.com/2011/10/after-shelley-duvall-bjarne-melgaard-on-his-unwieldy-show-at-maccarone/ (accessed 26 October 2014).

23 "Chaotic Expressionism," Bjarne Melgaard in conversation with Jennifer Krasinski, *Spike* 39 (Spring 2014), p. 75.

24 Dan Duray, "Bjarne Melgaard's Munch Museum Show will Feature a Soundtrack with Dolly Parton, Diana Ross," *Artnews*, (7 October 2014) http://www.artnews.com/2014/10/07/bjarne-melgaards-munch-museum-show-will-feature-a-soundtrack-with-dolly-parton-diana-ross/ (accessed 10 October 2014).

25 Signe Endresen, "Mannen og kunsten: Den mørke mannsfiguren i Edvard Munchs malerier 1891–1908," in

Kjønnsforhandlinger: Studier i kunst, film og litteratur, Anne Birgitte Rønning and Geir Uvsløkk, eds. (Oslo, 2013), pp. 216–30.

26 Allison Morehead, "'Are there bacteria in the rooms of Monte Carlo?' The roulette paintings 1891–93," in Ingebjørg Ydstie and Mai Britt Guleng, eds., *Munch Becoming "Munch": Artistic Strategies 1880–1892*, exh. cat., Munch Museum (Oslo, 2008), pp. 121–38.

27 Edvard Munch, in MM T 2734, Munch Museum Archives, translated in Morehead, p. 122.

28 Morehead 2008, p. 132.

29 Henri Matisse, quoted in Alfred H. Barr, Jr., "Matisse, His Art and His Public" (New York, 1951), p. 38.

30 Lyche 2014. Author's translation.

31 Yve-Alain Bois, *Painting as Model* (Cambridge MA, 1993), p. 3.

32 Edvard Munch, sketchbook 135-17R, translated in Gerd Presler, *Edvard Munch Werkverzeichnis der Skizzenbücher. Einsam wie ich immer war* (Karlsruhe, 2004), p. 53.

33 See Ann Wagner, "Rodin's Reputation," in *Eroticism and the Body Politic*, Lynn Hunt, ed. (Baltimore, 1991), pp. 191–242.

34 Patrick Maynard, *Drawing Distinctions: The Varieties of Graphic Expression* (Ithaca, 2005), pp. 190–96 and 217–25.

35 Bettina Pappenburg, "Touching the Screen, Striding through the Mirror: The Haptic in Film," in *What Does a Chameleon Look Like? Topographies of Immersion*, Stefani Kiwi Menrath and Alexander Schwinghammer, eds. (Cologne, 2013), http://www.academiz.edu/6561413/Touching_the_Screen_Striding_through_the_Mirror_THE_Haptic_in_Film, p. 126 (accessed 31 October 2014).

36 Laura. U. Marks, "Visitor's Voice. Haptic Visuality: Touching with the Eyes," in *The Finnish Art Review* (2 January 2004), p. 80.

37 Bjarne Melgaard, "Color Pulse," in *Art in America*, (November 2012), p. 77.

38 "Engaging Chaos and Seeking the Sublime: Bjarne Melgaard presents a New Novel at Luxembourg & Dayan," Press release, Luxembourg & Dayan, (9 November—22 December 2012), http://luxembourgdayan.com/exhibitions/a-new-novel-by-bjarne-melgaard/press (accessed 18 October 2014).